# Our Faith-Filled Heritage

The Church of Philadelphia

Bicentennial as a Diocese

1808–2008

THE CHURCH OF
*Philadelphia*

CELEBRATES BICENTENNIAL AS A DIOCESE
1808-2008

PREPARED BY THE ARCHDIOCESE OF PHILADELPHIA

**Cardinal Justin Rigali**
ARCHBISHOP OF PHILADELPHIA

**Most Reverend Robert P. Maginnis, D.D.**
AUXILIARY BISHOP
CHAIR, BICENTENNIAL COMMITTEE

**CONTRIBUTING AUTHORS**

Mr. Lou Baldwin
Monsignor Michael J. Carroll
Mr. Joseph J. Casino
Father John P. Collins
Mr. Shawn Weldon

**EDITORIAL CONSULTANTS**

Monsignor Francis A. Carbine
Monsignor James F. Connelly
Monsignor Louis A. D'Addezzio
Sister Joan Freney, R.S.M.
Sister Agnes Marie Gunn, S.S.J.
Monsignor James P. McCoy
Deacon David B. Schaffer


**Father Philip G. Bochanski, C.O.**
GENERAL EDITOR

Published by
**Éditions du Signe**
B.P. 94 – 67038 Strasbourg – Cedex 2 – France
Tel (+33) 388 789 191
Fax (+33) 388 789 199
info@editionsdusigne.fr


**Publishing Director**
Christian Riehl

**Director of Publication**
Joëlle Bernhard

**Publishing Assistant**
Marc de Jong

**Design and Layout**
Sylvie Tusinski

**Photographer**
John Glover

**Photoengraving**
Atelier du Signe - 106799

**Copyright Text**
Archdiocese of Philadelphia

© Éditions du Signe 2007
ISBN: 978-2-7468-1806-4

All rights reserved - Reproduction forbidden
Printed in China

## ACKNOWLEDGMENTS

A debt of gratitude is due to those who reviewed the manuscripts and offered corrections and helpful suggestions, especially Father Gregory Fairbanks, Mrs. Blanca Herrera, Monsignor Hugh Shields, Father Stephen Thorne, Monsignor Joseph Tracy, and Mrs. Anna Vega.

Sincere thanks are also offered to the following: Ms. Loretta Colucci and Mrs. Connie Hunt; the staff of the Philadelphia Archdiocesan Historical Research Center, particularly Mr. Colin Varga; Mrs. Michelle Laque Johnson and the staff of The Catholic Standard and Times; Mr. Kevin Riley and the staff of the Office for Printing and Duplicating Services; Sister Patricia Annas, S.S.J.; Mr. Gerard Burns; Ms. Susan Dilanni; Sister Helen Jacobson, O.S.F.; Sister Helena Mayer, S.H.C.J.; Dr. Stephanie Morris; Sister San Michel, I.H.M.; Dr. Nancy Shawcross.

The preparation of this commemorative history would not have been possible without the contributions of innumerable, often anonymous, clergy, religious and lay people—living and deceased—who prepared the many parish and school histories consulted by the authors and editor of this volume. Thanks are extended particularly to the pastors and parish staff members who prepared new material for this project, and who answered queries from the authors.


Every effort has been made to ensure that the information contained herein is accurate at the time of writing (2006). The General Editor assumes responsibility for any errors.

# TABLE OF CONTENTS

## Part I    page 15

### "Many Desired to See What You See"

Pastoral Reflections on the Occasion of the Opening at Easter 2007 of the Bicentennial of the Church of Philadelphia

• Two Centuries of Change at a Glance

## Chapter 1:    page 24
### Planting the Faith (1680–1808)

• Beginnings
• William Penn
• Early Catholic Community
• Jesuit Missions and Saint Joseph's Chapel
• Mission to the Germans
• Catholics under Suspicion
• Saint Mary's Church
• Catholic Loyalties
• Catholic Life in the New Nation
• The First Diocese for the United States
• Anti-Immigrant Attitudes
• Trustees of Holy Trinity
• Yellow Fever Epidemic
• Saint Augustine's Church

## Chapter 2:    page 42
### Defending the Faith (1808–1860)

• Bishop Egan
• Trustees of Saint Mary's
• Selecting a New Bishop of Philadelphia
• Bishop Conwell
• Hogan Schism
• The State of the Diocese
• Bishop Kenrick and the Trustees
• Foundation of the Seminary
• Responding to the Needs of Immigrants
• Anti-Catholicism, Nativism and Riots in Kensington
• Riots at Saint Philip Neri Church
• Cathedral of Saints Peter and Paul
• New Parishes
• Bishop Kenrick Proposes a Successor
• Bishop Neumann
• Bishop Neumann's Commitment to Catholic Education
• Appointment of a Coadjutor Bishop
• Death of Bishop Neumann

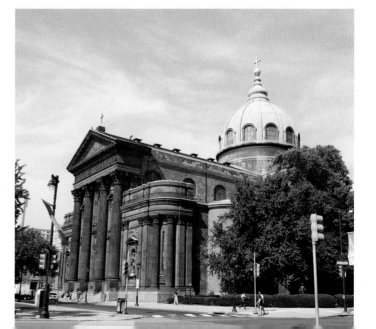

**Chapter 3:** page 62
**Expanding the Faith (1860–1911)**

- The Civil War
- Catholic Education
- Reorganizing Pennsylvania's Dioceses
- Molly Maguires
- Last Years of Archbishop Wood
- Archbishop Ryan
- Caring for New Groups of Immigrants
- Ministry to African Americans and Native Americans
- Mother Katharine Drexel
- Development of Archdiocesan High Schools
- New Bishops from Philadelphia
- Last Years of Archbishop Ryan

**Chapter 4:** page 78
**Living the Faith (1911–1960)**

- Archbishop Prendergast
- Constant Care for Immigrants
- Fostering a Life of Prayer
- The Great War
- Archbishop Dougherty
- The Great Influenza Epidemic
- Archdiocesan Celebrations
- New Seminary Building
- The Great Depression
- Catholic Presence in Civic Life
- Devotional Life
- Legion of Decency
- Ministry to African Americans in the 1930s and 1940s
- Orphanages and Other Institutions
- World War II
- Last Days of Cardinal Dougherty
- Archbishop O'Hara
- Addressing Immigration and Racism
- Education Expansion
- Death of Mother Katharine
- Care for Children and Families
- Going Home

**Chapter 5:** page 100
**Renewing the Faith (1960–2008)**

- Archbishop Krol
- Preparing for the Second Vatican Council
- Archdiocesan Celebrations
- Response to Difficult Times
- Implementation of Vatican II
- Archdiocesan Outreach
- Advocacy in Defense of Human Life
- Holy Year and Bicentennial
- Papal Visit
- Retirement of Cardinal Krol
- Arrival of Archbishop Bevilacqua
- Catholic Faith and Life 2000
- Social Advocacy
- Parish and School Closings
- Canonization of Mother Katharine
- Ensuring a Safe Environment
- Leading in the Third Millennium
- Cardinal Rigali
- Death of Pope John Paul II

- For Further Reading      page 262
- Photo Credits      page 264

**Part II** page 125

**The Fruits of Faith:**
The Parishes of the Archdiocese of Philadelphia

## Center City

Saint Joseph
Saint Mary
Holy Trinity
Saint Augustine
Saint John the Evangelist
Saint Patrick
Cathedral Basilica of Saints Peter and Paul
*Saint Peter Claver*
Holy Redeemer

## Germantown, Chestnut Hill & Mt Airy

Saint Vincent de Paul
Our Mother of Consolation
Holy Cross
Saint Francis of Assisi
Immaculate Conception
*Saint Catherine of Siena*
*Saint Michael of the Saints*
*Saint Brendan*
Saint Benedict
Saint Therese of the Child Jesus
Saint Madeline Sophie
*Our Lady of the Rosary*
Saint Athanasius
Saint Raymond of Peñafort

## Roxborough and Manayunk

Saint John the Baptist
Saint Mary of the Assumption
Saint Bridget
Holy Family
Saint Josaphat

Saint Lucy
Immaculate Heart of Mary

## Kensington

Saint Michael
Saint Peter the Apostle
Immaculate Conception B.V.M.
Saint Laurentius
Ascension of Our Lord
Holy Name of Jesus
*Saint Agnes*
Saint Agnes–Saint John Nepomucene
*Sacred Heart*

## Frankford, Bridesburg & Port Richmond

Saint Anne
Saint Joachim
All Saints
Nativity B.V.M.
Our Lady Help of Christians
Saint John Cantius
Saint George
Saint Adalbert
Mater Dolorosa
Saint Joan of Arc
Mother of Divine Grace
Holy Innocents

## Northeast Philadelphia

Saint Leo
Saint Cecilia
Our Lady of Consolation
Saint Bartholomew
Saint William
Saint Martin of Tours
*Saint Hubert*
Saint Bernard
Saint Matthew
Saint Timothy
Resurrection of Our Lord
Our Lady of Ransom

## Far Northeast Philadelphia

Saint Dominic
Maternity B.V.M.
Saint Katherine of Siena
Saint Christopher
Saint Jerome
Our Lady of Calvary
Saint Anselm
Christ the King
Saint Martha

## Fairmount and Spring Garden

Saint Francis Xavier
*Assumption B.V.M.*
*Saint Ludwig*
*Saint Hedwig*
*Our Lady of the Blessed Sacrament*
Our Lady of the Miraculous Medal/La Milagrosa
Saint Andrew

# CITY OF PHILADELPHIA

### Lower North Philadelphia

Saint Malachy
*Church of the Gesu*
*Saint Elizabeth*
*Our Lady of Mercy*
*Saint Columba*
*Most Precious Blood of Our Lord*
*Saint Mary of the Eternal*
*Corpus Christi*
Saint Martin de Porres

### Upper North Philadelphia

*Saint Stephen*
*Saint Edward the Confessor*
*Saint Boniface*
Saint Veronica
Visitation B.V.M.
*Saint Bonaventure*
*Saint Ladislaus*
*Holy Child*
*Our Lady of the Holy Souls*
*Our Lady of Pompeii*
*Saint Henry*
Saint Hugh of Cluny
Our Lady of Hope

### Olney

Holy Angels
Incarnation of Our Lord
Saint Ambrose
Saint Helena

### South Philadelphia

Saint Philip Neri
Saint Paul
*Saint Alphonsus*
*Saint Mary Magdalen de Pazzi*
*Saint Teresa of Avila*
Annunciation B.V.M.
Sacred Heart of Jesus
Epiphany of Our Lord
*Saint Stanislaus*
Saint Casimir
Saint Monica
Our Lady of Mount Carmel
*Our Lady of Good Counsel*
Saint Nicholas of Tolentine
*Saint John Nepomucene*
Saint Rita of Cascia
Saint Richard
Stella Maris
Holy Spirit

### Grays Ferry and Point Breeze

Saint Charles Borromeo
Saint Thomas Aquinas
*Saint Anthony of Padua*
*Saint Aloysius*
Saint Gabriel
Saint Edmond
*King of Peace*

### West Philadelphia

*Saint James the Greater*
Our Mother of Sorrows
*Saint Agatha*
Saint Agatha–Saint James
*Our Lady of the Rosary*
Saint Francis de Sales
Saint Ignatius of Loyola
Our Lady of Lourdes
*Saint Gregory*
*Our Lady of Victory*
Our Lady of the Blessed Sacrament
Most Blessed Sacrament
*Transfiguration of Our Lord*
*Our Lady of Angels*
Saint Donato
*Saint Carthage*
Saint Cyprian
Saint Barbara
Saint Rose of Lima
Saint Callistus

### Southwest Philadelphia

*Saint Clement*
*Saint Raphael*
Saint Barnabas
*Good Shepherd*
*Saint Mary of Czestochowa*
*Our Lady of Loreto*
*Saint Irenaeus*
Divine Mercy

_____

*Italics denotes closed or consolidated parishes.*

## Upper Bucks County

Saint John the Baptist, Ottsvile
Saint Isidore, Quakertown
Saint Agnes, Sellersville
Our Lady of the Sacred Heart, Hilltown
Saint Lawrence, Riegelsville

## Doylestown and Vicinity

Our Lady of Mount Carmel, Doylestown
Saint Martin of Tours, New Hope
Saint Jude, Chalfont
Saint Cyril of Jerusalem, Jamison
Saint Vincent de Paul, Richboro
Our Lady of Guadalupe, Buckingham

## Warrington, Warminster and Vicinity

Saint Joseph, Warrington
Saint John Bosco, Hatboro (Montgomery County)
Nativity of Our Lord, Warminster
Saint Catherine of Siena, Horsham (Montgomery County)
Saint Robert Bellarmine, Warminster

## Bristol, Bensalem and Vicinity

Saint Mark, Bristol
Saint Charles Borromeo, Bensalem
Saint Ann, Bristol
Our Lady of Grace, Penndel
Saint Thomas Aquinas, Croydon
Our Lady of Fatima, Bensalem
Saint Ephrem, Bensalem
Saint Elizabeth Ann Seton, Bensalem

## Newtown and Vicinity

Saint Andrew, Newtown
Our Lady of Good Counsel, Southampton
Assumption B.V.M., Feasterville
Saint Bede the Venerable, Holland

## Morrisville, Levittown and Vicinity

Holy Trinity, Morrisville
Saint Ignatius of Antioch, Yardley
Saint Frances Cabrini, Fairless Hills
Saint Michael the Archangel, Levittown
Immaculate Conception B.V.M., Levittown
Queen of the Universe, Levittown
Saint Joseph the Worker, Fallsington
Saint John the Evangelist, Lower Makefield

*Italics denotes closed or consolidated parishes.*

## West Chester, Downington & Vicinity

Saint Agnes, West Chester
Saint Joseph, Downingtown
Saints Philip and James, Exton
Saints Simon and Jude, West Chester
Saints Peter and Paul, East Goshen
Saint Maximilian Kolbe, West Chester
Saint Elizabeth, Upper Uwchlan

## Phoenixville and Vicinity

Saint Mary of the Assumption, Phoenixville
Sacred Heart, Phoenixville
Holy Trinity, Phoenixville
Saint Ann, Phoenixville
Saint Joseph, Spring City
Saint Basil the Great, Kimberton
Saint Thomas More, South Coventry

## Parkesburg, Coatesville and Vicinity

Our Lady of Consolation, Parkesburg
Saint Cecilia, Coatesville
Saint Stanislaus Kostka, Coatesville
Our Lady of the Rosary, Coatesville
Saint Joseph, Coatesville
Saint Peter, West Brandywine

## Kennett Square and Vicinity

Saint Patrick, Kennett Square
Assumption B.V.M., West Grove
Sacred Heart, Oxford
Saint Cornelius, Chadds Ford
Saint Gabriel of the Sorrowful Mother, Avondale
Misión Santa María Madre de Dios

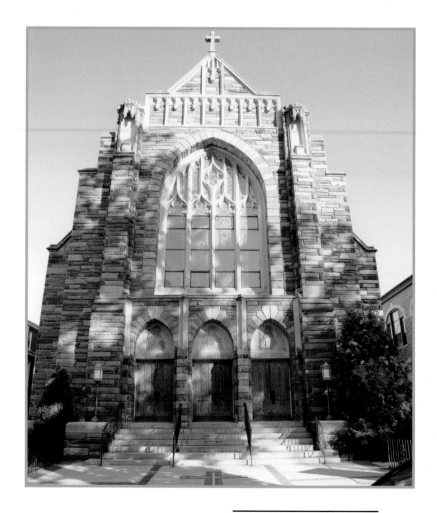

*Italics denotes closed or consolidated parishes.*

## Chester Heights, Media & Springfield

Saint Thomas the Apostle, Chester Heights
Nativity B.V.M., Media
Saint Francis de Sales, Lenni
Saint Francis of Assisi, Springfield
Holy Cross, Springfield
Saint Eugene, Primos
Saint Kevin, Springfield
Saint Mary Magdalen, Media

## Havertown and Vicinity

Saint Denis, Havertown
Saint Anastasia, Newtown Square
Annunciation B.V.M., Brookline
Sacred Heart, Manoa
Saint Pius X, Broomall

## Chester and Vicinity

*Saint Michael, Chester*
*Immaculate Heart of Mary, Chester*
*Resurrection of Our Lord, Chester*
*Saint Hedwig, Chester*
*Saint Anthony of Padua, Chester*
*Our Lady of Vilna, Chester*
*Saint Robert, Chester*
Saint Katharine Drexel, Chester
Holy Saviour, Linwood
Immaculate Conception of Lourdes, Marcus Hook
Saint Joseph, Aston
Our Lady of Charity, Brookhaven
Saint John Chrysostom, Wallingford
Saint John Fisher, Boothwyn

## Drexel Hill, Upper Darby and Vicinity

Saint Charles Borromeo, Drexel Hill
Saint Philomena, Lansdowne
Sacred Heart, Clifton Heights
Saint Andrew the Apostle, Drexel Hill
Saint Laurence, Highland Park
Saint Alice, Upper Darby
Saint Louis, Yeadon
Saint Cyril of Alexandria, East Lansdowne
Saint Bernadette, Drexel Hill
Saint Dorothy, Drexel Hill

## Eddystone, Ridley Park and Vicinity

Saint Rose of Lima, Eddystone
Saint Madeline, Ridley Park
Our Lady of Perpetual Help, Morton
Saint Gabriel, Norwood
Our Lady of Peace, Milmont Park
Saint Margaret Mary Alacoque, Essington
Notre Dame de Lourdes, Swarthmore

## Sharon Hill, Darby and Vicinity

Holy Spirit, Sharon Hill
Blessed Virgin Mary, Darby
Saint Joseph, Collingdale
Saint George, Glenolden
Our Lady of Fatima, Secane

*Italics denotes closed or consolidated parishes.*

### Norristown and Vicinity

Saint Patrick, Norristown
Holy Saviour, Norristown
Saint Teresa of Avila, Norristown
Saint Helena, Blue Bell
Saint Francis of Assisi, Norristown
Visitation B.V.M., Trooper
Epiphany of Our Lord, Plymouth Meeting
Saint Titus, East Norriton
Saint Paul, Norristown

### Conshohocken and Vicinity

Saint Matthew, Conshohocken
Saint Gertrude, West Conshohocken
Saint Augustine, Bridgeport
Saint Mary, Conshohocken
Sacred Heart, Swedesburg
Saints Cosmas and Damian, Conshohocken
Our Lady of Mount Carmel, Bridgeport
*Our Mother of Sorrows, Bridgeport*
Saint Philip Neri, Lafayette Hill
Mother of Divine Providence, King of Prussia

### Pottstown and Vicinity

Saint Aloysius, Pottstown
*Holy Trinity, Pottstown*
Saint Eleanor, Collegeville
Saint Philip Neri, Pennsburg
*Saint Peter, Pottstown*
Saint Mary, Schwenksville
Saint Gabriel of the Sorrowful Mother, Stowe
*Saint Clare, Linfield*
Blessed Teresa of Calcutta, Limerick
Sacred Heart, Royersford

### Lansdale and Vicinity

Saint Stanislaus, Lansdale
Saint Anthony of Padua, Ambler
Saint Joseph, Ambler
Saint Rose of Lima, North Wales
Saint Maria Goretti, Hatfield
Saint Alphonsus, Maple Glen
Corpus Christi, Upper Gwynedd
Mary, Mother of the Redeemer, North Wales

### Glenside and Vicinity

Saint Luke the Evangelist, Glenside
*Seven Dolors, Wyndmoor*
Saint David, Willow Grove
Holy Martyrs, Oreland
Saint Genevieve, Flourtown
Saint John of the Cross, Roslyn
Our Lady, Help of Christians, Abington
Queen of Peace, Ardsley

### Jenkintown and Vicinity

Immaculate Conception B.V.M., Jenkintown
Presentation B.V.M., Cheltenham
Saint Joseph, Cheltenham
Saint James, Elkins Park
Saint Albert the Great, Huntingdon Valley
Saint Hilary of Poitiers, Rydal

### The Main Line

Saint Thomas of Villanova, Villanova/Rosemont
Our Mother of Good Counsel, Bryn Mawr
Saint Katharine of Siena, Wayne
Saint Monica, Berwyn
Saint Margaret, Narberth
Saint Matthias, Bala Cynwyd
Saint Colman, Ardmore
Our Lady of the Assumption, Strafford
Saint Patrick, Malvern
Saint John Baptist Vianney, Gladwyne
Presentation B.V.M., Wynnewood
Saint Norbert, Paoli
Saint Justin Martyr, Penn Valley
Saint John Neumann, Bryn Mawr
Saint Isaac Jogues, Wayne

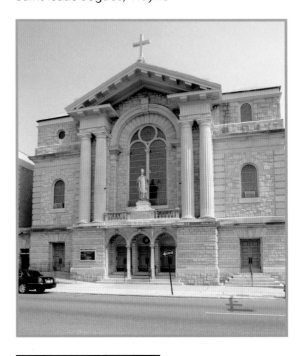

*Italics denotes closed or consolidated parishes.*

**Pope Benedict XVI**

**Cardinal Justin Rigali**
Archbishop of Philadelphia

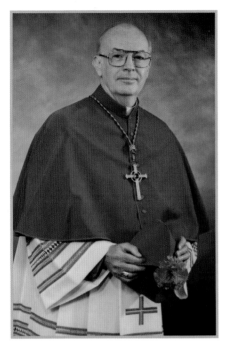

**Most Reverend
Robert P. Maginnis**

Titular Bishop of Siminina
and Auxiliary to the
Archbishop of Philadelphia

**Most Reverend
Joseph R. Cistone**

Titular Bishop of Case Mediane
and Auxiliary to the
Archbishop of Philadelphia

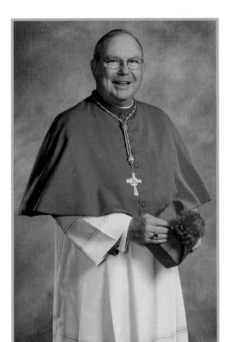

**Most Reverend
Joseph P. McFadden**

Titular Bishop of Orreomargo
and Auxiliary to the
Archbishop of Philadelphia

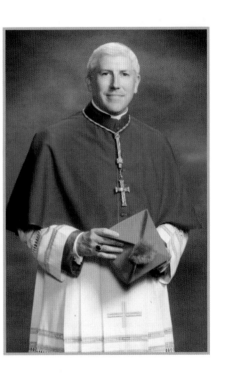

**Most Reverend
Daniel E. Thomas**

Titular Bishop of Bardstown
and Auxiliary to the
Archbishop of Philadelphia

*"I will give you shepherds after my own heart, who will feed you with knowledge and understanding."*

Jeremiah 3:15

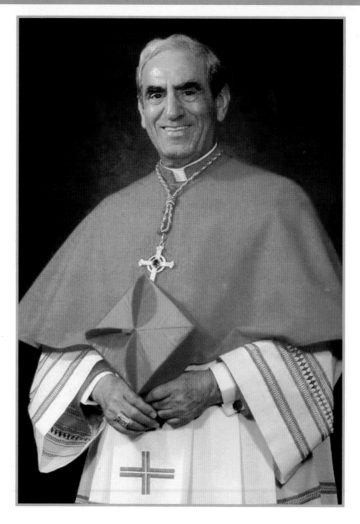

**Cardinal Anthony J. Bevilacqua**

Archbishop Emeritus of Philadelphia

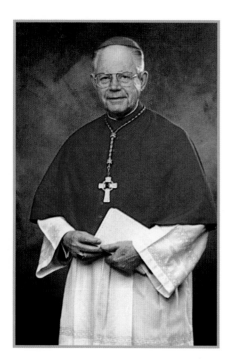

**Most Reverend
Martin N. Lohmuller**

Titular Bishop of Ramsbury
and Retired Auxiliary to the
Archbishop of Philadelphia

**Most Reverend
Louis A. DeSimone**

Titular Bishop of Cillio
and Retired Auxiliary to the
Archbishop of Philadelphia

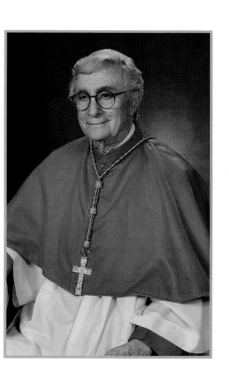

# "Many Desired to See What You See"

## Pastoral Reflections on the Occasion of the Opening at Easter 2007 of the Bicentennial of the Church of Philadelphia

*Jesus said to them, "Blessed are the eyes that see what you see!*
*For I say to you, many . . . desired to see what you see, but did not see it,*
*and to hear what you hear, but did not hear it."*

*(Luke 10: 23–24)*

The Church throughout the world raises her voice today to celebrate the solemn feast of Easter, and to proclaim her faith in the Resurrection of Jesus Christ, true God and true Man. We in the Archdiocese of Philadelphia have special reason to give praise and thanks to God our Father through His Son, our Risen Lord, as we open the Year of Jubilee that will celebrate the Bicentennial of the Church of Philadelphia, established as a diocese by Pope Pius VII on April 8, 1808. On this historic day we recall the words that Jesus spoke to His disciples, who were rejoicing with Him over the many miracles they were able to accomplish in His name: "Blessed are the eyes that see what you see!" Then He told them that "many... desired to see what you see, but did not see it" (Luke 10: 23–24).

### Early Days

On the threshold of a new century of faith and life as the Church of Philadelphia, we are privileged to behold the work that God has accomplished in our midst. Who among our ancestors could have predicted the transformation that has occurred in this Archdiocese over the past two hundred years? In those early days, a handful of missionary priests served a few thousand families scattered throughout a vast wilderness. Many Catholic families were able to celebrate the sacraments only a few times a year. Generations of immigrants fled poverty and persecution in distant countries to establish homes in the New World—all too often under the hostile gaze of neighbors suspicious of their foreign language and traditions. Only eyes of faith and hope could foresee the fruits that the efforts of these pioneer Catholics would bear in our own days, when one and a half million faithful have become a visible and vibrant presence in a bustling metropolitan area. Many of our ancestors longed to see the harvest of faith that we too often take for granted. We who are witnesses to the results of their self-sacrifice bear the responsibility of nurturing and building upon the faith-filled heritage that has been entrusted to us.

In February 1732, when eleven people gathered for the first Mass in the tiny chapel of Saint Joseph in Willings Alley, theirs was the only Catholic church in the fifty-year-old City of Philadelphia. Who among them could imagine that the sprawling territory surrounding the two- and-a-half-square-mile city would one day be home to more than 150 parishes? Much less, perhaps, could the families who greeted visiting missionaries in the Ivy Mills estate of Thomas Willcox in 1729, or at the Haycock Mountain farm of Edward McCarty in 1743, foresee the hundreds of churches and schools that would be built at the heart of the cities and towns in the counties surrounding Philadelphia. We have the privilege of beholding with our own eyes what these first parishioners could only entrust to Divine Providence. How they would rejoice with us to see the growth of so many churches in a community where Catholics still tend to identify their places of origin by the names of their parishes rather than their neighborhoods.

### Renewing the Vision

Yet even as we celebrate our inheritance of faith, we recognize that the precious gifts of our parishes and churches must be protected and renewed if we are to hand them on to the generations that will follow us. Some of us have experienced firsthand the difficult situations that follow when local Catholic populations become too small to meet the demands of aging buildings and increasing expenses, and urban parishes are forced to close or consolidate so that scarce resources may be used most effectively. At the same time, we are witnessing the beginning of new parish communities in suburban areas that are experiencing rapid development. The movement of many Catholic families away from cities presents new challenges to the Church of Philadelphia, which our forebears would never have contemplated. Yet we will be able to face these new situations more effectively if we learn to see them through the eyes of those who have preceded us.

Our ancestors looked at every community, every neighborhood, as a place where the Church and the faith ought to grow, and so must we. The Archdiocese of Philadelphia does not—and must not—abandon the inner city. On the contrary, the realities that face us at the beginning of our third century call us to *a renewed commitment to evangelization,* particularly in urban areas. All of us in the Catholic community share in the responsibility to spread the Good News proclaimed by Jesus Christ, and to invite the people among whom we live and work to share the gift of faith that we ourselves have received.

In many cases, this will take the form of what the Servant of God Pope John Paul II often called *"the new evangelization"*—reaching out, with new ardor and new efforts, to our Catholic neighbors who have fallen away from the practice of the faith, to extend the Lord's call to conversion and fidelity. Likewise, by honest dialogue and patient good example, we ought to encourage those who have not yet heard the Gospel to "come and see" what it is—Who it is—that makes us who we are as Catholic Christians.

A cynical view could look at this work as one more burden on parish communities that are already struggling to meet the day-to-day responsibilities of ministry. The eyes of faith, however, strive to see with the vision of our pioneer forebears, and to recognize in this mission of evangelization a key to preserving and rebuilding the Catholic community in our archdiocese. It is a mission that has been entrusted to us all, urban and suburban dwellers alike, and that requires perseverance and commitment of time, energy and resources if it is to bear fruit. Yet we have many examples of success from our past to give us hope—too many examples, indeed, for us to shirk this responsibility in our own day.

## Saint John Neumann and Catholic Education

I am humbled by the fact that one of the most prominent of these exemplary Philadelphians was among my predecessors as Shepherd of this local Church. As a boy in what is now the Czech Republic, Saint John Neumann was inspired by the stories of American missionaries to respond to God's call and dedicate his life to serving the Church in the United States as a priest. After serving in parishes and institutions in several states, he spent the last decade of his life as the fourth Bishop of Philadelphia, where he expended constant effort to seek out and evangelize every member of the flock entrusted to his care.

Saint John Neumann is perhaps best remembered for his dedication to the work of Catholic education, especially of the young. His first pastoral letter encouraged the foundation of parish schools, but even his saintly eyes might have been amazed to see the hundreds of thousands of alumni and alumnae of those Catholic elementary and high schools that would be founded during the next century. For decades the Archdiocese of Philadelphia has enjoyed a well-deserved reputation for excellence and leadership in Catholic education.

Although the faith is unchanging, the way in which we hand on this faith is deeply influenced by changing times. The work of Catholic education stands in need of renewal in our own day, and we must work to meet the challenges that modern society poses to this ministry. Here, too, the realities of shifting Catholic populations and declining enrollment require many parishes to close schools or to seek new models of collaboration. Teachers and parents alike face increasing financial sacrifices in order to provide this essential service to our children. The rapid pace at which technology develops provides both unforeseen benefits and unexpected dangers, and our approach to education must keep pace with a changing world.

Most important, however, is the need to understand the apostolic mission of Catholic education. Eyes of faith will recognize the place of this ministry in the mission of evangelization, which must include strengthening the faith and the practice of Catholic students, and inviting non-Catholic students to appreciate the truth of the Gospel. This apostolate requires commitment from all those involved, and particularly from a child's parents, whom the Rite of Baptism prays will be "the best of teachers" in the ways of the faith. The lessons learned in classroom catechesis will not bear fruit unless they are tended and reinforced in the home.

Parents must lead their children, by word and example, to a deeper understanding of the faith, and to the regular celebration of the sacraments. For this reason, a commitment to adult faith formation is an essential part of the total commitment to Catholic education. In Catholic universities, and through the work of Campus Ministry in secular institutions, young adults must be formed as faithful disciples, and assisted to discern their vocations. Efforts to provide continuing opportunities for adult faith formation in parishes and clusters, classes offered at the Seminary and by Catholic colleges and universities, and the Rite of Christian Initiation of Adults all strengthen the Church by forming committed adult disciples of the Lord.

## The Priesthood and Consecrated Life

The legacy of education that we share in this archdiocese could not have taken root without the selfless dedication of tens of thousands of consecrated women and men, and of the priests, deacons and lay faithful who collaborated with them in this mission. Saint John Neumann, himself the first Redemptorist professed in the United States, founded a community of religious Sisters—the Sisters of Saint Francis of Philadelphia—and invited many others to the archdiocese, to undertake the work of education. Sadly, our own times have seen sharp declines in the number of people who enter and persevere in the religious life and the archdiocesan priesthood. If we are to preserve the heritage of faith entrusted to us, we must pray and work to encourage *vocations to the priesthood and to consecrated life* among the youth of our Catholic community.

Almighty God surely does not call fewer young people to the priesthood and consecrated life in our day than He did in previous generations. However, the voices of consumerism and secularism, attacks on the virtues of chastity and self-sacrifice, and other negative messages from society and the media combine to create a distracting noise that can make it very difficult for young people to hear Christ's voice. Eyes that look for God's presence, and ears that are trained to hear His voice, are required to discern God's call amid so many conflicting messages.

Here again *parents play a crucial role*. By remaining faithful to their mutual commitment and sacramental bond, and by striving to form families built on love and sacrifice, Catholic parents must guide and encourage their children to discern God's call, whether to marriage, the single life, or a religious vocation. Priests, sisters and brothers must also strive to encourage and invite the young people entrusted to their care to consider priestly and religious vocations. We will accomplish this most effectively by working every day to be *more faithful to our own vocation*—particularly to the charisms, vows and promises that shape our identity as servants of the Lord and His Church. The *faithful and reverent celebration of Mass and the other sacraments is moreover an important factor in helping young people to listen to the Lord's call.* A fervent concern for the celebration of the sacraments was a driving force in the life and ministry of Saint John Neumann.

## Welcoming Immigrants

The archdiocese in his day was welcoming hundreds of thousands of immigrants from Europe, many of whom were unfamiliar with the language and customs of the United States. Saint John, himself an immigrant, learned several new languages in order to minister to these new members of his flock in their native tongues, and he welcomed immigrant priests to the archdiocese to assist in their care. It is difficult for most of us to imagine how these new Americans felt when they saw their new home for the first time. But we can be sure that their faithful eyes were reassured by the sight of the Catholic churches that were filling the landscape in those years. It was in these churches that they gathered to feel at home in the New World and to enrich the Church of Philadelphia with the customs and traditions of their homelands.

Those of us who were born and reared in the Archdiocese of Philadelphia have benefited throughout our lives from the sacrifices of our immigrant ancestors. We must remember, however, that ours is still an immigrant Church. *In our own day we welcome new members to our parishes,* who ought to be able to look on their new home with the same hope and joy that filled the hearts of our own parents and grandparents. Catholics continue to arrive in the archdiocese from Europe, and are joined today by brothers and sisters from every continent around the globe. Irish and Italian families now worship side-by-side with neighbors from Indonesia, Korea, Liberia, Mexico and other countries. Chapels that still echo with the sounds of the Rosary in Polish and Slovak are also filled with prayers in Creole, Igbo, Urdu and Vietnamese.

All too often the presence of newcomers in our midst can be a motivation for misunderstanding, tension and even violence. But we must heed the voice of the Risen Lord—who "has broken down the dividing wall between us . . . through the Cross" (Eph 2: 14, 16)—and who calls upon us to welcome the stranger in His name (cf. Mt 25:35). We must commit ourselves to working together to obtain for today's immigrants the same opportunities for freedom, security and happiness that our ancestors worked so hard to provide for us. Above all, we must strive for mutual understanding and respect, and make a place for all of our brothers and sisters at the table of our Eucharistic Lord.

## Through the Eucharist
## Training the Eyes of Faith to See

It is precisely at this table that we are taught by the Lord Jesus to recognize His presence among us. For this reason, Saint John Neumann established *the tradition of the Forty Hours' Devotion,* an annual three-day period of Eucharistic adoration still celebrated in our parishes. It was a practice most dear to the heart of the first native-born Philadelphian to be numbered among the saints, our own Saint Katharine Drexel. Guided by loving parents, and priests and religious who shared the faith with her and her sisters, Saint Katharine learned at an early age to love the Lord Jesus, and to adore Him present in the Blessed Sacrament. The time she devoted to communicating with Him transformed her life, and teaches an important lesson to us who strive to "see what we see" with her eyes of faith.

The ability to acknowledge Jesus in the Blessed Sacrament is not automatic, but requires an act of faith, as we affirm in the hymn known as *Tantum ergo:* "Faith will tell us Christ is present/When our human senses fail." Over the course of many long hours gazing upon Jesus in the sacred Host, Saint Katharine trained her eyes *to recognize Him under the appearance of simple bread.* Because she persevered in seeking the Lord in the Eucharist, she also learned *to see Him in places and in people where many of her contemporaries had chosen to ignore His presence.* She shared this perception with a new religious community—the Sisters of the Blessed Sacrament—whom she gathered to serve "the least of His brethren" (cf. Mt 25:40) among the African American and Native American communities.

## Recognizing and serving Christ in others

As my predecessor, Cardinal Anthony Bevilacqua, affirmed in his 1998 pastoral letter, *Healing Racism Through Faith and Truth,* "Racism is a moral disease and it is contagious. No one is born a racist." Racism and prejudice are utterly incompatible with the faith we profess as Catholic Christians, and Saint Katharine's example remains a model and a challenge for us as we strive to eradicate all forms of bigotry from our hearts and our communities. By God's providence, however, holiness and truth are also "contagious," and the first step to forming a more just and

tolerant society is found in our *personal commitment to holiness.* In the Blessed Sacrament we find both the motivation and the grace to transform our hearts and minds and to reach out to our brothers and sisters of every race and nation.

To see Christ present in the Blessed Sacrament also trains us *to recognize His presence* in others. He calls upon us to look for Him and to protect Him in every human life, from the tiny person in the womb waiting to be born into the world, to the sick or elderly person waiting patiently for God's call to be reborn into eternal life. We must learn to see and serve Him in those who reach out to us in their need, in search of clothing, food and proper housing. We must train our ears to hear His voice resound from the mouths of those who cry out in physical or emotional pain, of those who lead lonely lives on the margins of society. We must learn to greet Him with dignity and respect in those who face disabilities in mind and body, but have no difficulty in experiencing His loving presence. Christ leads us to seek peace through justice, to eradicate war and violence, and to do our part to establish the Kingdom of God in the world.

## New opportunities to build the Kingdom of God

At the beginning of this new century we have opportunities for building the Kingdom of God that our Catholic ancestors might never have imagined. For too much of our early history, Catholics were restricted or even excluded from participation in civic life. In particular, the Church of Philadelphia in the mid-nineteenth century experienced suspicion, hostility and violence from so-called "Nativist" politicians, as well as persecution and ridicule in public schools and other institutions. By God's grace such terrible conditions no longer exist. On the contrary, Catholics now enjoy full freedom to *participate in public life and public institutions* at every level, and the faithful are able to use their God-given abilities to *make contributions to the Church and to the community* through politics, business, science, education, the arts, sports, entertainment—in virtually every field of human endeavor.

With this privilege of participation in society comes the responsibility to use our gifts wisely, and to perceive with the eyes of faith the proper way to build the community. One out of every three persons in the five counties that make up the Archdiocese of Philadelphia is Catholic. Because we are so visibly present in our communities, we have a responsibility to work together to promote the moral and social values that form the core of the Gospel message. As Archbishop of Philadelphia, I will continue to speak out on important issues; yet mine is not the only voice that must be heard. Every one of us, according to our vocation and responsibilities, must participate *in building a just society.* Catholics leaders must put their gifts at the service of the Gospel and of those whom they serve; they must make conscientious decisions regarding laws in order to defend and protect the dignity and rights of every person. The right of Catholic citizens to vote is also a responsibility to choose candidates who will uphold God's moral law. This too is part of our baptismal call to share in the mission of Christ to build the Kingdom of God in the world.

## A commitment to the Sacraments

As I have already said, the first step in this building up of God's Kingdom is a personal commitment to holiness, which in turn involves *a commitment to the sacraments, especially to Confession and to the Holy Eucharist.* In the colonial period, Catholic families were often far removed from parish churches. They often walked long distances and cherished the opportunities they had—sometimes only a few times a year—to talk to a priest and to confess their sins. Today the Sacrament of Reconciliation is available every week—and, in some communities, every day—and yet many people neglect this precious opportunity to receive forgiveness and to be restored and strengthened by God's grace. *Frequent confession* is a fundamental part of growing in holiness. It teaches us humility and dependence on God's grace, and prepares us most effectively for a *frequent and fruitful reception of Holy Communion,* the source and summit of our lives as Catholic Christian people.

Confession and Communion, and a daily striving to see the work of God in our midst with the eyes of faith, transform our hearts into places where the Holy Spirit can dwell and bear fruit. There, *in private and communal prayer,* "heart speaks to heart," as the Venerable John Henry Newman said. It is precisely in this conversation that the definitive conversion and transformation of our hearts takes place. For this reason, my predecessor Archbishop James Wood solemnly consecrated the Archdiocese of Philadelphia to the Most Sacred Heart of Jesus in 1873, and Cardinal John O'Hara solemnly consecrated the Archdiocese to the Immaculate Heart of Mary in 1952. In the union of these two hearts—the pierced heart of God made Man, and the faithful heart of His first disciple—eyes of faith discern the pattern of the Christian life. The love that flows to us from the hearts of Jesus and Mary draws and calls us to a new and more abundant sacramental life.

## Blessed are the eyes that see what we see!

In this year of jubilee, we take time to offer thanks to God for the miracles of grace that He has worked in our midst. We stand in awe of the thousands of unsung heroes among the laity, religious and clergy who have gone before us and who have entrusted to us the faith-filled heritage that makes us who we are as the Church of Philadelphia. We celebrate the intercession and protection of our heavenly patrons, Saint Peter and Saint Paul, who call us to the work of evangelization; Saint John Neumann, who inspires us to spend our lives in the service of God's people; and Saint Katharine Drexel, who teaches us to recognize Jesus in the least of His brethren and in the Breaking of the Bread. We call upon our Mother, the Blessed Virgin Mary, who loves us with all the love of her Immaculate Heart, and whose footsteps we follow as disciples of her Son.

How blessed we are, indeed, to have received these great gifts from the Most Sacred Heart of Jesus through the Immaculate Heart of Mary; and how great a responsibility is placed on us to *preserve, renew and hand on the legacy of faith* with which we have been entrusted. We will fulfill this responsibility by following the example of the generations who went before us. Like them, let us seek with eyes of faith the Face of Christ—in the Blessed Sacrament, in the Church, and in all our brothers and sisters—and freely give our lives to the service of Him who gave His life for us.

**Cardinal Justin Rigali**
*Archbishop of Philadelphia*

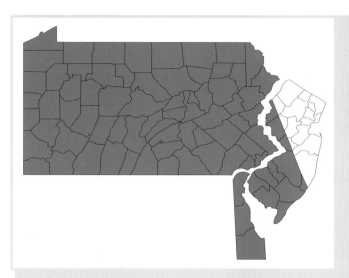

At its founding on April 8, 1808, the Diocese of Philadelphia served 30,000 Catholics scattered over about 53,000 square miles in the Commonwealth of Pennsylvania, the State of Delaware, and the western part of the State of New Jersey.

Two centuries later, nearly 1.5 million Catholics in the Archdiocese of Philadelphia live in an area of 2,182 square miles in five counties—Bucks, Chester, Delaware, Montgomery and Philadelphia— in southeastern Pennsylvania.
Eleven other dioceses now serve Catholics in territory once part of the Diocese of Philadelphia.

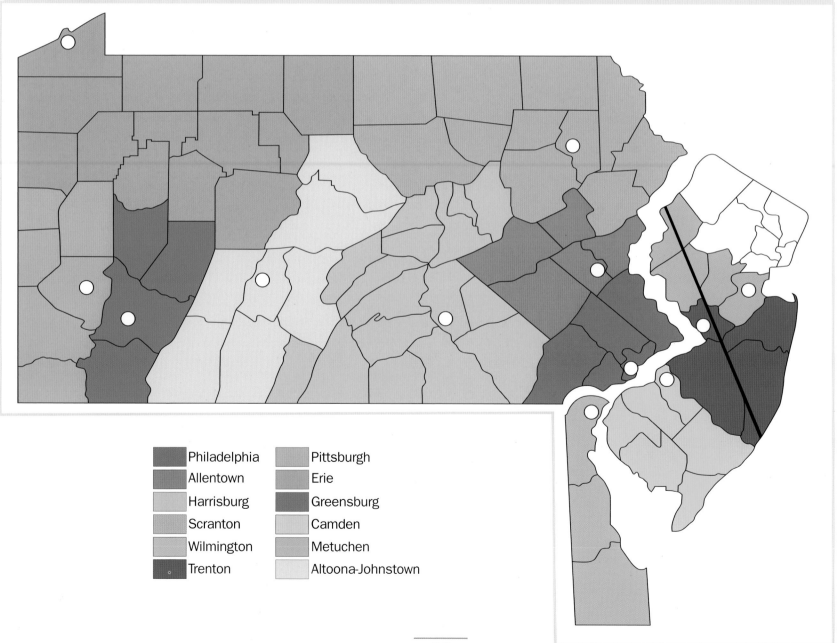

| | |
|---|---|
| Philadelphia | Pittsburgh |
| Allentown | Erie |
| Harrisburg | Greensburg |
| Scranton | Camden |
| Wilmington | Metuchen |
| Trenton | Altoona-Johnstown |

# TWO CENTURIES OF CHANGE AT A GLANCE

| | Total Area (sq.mi.) | Total Population | Catholic Population | Percent Catholic | Parishes and Missions | Diocesan Priests | Religious Priests | Permanent Deacons | Religious Brothers | Religious Sisters |
|---|---|---|---|---|---|---|---|---|---|---|
| 1810 | *about 53,000* | *998,000* | *30,000* | *3%* | *20* | 11 | | — | N/A | N/A |
| 1820 | | *1,176,700* | *59.000* | *5%* | 33 | 18 | | — | N/A | N/A |
| 1830 | | *1,567,400* | *100,000* | *6%* | 62 | 37 | | — | N/A | N/A |
| 1840 | | *1,971,500* | *150,000* | *7.5%* | 91 | 59 | | — | N/A | N/A |
| 1850 | *about 30,000* | 1,915,434 | *170,000* | *9%* | 92 | 93 | | — | N/A | 34 |
| 1880 | 5,043 | 1,502,365 | *300,000* | *20%* | 132 | 242 | | — | N/A | 981 |
| 1900 | | 2,264,971 | *475,000* | *21%* | 234 | 393 | 110 | — | 115 | 2,301 |
| 1910 | | 2,712,708 | *525,000* | *19%* | 312 | 490 | 124 | — | 81 | 2,610 |
| 1920 | | 3,176,549 | *711,300* | *22%* | 338 | 620 | 188 | — | 92 | 3,422 |
| 1930 | | 3,593,184 | *820,000* | *23%* | 388 | 750 | 273 | — | 119 | 5,133 |
| 1940 | | 3,653,120 | *852,000* | *23%* | 389 | 1,033 | 407 | — | 174 | 5,675 |
| 1950 | | 4,039,993 | 1,058,058 | 26.2% | 398 | 1,243 | 672 | — | 156 | 6,819 |
| 1960 | | 4,521,801 | 1,513,269 | 33.5% | 492 | 1,240 | 712 | — | 373 | 6,988 |
| 1970 | 2,182 | 3,865,810 | 1,355,435 | 35.1% | 328 | 1,137 | 667 | — | 342 | 6,534 |
| 1980 | | 3,682,709 | 1,359,987 | 36.9% | 319 | 987 | 553 | 1 | 225 | 5,884 |
| 1990 | | 3,728,909 | 1,402,753 | 37.6% | 315 | 884 | 489 | 95 | 213 | 4,638 |
| 2000 | | 3,849,647 | 1,418,575 | 36.8% | 295 | 781 | 404 | 169 | 127 | 3,764 |
| 2006 | | *3,890,181* | 1,458,895 | 37.5% | 277 | 633 | 358 | 218 | 111 | 3,054 |

NOTE: Figures in *italics* are estimates based on best available data.  N/A: No reliable data available.  Sources: 1810–1840: Philadelphia Archdiocesan Historical Research Center.  1850–1880: *The American Catholic Parish: A History from 1850 to the Present,* ed. Jay P. Dolan, Volume 1 (New York: Paulist, 1987), 111.  1900–2000: Total Population: US Census Bureau. All other data: *The Official Catholic Directory,* published by P.J. Kennedy and Sons, Inc. in corresponding years except 1900 (1905) and 1910 (1912).

# Part I

# The Church of Philadelphia:
## A Heritage of Faith

*God of hosts . . . look down from heaven and see.*
*Visit this vine, and protect it,*
*the vine your right hand has planted.*

*Psalm 80: 15-16*

The Bicentennial of the Church of Philadelphia provides a unique opportunity to look back at the wonders God has wrought. To accomplish His work, God called generations of believers to plant and tend the seeds of faith. The names of those faithful sons and daughters of the Church are mostly lost to history, at least outside of their own families and parishes. But the legacy of these Catholic pioneers is still very much a part of the fabric of life in this local church.

Generations of parishioners have left memorials of their skill and sacrifices in beautiful churches, imposing school buildings, and numerous Catholic institutions throughout the five counties that make up the Archdiocese of Philadelphia. However, the real monument to those dedicated men and women is not made of stone or stained glass. It is rather the vibrant legacy of faith that they planted and defended, that each of them lived out and renewed, and handed on from one generation to the next. The following pages strive to trace this faith-filled heritage, which by God's grace is alive and growing.

Part I of this book speaks of a living vine, transplanted from distant shores to bear fruit in the New World. It recounts the lives of those to whom charge of this vineyard has been entrusted over the years, and of those who labored with them, bearing the day's burden and the heat. Part II will tell the story of the fruit of the vineyard: the hundreds of parishes that have been at the heart of worship, catechesis and Catholic identity in every part of the archdiocese.

To celebrate the history of the Church of Philadelphia means more than simply relating names and dates. It is an acknowledgment of the pioneers who gave so much to spread the Gospel and to let it take root. It is a reminder of the debt that each generation owes to the ones that went before it, and that each generation pays by handing on the faith to the ones that come after it. Most of all, it is an invitation to hear again the call of the Lord Jesus: "You too go into my vineyard." (Mt 20:7)

# Planting the Faith

## (1680–1808)

The story of the Church in Philadelphia began long before the creation of the archdiocese—indeed, long before Philadelphia itself existed. Voyages of discovery in the fifteenth and sixteenth centuries had revealed new continents—a New World—that captured the imagination and ambition of monarchs, soldiers and common folk alike. Throughout the 1600s, indigenous peoples found themselves face to face with European settlers who came to America for varied reasons.

For some, the new continent held uncharted territories for conquest and adventure. Others sought new markets, untapped resources, and a chance to make their fortune. Many came in search of a new home and a fresh start, far away from the tyranny and oppression under which they were suffering. As they crossed the Atlantic Ocean to the eastern shores of North America, they brought with them the traditions, customs and culture of their homelands.

Among them, with names and faces largely unrecorded, sailed the sons and daughters of the Catholic Church. They had inherited a rich legacy from generations of martyrs and missionaries, pastors and parents who had labored for more than a millennium to plant the seeds of the Catholic faith throughout the known world. Now these immigrants carried shoots of that one faith to unknown regions.

## Beginnings

European settlement of the region around Philadelphia was begun by the Dutch, following Henry Hudson's travels through the region in 1609. Dutch influence survives in place names like Cape May and Schuylkill. Thirty years later, the Swedes arrived, and war between them and the Dutch erupted in the mid-1600s. The Dutch prevailed, but Swedish influence is still evident in names of streets like Swanson, Queen, and

Christian. The last two commemorate Queen Christina of Sweden, who abdicated the throne in 1654 when she was received into the Catholic Church.

In 1632, King Charles I of England granted Sir Edmund Plowden of Ireland a tract of land encompassing the present states of Pennsylvania, New Jersey, Delaware, and Maryland. Named "New Albion" by Sir Edmund, the proposed colony was to accord full religious liberty to its settlers. Opposition by the Dutch and Swedish to his claim, however, resulted in the failure of his enterprise.

**William Penn**

The English again laid claim to the area in 1664, when Charles II granted his brother James, Duke of York, all the territory of Maine, New Hampshire, Massachusetts, New York, Pennsylvania, New Jersey, and Delaware. After ten years of opposition by the Dutch, the claim was solidified when the Duke appointed Major Edmund Andros governor of the territory. Andros confirmed all previous grants of religious toleration in the territory, and appointed Lieutenant Anthony Brockholes, a Catholic, as his assistant and successor. In 1681, shortly after Brockholes assumed control over the territory, William Penn was granted a tract of that land, "bounded east by the Delaware River, from twelve miles northward of New Castle town, unto the three-and-fortieth degree of latitude."

## William Penn

As a member of the Society of Friends (who were also known as Quakers), Penn understood only too well the injustice of persecuting people for their religious beliefs. He and other Quakers had even been accused of being secret Catholics, and were taxed and persecuted under the same English statutes that outlawed the Catholic Church. Consequently, the Pennsylvania Assembly at Upland (Chester) passed the Great Law in 1682 which read:

> It is Enacted by the Authority Aforesaid that no Person now or at Any time hereafter Living in this Province who Shall Confess and acknowledge one Almighty God to be the Creator Upholder and Ruler of the World and that Professeth him or herself Obliged in Conscience to Live Peaceably and Justly under the Civil Government shall in any case be Molested or Prejudiced for his or her Conscientious Persuasion or Practice nor shall he or she at any time be Compelled to frequent or Maintain any Religious Worship place or Ministry whatever Contrary to his or her mind but shall freely and fully Enjoy his or her Christian Liberty without any Interruption or reflection and if any Person shall abuse or deride any Other for his or her Different Persuasion and Practice in Matters of Religion Such shall be Looked upon as a disturber of the Peace and be punished accordingly.

Penn was criticized because of his liberality to Catholics. By the beginning of the 18th century, after freedom of religion had been abolished in New York, New Jersey, and Maryland, Penn's colony was the only place in British North America where Catholics could openly practice their religion. In 1686, Penn was compelled to defend his principle of toleration against the attacks of the Archbishop of Canterbury, John Tillottson. "I am a Catholic," Penn wrote in answer, "though not a Roman. I have bowels for mankind, and dare not deny others, what I crave for myself."

*In colonial Pennsylvania, it was not uncommon for traveling Protestant ministers to be mistaken for Catholic priests. Jasper Dankers and Peter Sluyter, two ministers of the Pietist sect known as the Labadists, passed through the region in the 1670s. Catholic colonials, believing they were Jesuit missionaries, sought them out and begged them to celebrate Mass, baptism, and confession.*

*When Jankers and Sluyter reached Maryland, they purchased 4,000 acres of land in Cecil County. for a Labadist settlement. Coincidentally, a portion of this tract was bought by the Jesuits in 1706. It became the site of Bohemia Manor, the "headquarters" for Jesuit missionary activity in Pennsylvania.*

The pro-Catholic policies of Penn's friend, King James II, also stirred up resentment in England against the liberties extended to Pennsylvania, and when James was deposed in the "Glorious Revolution" of 1688, the situation worsened for Penn. By 1708, he was in a London jail for debt, and widely criticized for what people viewed as pro-Catholic sympathies.

## Early Catholic Community

The first Pennsylvania convert to Catholicism, a Susquehannock Indian named Arenhouta (who took the Christian name of Etienne), had been baptized in Canada in 1638. Thirty-six years later, a French Jesuit, Father Jean Pierron, on a journey from his mission among the Mohawk in New York, stopped at the Susquehannock village in Pennsylvania and began a mission there. Throughout the 1670s, while passing through Pennsylvania, Jesuit missionaries from Maryland encountered other Catholic Susquehannocks.

In the eighteenth century, the "Middle Colonies"— New York, New Jersey, Pennsylvania, and Delaware— were the most ethnically and religiously diverse of all colonies in British North America. The eastern part of Pennsylvania, especially the counties immediately adjoining Philadelphia, was settled by a homogeneous population principally of British descent; however, there was a sizable German community near Philadelphia at Germantown. The Welsh had come to Pennsylvania before 1682, and were the most numerous group of immigrants to that date. For the most part, they lived west of the Schuylkill River, in an area known as "the Welsh Tract".

**A warrior of the Susquehannock tribe**

From the first, Penn's colony became a magnet for Catholics from Europe. They came from all walks of life and social classes. In 1683, a man known simply as a "Romanist" servant of Daniel Pastorius (the founder of Germantown) may have been the first Catholic resident of Philadelphia. Much more is known about John Gray, also known as John Tatham, a "Gentleman" of some prominence who came from London and settled in the province in 1685. His land holdings in Pennsylvania were quite extensive, largely in Bensalem Township and on both sides of Neshaminy Creek. His Burlington residence, described as "a great and stately mansion, the best in the province," was a mission stop for Jesuit priests, who made frequent trips between New York and Maryland to minister to the scattered Catholic population. His library was among the largest in the colonies, and its 478 volumes included theological, philosophical and scientific works. For a short time in 1690-91, Tatham served as acting governor of New Jersey. However, his Catholic faith prevented him from taking an oath of allegiance to King William and Queen Mary, and Tatham could not be confirmed as governor by the New Jersey Assembly.

Probably the first European to become a Catholic in Philadelphia was Lionel Britten. An immigrant of some means, Britten had arrived in Pennsylvania in 1680, from Alny (Berkshire), England, and purchased land adjacent to Tatham's property in Bensalem. In 1688, Britten moved to a house in Philadelphia on Second Street below Market. He was received into the Catholic Church in 1707 during a public Mass celebrated in this house. Although the Catholic community in Philadelphia at that time included fewer than ten members over the age of twelve, the event stirred up anti-Catholic suspicion in Philadelphia and in Great Britain.

During the first quarter of the 18th century the Catholic population in Pennsylvania began to increase. In the 1720s, Pennsylvania received many Catholic immigrants from Germany and Ireland, including indentured servants and convicts. Many Catholics in Pennsylvania were poor, although there were some Catholics in Philadelphia—merchants and sea captains—who were better off financially. In Philadelphia most immigrants worked as domestic servants or artisans; beyond the city limits, most were farmers.

In the 1690s, a small French Catholic community existed in southeastern Pennsylvania. One of its prominent members was Peter Dubuc, one of the wealthiest men in Philadelphia. When he died in 1693, Dubuc left a sum of money to a "Father Smith"—a name used by many Jesuit priests who had to hide their true identity because colonists were generally hostile to Catholics. This particular "Father Smith" was really

Father Thomas Harvey, S.J., chaplain to the Catholic governor of New York, Thomas Dongan. When Dongan was overthrown in a rebellion led by Jacob Leisler in 1689, Father Harvey was forced to flee to Talbot County, Maryland. But for many years before his eviction from New York, Father Harvey ministered to the religious needs of Philadelphia Catholics as he passed back and forth between Maryland and New York.

*Beginning in the early 17th Century, French Catholics settled in Acadia, Nova Scotia. In 1713, their homeland was captured by the British. They initially professed allegiance to the British, promising not to give aid to the French and their Indian allies. But when the British governor, Edward Cornwallis, insisted on an oath of unconditional loyalty to the British crown, the Acadians refused. Many Acadians fled to Quebec, and those who stayed in Acadia strove to remain neutral.*

*In 1755, at the outbreak of another war between England and France, British soldiers seized Acadian property, and arrested their Catholic priests. Lieutenant-Governor Charles Lawrence expelled nearly 12,000 Acadians from the territory. They were taken by ship to various points along the east coasts of North and South America. One-fifth of the deportees died en route.*

*In November 1755, three ships, the Hanna, the Three Friends, and the Swan, docked in Philadelphia. These vessels carried 454 Acadian refugees. Their arrival caused considerable concern among Philadelphians and British authorities, who worried that Acadians would convey intelligence to the French enemy and foment violence in Pennsylvania in "conjunction with the Irish and German Catholics in this and neighboring Provinces."*

*Father Robert Harding and Anthony Benezet, a Quaker, cared for the refugees—many of whom were sick with smallpox—in "neutral huts" on Pine Street above Fifth Street. Later Father Harding and Mr. Benezet helped to find homes for the Acadians in various townships around Philadelphia.*

*Although the Treaty of Paris in 1763 allowed Acadians to return home, many decided to remain in Philadelphia. In 1771, the Philadelphia Overseers of the Poor listed 22 Acadian families—totaling 78 individuals—still in the city. Many of them were suffering from poverty and disease.*

*Sacramental registers at Saint Joseph's record several marriages of Acadians, some to non-Acadian Philadelphians. The dead were often buried in Potter's Field, now Washington Square, at Seventh and Walnut Streets.*

## Jesuit Missions and Saint Joseph's Chapel

Jesuit missionaries made these journeys throughout the colonial period, periodically visiting Catholic settlers at an agreed-upon meeting place—usually the house of community leaders like Tatham or Dubuc. There these missionaries celebrated Mass, heard confessions, baptized children, witnessed weddings, and comforted and anointed the sick. In 1706, the Jesuits built the mission of Bohemia Manor, in Cecil County, Maryland. This mission became the center for missionary activity and journeys into Pennsylvania.

In 1720, a priest arrived at Bohemia Manor who would become a pioneer in helping the Catholic faith take root in the Philadelphia region. Joseph Greaton had been born in England, around 1680, and became a Catholic in 1694. In 1708, he became a Jesuit and devoted his life to service in the New World. From Bohemia Manor, he regularly traveled through Cecil, Harford, and Baltimore counties in northern Maryland, and on to Conewago and Lancaster in Pennsylvania. From there he made his way to Philadelphia. Here he rested, and celebrated the sacraments for the faithful in several places. These included a house owned by a Quaker named Dickinson at Front and Walnut Streets, and the home of John Dixon, a Catholic surgeon-barber, near the corner of Second and Chestnut Streets. On the way to Philadelphia, Father Greaton often stopped at the Ivy Mills estate of Thomas Willcox in Concord Township, Pennsylvania.

By 1729, the Catholic population of Philadelphia had increased to the point that Father Greaton was appointed the first residential priest in the city. He could now stay in one place and concentrate on nourishing the faith on a more permanent basis. As he carried out his ministry—often dressed in the garb of a Quaker schoolmaster—it quickly became apparent that he needed a more permanent habitation. He also needed an assistant to take care of the Catholics beyond Philadelphia.

Through the auspices of John Dixon, Father Greaton was able to obtain a plot of land at Fourth and Walnut Streets, and bordering the Quaker almshouse. Here he built a two-story brick house connected to a chapel. Known as Saint Joseph's, the small chapel—only 18 feet by 28 feet—was the first public Catholic chapel built in the British colonies in North America (although there were several private chapels in Maryland). Here, eleven people gathered for the first Mass on February 22, 1732. The first congregation at Saint Joseph's consisted of 22 persons of Irish descent, and 15 of German heritage.

In 1741 Father Greaton received an assistant, Father Henry Neale, S.J. Father Neale was born in England in 1702, and at the age of 22 entered the Society of Jesus. When he arrived in Philadelphia, Father Neale assumed responsibility for the faithful in outlying rural areas, while Father Greaton continued to serve Catholics in and around the city.

---

*Thomas Willcox was born in Exeter (Devonshire), England. He immigrated to America in 1712, and six years later settled in Concord Township. In 1727 he married Elizabeth Cole, an Irish immigrant then living in Chester, and showed himself to be an exemplary Catholic.*

*Willcox had been trained as a paper maker in England, and built a paper mill on the West Branch of Chester Creek, which came to be known as Ivy Mills. Willcox paper was used for colonial and United States currency for more than a century. Benjamin Franklin often purchased paper from the mill for his Philadelphia printing press.*

*By 1729, Father Greaton and others were making regular stops at the Willcox home, located behind the mill, to minister to the small number of Catholics in the area. When Willcox died in 1779, his son Matthew continued to*

**The Willcox home at Ivy Mills**

*welcome visiting priests—Jesuits from Philadelphia and, from 1790, Augustinians from Saint Mary's in White Clay Creek, New Castle County, Delaware (also known as Coffee Run). The original Willcox home was demolished in 1837 and replaced with a larger one. Mass continued to be celebrated in the new house until Saint Thomas the Apostle Church was built in 1853, in Chester Heights. In 1819, Thomas' son, James Mark, married Mary Brackett, a Protestant from Massachusetts. It is said that Mary protested living in a Catholic house by banging pots and pans in the kitchen while Mass was taking place in the parlor. Nevertheless, she became a Catholic twenty years later. Beginning in 1842, she and her husband offered the use of their house to seminarians for a summer retreat and a place of convalescence.*

**The "Willcox Chalice"**
**used by Father Greaton at Ivy Mills**

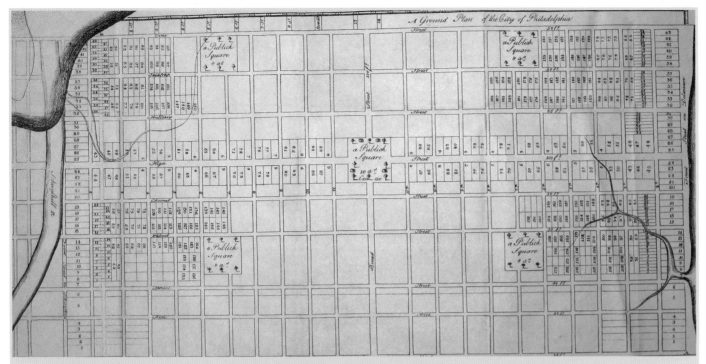

A 17th-century map of the City of Philadelphia shows William Penn's grid of streets around five public squares, and the development of housing close to the Delaware River (at right) and Schuylkill River (at left).

funds for Catholic missions in the colony of Pennsylvania. A legacy of £4,000 —which came to be known simply as the "Sir John James Fund" — provided an annual income of £40 to support priests in London, and £80 for priests in Pennsylvania. This sum was divided equally among the missions of Saint Mary, Philadelphia; Saint John Nepomucene, Lancaster; Saint Francis Regis, Conewago; and Saint Paul, Goshenhoppen (after 1837 known as Blessed Sacrament Church, Bally) in Berks County.

Each mission in Pennsylvania received the 2005 equivalent of about $4,300 a year from the Sir

During these early years, the Jesuits in the Pennsylvania missions received much-needed assistance from a wealthy English aristocrat, Sir John James. Sir John had been raised in the Church of England, but became a Catholic after reading the life of Saint Francis Xavier, a sixteenth-century Jesuit missionary in India and the Far East. After Sir John entered the Catholic Church, he became a friend of Bishop Richard Challoner, who as coadjutor Vicar Apostolic of the London District was responsible for the American missions. When Sir John died in 1741, he left part of his estate to provide

John James Fund. While a great boon to missionary priests, the Fund did not stretch far, since prices in America were higher than in London. On his arrival in Philadelphia in 1741, Father Neale wrote to Sir John about the conditions for Catholics in the region:

*[I] must of necessity keep a horse in order to assist poor People up and down ye country, some twenty miles, some sixty, some farther off. For at present he alone is sufficient for ye service of ye Town, (tho' 'tis a growing Congregation, & will in all likelihood soon require both more hands, and a large house.) Now traveling expenses in my regard will be considerable, since little or nothing can be expected from ye Country Catholics, who, tho' very numerous, are most of them servants, or poor tradesmen, & more in need oftentimes of charity themselves, than capable of assisting others.*

An artist's impression of the original chapel and house at Saint Joseph's Church, Philadelphia

Father Neale died in 1748. The following year Father Greaton, after nearly twenty years service in Philadelphia, retired to Maryland, where he ended his fruitful ministry in 1753. Succeeding him at Saint Joseph's was Father Robert Harding, S.J., born in Nottinghamshire, England, in 1701. He came to America in 1732, and assumed leadership of the Philadelphia community in 1749. Here he labored for twenty-three years. During his tenure the growth of the Catholic population of Philadelphia necessitated an enlargement of Saint Joseph's. In 1757, the original chapel was torn down, and a new one—40 by 60 feet in size—was erected.

## Mission to the Germans

In the 1740s two distinguished German priests abandoned comfortable careers in their homeland to take on the rigors of missionary life. Father William Wappeler, born in Westphalia in 1711, entered the Society of Jesus and emigrated to Pennsylvania in 1741. He traveled by boat up the Susquehanna River to Lancaster. Here he lodged with an Irish Catholic named Thomas Doyle. Father Wappeler served Catholics in the Pennsylvania missions until he returned to Germany in 1748.

A letter from Father Wappeler gives a description of the Catholic community in this period. He found that "… the little band of Catholics is so small and so scattered throughout the country that it is difficult for the missionaries to gather them for Divine Service and especially to instruct them in the Faith. There were very few German Catholics here at our arrival, about 200 in all." He established three places of worship for his flock, each about ten hours' journey from the others, and he visited each once a month. A log chapel-house in Lancaster, which contained living quarters for the priest along with a room in which services were held, was known as Saint Mary of the Assumption. The second was located near the iron and steel forges—New Forge, New Furnace, Durham Furnace, and Branson's Iron Works—around the mission of Saint Paul, Goshenhoppen (Bally). At the small agricultural settlement of Conewago, Adams County, he built a log chapel to look like a private dwelling, which he called the Church of the Assumption.

Father Wappeler eventually had six stops every month on his circuit. He described his usual routine:

*Usually I preface all activities with the Holy Sacrifice of the Mass. After that I read the Gospel from an English book, until I know the language more thoroughly, for the English members who often mingle with the Germans. Then I address an allocution to my compatriots in their native tongue. Lastly, I take a catechism question and discuss it full for the necessary instruction of both young and old… If there are some present who wish to be reconciled to God through the Sacrament of Penance, to enter the marriage bond, or through Holy*

*Baptism become a member of the Church, I dispense these sacraments with the usual ceremonies of our holy religion… For all these sacraments I require previous necessary preparation which often entails toil and prolonged consumption of time for me.*

It is also apparent from his correspondence also that many non-Catholics in the region attended his services, and had their children baptized by the Catholic priest, because, unlike Protestant ministers, he did not charge for the service. He mentions Irish, British, and Africans on his circuit, as well as the non-Catholic spouses of Catholics, who regularly attended the liturgy and some-times became Catholics themselves.

Father Theodore Schneider, born in the Rhine Palatinate in 1703, entered the Jesuits at the age of eighteen. Shortly after his ordination in 1733, Father Schneider was appointed professor at the Jesuit Seminary in Liege, Belgium, and later rector of the University of Heidelberg, Germany. He desired to serve as a missionary, and so immigrated to Penn-sylvania, where he ministered to the German Catholics in Goshenhoppen. Every Sunday he celebrated Mass at Saint Joseph's in Philadelphia. During the week, he visited the faithful "sometimes in forest, sometimes on the banks of rivers."

After Father Wappeler returned to Europe in 1748, Father Schneider was the only priest left to ride these far-flung circuits. He received help in 1752 from two new Jesuit missionaries: Father Mathias Sittensberger (known in America as Father Manners), who was 33 years old and from Landsberg, Germany; and Father Ferdinand Steinmeyer (known as Father Farmer), from Weissenstein in Wuertemberg. These missionary priests rode between 150 and 250 miles each week to visit their scattered flocks, and faced many hazards along the way. Circuit riding demanded a sturdy physical constitution as well as mental discipline. Father Schneider wrote of the qualities necessary in a priest who would undertake this work:

*He must eat, drink, sleep, and be able to ride well, and not be too zealous. Outside of the city in the missions, where most time is spent,*

**An artist's impression of Father Farmer on a journey to one of the missions in New Jersey.**

*the parishioners are poor, and the food served is often coarse and badly prepared. As for drinking, he should drink little or no wine. He should drink cider also sour beer, however, it does not taste as well as water from the well. In regard to sleeping, he must sleep in bad huts, in common, on the straw where his sheep rest. Riding is the cause of the greatest inconvenience, both on account of the heat in summer and the raw winter weather, and very often without getting any rest between, because of the great distance between the places of assembly he must be constantly in motion and therefore on horseback.*

## Catholics under Suspicion

On November 5, 1605, a Catholic Englishman named Guy Fawkes was arrested for plotting to blow up the Palace of Westminster, the meeting place of the English Parliament. In the wake of this "Gunpowder Plot," suspicion fell upon all Catholics in Great Britain, and especially on Jesuits. Anti-Catholic laws were passed at this time and remained in effect until 1829.

Frequent wars with the French and Spanish between 1689 and 1763 also made the presence of the ever-growing number of Catholics in strategically-located Pennsylvania a source of concern to British authorities, and a source of some discomfort to the Catholics themselves. After the outbreak of another war between Great Britain and France in 1754, Catholics, and especially their priests, were suspected of being loyal to the French. There were rumors and suspicions that Catholics were, or could become, disloyal and violent toward Great Britain, and might join forces with hostile Indians on the frontier. During these tense years, Quakers were in the forefront of the defense of Catholic rights. In 1740 and again in 1755, axe-wielding mobs attempted to destroy Saint Joseph's Church, and were only dissuaded by the intervention of Philadelphia Quakers.

In 1757, the total number of Catholics in Pennsylvania over the age of 12 was only 1,365; however, during a time of war this number was inflated in the popular imagination. In that year, Catholics throughout

*Some* THOUGHTS *upon* America, *and upon the* Danger *from* Roman Catholicks *there.*

**The title of an anonymous broadside published in London around 1739 or 1740. The author plays on fears of an alliance with France to discourage allowing Catholics to settle in the colonies.**

*B*enjamin Franklin (seen here in his printing shop) joined in publicly questioning Catholic loyalties in colonial Philadelphia. In articles in his newspaper The Gazette, and a 1744 pamphlet titled Plain Truth, he pondered the prospect of the Iroquois on the Pennsylvania frontier joining forces with the Catholic French in Canada. He and other prominent Protestants advocated restrictions on German Catholics, including limits on immigration, prohibitions against them holding public office or military commissions, and bans on the importation of German books.

Although the charges were baseless—relatively few Iroquois, and only one percent of Germans, were actually Catholic—public speculation like Franklin's worked to intensify anti-Catholic suspicions among Philadelphians.

Pennsylvania, forced to register with colonial authorities, were prohibited from carrying firearms or serving in the militia, and compelled to pay double taxes. An attempt to make it impossible for Catholics to own land in the colony was stopped only by the intervention of Governor William Denney. As the resident priest at Saint Joseph's, Father Harding did his best to calm non-Catholic fears, saying that, though staunchly Catholic in his religious beliefs, he was an Englishman through and through with an "English heart," and he would be appalled at the idea of the French possessing a foot of English America.

In colonial days, Catholics were few, widely scattered, without visible places of worship, and almost invisible. However, when their population began to grow and church buildings began to appear in prominent places like Philadelphia, colonial Catholics began to be viewed much differently. When Anglicans and Presbyterians could see that Catholics were just like themselves—with buildings, resident clergy, and permanent congregations gathering to worship publicly—anti-Catholic anxieties were calmed for a time.

## Saint Mary's Church

The expansion of Saint Joseph's in 1757 eliminated much of the space that could be allocated for a cemetery. On May 10, 1759, Father Harding purchased ground for a Catholic cemetery at Fourth and Walnut Streets. Subscribers to the fund to purchase the land included wealthy Catholic merchants and craftsman in Philadelphia, as well as country residents like Thomas Willcox of Ivy Mills. In addition to the cemetery, part of the plot was used as the site for a much larger church.

Saint Mary's Church was opened in 1763, and as it became the parish church it was associated with a wealthy congregation of Irish and British Catholic merchants and sea captains. Both Saint Mary's and Saint Joseph's

**Saint Mary's Church, Philadelphia, viewed from the parish cemetery**

were served by the same priest, who celebrated a solemn Mass on Sundays at Saint Mary's, and other Sunday and weekday Masses at Saint Joseph's. At 50 feet by 80 feet, Saint Mary's was eight times larger than the original Saint Joseph's.

Father Ferdinand Farmer had come from Lancaster to minister to the Germans of Philadelphia in 1758, and he was still in Philadelphia when Father Harding died in 1772. For almost a year, the whole mission in Philadelphia fell on Father Farmer's shoulders, with occasional assistance from circuit riders from Bohemia Manor. He also continued his ministry beyond the city. Until his death in 1786, he made monthly visits to missions as far away as New York.

## Catholic Loyalties

**Father Robert Molyneux, S.J.**

Father Harding was succeeded at Saint Mary's by Father Robert Molyneux, S.J. Born in Lancashire, England, in 1738, he entered the Society of Jesus in 1757. He became pastor of Saint Mary's in 1773, when the Boston Tea Party and the closing of Boston Port were poisoning relations between American colonists and the British. Father Molyneux was now in charge of the largest Catholic parish in the thirteen colonies. In the coming years, the pews of Saint Mary's would be filled at times by wealthy and prominent persons from around the world.

In 1774, the British Parliament passed the Quebec Act, which expanded the province of Quebec to include territories west of Pennsylvania that had been won in the French and Indian War. Because the Act also permitted new French Canadian subjects to practice the Catholic religion openly, Pennsylvania opponents deplored the Quebec Act as "openly countenancing Popish conspiracies" designed solely for the destruction of Protestant Americans by Catholic Canadians. "We may live," one excited writer declared, "to see our churches converted into mass houses and our lands plundered by tythes for the support of the Popish clergy." Another wrote that the logical outcome of the Act was that "the Inquisition may erect her standard in Pennsylvania and the city may yet experience the carnage of Saint Bartholomew's Day." This allegation referred to Catholic mob violence against Protestants Huguenots in France in 1572.

Sermons against the Act were preached throughout the colony, and Presbyterian clergy of Pennsylvania appealed to the memory of past warfare against the Catholic Church in their *Address to the Ministers and Presbyterian Congregations in North Carolina.* The newly formed Continental Congress meeting in Philadelphia drew up appeals to the King and people of Great Britain "in order that their [Protestant] Religion, Laws and Liberties may not be subverted."

In 1774, Philadelphia Catholics wondered what this all would mean for them, as the city became a hub of revolutionary activity. Citizens representing the thirteen colonies met in Carpenter's Hall, promenaded through the streets, and filled inns and coffee houses with talk of resistance and the rights of British subjects. Saint Joseph's and Saint Mary's were located in the heart of all this activity, and contacts between Protestants and Catholics were unavoidable. George Washington worshiped at Saint Mary's on at least two occasions in 1774. Puritan-born John Adams was also present, and in a letter to his wife Abigail he expressed his misgivings:

> This afternoon, led by curiosity and good company, I strolled away to the mother Church, or rather grandmother Church, I mean the Romish chapel… This afternoon's entertainment was to me most awful and affecting; the poor wretches fingering their beads, chanting Latin, not a word of which they understood; their Pater Nosters and Ave Marias; their holy water; their crossing themselves perpetually; their bowing to the name of Jesus whenever they heard it; their bowing and kneeling and genuflecting before the altar.

Father Molyneux and Father Farmer skillfully guided the infant Church in Philadelphia during the stormy days of the Revolution. Like most Philadelphia Catholics, these priests remained neutral while hateful charges were leveled against Catholics and the Catholic Church over the Quebec Act. At the same time, patriots were appealing for Catholic

*Charles Carroll, of Carrollton, Maryland, was the only Catholic to sign the Declaration of Independence. It is said that he signed his name as "Charles Carroll of Carrollton" to make sure that King George III knew exactly which Carroll from Maryland had risked everything by signing the Declaration.*

*Carroll was the last surviving signer of the Declaration when he died on November 14, 1832.*

support for the revolutionary cause. During these years, enthusiasm for a complete separation from Great Britain was lacking among most non-Catholics outside New England, and Philadelphia sat in the heart of the region of greatest resistance to the appeal for independence.

A major shift occurred in 1777, when the possibility of an alliance with Catholic France seemed imminent. On September 18, the Continental Congress attended a funeral Mass at Saint Mary's for General Philippe du Coudray, a French Catholic engineer who had drowned in the Schuylkill River while serving with the American revolutionary forces. In 1778, after an alliance was signed between the United States and France, banquets were held in Philadelphia which included toasts in honor of the French. Speeches before American regiments were soon celebrating the entrance into the war of a second Catholic ally, King Charles III of Spain. The prominent Philadelphia physician Benjamin Rush, stated that he "had always been taught to consider [Catholicism] as unfriendly to humanity." Now he saw the rapid shift away from anti-Catholicism and toward an alliance with France and Spain as a sign that "human nature" had "turned inside outwards."

For its own purposes, the Loyalist side in the conflict retained the anti-Catholic fervor of the pre-Revolutionary era. *The Pennsylvania Ledger* and the *Pennsylvania Evening Post* railed against the French alliance and the supposedly pro-Catholic trend in Congress. Throughout the war, *Rivington's Gazette*, based in New York City, ridiculed Congress' attendance at Catholic services at Saint Mary's Church, and spread rumors that Benjamin Franklin had renounced his Protestant religion and received the papal honor of a knighthood in the Order of the Holy Cross of Jerusalem. Drafters of the Pennsylvania Constitution in 1776 were criticized because it now opened government offices in the Commonwealth to all candidates, regardless of religion. Benjamin Rush refused to attend the Requiem Mass for the Spanish Agent, Don Juan de Miralles, at Saint Mary's Church on May 8, 1780, because Rush considered it "as not compatible with the principles of a Protestant."

The presence of the members of the (mostly Protestant) Continental Congress at Catholic liturgies could lead to misunderstandings. The Marquis François de Barbe-Marbois (pictured) wrote to a friend in Paris, to describe one such incident at the funeral of Don Juan de Miralles in 1780:

I will not tell you of the funeral except that Congress was present, and we thought there would be a scene. Our chaplain, following the custom, threw holy water on the people. An American officer received a little more abundantly than the others. He felt insulted, and it was not without some difficulty we made him understand that he ought to be especially grateful, that it was a special favor which the priest had done him, and that we looked upon it as a blessing to be well drenched by him.

Benedict Arnold, who did attend the Requiem Mass, revealed his real feelings about the experience five months later in an address to his troops:

*Do you know that the eye which guides this pen, lately saw your mean and profligate Congress at Mass for the soul of a Roman Catholic in Purgatory, and participating in the rites of a church against whose anti-Christian corruptions our pious ancestors would have witnessed with their blood?*

Catholics were ambivalent about allying themselves with such people, a fact well understood by the French minister, André Conrad Gerard. To bring the two sides together, he recommended that the third anniversary of the Declaration of Independence be celebrated in Saint Mary's on July 4, 1779. Gerard invited "the President of the Congress, the President of the State, the Council officers, civil and military, and a number of the principal gentlemen and ladies of the city." His purpose was to bring all Catholics over to the Revolutionary side.

Determining the loyalties of most Philadelphia Catholics during the Revolution is impossible. Several Pennsylvania Catholics—including John Barry, Thomas FitzSimons, Stephen Moylan, and George Meade—served with distinction in the revolutionary cause, but they represent only a prominent minority. Most Catholics remained silent, as did their religious leaders.

The British made much of Catholic attachment to the royalist cause, and could point to the number of Catholics who remained in Philadelphia

Stephen Moylan was born in Ireland in 1734. He received his education in Ireland, but resided for some time in Great Britain. He also traveled on the Continent before immigrating to the British colonies in America. Settling in Philadelphia, he became a member of Saint Mary's Parish. He was caught up in the patriot cause, and hastened to join the Continental Army surrounding the British in Boston in 1775. John Dickinson recommended him for a position in the Commissariat Department, and Moylan was appointed an aide-de-camp to General Washington in March 1776. Moylan was soon appointed Commissary General of the Continental Army. The following year, he re-signed this position to form a troop of light dragoons, the First Pennsylvania Regiment of Cavalry. Under his command, the troop served at the battle of Germantown and through the trying winter of 1777–78 at Valley Forge. Later Moylan's troops operated on the Hudson River; in Connecticut; with General Anthony Wayne in Pennsylvania; and finally with General Nathanael Greene in his southern campaign against General Charles Cornwallis in the last year of the war. In 1782, in recognition of Moylan's contributions and undoubted bravery, he was brevetted a brigadier-general.

When the war ended, Moylan returned to civilian life, resuming his mercantile pursuits in Philadelphia and living on a farm in Chester County. In 1792 he became Register and Recorder of Chester County, and was appointed by President Washington as Commissioner of Loans of Pennsylvania. He died in 1811 at the age of 74, and is buried in Saint Mary's cemetery.

**Commodore John Barry (1745-1803) was captain of the U.S.S. Lexington, the first American naval vessel to capture a British warship (1776). He is buried in Saint Mary's Cemetery.**

during the British occupation of 1777-78. One of these was James Oellers, an innkeeper and a parishioner at Saint Mary's. On the evening of February 7, 1778, Oellers was arrested by a British guard for violating the curfew imposed the previous month. Oellers explained that he, along with Catherine Haffner, and Henry Horn and his wife, were on their way to Saint Mary's Church so that he could be married to Miss Haffner. Eventually convinced that his being out after curfew posed no threat to British security, the British commander sent a military guard with them on their way to Saint Mary's. Here the wedding ceremony was performed by Father Farmer as the British soldiers looked on.

However, the mere presence of Catholics in the occupied city was no sure indicator of Catholic loyalties. The British attempted to raise a regiment of Catholics in the city to fight against their fellow Americans, but this plan met with little success. The Roman Catholic Volunteers, commanded by Alfred Clifton, a member of Saint Mary's congregation, attracted mostly deserters from Washington's army at Valley Forge, and not Catholics from Philadelphia. Father Farmer declined an offer from General Sir William Howe, the Commander-in-Chief of British forces in North America, to become chaplain of the regiment. The unit was disbanded by the end of 1778.

## Catholic Life in the New Nation

In the evening of March 1, 1781, Saint Joseph's Church was splendidly illuminated to celebrate the final ratification of the Articles of Confederation. The thanksgiving hymn *Te Deum* was chanted as part of a solemn ceremony celebrated by Father Farmer and Father Molyneux. The French ambassador, Anne-César de la Luzerne, and his entire entourage were present for this ceremony, and returned on August 25 for another celebration marking the birthday of King Louis XVI. On November 4, members of Congress, the Pennsylvania Supreme Executive Council, and the Pennsylvania Assembly attended another *Te Deum* liturgy to celebrate the surrender in the previous month of the British at Yorktown. Soon there would be peace, and a new government under a new Constitution.

At the time of the adoption of the United States Constitution in 1787, there were about 35,000 Catholics in the nation out of a total population of about four million. The majority were in Maryland (20,000) and Pennsylvania (7,000). To care for this population, and also for Catholics scattered throughout other states, there were only about 34 priests, with only four or five in Pennsylvania. Catholics in rural areas were visited by a priest four or five times a year. A handful of priests from Philadelphia was responsible for congregations throughout Pennsylvania and New Jersey, and in parts of New York.

*The two Catholic signers of the United States Constitution.*

*D*aniel Carroll (above) was the cousin of Charles Carroll of Carrollton, who signed the Declaration of Independence, and the brother of John Carroll, first Archbishop of Baltimore.

*Irish-born Thomas FitzSimons (right) represented Pennsylvania in the Continental Congress and the Constitutional Convention. He also served three terms in the U.S. House of Representatives. He is buried in the churchyard at Saint Mary's.*

With few priests and chapels, lay Catholics were more or less left to themselves and to their private devotions for most of the year. The prayer books and devotional works available to them emphasized a type of religious practice well-suited to a frontier environment. Bishop Richard Challoner, Vicar Apostolic of the London District from 1758 to 1781, published a number of books with titles like *Think Well On't* (1728), *The Garden of the Soul* (1740), and *Meditations for Every Day of the Year* (1753). The devotions suggested in such works were rooted in a personal relationship between the individual Christian and God, and demanded few external rituals. The Catholic was urged to be sober, disciplined, and engaged in the world as a Christian. In a potentially hostile and widely-scattered colonial society, these works made a virtue out of the necessities of life.

Attendance at Mass on Sundays and feast days, enjoined by all Catholic religious teachers and writers, was often impossible in the colonies. Consequently, Catholics resorted to celebrating "Mass in Spirit" by reading the prayers in one of their manuals, alone or with their families. Catholic missionaries feared that conditions in America led to few conversions and many defections from the faith. Estimates suggest that as many as 24,000 Catholics may have fallen away from the faith during the colonial and revolutionary period.

During the last years of the American Revolution, Saint Mary's and Saint Joseph's were renovated and redecorated, and Father Molyneux began to provide for a parish school. A Quaker school northeast of Saint Joseph's and connected with the Quaker almshouse had fallen on hard times during the Revolution and had to be sold. In February 1781, this building was purchased, repaired, and opened in May 1782 as Saint Mary's School, the first Catholic parish school in Philadelphia.

When Father Farmer died in 1786, Father Molyneux became the parish priest for the Catholic community in Philadelphia. Occasionally, Father Huit de la Valienire visited the French Catholics in the city, and Father T. Hassett ministered to the faithful who spoke Spanish. For a short time in 1786 Father William O'Brien, O.P., assisted Father Molyneux, and in 1787 Father Francis Beeston arrived as a permanent replacement for Father Farmer.

Francis Beeston was born in Lincolnshire, England. He studied classics at the English Jesuit College at St. Omer in Flanders, and became a

Master at the Academy of Liege before his ordination to the priesthood. After arriving in Philadelphia, he continued the missionary journeys of Father Farmer through New Jersey and New York. Father Beeston spoke no German, however, leaving German immigrants without a priest of their own for much of this period. Father John Causé spent eight months among the Germans in eastern Pennsylvania before moving on to Lancaster. He was succeeded by Father Lorenz Graessl, who came to Philadelphia from Bavaria in 1787.

Large numbers of immigrants arrived in Philadelphia in the 1790s from Europe and the Caribbean. Irish immigrants were fleeing religious and political persecution. In addition, economic distress had provoked uprisings and violent suppression in their native land. Many of the refugees were penniless, and conditions on immigrant ships were life-destroying. In 1792 Father Keating and Father Fleming were cited by the Hibernian Society for their tireless efforts to assist sick and dying immigrants on ships arriving in Philadelphia from Ireland.

**Irish immigrants arrived in Philadelphia in large numbers in the 1790s, fleeing religious persecution by British officials in their homeland.**

During the 1790s Philadelphia also welcomed numerous French-speaking Catholics, who were fleeing the turmoil of the French Revolution that had begun in 1789. Saint Mary's became home for many of them, including the future King Louis-Philippe and his two brothers. French-speaking Catholics also arrived from the colony of Saint-Domingue on the Caribbean island of Hispaniola, where a slave revolt in 1791 led to the founding of the world's first black republic, Haiti, in 1801. Catholics from the island had strong ties to Philadelphia's merchants, who imported large quantities of sugar and coffee from Saint-Domingue.

Philadelphia's three Catholic churches—including Holy Trinity, founded in 1788—were all located near the waterfront, where most of the French refugees found lodgings. These small congregations were now transformed into biracial and bilingual communities. Africans had long been part of the Catholic community in Philadelphia, though in small numbers, and Father Schneider's sacramental registers from Goshenhoppen (Bally) note some black men and women among his early converts. In 1743, a man named James—whose mother was a slave— had been baptized in James Hoffman's house in Philadelphia. In 1744, Christiana, a slave of John Michael Browne, M.D., was baptized at Doctor Browne's house in Nicetown. In 1763, a slave of Peter Hegnan named Elizabeth was a sponsor at baptism for another black woman, also named Elizabeth.

**The Baptism register of Old Saint Joseph's Church shows the first African American baptism recorded in Philadelphia:**

*17 April Philadelph. in domo Jacobi Hoffman bapt. est Jacobus fil. leg. cujusda. nigrae. Patrini erant Jacob. Hoffman et uxor ej.*

**"17 April [1743], Philadelphia: In the house of James Hoffman was baptized James, the legitimate son of his black woman. The sponsors were James Hoffman and his wife."**

After the Revolution, there were definite signs that Catholics had achieved a significant degree of acceptance by non-Catholics. Catholics had served faithfully in civilian and military capacities during the war. Thomas FitzSimons, a Philadelphia Catholic, was a signer of the new Constitution in 1787. When Father Farmer died in 1786, his funeral was attended by Philadelphia's Protestant clergy, members of the American Philosophical Society, professors and trustees of the University of Pennsylvania (which he had served as Trustee since 1779), and large numbers of non-Catholics. On the feast of the Epiphany in 1790, Jacob Hiltzheimer, a Protestant member of the Pennsylvania House of Representatives, visited the newly-constructed Holy Trinity church. He walked into the church just as its first Confirmation of young Catholics was about to take place. He related that

*shortly after being seated, a gentleman came Over to me and very politely asked me to take a pew nearer the altar and took me to one in which was the Rev. Mr. Blackwell. When the collection plate was handed around we put on a dollar each. In addition to the officiating priests, there were 12 boys and 14 girls dressed in white each with a candle. I counted 98 candles burning.*

A dollar in the collection plate was a substantial contribution for a Protestant to make to a Catholic church in 1790. Hiltzheimer may not have been aware of the significance of his presence or his contribution; however, both indicate how much the American Revolution in Philadelphia had modified the attitudes of many Protestants toward Catholics.

## The First Diocese for the United States

The Catholic Church in the United States had to be reorganized after the Treaty of Paris in 1783, which formally ended the Revolutionary War. Now Catholic life was no longer to be supervised by the Vicar Apostolic in London. On June 9, 1784, the prefect of the Congregation for the Propagation of the Faith, Cardinal Leonardo Antonelli, issued a decree establishing the Catholic Church in the United States as a distinct administrative area. He also appointed Father John Carroll, from Bohemia Manor, as Prefect Apostolic, with faculties to administer Confirmation. Father Carroll visited in Philadelphia in October 1785 to celebrate Confirmation here for the first time.

In 1789, a committee of clergy met at Whitemarsh, Maryland, to petition the Holy See to appoint an American

**Archbishop John Carroll
First Bishop of Baltimore, 1790–1808
First Archbishop of Baltimore, 1808–1815**

bishop, and nominated Father Carroll for the post. Father Carroll was appointed the first Bishop of Baltimore on November 6, 1789, with jurisdiction over what was then the entire United States. He traveled to Great Britain and was ordained a bishop in the chapel of Lulworth Castle, Dorset, on August 15, 1790.

In 1789, Father Thomas Keating arrived in Philadelphia from Ireland. However, he was soon transferred by Bishop Carroll to Charleston, South Carolina, because Saint Mary's parish could not afford to support a third priest. Eventually a newly-formed group of "Trustees of the Roman Catholic Society Worshipping at the Church of Saint Mary's in the City of Philadelphia" did raise enough money for a third priest, and Father Francis Fleming, O.P., arrived as assistant priest. When Father Beeston retired to Bohemia Manor in 1790, Father Christopher Keating, O.P., succeeded him, but was soon transferred to Maryland. To fill the vacancy, Father Thomas Keating was recalled from Charleston.

**Archbishop Leonard Neale**
**Coadjutor Bishop of Baltimore, 1800–1815**
**Second Archbishop of Baltimore, 1815–1817**

In December 1793, Father Leonard Neale arrived as pastor of Saint Mary's. Born at Port Tobacco, Maryland, in 1746, he was educated at Saint Omer, Bruges and Liege in Belgium. He carried out his ministry in several locations in Europe before returning to Maryland in 1783. In September 1793, Father Graessl was appointed as coadjutor bishop to Bishop Carroll in Baltimore; however, Father Graessl died of yellow fever before he could be ordained bishop. In 1795, Father Neale was appointed as coadjutor bishop; however the documents conveying the appointment were lost in transit, and official notification did not arrive until 1800.

## Anti-Immigrant Attitudes

In the 1790s, England and France were again at war, and French leaders looked for assistance from former allies in America. President Washington declared the neutrality of the United States. After his retirement in 1796, the administration of John Adams moved further away from any pro-French policies. In 1798, Congress passed four laws known as the "Alien and Sedition Acts." The "Naturalization Act" extended the period for becoming a citizen of the United States from five to fourteen years. The "Alien Friends Act" gave the President authority to deport any foreigner dangerous to American security. The "Alien Enemies Act" gave the President authority to imprison or deport any national of a country at war with the United States. The "Sedition Act" gave the President authority to fine or imprison anyone who opposed policies of the government or incited riot or rebellion against the government.

German and Irish immigrants in Philadelphia were outraged. Many Irish immigrants saw the Acts as a pro-British ploy to silence Irish newspapers and shut down Irish organizations. As a result, many immigrants joined the Democratic-Republican Party, which opposed the Federalist Party. Germans and Irish in Philadelphia held mass meetings in 1799 to petition Congress to repeal the Acts. To expedite the collection of signatures, petitions were circulated at Catholic and Presbyterian churches on the Sunday preceding the meeting of Congress. A notice was posted on the door of Saint Mary's asking Irishmen of the parish to sign the petition in the churchyard after Mass.

One of Saint Mary's trustees, John O'Hara, was indeed Irish, but was no friend to the petition movement; consequently, he tore down the notice. When other copies were put up, they were again torn down by James Gallagher, Jr. He was confronted by Samuel Cummings, one of the petitioners. The argument escalated over the next several hours into a mob confrontation during which a firearm was drawn, but not discharged. Constables arrived and arrested several participants.

**Father Matthew Carr, O.S.A.**

The trial of the rioters divided the Catholic community, including the parish priests. Father Matthew Carr, an Augustinian who had arrived from Dublin in 1795, testified that the practice of signing petitions after

Mass was customary in Ireland, and therefore there should have been no interference with the process at Saint Mary's. But American-born Father Leonard Neale maintained that posting the petition had been contrary to his orders and an insult to him and the Board of Trustees. In fact, Father Neale had advised several of his parishioners to prevent posting of these petitions.

## Trustees of Holy Trinity

For several years, the substantial German Catholic community in Philadelphia had desired a parish of their own. This wish was fulfilled in 1788 when the parish of Holy Trinity was incorporated under the direction of a Board of Trustees led by Adam Premir. Premir oversaw the building of a church at Sixth and Spruce Streets. He deeded the property to the trustees in 1791, with a document naming Father John Heilbron, a Capuchin friar, as pastor. Father Heilbron's appointment was confirmed by Bishop Carroll in August of that year; however, the trustees were left with the impression that they had the power to appoint the pastor.

### TRUSTEEISM

*C*hurches in eighteenth-century America were frequently founded by groups of laymen, who formed Boards of Trustees to fund and administer the church. Because they funded the church, these trustees expected to have a say in matters affecting the parish's financial administration—a policy endorsed by Bishop Carroll.

*Problems developed, however, when some trustees tried to usurp the authority of the bishop by appointing their own pastors. Some also sought to control the administration of the church and influence the decisions of the pastor by withholding salaries and other necessary funds.*

*Bishop Carroll had to resist the claims of lay trustees in several areas, beginning with New York in 1785, when he was still Prefect Apostolic. In addition to the Holy Trinity incident in the 1790s, Bishop Carroll faced further problems in the early 1800s in Charleston, South Carolina, and New Orleans, Louisiana.*

*After the division of the Diocese of Baltimore in 1808, lay trustee problems became even more frequent and divisive. Pope Pius VII, in the papal brief* Non Sine Magno *(1822), restated the canonical norm that church property was under the control of the pastor and the bishop, not the trustees. The First Provincial Council of Baltimore in 1829 insisted that church property be deeded to the bishop before the dedication of any new church, and defined penalties for priests and laymen who disobeyed this rule.*

**Drawing by architect William Palmer of Holy Trinity Church, Philadelphia, 1788**

Father John Heilbron immediately left to raise money in Europe, and was succeeded by his brother, Father Peter Heilbron, who was also a Capuchin. He arrived from Bally in 1792. A year later, he was joined by Father Lawrence Phelan. Soon afterwards, Father John Goetz, who had been a professor and preacher at the Royal Imperial Academy in Wiener Neustadt, Austria, was appointed by Bishop Carroll and elected by the trustees as an assistant to Father Peter Heilbron at Holy Trinity. Dissatisfied with this subordinate role, Father Goetz appealed to the trustees in 1796 to be made co-pastor.

Father Peter Heilbron refused to accept the decision of the trustees. In retaliation, the board ordered him to surrender the property of the church to them or face legal prosecution. To avoid scandal among the laity, Father Heilbron moved to Saint Joseph's. Here he continued to minister to the members of Holy Trinity who felt the trustees had overstepped their legitimate authority. The trustees elected Father Goetz as pastor in November 1796, and although Bishop Carroll threatened Father Goetz with suspension, he continued to act as pastor of Holy Trinity, assisted by Father William Elling.

Both priests were excommunicated by Bishop Carroll at the end of February 1797. The two priests had a falling out soon after, and the trustees elected Father Elling as the pastor in November. Bishop Carroll traveled to Philadelphia where he was immediately served with a writ and brought into court. There the lawyer for the trustees claimed that the only power the bishop had was to impose hands on the person whom the people presented as their chosen minister. Anything beyond that, they insisted, would be contrary to American law.

Over time, the supporters of the trustees dwindled, and by 1802 Father Elling had begun to see the hopelessness of his position. When he finally submitted to the authority of the Bishop, the trustees also admitted that their position had been erroneous. James Oellers went to the other trustees to have them sign a document which stated that they were subject to the episcopal authority and jurisdiction of the Bishop of Baltimore. The censure was removed from Father Elling, who was then officially appointed by Bishop Carroll as pastor of Holy Trinity.

Holy Trinity's financial affairs were ruined by the schism, and money was a source of constant tension between Father Elling and the trustees. When Father Elling retired in 1806, he was succeeded by Father Adam Britt. He soon found that many members of the parish had not attended Mass for years and lacked even basic knowledge of the truths of the faith.

## Yellow Fever Epidemic

An epidemic of yellow fever struck Philadelphia in July 1793. Unknown to the medical profession at the time, mosquitoes from the tropics were the cause of the epidemic. The carriers of the disease arrived on ships bringing refugees from the revolutionary chaos in Haiti. Doctor Benjamin Rush noted in his diary that mosquitoes in the city were particularly numerous.

Remedies endorsed by physicians—ringing bells to break up the bad air, wearing garlic to ward off infection—were futile. The bleeding of patients triggered weakness that was often fatal. Panic set in, and more than half of the city's population fled to the countryside. As the weeks wore on, roads leading out of Philadelphia were choked with coaches, wagons, carts and pedestrians. Shops and houses were shuttered, theaters closed, and church services were suspended. Families were split, sick children abandoned by parents, and infected spouses deserted. There was no work, since most businesses had closed, and the quarantine imposed on Philadelphia by fearful surrounding communities meant that the usually bustling port on the Delaware was absent of incoming ships.

In this hour of crisis, prominent heroes emerged. The financier, Stephen Girard; Matthew Carey, a Philadelphia printer; and Benjamin Rush took steps to educate the public and care for the sick. Assisting victims of the yellow fever meant taking the risk of being exposed to the disease. Both Father Graessl and Father Fleming died of yellow fever and were buried at Saint Joseph's cemetery. When the epidemic revisited the city a few years later, three more priests succumbed—Father Michael Ennis, Father Joseph La Grange, and Father John Burke.

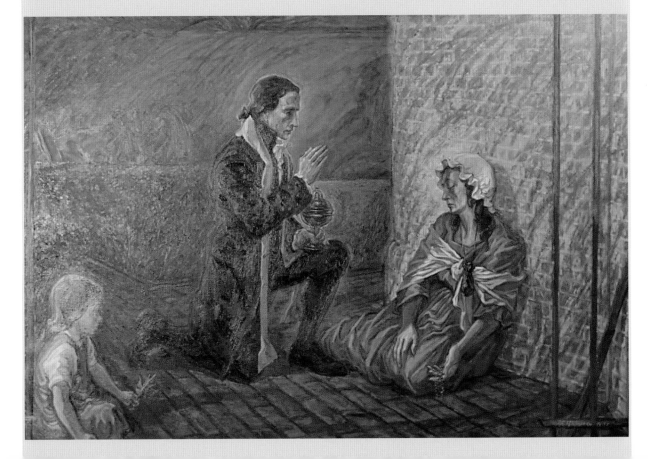

A 1976 painting by Philadelphia Catholic artist Robert McGovern depicts Father Lorenz Graessl ministering to a victim of Yellow Fever. In 1793, Father Graessl would himself succumb to the disease.

Posters like this one—listing burial totals from Philadelphia churches from 1792 to 1795—were powerful reminders of the toll that Yellow Fever took on city residents.

Parishioners from Saint Mary's, Saint Joseph's and Holy Trinity cared for victims of yellow fever, and children whose parents had died from the epidemic throughout the 1790s. In 1806, a group met at Saint Joseph's to incorporate "The Roman Catholic Society of Saint Joseph for the Maintenance and Education of Orphans," which opened Saint Joseph's Orphan Asylum at Sixth and Spruce Streets in 1808.

*One Catholic layman who gained prominence during the Yellow Fever epidemics was Matthew Carey. When the disease struck in 1793, Carey was appointed to the Committee of Health to provide relief to those stricken by the disease, and to try to prevent its further spread. His investigations on the subject were published as the* Rise, Progress, Effects, and Termination of the Disease, *which went through five editions.*

*Matthew Carey was born in Ireland in 1760, and despite his father's objections became a printer and bookseller. His pamphlets on equality for Irish Catholics attracted the attention of British and Irish authorities, and he fled to France, was jailed in Great Britain for a time, and finally immigrated to America.*

*In Philadelphia he became a member of Saint Mary's parish, and produced a number of Catholic books and pamphlets, including the first edition of the Douay translation of the Bible printed in America. His Columbian Magazine, which he began in 1786, lasted less than a year, but his journal* The American Museum *had more success, and was published from 1787 to 1792. Dedicated to "Dr. Carroll, Bishop-elect of the Catholic Church," the* Museum *reprinted articles from various newspapers as well as documents of general interest and worthy of preservation.*

*In 1793, Carey convinced prominent Irishmen in Philadelphia to establish the "Hibernian Society for the Relief of Immigrants from Ireland." In 1796, he helped to found the "Sunday School Society", the first of its kind in the United States. Carey died in 1839 and was buried in Saint Mary's cemetery.*

A SHORT
ACCOUNT
OF THE
MALIGNANT FEVER,
LATELY PREVALENT IN
PHILADELPHIA:
WITH A STATEMENT OF THE
PROCEEDINGS
THAT TOOK PLACE ON THE SUBJECT IN DIFFERENT
PARTS OF THE
UNITED STATES.

TO WHICH ARE ADDED,
ACCOUNTS
OF THE
Plague in London and Marseilles;
AND A LIST OF THE DEAD,
From August 1, to the middle of December, 1793.

BY MATHEW CAREY.

FOURTH EDITION, IMPROVED.

PHILADELPHIA:
PRINTED BY THE AUTHOR.
January 16, 1794.

## Saint Augustine's Church

The churches of Saint Joseph, Saint Mary and Holy Trinity were all close together in the southern part of Philadelphia; however, the Catholic population in the 1790s was growing in the city's northern areas. Irish Augustinians had been seeking to establish a house in the United States, and Father John Rosseter, O.S.A., and Father Matthew Carr, O.S.A. sought donations to build a new church. Contributions came from both Catholics and non-Catholics. Donors included George Washington, John Barry, Thomas FitzSimons, and Stephen Girard.

President Washington and Pennsylvania Governor Thomas McKean attended the laying of the cornerstone of the new church in September 1796, and after many delays—especially as a result of a return of yellow fever—Saint Augustine Church was dedicated on June 7, 1801. At 125 feet by 62 feet, with a steeple 75 feet high, the church at Fourth and Vine Streets was the largest in Philadelphia at that time. Michael Fagan was the architect, and all of the lumber for its construction was donated by Fagan's father-in-law, Captain John Walsh, a privateer during the American Revolution.

In 1803, separate parish boundaries were drawn for Saint Mary's and Saint Augustine's. Market Street was the dividing line. The two parishes also included the faithful beyond the city limits. Sacramental registers for both parishes show marriages and baptisms taking place in a number of villages in Philadelphia County and also in New Jersey and Delaware. During the trustee troubles at Holy Trinity, many parishioners who objected to the position of the trustees attended Saint Augustine's. During construction of Saint Augustine's, Father Carr lived at Saint Joseph Church. He moved to a residence near Saint Augustine's in 1802.

The trustees of Saint Mary's petitioned Bishop Carroll to appoint a new pastor. In 1803, Father Michael Egan, O.S.F., a Franciscan priest who had been stationed at Lancaster, became co-pastor with Father Rosseter.

**Matthew Carey's account of the Yellow Fever epidemic, printed in 1794.**

## CATHOLIC SCHOOLS IN THE EARLY 1800s

*In a 1792 pastoral letter, Bishop Carroll had stressed the "necessity of a pious and catholic education of the young to insure their growing up in the Faith." His exhortation gave great impetus to the founding of Catholic schools in the new United States.*

*The first Catholic school in the Philadelphia area was opened by Father Theodore Schneider in Goshenhoppen (Bally) in 1741, and welcomed children of all religions. At Bohemia Manor, Father Thomas Poulton created an elementary and preparatory school in 1747, which counted the future Bishop Carroll among its alumni. The tuition was too high for most Catholics, but prominent Philadelphia Catholics sent their boys there to prepare them for higher education in Europe. Other Catholic schools were founded in places like Conewago, York, Reading and Haycock Run (present-day Ottsville).*

*Saint Mary's had operated a school since at least 1782, and Holy Trinity since 1787. These were supported by contributions from both parishes, as well as by special collections taken up at regular intervals. Students at Saint Mary's received instruction in reading and spelling, in addition to catechetical exercises. By 1805 more than forty boys and girls attended Saint Mary's Free School, necessitating an expansion of the building in 1810.*

*Additional private Catholic schools were founded in the early 1800s. Charles Carre, a Catholic immigrant from Alsace (on the border of France and Germany) opened a private school in 1806 called Clermont Seminary. This school was located on the road from Frankford to Germantown. Father Francis Brosius founded a private school in Mount Airy in 1807. In addition to religion, the course of study included French, English, Latin and Greek, ancient and modern history, geography, arithmetic, algebra, geometry, dancing, drawing and music—a far cry from the primitive education available to Catholics just a century before.*

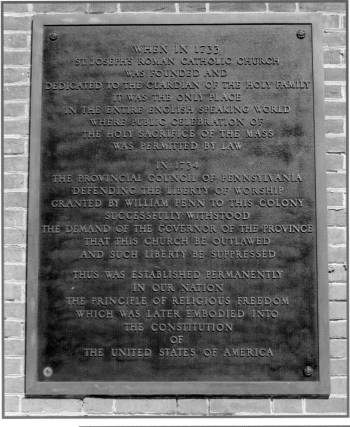

The Catholic community that Father Egan encountered in 1803 looked much different than it had when the City of Philadelphia had been founded over a century before. Once-isolated mission communities were being built up into vibrant parishes. Priests still had long journeys to make to tend to the faithful, but now these priests had permanent homes and public places in which to worship and teach. Generations of Catholics had withstood hardship, labor and years of war to plant the faith firmly in the heart of the new nation.

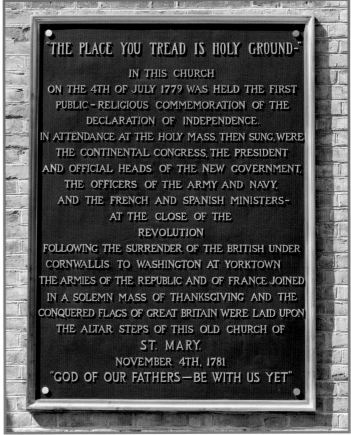

# Defending the Faith
## (1808–1860)

The growth of the Church in the United States at the beginning of the nineteenth century put increasingly greater demands on Bishop Carroll and his coadjutor, Bishop Neale. The Diocese of Baltimore now encompassed seventeen states, and in 1805 Bishop Carroll had also been appointed Apostolic Administrator of the huge territories acquired by the Louisiana Purchase. Communicating with congregations and pastors scattered over half a continent was immeasurably difficult. These congregations continued to expand, and leaders began to emerge in each local church. The time was right to ask the Holy See to take the next step in building the Church in America.

### Bishop Egan

On April 8, 1808, Pope Pius VII issued the solemn documents called bulls (from the lead seal or *bulla* with which each was authenticated) which established Baltimore as the first archdiocese in the United States, and created four new dioceses: Philadelphia, Boston, New York and Bardstown, Kentucky. On the same date, Father Michael Egan, O.S.F., the pastor of Saint Mary's, was appointed as the first Bishop of Philadelphia.

Michael Francis Egan was born in Limerick, Ireland in 1761. He joined the Franciscans in Ireland and was educated at Louvain, Belgium, and Prague, where he was ordained. He worked in Rome from 1787 to 1790, and in Ireland for an additional seven years, before immigrating to America in 1798. Archbishop Carroll called him "truly pious, learned, religious, remarkable for his great humility but deficient, perhaps, in firmness and without great experience in the direction of affairs."

Although he was appointed in 1808, Bishop Egan was not consecrated as bishop until October 28, 1810. The turmoil of European wars meant that it took over two years for the documents of appointment to arrive in

Bishop Michael Francis Egan, O.S.F.
First Bishop of Philadelphia, 1810-1814

The new Diocese of Philadelphia, established in 1808, comprised the entire Commonwealth of Pennsylvania, the entire State of Delaware, and the western part of the State of New Jersey— a total area of about 53,000 square miles.

the United States. In the interim he served as Vicar General and Administrator of the diocese.

In October 1808, Archbishop Carroll sent a letter to the parishes of the City of Philadelphia urging them to create a means of financial support for their new bishop. Representatives of Saint Mary's, Holy Trinity and Saint Augustine's agreed on an annual sum of $800.00, to be paid quarterly. Half would be paid by Saint Mary's, which would serve as pro-cathedral, and where the bishop would serve as pastor. The trustees of Saint Mary's voted on May 10, 1809, to enlarge the church and decorate it in a manner appropriate for a cathedral. They began a subscription among all of the city's Catholic churches to cover the $22,000 cost of renovating and expanding the church and school. The project, however, left the trustees $5,000 in debt.

## Trustees of Saint Mary's

On April 9, 1812, the trustees of Saint Mary's issued a report on the financial condition of this church. To relieve the debt they recommended that the salaries of the parish clergy be decreased, and the number of priests reduced from three to two. In July the trustees remitted only a third of the usual stipend. The following month, Bishop Egan and his assistants, Father William Harold, O.P., and his uncle Father James Harold, placed in the pews a printed "statement of grievances" against the lay trustees.

**Father William Harold**

The trustees responded with several written appeals to members of the parish, and the dispute continued throughout the autumn of 1812. In an attempt to reconcile with the trustees, Bishop Egan agreed to remove Father James Harold from the parish. Now both Father James and Father William Harold resigned, and the bishop's acceptance of their resignations caused a rift among the parishioners. Those who supported Father James Harold elected a new Board of Trustees on April 20, 1813, which demanded Father James's reinstatement. They also voted to reduce by two-thirds the salaries provided to the bishop and parish clergy. When Bishop Egan protested, the board voted to remove him as President of the Board.

Amid this turmoil, Bishop Egan's already fragile health was deteriorating. He had made out his will on July 6, 1814, and by the middle of that month he was seriously ill. After suffering for several weeks, on Friday, July 22, he asked to be laid on the floor of his room in front of a portrait of Saint Francis of Assisi, the founder and patron of his Order. He received the sacraments, extended his arms in the form of a cross, and died peacefully at the age of 53. His body was dressed in vestments and lay in state overnight in Saint Mary's Church. His funeral was celebrated there the next day, and his body was buried in the churchyard of Saint Mary's.

## Selecting a New Bishop of Philadelphia

On July 20—two days before his death—Bishop Egan named Father Louis de Barth, a French Sulpician and pastor at Conewago, as his Vicar General. After Bishop Egan's death, Archbishop Carroll named Father de Barth administrator of the diocese. Father de Barth did not want the appointment, and begged Archbishop Carroll to withdraw it, writing that "Death would not be so frightful to me as Philadelphia." At the archbishop's insistence, Father de Barth eventually accepted. He spent as little time in Philadelphia as possible, and delegated pastoral duties to his assistant, Father Terrence McGirr.

After Bishop Egan's death, Philadelphia had no bishop for nearly five and a half years. Poor communications between America and Europe, uncertainty over the procedures to be followed for the nomination of bishops in the United States, and attempts by various European factions to influence the appointments made the process a slow one. But the biggest problem was the state of the Catholic Church in Philadelphia. Bishop Egan and the trustees of Saint Mary's had been fighting at the time of his death, and the trustees repeatedly petitioned Archbishop Carroll for the appointment of Father William Harold as pastor. They also lobbied for his appointment as Bishop of Philadelphia.

Early nominees for the post refused the appointment, including Father de Barth, who wrote to Archbishop Ambrose Maréchal, third Archbishop of Baltimore, in late 1818:

> I declare to you Monsigneur, that if you do not forward my objections to the Holy See, and His Holiness sees and weighs them, I will not accept but will kneel down and devoutly put the bulls in the fire… and then, farewell, Monsigneur. Neither you nor anyone else shall ever know the corner of the globe where I will vegetate the few years still left me to live.

Father de Barth continued as administrator, but discipline became more relaxed as he deferred decisions to a bishop who had yet to be appointed. The news finally arrived in 1820 of the appointment of Bishop Henry Conwell as second Bishop of Philadelphia.

## Bishop Conwell

Born in Moneymore (County Derry), Ireland in 1747, Henry Conwell was ordained in

**Bishop Henry Conwell,**
**Second Bishop of Philadelphia, 1820–1842**

1776, and around 1785 became a parish priest in the Archdiocese of Armagh. He was appointed Vicar General of Armagh in 1795. In 1817, when the Archbishop of Armagh died, priests of the archdiocese asked the Holy Father to appoint Father Conwell as Archbishop. This was opposed by the British government as well as by the three other archbishops in Ireland. Instead of the Archdiocese of Armagh, Father Conwell was given the choice of two dioceses: Madras, in India, or Philadelphia. He chose the latter, and was ordained a bishop in London on September 24, 1820.

Bishop Conwell arrived in Philadelphia on December 2, 1820. At 73 years of age, he was unaccustomed to the ways of America, and his critics accused him of being stubborn and hard-headed. Archbishop Patrick Curtis, who was appointed Archbishop of Armagh in 1819, said that Bishop Conwell's appointment "was almost as impossible as to believe he had been made Emperor of China."

When he arrived in Philadelphia, Bishop Conwell immediately had to deal with the trustees of Saint Mary's. They continued to seek the return of Father Harold as pastor of Saint Mary's, and in February they had unsuccessfully attempted to change the charter of the parish to exclude clergy from the Board of Trustees. But a more pressing problem was created by the presence of a priest who had been appointed to Saint Mary's by Father de Barth: Father William Hogan.

## Hogan Schism

William Hogan was born in the Diocese of Limerick, Ireland, and came to America in late 1819, ministering in Albany, New York. On his way to Baltimore to attend the ordination of his cousin Father George Hogan in March 1820, William passed through Philadelphia and offered his services to Father de Barth, who accepted him based on a letter of recommendation from the Bishop of Limerick. Young, handsome, sociable, and admired for his preaching ability, Father Hogan quickly became popular at Saint Mary's, especially with women and youth. He revived religious instruction at the church, revitalized the Sunday School and was active in charitable work. However, his critics, including almost all of his fellow priests, considered his first priority to be socializing.

Father Hogan preached the sermon at Bishop Conwell's installation, and used the occasion to attack Father de Barth. Bishop Conwell ignored the attack, but ordered Father Hogan—who at this time was living in a private residence—to return to the priests' house at Saint Joseph's. During another sermon on December 10, Father Hogan declared that no one could tell him where to live, and that he would not submit to the directive of Bishop Conwell. Two days later, the bishop suspended Father Hogan.

Bishop Conwell refused a request from parishioners of Saint Mary's to reinstate Father Harold, and over the next few months the Board of Trustees voted to remove Bishop Conwell from the board. They appointed

**Father William Hogan**

the suspended Father Hogan as pastor of Saint Mary's and chairman of the Board of Trustees. This defiance of the bishop's authority amounted to schism— a public break from the unity of the Church. Bishop Conwell declared Father Hogan excommunicated, placed the parishioners of Saint Mary's under interdict, and forbade them to receive the sacraments.

A public war of words continued for more than a year, and on April 9, 1822, the crisis escalated to violence in Saint Mary's churchyard. In August 1822, Pope Pius VII addressed an apostolic letter to all of the clergy and laity of the United States, condemning the trustees' actions and Father Hogan's defiance.

By June 1823 the dissenters were losing support, and they opened negotiations with Bishop Conwell to settle the dispute. However, they made repeated attempts to appoint their own pastors. Conflicts over these appointments protracted the dispute for three more years. An agreement was finally reached on October 9, 1826. The "Pact," as it was called, contained nine articles setting "the terms and conditions upon which the reconciliation and union shall be effected." It gave the trustees responsibility for the temporal affairs of the parish, and acknowledged the bishop's responsibility to provide for the spiritual life of the parishioners and to appoint pastors. The Pact allowed trustees to raise objections to the bishop's choice of pastor, which would be settled by a board of arbitrators.

As both sides awaited approval of the Pact by the Holy See, Bishop Conwell lifted the interdict and returned to Saint Mary's as pastor, assisted by Father William Harold and Father Thomas Heyden. Parishioners from both sides of the dispute organized to form "The Vindicators of the Catholic Religion from Calumny and Abuse," to defend and restore the nearly ruined reputation of the Catholic Church in Philadelphia. However, Father William Harold and some diocesan clergy publicly criticized the Pact and the bishop's actions. Bishop Conwell

suspended Father Harold in April 1827. A committee of parishioners protested this decision, and criticized Bishop Conwell in pamphlets and public meetings.

---

*CATHOLIC NEWSPAPERS AND JOURNALS*

*T* *he trustee crisis of the 1820s led many non-Catholics to criticize both Bishop Conwell and the Catholic faith itself. Father John Hughes, the pastor of Saint John the Evangelist Church and future Bishop of New York, spoke privately and publicly in defense of the bishop and the diocese. In December 1832 the secretary of the Board of Education of the Presbyterian Church, John Breckinridge, invited any Catholic priest or bishop to a public debate on the truths of the faith, and Father Hughes took up the challenge.*

*Mr. Breckinridge printed his arguments in the weekly journal* The Presbyterian, *but at the time there were no Catholic papers in Philadelphia. With financial backing from friends, Father Hughes published the first issue of* The Catholic Herald *on January 8, 1833, headed by a letter to Mr. Breckinridge.*

*The* Herald *continued to be published even after the debates ended in September 1833, and grew to become the official publication of the Diocese of Philadelphia. Its pages contained news of the Church both local and national, and it reported on Catholic events in Ireland and Rome. Speeches and sermons of prominent priests and diocesan spokespersons were reprinted, along with articles defending the faith against attack and misunderstanding.*

*The Catholic Visitor began in 1856, and the next year merged with the* Herald *to form* The Catholic Herald and Visitor, *which was published into the 1860s. In 1866 it was joined by* The Catholic Standard, *published by Father James Keogh, a theology professor at Saint Charles Seminary. A third paper,* The Catholic Times, *came out in 1892.*

*Mr. Francis T. Furey, a professor at Saint Joseph's College who also taught at Roman Catholic High School, oversaw the merger of these two papers to form* The Catholic Standard and Times, *which first appeared on December 7, 1895. This weekly paper is still the official publication of the Archdiocese of Philadelphia.*

---

Bishop Conwell was also coming under increasing criticism from other American bishops. Many thought that the Pact set a bad precedent, and would embolden opposition to Church authority. Archbishop Maréchal of Baltimore wrote to the Congregation for the Propagation of the Faith urging the transfer of Bishop Conwell to Ireland. "As long as Bishop Conwell remains bishop," he wrote, "there is no ground for hoping that religion can ever flourish… Faith and piety will be totally uprooted from the hearts of the faithful."

On May 19, 1827, letters were sent from Rome notifying Bishop Conwell that the Pope had rejected the Pact. In August 1827 Bishop Conwell was ordered by the Holy See either to resign as Bishop of Philadelphia and return to Ireland, or to come to Rome. On his arrival in Rome in September 1828, Bishop Conwell was told to remain in the city and to prepare a report on the events in Philadelphia. He fled to Paris during the night of April 12, 1829, and sailed for America in August. The Congregation for the Propagation of the Faith wrote to Father William Matthews, who was serving as administrator of the Diocese of Philadelphia, to inform him that Bishop Conwell was suspended and his jurisdiction removed.

**Bishop Francis Patrick Kenrick**
**Coadjutor Bishop of Philadelphia, 1830-1842**
**Third Bishop of Philadelphia, 1842-1851**

small missions. Only eleven priests served the diocese, and five were in Philadelphia. By the time Bishop Kenrick arrived in Philadelphia in 1830, the Catholic population of the diocese had increased to 100,000, and 35 priests staffed approximately 50 churches and missions. Due to the trustee crisis, the "Hogan Schism," and the two-year absence of Bishop Conwell, the state of Catholicism in the city was at a low point. On March 24, Father John Hughes, pastor of Saint John the Evangelist Church, had written to a friend that the Catholic Church in Philadelphia was "really in a deplorable plight," and that the new coadjutor would need "all his prudence and piety to steer the vessel whose helm has been so long in unconsecrated hands."

Francis Patrick Kenrick was born in Dublin, Ireland, on December 3, 1797. He was educated at the Urban College in Rome (founded in the sixteenth century to train priests for work in the missions), and ordained in 1821. After his ordination, he became the first alumnus of the Urban

In October 1829, Bishop Conwell appealed to the First Provincial Council, a meeting of all American bishops. The Council—held in Baltimore— asked the Holy See to reinstate Bishop Conwell, and suggested that he be given a coadjutor—a bishop to assist him in the administration of his diocese and succeed him. On March 13, 1830, the Congregation for the Propagation of the Faith agreed to this request, and appointed Father Francis Kenrick, of the Diocese of Bardstown, Coadjutor Bishop of Philadelphia. Bishop Kenrick was entrusted with all administrative power in the Diocese of Philadelphia; however, this arrangement was kept secret to spare Bishop Conwell embarrassment.

## The State of the Diocese

In October 1811, Bishop Egan had written to Archbishop Carroll to report that there were 30,000 Catholics in the Diocese of Philadelphia (15,000 of them in the city of Philadelphia), served by sixteen churches and several

College to travel to America where he was assigned to the Diocese of Bardstown, Kentucky. In addition to pastoral work in missions scattered over a thousand square miles, Father Kenrick regularly took part in public debates on theological topics with local Protestant ministers. On June 6, 1830, in the Cathedral of Saint Joseph in Bardstown, he was ordained as titular Bishop of Arath and Coadjutor Bishop of Philadelphia. According to an ancient tradition, the principal celebrant of the ordination of a bishop is joined by two other bishops called co-consecrators. Bishop Kenrick was ordained a bishop by the Bishop of Bardstown, Bishop Benedict Flaget, and Bishop Conwell served as one of the co-consecrators. A few days later, Bishop Conwell and Bishop Kenrick set out together on the journey to Philadelphia, where they arrived on July 7.

Almost immediately, Bishop Kenrick made plans for his first visitation of the diocese. He traveled to western Pennsylvania from September 5 to November 7, 1830. On his return to Philadelphia, he announced the celebration of the Jubilee which had been declared in 1829 to commemorate the election of Pope Pius VIII in March of that year. Jubilee celebrations began on November 14, 1830, and continued for two weeks, and with excellent results. The bishop wrote that "the jubilee indeed did immense good here… Thousands crowded to the Tribunal of Penance, and to the Divine Banquet. How many prodigals return to their Father's house to be clasped in his affectionate embrace?"

The first problem Bishop Kenrick had to solve as Coadjutor Bishop of Philadelphia was the question of jurisdiction. Because of circumstances of his appointment, many priests of the diocese were unsure who held jurisdiction, and factions were formed supporting each bishop. It was not until September 9, 1831, that Pope Gregory XVI issued a papal brief confirming that Bishop Kenrick had jurisdiction in Philadelphia, and gave permission to publish the fact throughout the diocese.

The relationship between the two bishops was marked by tension, as the elderly Bishop Conwell referred to the 33-year-old Bishop Kenrick as "the boy." Bishop Kenrick had to find his own lodgings apart from Bishop Conwell's residence, and was concerned that Bishop Conwell would use the civil law and his political connections—he was friendly with President Andrew Jackson—to press a claim to authority in the diocese. Suffering from the stress of this arrangement, Bishop Kenrick suggested that the Diocese of Philadelphia be divided, and that he be appointed as Bishop of a new diocese in Pittsburgh. Although Pope Gregory XVI initially approved this suggestion, he later decided to wait until the next Provincial Council would meet in Baltimore.

Bishop Conwell's advanced age (he was already 83 years old when Bishop Kenrick was appointed), as well as the blindness with which he was stricken for nine years, made this once-powerful man increasingly dependent on others during the last decade of his life. He remained at the residence at Saint Joseph's until his death on April 22, 1842, at the age of 95. After his funeral on April 26, his body was taken from Saint Joseph's to the cemetery known as "The Bishop's Grounds," located at Passyunk and Washington Avenues in South Philadelphia.

## Bishop Kenrick and the Trustees

Bishop Kenrick needed to deal with the trustee issue at Saint Mary's. On December 27, 1830, he named himself pastor of Saint Mary's, and decreed the establishment of the parish of Saint John the Evangelist, which would have no trustees. When the trustees of Saint Mary's refused to recognize him as pastor of the parish, Bishop Kenrick placed the parish under interdict on April 17, 1831. This time the trustees had little support among parishioners, and by May 21 they had submitted to the bishop's authority and relinquished the right to appoint their own pastors. By the end of May the interdict was lifted from the parish.

Bishop Kenrick became a citizen of the United States on June 29, 1831. This status gave him the right to own church property in his own name. He soon established that he would hold the title to parish property throughout the Diocese of Philadelphia, rather than parish trustees, and removed pastors who did not comply with this arrangement. He codified these regulations as part of the First Diocesan Synod, which met in May 1832.

This was the first of three synods that Bishop Kenrick convoked during his tenure as Bishop of Philadelphia. At the synods he established regulations organizing many facets of the administration and ministry of the diocese, and introduced statutes aimed at increasing clerical discipline and regularizing parish administration. He also established a uniform catechism for the diocese, and ordered that books of a religious nature had to be approved by the bishop or his representative.

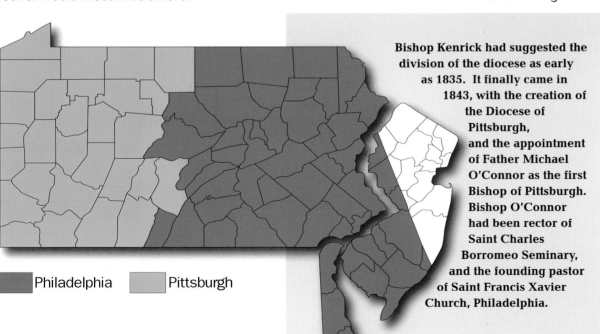

Bishop Kenrick had suggested the division of the diocese as early as 1835. It finally came in 1843, with the creation of the Diocese of Pittsburgh, and the appointment of Father Michael O'Connor as the first Bishop of Pittsburgh. Bishop O'Connor had been rector of Saint Charles Borromeo Seminary, and the founding pastor of Saint Francis Xavier Church, Philadelphia.

Philadelphia    Pittsburgh

*B*ishop Kenrick convoked the First Diocesan Synod in May 1832.  A synod gathers the members of the local Church to consider prayerfully and seriously the current state of the Church's life in order to create a vision and a plan for the future. The purpose of the synod is to assist the archbishop in his office of guiding the Church as Shepherd of the faithful.  The word synod comes from two Greek words meaning "together on the way."

There have been ten synods in the history of the Archdiocese of Philadelphia.  The Tenth Synod, in 2002, was the first to include among its members not only priests but also deacons, lay men and women, and men and women in consecrated life.

After each synod the bishop or archbishop issued decrees concerning various aspects of the life of the Church in Philadelphia.

| SYNOD | CONVOKED BY | IN | TOPICS OF DECREES |
|---|---|---|---|
| I. | Bishop Kenrick | 1832 | re-promulgation of decrees of the First Provincial Council of Baltimore; parish leadership and the rights of the pastor; Catholic education; celebration of the sacraments |
| II. | Bishop Kenrick | 1842 | promulgation of decrees of the Second Provincial Council of Baltimore; strict observance of parish boundaries; relationships between pastors and assistants; regulations for confession and confessionals; approval of new Catechisms in English and German; obligations of priests to attend clergy conferences four times a year |
| III. | Bishop Kenrick | 1847 | promulgation of decrees of the Fifth and Sixth Provincial Councils of Baltimore; procedures for financial affairs; the Sacrament of Matrimony, particularly the banns of marriage; clerical attire; rights of certain religious orders who administered parishes in the diocese |
| IV. | Bishop Neumann | 1853 | importance of faith in the life of the Christian; Catholic education of children and adults |
| V. | Bishop Neumann | 1855 | promulgation of the decrees of the First Plenary Council of Baltimore; construction of the Cathedral; petition for designation of Saints Peter and Paul as diocesan patrons; appointment of counselors to the bishop; Catholic education |
| VI. | Bishop Neumann | 1857 | preparation of children and adults to receive the sacraments; role of the pastor in Catholic education; liturgical rubrics, especially recent decisions from the Holy See; teaching on the indissolubility of marriage |
| VII. | Archbishop Ryan | 1886 | promulgation of decrees of the Third Plenary Council of Baltimore; Catholic education; creation of Archdiocesan School Board |
| VIII. | Archbishop Prendergast | 1912 | promulgation of decrees of First Provincial Council of Philadelphia; appointment of five vicars forane; sacramental celebrations, especially Sunday Mass; national parishes; annual parish visitations; Sunday school instruction for children; financial regulations |
| IX. | Cardinal Dougherty | 1934 | attire and lifestyle of archdiocesan priests; sacraments, Sunday worship especially the homily; times for the first and last Masses on Sundays; fast and abstinence; obligation of parents to send children to Catholic schools; financial administration in parishes; annual collection for support of Saint Charles Seminary |
| X. | Cardinal Bevilacqua | 2002 | spirituality and sacraments; roles of service in the Church; marriage and family; youth and young adults; Catholic education; adult faith formation; moral and social issues; liturgy; evangelization |

*B*ishop Kenrick became well-known for frequent visitations to rural areas of his diocese, something his predecessors had been unable to do. Bishop Egan made only one visitation, a three-month trip to Pittsburgh, by way of the missions in Lancaster and Conewago.  He dedicated St. Patrick's Church in Pittsburgh, and administered Confirmation to over 1,500 people. The aged Bishop Conwell made four short visitations of the diocese beyond the Philadelphia area. He visited Conewago in 1821, Lancaster in 1823, Carlisle in 1825 and Harrisburg in 1827. But the difficulty of traveling left the northern and western areas of the diocese unvisited in these years.

## Foundation of the Seminary

During his twenty-one years as Bishop of Philadelphia, Bishop Kenrick made nineteen official visitations to parishes and other Catholic settlements throughout the diocese.  During his first visitation, from September to November 1830, Bishop Kenrick was struck by the scarcity of priests to serve his widely-scattered flock.  He determined to establish a seminary where he could train priests specifically for service in the diocese, ensuring uniformity of training and fostering a spirit of fraternity among the clergy. In May 1832 Bishop Kenrick was informed of a grant from the Leopoldine Association of Vienna, Austria, to be used "for the more urgent needs of the diocese." This charitable organization—named for Leopoldina, the daughter of Emperor Francis I of Austria—had been founded in 1829 by an American priest, Father John Reze of Cincinnati, Ohio, to collect funds to support missionary work in America. Bishop Kenrick decided to use the 25,000 francs ($4,803; equivalent to about $94,000 in 2005 terms) that he received to help found a diocesan seminary.

Saint Charles Borromeo Seminary had its first home in the upper rooms of the bishop's residence at Saint Mary's, and its first student—Patrick Bradley, a native of the Diocese of Derry, Ireland—arrived on June 26, 1832. By September, there were three seminarians studying in Bishop Kenrick's house. The bishop acted as rector and professor of theology, and Father Francis Guth taught philosophy.

The beginnings of the seminary were slow: Patrick Bradley was dismissed in 1833, and of the other four members of that first class only one, Henry Fitzsimmons, became a priest. Father Fitzsimmons was ordained by Bishop Kenrick at Saint Mary's on August 15, 1836, but the new priest died before he could celebrate his first solemn Mass. It would be three more years until the first Philadelphia-born seminarian, Daniel Devitt, was ordained, on September 21, 1839.

The course of study at the seminary was determined by Bishop Kenrick's schedule and the ability of the individual student, and focused more on the practical problems of parish life than on theological issues. When the seminary moved out of the bishop's residence in 1836, and into a house adjoining Saint Mary's Church, conditions somewhat improved. By the following year the seminary had established a regular curriculum of theology courses. On April 13, 1838, the seminary was officially incorporated by the Pennsylvania Assembly, under the title of the Philadelphia Theological Seminary of Saint Charles Borromeo.

In 1838, a new seminary building was purchased at the corner of present-day Eighteenth and Race Streets at the cost of $12,000. In September, Bishop Kenrick requested a collection for support of the new building. This appeal raised more than $5,000. On January 22, 1839, ten students arrived, together with the new rector, Father Michael O'Connor, the future founding Bishop of Pittsburgh. Two years later, Bishop Kenrick invited priests of the Congregation of the Mission (Vincentians) to staff the seminary. They began this ministry on July 10, 1841, under the direction of rector Father Mariano Maller, C.M.. This arrangement with the Vincentians allowed diocesan priests to attend more freely to the needs of parishes in the diocese.

## Responding to the Needs of Immigrants

Waves of immigration flooded the diocese from the 1830s through the 1860s. The largest group was from Ireland, and the majority of the Irish were Catholics from the southern and western counties. Large numbers of these Irish Catholics were unskilled or semi-skilled men and young women, who tended to travel alone, and were almost penniless when they arrived in America. The men were generally employed as laborers in building trades, digging canals or hauling freight on the rivers. The women usually found employment as domestic servants.

This Irish immigration had a tremendous impact on the Catholic Church in Philadelphia. By 1860 more than 95,000 people of Irish descent lived in Philadelphia County, comprising 17 percent of the total population. As Catholic population within the diocese increased, more churches and schools were founded to meet spiritual and educational needs. Due to growing anti-Catholic hostility, other institutions were also needed to provide social services to Catholics.

*M*arc Frenaye was born into a wealthy family on the French colony of Saint-Domingue (present day Haiti) on February 5, 1783. He immigrated to Philadelphia in 1807, and became a bookkeeper to a silk merchant. He quickly worked his way up to partner. Over the next twenty years, he became wealthy through his business and real estate investments. After pursuing business ventures outside the city during the 1820's, he settled in Philadelphia permanently in 1829.

*Frenaye's return to Philadelphia marked the beginning of over forty years of service to the Catholic Church in Philadelphia. He served nearly thirty years without pay as financial agent and treasurer of the diocese. Frenaye was instrumental in the establishment of St. Charles Seminary and served as treasurer and member of the board of trustees from its incorporation until his death in 1873. He purchased the ground that became the site of the Cathedral and contributed greatly to its construction. He also lent money to build St. John the Evangelist Church.*

*From 1830 to 1865, Frenaye acted as purchasing agent for many Western and Southern dioceses and missions, obtaining church goods of all kinds. When Frenaye died on January 4, 1873 he was buried in Cathedral Cemetery, established on land which he had helped to purchase.*

## THE TEMPERANCE MOVEMENT

*An 1840 pastoral letter from Bishop Kenrick urged the faithful to practice temperance—that is, moderation—in their consumption of alcohol. Within a few years most parishes had "temperance societies" which supported this movement. Fourth of July parades from 1841 to 1843 frequently included parish temperance societies, who marched with bands and displayed their banners. After the 1844 riots, the parades were discontinued and the temperance movement declined among Catholics.*

*Father Theobold Mathew (pictured), an Irish Capuchin priest known as "The Apostle of Temperance", visited the United States in 1849 to promote the cause of total abstinence from alcohol. His visit to Philadelphia in late November was greatly anticipated by both Catholics and Protestants alike. He stayed twelve days with Bishop Kenrick, and a steady stream of visitors came to him to "take the pledge" to abstain. Father Mathew was honored with receptions by the temperance groups of the city and by the Mayor and City Council.*

By 1830, Saint Joseph's and Saint John's Orphan Asylums were already established for boys and girls, but both institutions were badly overcrowded. In November 1834, Father Francis Guth, pastor of Holy Trinity, established Saint Vincent's Orphan Asylum exclusively for boys. In 1836 Saint Joseph's was designated exclusively for girls, and Saint John's and Saint Vincent's merged to be a boys' orphanage, now called Saint John's. In the summer of 1855, the pastors of Holy Trinity and Saint Peter's formed Saint Vincent's Orphan Society to serve the needs of German Catholic orphans. On Thanksgiving Day, 1855, these pastors laid the cornerstone of a new Saint Vincent's Orphanage—in the Tacony neighborhood of Philadelphia—which was placed under the administration of the School Sisters of Notre Dame. In March 1857, sixteen orphans from Saint Peter's parish took up residence.

**A contemporary cartoon emphasizes the poverty of the Irish immigrants who fled the famine in their homeland in the 1840s.**

**The terrible conditions that Irish immigrants endured during the transatlantic voyage earned the nickname "coffin ships" for the vessels that carried them.**

Thousands of poor Irish immigrants poured into Philadelphia as a result of the potato famine that began in 1845. On February 10, 1848, Father Felix Barbelin, S.J., pastor of Saint Joseph's Church, organized "The Saint Joseph's Society for the Relief of Distressed Immigrants from Ireland, and for the Establishment of a Hospital." On November 13, the society organized a plan for Saint Joseph's Hospital, which was incorporated on March 12, 1849, at Sixteenth Street and Girard Avenue.

On May 24, 1849, the Sisters of the Good Shepherd opened Saint Anne's Widows' Asylum on Second Street below Christian Street, near Saint Philip Neri Church, for widows who had no means of support. When the Sisters of Saint Joseph took over Saint Anne's in 1850, the Good Shepherd Sisters opened their House of the Good Shepherd at 22nd and Walnut Streets to "afford a retreat to those females who have had the misfortune of falling into crime, and who wish to reform their lives." In 1859 the Sisters opened a Magdalene Asylum as a refuge for prostitutes.

Father Joseph Felix Barbelin, S.J., pastor of Saint Joseph's Church, was a founder of Saint Joseph's Hospital, on Girard Avenue, and Saint Joseph's College.

and unemployment were blamed on recent immigrants, and especially on the Catholic Irish. Conspiracy theories abounded, and Nativists played on fears and prejudice to rally "native born" Americans against immigrants. Catholic immigrants, they suggested, were being sent by the Pope to lay the groundwork for a Catholic conquest of America, by sheer numbers and possibly by armed conflict.

Increasing anti-Catholic hostility in the 1840s became evident in the matter of the use of the Bible in public schools. Although the state-wide school system in Pennsylvania was nominally secular and non-sectarian, each school day included reading from the Authorized ("King James") Version of the Bible, and prayers taken from various Protestant texts. On November 14, 1842, Bishop Kenrick addressed a letter to the Controllers of the public school system, asking that the 5,000 Catholic students in Pennsylvania public schools be permitted to use a Catholic version of the scriptures, or be excused from class during Bible reading. He also protested the recitation of Protestant prayers and the inclusion of anti-Catholic remarks in some textbooks.

## Anti-Catholicism, Nativism and Riots in Kensington

The increase of the number of Catholic immigrants to Philadelphia coincided with growth in anti-Catholicism throughout the United States. This hostility was due in part to a Protestant evangelical revival that had begun in the late 1820s. As the Catholic population grew, and the diocese became more organized and its institutions more visible, some saw the Church as a threat to traditional American values. Growing intolerance was accompanied by a torrent of anti-Catholic literature, based mostly on lies and sensationalist innuendo. Philadelphia was second only to Hartford, Connecticut, in the quantity of anti-Catholic material published during the 1840s.

Closely tied to this intensifying anti-Catholicism was a political movement known as Nativism. Immigration, together with revolutionary developments in transportation and industry, had dramatically changed the conditions of life in cities of the nation. Social ills such as overcrowding

The bishop's letter provoked a storm of controversy in Nativist publications. Some alleged that Bishop Kenrick had requested a complete ban on the reading of the Bible in school. The same charge was made against Hugh Clark, an Irish Catholic alderman and school inspector in the district of Kensington. In February 1844, a teacher complained to Clark of the disruption caused by Catholic students leaving class. In response, Clark suggested that Bible reading be suspended temporarily until a solution could be reached. Rumors quickly spread that Clark had forbidden a Protestant teacher to read the Bible in school, and "Save the Bible" rallies were organized.

In May 1844 the general atmosphere of hostility combined with the Nativist agenda with catastrophic results. On Friday, May 3, Nativist leaders held a rally at Second and Master Streets. Here was the heart of the Irish neighborhood of Kensington. By late afternoon, a crowd of about 300 Nativists had gathered, and several leaders began making speeches.

Fight between the Rioters in Kensington.

**An artist's impression of the 1844 riots in Kensington
(from the 1845 Philadelphia Almanac)**

Irishmen in the crowd repeatedly heckled the speakers and the Irish began to tear down the platform. The Nativists quickly retreated, but scheduled another rally for the following Monday, May 6.

Three thousand people were at Monday afternoon's rally, which was disrupted by a rainstorm around 4:00 p.m. As the crowd ran for shelter to the Nanny Goat Market on Third Street—in the center of the Irish neighborhood—the inhabitants were determined to keep the Nativists out. Fighting erupted, and musket fire came from the nearby houses and from

the Hibernia Fire Company on Cadwallader Street. The Nativists retreated, but returned with reinforcements around 4:30 p.m. to drive the Irish from their homes. At 5:00 p.m. Sheriff Morton McMichael arrived with a posse. The fighting ceased around the market, but Nativists continued to roam the neighborhood, attacking houses of Irish Catholics.

The following day, May 7, Bishop Kenrick had placards posted throughout the city warning Catholics to stay indoors. The bishop himself departed to the home of the Willcox family in Ivy Mills where he and a few of his priests remained during the riots. At 3:30 p.m. on Tuesday, a crowd of over 3,000 armed Nativists marched to Kensington, where they attacked the Hibernia Fire Company. The marchers were met with gunfire from the hose company and surrounding houses. This time the Nativists responded with arson, setting the hose company and many of the surrounding houses ablaze to drive the Irish from cover. The militia arrived at around 5:00 p.m. to restore order, and many of the Irish in the neighborhood fled to Camac's Woods, north of Kensington, for shelter.

In the early afternoon of Wednesday, May 8, the Nativists returned to Kensington, and set fire to Saint Michael Church and rectory, as well as to the convent of the Sisters of Charity. Nativists prevented firemen from putting out the fire. As night fell, the mob started to march to Saint Augustine's Church at Fourth and Vine Streets. At Saint Augustine's

Destruction of the Market House in Kensington.

Conflagration of St. Augustine Church, Fourth street.

**The Philadelphia Almanac for 1845 included accounts of the fire in the Market House in Kensington (left) and the burning of Saint Augustine's Church (right).**

they were met by Mayor John Morin Scott and a group of volunteer militiamen. As the two sides confronted each other, someone slipped into the church and set it aflame. The fire soon engulfed the church, rectory and library—one of the finest collections in the country.

Now that the violence spread from the Kensington district to the City of Philadelphia itself, local authorities and citizens finally took action. On Thursday, May 9, Philadelphia County was placed under martial law, and militia units poured into the city. Several thousand law-abiding citizens now held a meeting in the State House yard and formed into divisions of "Peace Police" to assist the militia in guarding Catholic churches for the next several days. On May 10, Bishop Kenrick suspended all public worship in Catholic churches for the following Sunday. Father Patrick Rafferty, pastor of Saint Francis Xavier Church in Fairmount, was the only priest in the county to ignore the bishop's order, and celebrated Mass in defiance of the Nativist threat.

Father Patrick Moriarity, O.S.A., was rector of Saint Augustine Church at the time of the riots in 1844.

In early July, Father John Dunn, pastor of Saint Philip Neri Church in the Southwark district, was warned of possible violence against the church. He then obtained permission from the governor to draw rifles from the Frankford Arsenal (in the Bridesburg district) to protect the church. On July 5, when people saw rifles being taken into the church, a crowd of several thousand Nativists gathered outside. Sheriff Morton McMichael arrived with a posse of only a hundred men, and to placate the crowd he removed the guns from the church. Not satisfied, the crowd searched the church on their own, and found and removed more muskets. The Pennsylvania militia soon arrived and dispersed the crowd.

## Riots at Saint Philip Neri Church

On June 17, a Nativist-dominated grand jury issued its report on the causes of the riots. The jury determined that the riots were caused by poor law enforcement, Catholic attempts to exclude the bible from public schools, and Irish disruption of the Nativist rally in Kensington. The Nativists were temporarily appeased, but it was not long before violence resumed.

The next day the crowd gathered again. Sheriff McMichael arrived with a posse to disperse the crowd in Queen Street, and General George Cadwalader arrived with the militia at about 11:00 p.m. to clear the entire area around the church. When the Nativists began throwing bricks and stones at the militia, General Cadwalader ordered the troops to fire. Charles Naylor, a former United States Congressman, jumped in front of the muskets to prevent their firing. He was arrested and placed in custody in the church, under the protective guard of the Montgomery Hibernia Greens, an Irish Catholic militia unit.

On July 7, a crowd of several thousand again gathered and demanded Naylor's release. The Hibernia Greens were besieged in the church, and the mob brought up a cannon and fired on the church several times. An agreement was finally reached: if the Hibernia Greens would leave the church, Nativist leaders would guarantee their safety. However, as men of the militia were marching from the church, they were attacked by the mob. Several Irish men were injured.

An artist's impression of the riots near Saint Philip Neri Church in Southwark. The church is visible in the right rear of the scene.

For the remainder of the day, the crowd milled around the church and individuals made several attempts to set it on fire. However, Nativist leaders stood by their agreement and prevented further damage. By evening the situation was easing. General Cadwalader then took control of the church and ordered his militia to clear the surrounding area. When some of the mob attacked the militia, the troops opened fire.

A full-scale battle erupted between the Nativist mob and the militia. Cannons were brought up from the Southwark docks and fired on the soldiers. Gunshots were fired from nearby houses. Militia cavalry charged the crowd who tied ropes across the street to trip the horses. Women crept along rooftops and threw pots of boiling water on the militia. The battle raged into the early morning. When the fighting finally ended there were 14 dead, including two militiamen. Approximately 50 men were wounded.

Philadelphia architect John Notman, who took over the Cathedral project after the resignation of LeBrun

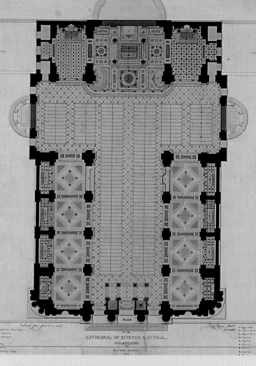

Napoleon LeBrun's original plan for the Cathedral of Saints Peter and Paul

As in May, militia and private citizens patrolled the streets to maintain order. The situation returned to normal. By July 10, militia troops were leaving the city. Bishop Kenrick urged Father Dunn and Father Patrick Moriarity, O.S.A. to leave the city for a time, since both were prominent critics of the Nativists and the presence of these priests might keep passions enflamed. Under an 1841 Act that permitted property owners to sue county governments for property destroyed by violence, lawsuits were filed by Saint Michael's and Saint Augustine's churches against the County of Philadelphia for damage caused during the Kensington riots. The County of Philadelphia was ordered to pay $27,090 to Saint Michael Church and $47,433 to Saint Augustine Church.

## Cathedral of Saints Peter and Paul

On June 29, 1846, the feast of Saints Peter and Paul, Bishop Kenrick issued a pastoral letter to solicit funds for building a cathedral for the diocese. He planned to build it on a plot adjoining the seminary, now located at Eighteenth and Race Streets, and fronting Logan Square. The bishop noted that a cathedral close to the seminary would allow the seminarians to practice sacred rites and ceremonies. Its position on a large public space like Logan Square would give the church a higher public profile. He called the priests of the diocese to a meeting on July 7, which was also attended by more than 800 lay people. To avoid incurring large debts, the group decided that work would be done only as the money was received. The cornerstone was laid on September 6, 1846, with 8,000 people in attendance.

The Philadelphia architect Napoleon LeBrun was selected to plan the cathedral. Although he was only twenty-five years old at the time, he had already gained prominence as the architect of the Catholic churches of Saint Patrick (Twentieth and Locust Streets, 1841) and Saint Peter (Fifth Street and Girard Avenue, 1843), as well as several Protestant churches. LeBrun soon resigned, however, and was replaced by the Scottish-born architect John Notman, whose work in Philadelphia includes Laurel Hill Cemetery, the library and museum of the Philadelphia Athenaeum on South Sixth Street, and the Episcopal Church of the Holy Trinity on Rittenhouse Square. Criticism from some priests and laity, and a severe economic depression in 1847 caused the building of the cathedral to be protracted for long periods.

## New Parishes

By 1830, the population of the areas of Philadelphia County outside the city proper exceeded the population within the city. Here the population was also shifting as the area west of Seventh Street was developed. Saint John the Evangelist Church, founded in 1830 on Thirteenth Street just south of Market Street, was the first parish in the city west of Sixth Street. In 1831, Saint John the Baptist Church was established to serve mill and canal workers in the manufacturing center of Manayunk, and so was the first parish established in Philadelphia County outside the original city limits.

In 1842, Saint Peter the Apostle was founded at Fifth Street and Girard Avenue, to provide a national parish for German Catholics living north of the city. Likewise, in 1849, Saint Mary of the Assumption was founded to serve the growing German population in the area of Manayunk, along the east bank of the Schuylkill River. Other parishes reflected the growth of Catholic communities in outlying areas of the county. Both Saint Stephen (founded 1843) in Nicetown, and Saint Vincent (1851) in Germantown were founded to serve settlements of railroad workers. In 1845 Saint Joachim was founded in Frankford, and Saint Anne in Port Richmond. In 1849 Saint Dominic was founded in Holmesburg—near the Bristol Canal and railroad camps—and in 1850, Saint James on 38th Street became the first parish in West Philadelphia. During his time as bishop, Bishop Kenrick established twenty-six parishes in Philadelphia and outlying areas.

It is important to remember that, although parishes were officially founded by the decree of the bishop, the work of building the parish church rested on the people and their pastors. Many parishes were blessed by the generosity of a few wealthy individuals who contributed to the construction of the church and parish buildings. Most parishes in this era, however, relied on the steady commitment of ordinary people to raise money and organize labor to make a beautiful church a reality. Parishioners who were artisans and craftsmen often took part in construction, and the architecture and decoration of parish churches bear witness to the cultural heritage of their people. Many parishes were, in a real sense, built upon the nickels and dimes, and the prayers and labors of faithful parishioners.

## Bishop Kenrick Proposes a Successor

After twenty-one years of service in Philadelphia, Bishop Kenrick was appointed Archbishop of Baltimore in October 1851. Father Edward Sourin, pastor of Saint John the Evangelist, was appointed Administrator of the Diocese of Philadelphia until a successor was appointed. Shortly after arriving in Baltimore, Bishop Kenrick went to confession at Saint Alphonsus Church. He was greatly impressed by the holiness and spirituality of the priest who heard his confession, Father John Neumann, C.SS.R., pastor of Saint Alphonsus.

John Nepomucene Neumann was born March 28, 1811, in Prachatitz, Bohemia. He studied for the priesthood in the Diocese of Budweis, but was not ordained there because of the large number of priests already serving that diocese. He was inspired by stories of American missionaries—such as Slovenian-born Bishop Frederic Baraga, who worked with miners and Native Americans in Michigan—and decided to immigrate to the United States. He sailed from Le Havre, France, to New York, where he presented himself to Bishop John DuBois, and was ordained on June 25, 1836.

Father Neumann was sent to missions in the western part of New York, near Buffalo. During his four years there, he was impressed by the priests of the Congregation of the Most Holy Redeemer, with whom he often collaborated. On November 30, 1840, he entered the Redemptorists at

---

*T*he growth of the Church in the United States changed the focus of religious practices from the individual in the home to organized devotions at the parish level. A number of groups known as confraternities were established in the 1830s and 1840s, to promote devotion to the Blessed Sacrament, the Immaculate Heart of Mary, the Scapular and the Rosary. There was even a group known as the Confraternity for a Good Death.

The Society for the Propagation of the Faith was established in the diocese in the early 1850s to support missionaries. The Sodality for the Conversion to the Faith was formed to invite Protestant Christians to enter the Catholic Church. The St. Vincent de Paul Society was established in many parishes in the late 1850s and 1860s to provide assistance to the poor.

The 1850s also saw an increase of devotion to the Blessed Virgin Mary. New Marian hymns and prayers were composed for the popular May Processions held in many parishes. Many Catholic homes had an image

of the Virgin Mary, and Mass and devotions on the feasts of Our Lady were well attended.

Bishop Kenrick introduced the custom of the Forty Hours' Devotion—a three-day celebration of adoration of the Blessed Sacrament in the parish church. Bishop Neumann encouraged this celebration in every parish. He also arranged a schedule so that the devotion was always going on at some parish in the diocese. He celebrated the Forty Hours himself at Saint Philip Neri Church, Philadelphia, on May 26, 1853—the feast of Saint Philip and, that year, the feast of Corpus Christi.

Jesuits, Redemptorists and other priests preached parish missions to encourage the faithful and to bring back those who had strayed from the Church. Missions often lasted for several days, and included numerous sermons and devotions—often geared for specific age or gender groups. These missions also provided an opportunity to celebrate the Sacrament of Reconciliation.

Pittsburgh. On January 6, 1842, he professed his vows in Baltimore, the first member of his Congregation to be professed in the United States. In March 1844, he was named superior of the Redemptorist foundation in Pittsburgh, and served in that position for two years before returning to Baltimore as Vice-Provincial and pastor of Saint Alphonsus Church.

Since Father Neumann's German background would appeal to the significant German population of the diocese, Archbishop Kenrick considered this immigrant priest an ideal candidate to be Bishop of Philadelphia. The humble Father Neumann wanted no part of this plan, and tried to get his appointment blocked. Nonetheless, he was appointed Bishop of Philadelphia on February 1, 1852. He was ordained a bishop on March 28—his forty-first birthday—in Saint Alphonsus Church, Baltimore. Two days later, when he arrived in Philadelphia, the new bishop asked the priests who came out to meet him to use the money set aside for a celebration in his honor to build a new Catholic school.

## Bishop Neumann

Bishop Neumann continued Bishop Kenrick's policy of liturgical, sacramental and administrative reform, convoking diocesan synods in 1853, 1855 and 1857. He decreed that the Litany of the Blessed Virgin Mary be sung in parish churches on all Sundays and holy days before the principal Mass, and that Vespers, the evening prayer of the Church, be celebrated on Sunday. Bishop Neumann was particularly interested in religious instruction, and passed statutes organizing the religious instruction of students preparing to receive the sacraments. He established the Confraternity of Christian Doctrine in every parish to further the cause of religious education, and set up the diocesan Society for the Propagation of the Faith.

Bishop Neumann kept a watchful eye on affairs at Saint Charles Seminary. He spent a great deal of time at the seminary, and personally instructed seminarians in pastoral theology. He added several courses of study to the curriculum, expanded the program to six years, and arranged for seminarians to use the facilities of Saint Joseph's College (located near Old Saint Joseph's Church) for science courses. Bishop Neumann was greatly disappointed when the Vincentian priests who staffed the seminary were forced to withdraw in 1852 because they did not have a sufficient number of priests available for the work. He invited the last Vincentian rector, Father Thaddeus Amat, C.M., to accompany him to the First Plenary Council in Baltimore in May 1852. At the Council, Father Amat was nominated as Bishop of Monterey, California.

Perhaps Bishop Neumann's most significant contribution to the seminary was the establishment of a preparatory or "minor" seminary for younger students. He felt that vocations would be increased, and education for the priesthood more effective, if training for the priesthood started at an earlier age than the usual eighteen or twenty years. In 1859, he purchased the former Ashton Ridge Female Academy in Glen Riddle, Delaware

## THE CAMP HILL DISASTER

On the morning of July 17, 1856 the first of two excursion trains pulled out from Master Street Station, its ten cars filled with nearly 700 children and their chaperones from St. Michael's parish in Kensington. The young people and their pastor, Father Daniel Sheridan, were on an outing to the country, in the area of Fort Washington, Montgomery County.

The line to Fort Washington was a single track—if a train was coming in the opposite direction, the engineer would pull off onto a "siding" to allow it to pass. Standard practice required outbound trains running behind schedule to pull off and wait for the inbound train from Gwynedd to pass on its way to Philadelphia. Although the St. Michael's train was running 35 minutes late, the engineer ignored the rule about pulling off, and tried instead to make up the time.

At Camp Hill, just outside Fort Washington, the two trains collided on a blind curve. The two engines hit head-on with such force that both rose on end and crashed onto their sides. The first three cars of the excursion train were smashed to pieces, and burning coals from the engine box set other cars on fire.

Local residents rushed to the site to lend assistance and pull survivors from the burning wreck. Among them a Quaker woman named Mary Ambler played a prominent role. The Reading Railroad was so grateful that they named the nearby Wissahickon Station after her. In 1869, the Village of Wissahickon was incorporated as the Borough of Ambler.

When news of the disaster reached Philadelphia around 9:00 a.m., crowds flocked to the train station. A relief train carrying doctors and nurses, including Sisters of Charity, rushed to the scene, with frantic parents hanging from the side. A convoy of wagons, carts and any other available means of transportation made its way up Germantown Pike to the crash site.

When the fires were extinguished and the victims recovered from the shattered carriages, 59 people were dead, including Father Sheridan and 47 young people, aged 9 to 21—the worst train tragedy in the world to that date.

County. In September 1859, twenty-six students and four professors moved into the new preparatory seminary.

Bishop Neumann spent five months out of each of his first three years on diocesan visitations. He visited the more populous areas of the diocese every year, and less-populous communities every two years. During his visit, the bishop conferred the Sacrament of Confirmation in churches, public halls and courthouses. He also examined parish property, financial accounts and sacramental records. The "little bishop" (as he was called because of his short stature) gave religious instruction, preached in both German and English, and visited the sick. He carried a portable altar with him so that he could celebrate Mass in homes. His ability to speak several languages allowed him to preach to and hear the confessions of many people who previously had no opportunity to confess their sins in their native tongues. Bishop Neumann even taught himself enough Gaelic to hear confession in that language. He once rode 25 miles from Bellefonte to Snowshoe—both in Centre County, now in the Diocese of Altoona-Johnstown—to confirm a single child. When someone suggested the journey would be too difficult, Bishop Neumann simply replied, "Has not the child a soul to save?"

The continued pace of immigration in the 1850s led Bishop Neumann to continue the establishment of new churches to serve the growing Catholic population. In 1852 there were 170,000 Catholics in the diocese. The following year, on July 29, 1853, seven counties in western New Jersey that had been part of the Diocese of Philadelphia were separated to form the new Diocese of Newark. Nevertheless, by 1858 the population of the Diocese of Philadelphia had increased to 250,000. During his time as bishop, Bishop Neumann rebuilt ten churches, completed six begun by Bishop Kenrick, and founded 72 new parishes, most outside the city of Philadelphia. Notable among the new churches was Saint Mary Magdalen de Pazzi in South Philadelphia. This was the first national parish for Italian immigrants in the United States.

Bishop Neumann had to deal with problems at Holy Trinity Church, now exacerbated by a rift between German-speaking and English-speaking trustees. As the crisis worsened, the trustees were put under interdict, and some were even jailed for contempt of court. To care for German-speaking Catholics in the meantime, Bishop Neumann founded a new national parish, Saint Alphonsus Church, on South Fourth Street.

When Bishop Neumann arrived in Philadelphia, there were no financial resources for completion of the Cathedral. Bishop Neumann continued

Bishop Kenrick's plan of doing no work on the Cathedral until the funds were available. In his first pastoral letter in 1852, he urged the faithful to contribute to this project. The dome of the Cathedral was completed on September 18, 1859, and 10,000 people crowded Logan Square to see the cross placed on top of the dome.

## Bishop Neumann's Commitment to Catholic Education

Although a number of Catholic schools were already operating before 1850, Bishop Neumann is considered the real founder of the parochial school system in Philadelphia. He was concerned that Catholic children be given a sound education in the principles of the Catholic faith, and felt that the school, with its own building, adequate staff and proper resources, should be a major component of every parish. In his first pastoral letter—

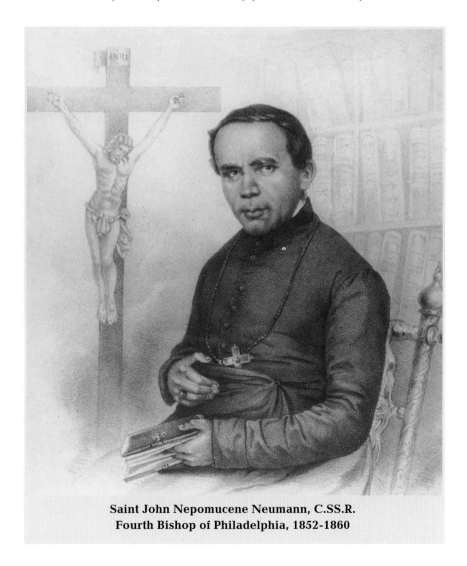

**Saint John Nepomucene Neumann, C.SS.R.**
**Fourth Bishop of Philadelphia, 1852-1860**

## CATHOLIC UNIVERSITIES

*I*n October 1841, Father Patrick Moriarty and Father Thomas Kyle, Augustinian priests from Saint Augustine Church, purchased an estate called "Belle Aire" in Radnor Township as the site for an academy for boys. The school opened in September 1843 under the title of the Augustinian College of Villanova. It was the beginning of Villanova College, later renamed Villanova University.

Financial difficulties caused by the damage to Saint Augustine's in the 1844 riots, and by the economic downturn known as the Panic of 1857, closed Villanova several times in its early years. The school reopened permanently in September 1865.

In September 1851, the Jesuits opened St. Joseph's College, in a building adjacent to St. Joseph's Church. Father J. Felix Barbelin, pastor of St. Joseph's Church, was the first president.

In 1855, the Jesuits took charge of St. John the Evangelist Church, on 13th Street, and the college was moved to St. John's large school building at Juniper and Filbert Streets. In 1860, the Jesuits withdrew from the Saint John's, and moved the college back to Saint Joseph's. It would be moved twice more—to 17th and Stiles Streets in 1889, and to its present location on City Avenue in 1927.

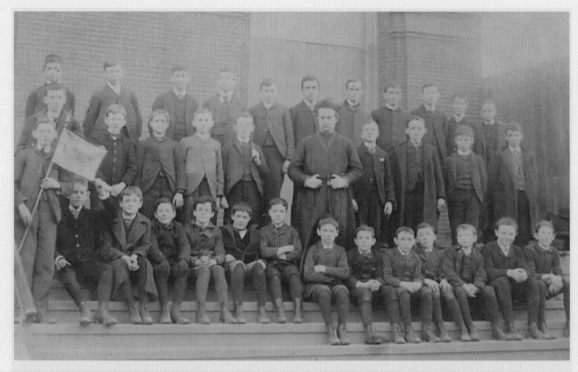

**Students of Saint Joseph College with Fr Barbelin, SJ, in 1889.**
**The school educated boys and teens as well as college-age young men.**

**Some of the Augustinian Priests of Villanova College, 1867**

written barely a week after he arrived in Philadelphia—Bishop Neumann also urged pastors to spare no effort to establish schools in their parishes. Later in the same month he called a general meeting of all interested Catholics to further the cause of Catholic education.

## NINETEENTH-CENTURY CATHOLIC SCHOOLS

*Although Bishop Neumann is known as the builder of the Catholic School system in Philadelphia, there were a number of parish and private schools operating in the 1830s and 1840s:*

*Saint Mary's free school admitted parish children from the 1780s*

*Saint Patrick Church, founded in 1839, opened a school that year. Saint Philip Neri in Southwark followed in 1841, Saint Augustine in 1842, and Saint Francis Xavier in 1845.*

*The Misses Lloyd conducted a school for girls in their home on Fifth Street in the 1830s.*

*The Young Ladies French and English Academy for adolescent girls was opened by Les Dames de la Retraite in 1832. Rodrigue's Academy for Young Ladies opened on Chestnut Street in 1833.*

*St. Joseph's English and Classical Academy was located on Willings Alley from 1840 to 1850, and welcomed boys to a place "without the fear of their being... insulted on account of their religion."*

*Miss Mary Kelly opened a school on Richmond Street in 1845, the precursor of St Anne's School.*

*Mrs. Holmes Seminary for Young Ladies and Saint Mary's Classical Academy both opened in 1845.*

*The Ladies of the Sacred Heart opened a school for girls on Logan Square in 1846, near the site of the planned Cathedral. They moved in 1847 to Eden Hall, in the Torresdale section of the city.*

**Students of Sacred Heart Academy, Eden Hall**

*Agnes Repplier, an acclaimed American author and essayist, was born in Philadelphia in 1855. Her memoir* In Our Convent Days *recalls fondly her days as a student at Eden Hall, under the supervision of the Ladies of the Sacred Heart. She also attended Agnes Irwin's West Penn Square Seminary for Young Ladies, but was expelled after three terms for disobedience to the headmistress. She kept in contact with Mrs. Irwin, however, and in 1914 wrote a biography of her former teacher.*

*Her stories and poetry—which she began to publish at the age of twenty in journals like* Catholic World, The Atlantic Monthly, Commonweal *and* Life—*are known for their straightforward common sense, wit and humor. She published more than two dozen books between 1888 and 1937, including such titles as* Essays in Idleness *(1893),* Points of Friction *(1920) and* To Think of Tea! *(1931).*

*In later years Miss Repplier was invited by the secular press to contribute articles on religious subjects, including a remembrance of Pope Pius XI for* The Philadelphia Inquirer *after the Holy Father's death in 1939. She also published biographies of the North American missionaries Père Jacques Marquette, Mère Marie de l'Incarnation and Father Junipero Serra.*

*Agnes Repplier died in 1950 at the age of 95. She is buried in the parish cemetery of Saint John the Evangelist.*

At a meeting in the bishop's residence on April 28, 1852, a diocesan Board of Education was established, with the bishop as president, and pastors and two laymen from each parish as members of the board. The duties of the board were to arrange general appeals to the faithful for financial aid, and to recommend a general plan for hiring teachers. Each pastor would be responsible for hiring a faculty and providing administration for his school.

During his visit to Rome in 1854, Bishop Neumann reported that there were thirty-four parochial schools in the diocese, serving almost 9,000 students. By 1857 the number had increased to forty-three, and most were staffed by lay teachers. A number of religious orders and congregations were also serving in the ministry of Catholic education, including Jesuits, Augustinians, and Vincentians. The Sisters of Saint Joseph—founded in Le Puy, France, in 1650—had served in the Diocese of St. Louis since 1836. Bishop Kenrick had heard of the Sisters'

# RELIGIOUS COMMUNITIES IN THE ARCHDIOCESE OF PHILADELPHIA

*Over its 200-year history, the Archdiocese of Philadelphia has been blessed with the presence and prayerful ministry of consecrated virgins and hermits, more than 80 communities of women, and nearly 40 communities of men.*

## Religious Communities of Women

- Adrian Dominican Sisters
- Armenian Sisters of the Immaculate Conception
- Bernardine Sisters of the Third Order of Saint Francis
- Carmelite Sisters for the Aged and Infirm
- Comboni Missionary Sisters
- Congregation of the Sisters of the Holy Cross
- Corpus Christi Carmelite Sisters
- Daughters of Charity of Saint Vincent de Paul
- Daughters of Mary of the Immaculate Conception
- Daughters of Saint Mary of Providence
- Daughters of Saint Paul
- Daughters of the Divine Redeemer
- Daughters of the Heart of Mary
- Daughters of the Most Holy Redeemer
- Discalced Carmelite Nuns
- Dominican Sisters of Hope
- Dominican Sisters of Our Lady of the Rosary of Fatima
- Dominican Sisters of Saint Catherine de Ricci
- Dominican Sisters of the Third Order
- Dominican Sisters, Congregation of Saint Rose of Lima
- Franciscan Sisters of Allegany, New York
- Franciscan Sisters of the Martyr Saint George
- Grey Nuns of the Sacred Heart
- Handmaids of the Sacred Heart of Jesus
- Ladies of the Sacred Heart
- Les Dames de la Retraite
- Little Servant Sisters of the Immaculate Conception
- Little Servants of the Holy Family of Seoul
- Little Sisters of the Assumption
- Little Sisters of the Holy Family
- Little Sisters of the Poor
- Little Workers of the Sacred Heart
- Medical Mission Sisters
- Missionaries of Charity
- Missionary Franciscans of the Immaculate Conception
- Missionary Servants of the Most Blessed Trinity
- Missionary Sisters of Our Lady of the Holy Rosary
- Missionary Sisters of the Most Sacred Heart of Jesus
- Missionary Sisters of the Precious Blood
- Missionary Sisters of the Sacred Heart of Jesus
- Missionary Sisters of the Third Order of Saint Francis
- Missionary Sisters of Verona
- Oblate Sisters of Providence
- Oblate Sisters of Saint Francis de Sales
- Order of the Visitation of Holy Mary
- Poor Clare Nuns
- Poor Servants of the Mother of God
- Religious of the Assumption
- Religious Teachers Filippini
- School Sisters of Notre Dame
- School Sisters of the Third Order of Saint Francis
- Servants of the Lord and the Virgin of Matara
- Sister Servants of the Holy Spirit of Perpetual Adoration
- Sister Servants of the Most Sacred Heart of Jesus
- Sisters of Bon Secours
- Sisters of Charity of Nazareth
- Sisters of Charity of the Blessed Virgin Mary
- Sisters of Christian Charity
- Sisters of Jesus Crucified
- Sisters of Mercy of the Americas
- Sisters of Notre Dame de Namur
- Sisters of Our Lady of Charity of the Good Shepherd
- Sisters of Our Lady of Mercy
- Sisters of Saint Basil the Great
- Sisters of Saint Casimir
- Sisters of Saint Felix of Cantalice (Felicians)
- Sisters of Saint Francis of Assisi
- Sisters of Saint Francis of Philadelphia
- Sisters of Saint Joseph of Cluny
- Sisters of Saint Joseph of Philadelphia
- Sisters of Saints Cyril and Methodius
- Sisters of the Blessed Sacrament
- Sisters of the Catholic Apostolate (Pallotines)
- Sisters of the Divine Compassion
- Sisters of the Divine Redeemer
- Sisters of the Holy Cross
- Sisters of the Holy Family of Nazareth
- Sisters of the Holy Redeemer
- Sisters of the Most Holy Crucified
- Sisters of the Most Holy Trinity
- Sisters of the Third Order of Saint Augustine
- Sisters, Servants of the Immaculate Heart of Mary (Immaculata)
- Sisters, Servants of the Immaculate Heart of Mary (Scranton)
- Society of the Holy Child Jesus
- Third Order Franciscans of the Immaculate Conception
- Ursuline Sisters of the Immaculate Conception
- Vietnamese Sisters of the Holy Rosary

## Religious Communities of Men

- Brothers of Charity
- Brothers of the Christian Schools (De La Salle Christian Brothers)
- Carmelite Fathers
- Catholic Foreign Mission Society of America (Maryknoll)
- Columban Fathers
- Congregation of the Holy Cross
- Congregation of the Holy Spirit
- Congregation of the Mission (Vincentians)
- Congregation of the Most Holy Redeemer (Redemptorists)
- Immaculate Heart of Mary Mission Society
- Institute of the Incarnate Word
- Legionaries of Christ
- Little Brothers of the Good Shepherd
- Marianists
- Marist Fathers
- Missionaries of Africa
- Missionaries of Our Lady of La Salette
- Missionaries of the Blessed Sacrament
- Missionaries of the Sacred Heart
- Missionary Servants of the Most Holy Trinity
- Norbertines (Canons Regular of Premontre)
- Oblates of Saint Francis de Sales
- Order of Friars Minor
- Order of Friars Minor Conventual
- Order of Friars Minor, Capuchin
- Order of Preachers (Dominicans)
- Order of Saint Augustine
- Order of Saint Paul the First Hermit
- Order of the Blessed Virgin Mary of Mercy (Mercedarians)
- Order of the Most Holy Trinity
- Order of the Pious Schools (Piarists)
- Passionists
- Philadelphia Congregation of the Oratory of Saint Philip Neri
- Saint Joseph's Society of the Sacred Heart (Josephites)
- Servants of Charity
- Society of Brother Servants of the Holy Spirit
- Society of Jesus (Jesuits)
- Third Order Regular of Saint Francis
- Third Order Regular of Saint Francis of Penance

---

work in religious education from his brother, Bishop Peter Kenrick of St. Louis, and invited them to the Archdiocese of Philadelphia in 1845. As the parochial school system grew during Bishop Neumann's administration, he continued to invite congregations of Sisters to carry out the work of teaching Catholic youth.

The Sisters, Servants of the Immaculate Heart of Mary—often known as the "I.H.M. Sisters" after the initials used after their names—had been founded in 1845 in a log cabin in Monroe, Michigan. Father Louis Gillet, C.SS.R.—a Redemptorist like Bishop Neumann—assisted three women, led by Mother Mary Theresa Maxis, to begin a religious community dedicated

to the apostolate of Catholic education. In 1858, Bishop Neumann invited the Sisters to staff Saint Joseph's School, Susquehanna, near Scranton. In 1859, the Sisters established a school at Saint Peter's in Reading, Berks County, where they also built a motherhouse for the community in Pennsylvania. In 1872, the motherhouse was transferred to West Chester, Chester County.

Bishop Neumann also founded a new religious community. During his visit to Rome in 1855, he had spoken with Pope Pius IX about inviting a religious order to Philadelphia to care for orphans and the sick, and the Holy Father suggested that he found his own Order of Saint Francis of

Assisi. At the time, Father John Hespelein was providing spiritual direction at Saint Peter's Church for three women who wanted to begin a religious order, and on April 9, 1855, Bishop Neumann vested these women—Anna Bachman, a widow; her sister, Barbara Ball; and their friend, Anna Dorn—with the religious habit. One year later they made their profession in the bishop's chapel as the Sisters of the Third Order of Saint Francis of Philadelphia. Following a Rule that Bishop Neumann composed for them, they began their ministry by visiting the sick and founding a shelter for homeless girls. These Sisters would become prominent in the diocese by teaching in parish schools and working in nursing and health care.

## Appointment of a Coadjutor Bishop

During his tenure as bishop, Bishop Neumann came under increasing criticism. No one doubted his holiness, but some were critical of his administrative abilities, especially in light of the debt that existed on diocesan property. Other criticism, on a more personal level, came from clergy who resented synodal legislation concerning finances, church property, and the transfer of responsibility for Saint John the Evangelist Church to the Jesuits.

Aware of the criticism, and feeling out of place in Philadelphia, Bishop Neumann suggested a division of the diocese and his transfer to the northern counties as Bishop of Pottsville. The bishops who received his suggestion at the Eighth Provincial Council, which met in Baltimore in May 1855, did not favor dividing the diocese. They did recommend, however, that Bishop Neumann be given an assistant. Two years later, Father James Wood was named coadjutor bishop of Philadelphia.

Few people would have expected James Frederic Wood, born in Philadelphia on April 27, 1813, to become the bishop of his native city. The Wood family belonged to the Unitarian Church, in which James practiced during his childhood. When he was fourteen years old, his family moved to Cincinnati, Ohio where he began a career in finance. He became friendly with the Archbishop of Cincinnati, John Purcell, who instructed him in the Catholic faith and, in 1838, received him into the Catholic Church. A year later James Wood expressed an interest in the priesthood, and was sent to Rome to study theology. After his ordination on the solemnity of the Annunciation (March 25, 1844), he returned to Cincinnati, to serve as pastor of Saint Patrick's Church. Pope Pius IX appointed him Coadjutor Bishop of Philadelphia on February 17, 1857.

With his background in banking, Bishop Wood was placed in charge of the temporal affairs of the diocese, including completion of the Cathedral. He also celebrated Confirmation within and beyond the City of Philadelphia, thus freeing Bishop Neumann to make visitations to rural areas. Bishop Wood, however, had misunderstood the terms of his appointment, and was under the impression that Bishop Neumann had planned to resign. Bishop Wood wrote to the Holy See to complain about the burden of diocesan finances, especially the huge debt, without authority to make decisions.

Fortunately, there was not a conflict like that between Bishop Conwell and Bishop Kenrick. Bishop Wood recognized Bishop Neumann's spiritual gifts and greatly admired him. Bishop Neumann was grateful for the relief Bishop Wood gave him from the responsibilities of temporal administration, and was sympathetic to Bishop Wood's feelings of frustration. At the Ninth Provincial Council of Baltimore in 1858, Bishop Neumann again proposed a division of the diocese, offering to go to a new diocese in Easton and leave Bishop Wood to become Bishop of Philadelphia. The Holy See delayed the decision until the next Plenary Council could meet in Baltimore.

## Death of Bishop Neumann

On January 5, 1860, Bishop Neumann was returning from the post office on a task typical of his personality. He was checking on the status of a chalice that had been sent to him by a priest in Bellefonte, Centre County, to be consecrated, and which had been lost in transit. On his way home, he collapsed on an icy sidewalk in front of a house at 1218 Vine Street. He was carried inside where he soon died. He was forty-eight years of age.

On January 9, Bishop Neumann's body was placed in the Cathedral chapel, where it was visited by thousands of mourners. A lengthy procession made its way from the chapel to Saint John the Evangelist Church—the pro-cathedral—for the funeral Mass, during which Archbishop Francis Kenrick preached the homily. Bishop Neumann's body was then taken to Saint Peter's Church where he had asked to be buried with his fellow Redemptorists.

The Diocese of Philadelphia had experienced a great deal of turmoil in the years that Bishop Wood had lived in Cincinnati. As Bishop of Philadelphia, however, Bishop Wood found himself at the head of a Catholic community that had emerged stronger from those difficult years. Philadelphia Catholics had fought to defend the faith that their parents had planted, and paid for it with hardship and sacrifice. Now Catholics in Philadelphia were able to hand on that faith to children and grandchildren who gathered in beautiful places of worship and attended Catholic schools that were a model for the nation. Much of this was the fruit of the efforts of Bishop Wood's saintly predecessor. It was likewise a testament to the new members of the flock—immigrants like their bishop—who banded together to preserve the heritage of faith that had been entrusted to them.

# 3

# Expanding the Faith

## (1860–1911)

Unprecedented numbers of Catholic immigrants to the Diocese of Philadelphia in the first half of the nineteenth century had changed the face of the Catholic Church in southeastern Pennsylvania. At the beginning of the 1860s, vibrant parish communities— inspired by the missionary zeal of the saintly Bishop Neumann and by their own experience of defending the faith—were poised to build on this firm foundation. As immigrants became an integral part of the society of their adopted homeland, and new groups arrived from foreign shores, the Church in Philadelphia expanded at a rapid pace. Before that could happen, however, priests and people would have to endure a new kind of turmoil: a civil war to preserve the unity of the nation.

## The Civil War

During his first year in office, Bishop Wood opened two new parishes. One was the Church of the Annunciation of the Blessed Virgin Mary, at Tenth and Dickinson Streets in South Philadelphia. He named this parish to honor of the feast on which he had been ordained a priest. The other was All Saints Church, in the Bridesburg section of the city, as a national parish for German-speaking Catholics. The summer of 1861, however, witnessed a halt to building projects in the diocese, as eleven Southern states seceded from the Union. Philadelphia and the nation mustered for war.

At the outbreak of the Civil War, Pennsylvania Governor Andrew Curtin asked Bishop Wood to release priests to serve as chaplains to the soldiers. One of them, Father John McCusker, died in the service of his country. Several religious orders of women sent Sisters to serve as nurses on battlefields and in hospitals. The Sisters of Saint Joseph served on hospital ships and tended to the wounded and dying on both sides of the struggle. The Sisters also served at the bloody Battle of Gettysburg in 1863. The Daughters of Charity staffed Satterlee Hospital in West Philadelphia, and also helped at Gettysburg and nearby Emmitsburg, Maryland.

The Sisters of Mercy were also prominent among the nursing Sisters during the Civil War. Founded in 1827 in Dublin, Ireland, by Catharine McAuley, in 1854 they opened their first school in the United States in Pittsburgh. In 1861, these Sisters came to Philadelphia, to the Church of

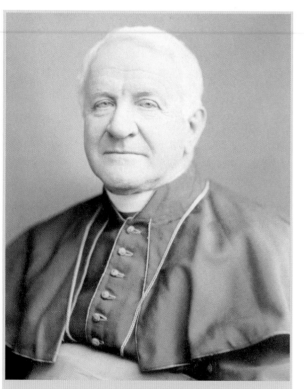

**Archbishop James Frederic Wood**
**Coadjutor Bishop of Philadelphia,**
**1857-1860**
**Fifth Bishop of Philadelphia,**
**1860-1875**
**First Archbishop of Philadelphia,**
**1875-1883**

**Sister Anselm Jennings, S.S.J., was one of fourteen Sisters of Saint Joseph officially recognized by Congress for their service as nurses during the Civil War. She was a nurse on a "floating hospital" on the James River near Yorktown, Virginia. She wrote of how the captain of the vessel would ask the Sisters to stand on deck when an enemy ship approached so that the ship would be recognized as a hospital vessel.**

the Assumption of the Blessed Virgin Mary, on Spring Garden Street. They soon founded an Academy for Young Ladies at the corner of Broad Street and Columbia Avenue. In addition to their work in education, the Sisters also tended to the sick and dying, both in their homes and in hospitals. Following the example of Catharine McAuley, the Sisters also visited inmates in Philadelphia prisons.

One of the fears of Bishop Wood was that the war might put a halt to the construction of the new Cathedral of Saints Peter and Paul. Building had begun in 1846 under Bishop Kenrick but had encountered many delays. Ten thousand people had gathered on

**A Daughter of Charity tends the sick in a field hospital near the battlefield in Gettysburg, 1863.**

September 18, 1859, to see the Cross placed on the dome, and Bishop Wood and the faithful eagerly anticipated the completion of the interior of the building. However, with the advent of war, Bishop Wood stopped the annual collection to lessen the burden on his people. During the war, Philadelphia became a leading manufacturing center, and the improved economic situation later allowed the faithful to respond generously to the project

Bishop Wood celebrated the Mass of Dedication in the new Cathedral on November 20, 1864. Archbishop Martin Spaulding, Archbishop of Baltimore, attended the dedication and preached the sermon. Five years

after the completion of the church, on March 16, 1869, the remains of Bishop Egan and Bishop Conwell were disinterred from Saint Mary's Cemetery and the Bishop's Cemetery on Washington Avenue, respectively, and were entombed in the Cathedral crypt.

## Catholic Education

In 1861, as a result of financial constraints, the Jesuits had to close Saint Joseph's College, which had opened in 1851. Bishop Wood turned to the Brothers of the Christians Schools (known as the Christian Brothers) to provide another Catholic college in Philadelphia. Brother Teliow, FSC, agreed to the bishop's request and began teaching advanced courses in the basement of Saint Michael's School in Kensington—one of three schools that the Christian Brothers staffed in the diocese. On March 20, 1863, Bishop Wood petitioned the state for an Act of Incorporation for "a college within the city limits of Philadelphia," and formed the board of directors of "LaSalle College in the City of Philadelphia" on May 18. The college was known in its early years as the Christian Brothers Academy, and classes began later in 1863 in Saint Michael's Hall. In 1864 the college moved to a three story building located at the corner of Juniper and Filbert Streets at the northeast corner of Centre Square (now the location of Philadelphia City Hall).

**The Daughters of Charity and the medical staff of Saterlee Hospital, Philadelphia**

The Society of the Holy Child Jesus was founded in 1846 by a Philadelphia native, Mrs. Cornelia Connelly. In 1835, Mrs. Connelly and her husband, Reverend Pierce Connelly—an Episcopal clergyman—were received into the Catholic Church in New Orleans. They moved to England, and agreed to separate so that they could both enter religious life. Mr. Connelly was ordained a priest, and Mrs. Connelly founded the Society of the Holy Child Jesus in Derby, England. In 1863 she sent some of her Sisters to staff the parish school at the Church of the Assumption B.V.M., Spring Garden Street. The following year they established a motherhouse in Sharon Hill, Delaware County. In 1868, they opened an academy at the corner of 39th and Chestnut Streets in West Philadelphia, called Saint Leonard's House.

Although many parishes had elementary schools, Catholic education for adolescent boys and girls in this period was mostly provided by the private academies and colleges operated by religious communities. In 1866, parishioners of Saint Matthew Church, Conshohocken, sought Bishop Wood's approval to begin a parish-based high school. Saint Matthew High School was staffed by Sisters of Saint Joseph, under the leadership of a lay principal, and operated as a parish high school for nearly ninety years. In 1955 it came under the direction of the Office of the Superintendent of Schools, and in 1966 was renamed Archbishop Kennedy High School, after Archbishop Thomas Kennedy (1857–1917), a graduate and former principal of Saint Matthew's High School.

Bishop Wood also consolidated the major and minor diocesan seminaries, and relocated the seminary campus. Concerned with the high rate of tuberculosis which had developed among seminarians and newly-ordained priests—which he attributed to the congestion and industries of the city—the bishop bought 137 acres in Overbrook (now Wynnewood), Montgomery County, at the intersection of Lancaster Avenue and the city boundary line. The bishop was severely criticized for spending $62,000 for land that was so far away (about six miles) from the center of the city, and the purchase was referred to as "Wood's Folly." The cornerstone was placed on April 4, 1866, and after several building delays due to lack of funds, the new seminary opened in August 1871 with two weeks of retreats for priests. On September 16, 1871, the seminary welcomed 128 students for the new academic year.

## Reorganizing Pennsylvania's Dioceses

Bishop Wood made four journeys to Rome between 1862 and 1869. During a visit in 1867, he asked Pope Pius IX to reduce the size of his diocese. A year later, the pope granted his request by creating two new dioceses in Pennsylvania: Scranton, with Bishop William O'Hara, formerly pastor of Saint Patrick's in Philadelphia as its first bishop; and Harrisburg, under the direction of Bishop Jeremiah Shanahan, rector of the minor seminary in Glen Riddle. The new bishops were consecrated by Bishop Wood at the Cathedral of Saints Peter and Paul on July 12, 1868, and then departed to begin the task of establishing their own dioceses.

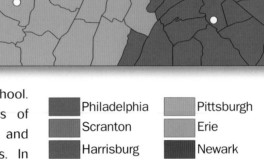

| | | | |
|---|---|---|---|
| ■ | Philadelphia | ■ | Pittsburgh |
| ■ | Scranton | ■ | Erie |
| ■ | Harrisburg | ■ | Newark |
| ■ | Wilmington | | |

A map of the dioceses in the original territory of the Diocese of Philadelphia in 1868, after the creation of the Dioceses of Harrisburg, Scranton and Wilmington

**Bishop William O'Hara**
**First Bishop of Scranton,**
**1868–1899**

**Bishop Jeremiah Shanahan**
**First Bishop of Harrisburg,**
**1868–1886**

The creation of these two new dioceses, as well as the Diocese of Wilmington, Delaware, removed a total of twenty-nine counties in northeastern and central Pennsylvania, and the entire State of Delaware, from the Diocese of Philadelphia—approximately 18,500 square miles in all. In the ten counties that remained in the Diocese of Philadelphia lived 200,000 Catholics, served by 121 priests, 491 religious Sisters and 59 religious Brothers. They lived in 76 parishes, of which 42 included parish schools.

As the Catholic population increased, and more dioceses were created to serve the faithful, it became more difficult for the Archbishop of Baltimore to oversee the many dioceses that surrounded his archdiocese. On March 15, 1875, Pope Pius IX established the Archdiocese of Philadelphia—as well as the Archdioceses of Boston, Milwaukee and Santa Fe—and reorganized dioceses into provinces under the leadership of these new archbishops. Archbishop Wood became the Metropolitan Archbishop of the Province of Philadelphia, and responsible for overseeing the other Pennsylvania dioceses of Pittsburgh, Erie, Harrisburg and Scranton. As Metropolitan, Archbishop Wood was responsible for calling Provincial Councils and coordinating church affairs on a state-wide basis.

In 1875, the formal installation of Archbishop Wood as Archbishop of Philadelphia included a procession to the Cathedral and the conferral of the pallium by Archbishop James Bayley of Baltimore

Archbishop Wood was formally installed as Archbishop of Philadelphia on June 17, 1875. During the Mass at the Cathedral the new archbishop received the pallium—a scapular-like vestment made of lamb's wool, which is blessed by the Pope and given to residential archbishops to signify a special unity between the Holy Father and the Church throughout the world. An archbishop receives the pallium either in person at the Vatican, or in his home archdiocese from an official representative of the Pope. Archbishop Wood received his pallium in the Cathedral of Saints Peter and Paul from the Archbishop of Baltimore, James Bayley.

## Molly Maguires

In the second half of the nineteenth century, America witnessed the formation of a number of secret societies, several of which—Masons, Oddfellows and the Ku Klux Klan—had agendas that opposed the Catholic Church. The church prohibited membership in these groups, and Bishop Wood informed the faithful of this prohibition in pastoral letters in 1864 and 1871.

Another secret society—the Molly Maguires—was made up of Irish Catholic coal miners in Schuylkill and Carbon Counties. Named for an Irish group which fought against their British landlords, the Mollies opposed the unscrupulous policies of mine owners and railroad magnates by blowing up tracks and allegedly murdering mine foremen. Franklin Benjamin Gowan, the president of the Philadelphia and Reading Railroad, employed the Allen Pinkerton Detective Agency to infiltrate the Mollies. Twenty Mollies were arrested, convicted of murder, and hanged between 1887 and 1889. The justice of the verdict is still contested.

## Last Years of Archbishop Wood

In 1873, Bishop Wood announced his intention to consecrate the entire diocese to the protection of the Sacred Heart of Jesus, and did so at the Cathedral on October 15. Bishop Wood presided at the Mass, celebrated by Bishop O'Hara of Scranton, and attended by great numbers of clergy and laity.

Several years later, Philadelphia and the entire nation observed the Centennial of American Independence. Bishop Wood decreed that "throughout our diocese the 4th of July [should] be religiously celebrated," and ordered the celebration of the Mass of the Trinity in all parishes of the diocese, followed by Exposition of the Blessed Sacrament, Benediction, and the singing of the *Te Deum*, a hymn of praise and thanksgiving. The ceremonies were concluded by the ringing of church bells throughout the city.

In the later years of his life, Archbishop Wood continued to establish new parishes, both in rural areas like Lansdale (Saint Stanislaus, 1876) and Newtown (Saint Andrew, 1880), and in various sections of the city. The last parish founded by the archbishop was the Polish national parish of Saint Laurentius in 1882, located at Memphis and East Berks Streets in Philadelphia.

After twenty years of service, Archbishop Wood's health declined, and he was forced to leave the archdiocese during the winter months. On May 3, 1882, faithful people from throughout the archdiocese gathered to celebrate his Silver Jubilee, the twenty-fifth anniversary of his ordination as a bishop. Sadly, the Mass and procession would be his last public appearance. His legs now became paralyzed and he was confined to bed. However, he continued to oversee the affairs of the archdiocese until June 20, when he appointed his Vicar General, Monsignor Maurice Walsh, as administrator of the archdiocese. Archbishop Wood died shortly after 10:00 that night.

On June 25, the archbishop's body was transferred to the Cathedral to lie in state for a day. His funeral Mass was celebrated the following day by Bishop O'Hara of Scranton. The body of Archbishop Wood was then entombed in the crypt of the Cathedral, the completion of which he had supervised.

## Archbishop Ryan

Patrick John Ryan was born in County Tipperary, Ireland on February 20, 1831. He studied for the priesthood in County Carlow, and completed his studies so quickly that he had not yet attained the required age for ordination. He immigrated to the United States and was ordained in the Archdiocese of St. Louis in 1853. Here he served until 1872 as pastor in three parishes, including the Cathedral parish. During the Civil War he served as a military prison chaplain, ministering to the soldiers of the

**As part of the celebrations of the Centennial of American Independence in 1876, the Catholic Total Abstinence Union built a fountain in west Fairmount Park, near the present site of the Mann Music Center. It portrays Moses (center), and prominent American Catholics: Charles Carroll of Carrollton, Archbishop John Carroll, Father Theobold Mathew, and Commodore John Barry.**

**Archbishop Patrick John Ryan**
**Second Archbishop of Philadelphia, 1884-1911**

*In June 1891, Reverend William McGarvey (pictured) and six fellow clergymen of the Episcopal Church founded a religious community, the Congregation of the Companions of the Holy Savior. They had been influenced by the Anglican revival known as the Oxford Movement, which was rediscovering the roots of Christianity in the writings of the Church Fathers. Their community followed a rule based on traditional Catholic forms of religious life, including the profession of vows of poverty, obedience and (unusual for the Episcopal Church) celibacy.*

*The 1907 General Convention of the Episcopal Church passed the "open pulpit canon"—a law that allowed ministers of other Christian denominations to preach in Episcopal churches. McGarvey found this incompatible with the teaching of the Church Fathers on the connection between authority to preach and ordination. Together with three other vicars—Maurice Cowl, William Hayward and William McClellan—McGarvey resigned his position at Saint Elizabeth's Episcopal Church (in the 1500 block of Mifflin Street) in 1908. These four clergymen and several seminarians asked to be received into the Catholic Church. With the permission of Archbishop Ryan, several of them entered Saint Charles Seminary to study for the priesthood. Father McGarvey was ordained a priest for the Archdiocese of Philadelphia in December 1910, and served at Holy Child Church and Saint James Church. He was named a monsignor in 1921, and was pastor of Saint James from 1918 until his death in 1924.*

*One of Father McGarvey's confreres, Father Edward Hawks, wrote a memoir of the events:* William McGarvey and the Open Pulpit, *published in 1935.*

Confederacy, and after the war he became secretary to Archbishop Peter Kenrick. In 1872, Father Ryan was appointed Coadjutor Archbishop of St. Louis—a position he held until June 8, 1884, when he was named by Pope Leo XIII to succeed Archbishop Wood.

Archbishop Ryan's arrival in Philadelphia was greeted with great joy by Catholics and non-Catholics alike. The *Evening Bulletin* described him as "vigorous with a commanding presence and a gracious manner, a highly cultivated man with the powers of eloquent oratory. He combines the powers of the pulpit with those of official administration in a very unusual degree and enjoys a familiar reputation to Catholics throughout the country." As the train that brought him from St. Louis neared the city, welcoming bonfires were lit by the students of Villanova College along the railroad tracks which bisect the campus. He arrived at the Broad Street Station on August 19, and was installed in the Cathedral the next day by Archbishop Gibbons of Baltimore.

Later, in November 1884, Archbishop Ryan attended the Third Plenary Council of Baltimore. The bishops were concerned with the pastoral care and education of new Catholic immigrants, and directed every pastor to build a school affiliated with the parish church. The Council

fathers also discussed a national center of Catholic higher education, and founded the Catholic University of America in Washington D.C. To assist catechists in the work of instructing children and adults in the faith, the Council formed a commission to prepare what came to be known as the Baltimore Catechism.

**Father Patrick Ryan after his ordination to the priesthood in 1853, with his sisters, Mrs. Bowen and Mrs. Maguire**

*The bishops assembled at the Third Plenary Council of Baltimore (1884) appointed a committee to draft a new catechism—a textbook for religious instruction—for the United States. The following year saw the publication of "A Catechism of Christian Doctrine, Prepared and Enjoined by Order of the Third Council of Baltimore."*

*The Baltimore Catechism, as it came to be known, presented the truths of the faith in question and answer format, with prayers, word lists, study questions, and exercises. Editions were prepared for various grade levels, and were used for religious instruction well into the 1950s and early 1960s.*

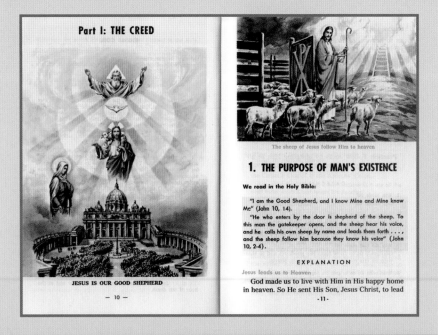

**One of Archbishop Ryan's first responsibilities was to attend the Third Plenary Council of Baltimore, which met at Saint Mary's Seminary in Baltimore in November 1884.**

## Caring for New Groups of Immigrants

When Archbishop Ryan returned to Philadelphia, he endeavored to implement the conciliar regulation to provide education for new immigrants. Many Irish had begun to establish themselves in civil service jobs, on the police force, and as teachers. As the Irish prospered, they built new houses in outlying sections of the city, and Archbishop Ryan founded a number of parishes in these new neighborhoods. He also established several German national parishes, where priests could preach and hear confessions in the newcomers' native language, including Our Lady Help of Christians in Port Richmond, Saint Bonaventure in North Philadelphia, Saint Ludwig in Brewerytown, and Saint Aloysius in South Philadelphia.

The largest group of Catholic immigrants during Archbishop Ryan's tenure was Italian. Between 1880 and 1910, the Italian population increased twenty-seven-fold. The first Italian national parish, Saint Mary Magdalen de Pazzi, had opened in South Philadelphia in 1852; however, as large numbers of Italians arrived and settled the area of South Philadelphia, there were too few churches to serve them. Archbishop Ryan saw the need to establish more national parishes, staffed by priests who were able to preach and minister to the people in their own language. Accordingly, he prevailed upon the Italian Augustinians to send several priests to Philadelphia. In 1898, the parish of Our Lady of Good Counsel, at 816 Christian Street, was formed for the approximately 25,000 Italians who lived west of Eighth Street in South Philadelphia. In 1907, Saint Rita of Cascia Church was founded at Broad and Ellsworth Streets. Italian parishes were founded in other areas of the city, as well as in Norristown, Chester and Strafford.

After the arrival of the Irish, Germans and Italians, the fourth and last major wave of immigrants to America prior to the First World War consisted of thousands of people fleeing Eastern Europe for political and religious reasons. Statistically prominent were the Polish, whose presence in Philadelphia rose from 146 in 1870 to 7,554 in 1900. Archbishop Ryan again faced the challenge of an insufficient number of priests who could minister to the Polish immigrants in their native language. The first Polish national parish, Saint Laurentius in North Philadelphia, had been opened by Archbishop Wood in 1882. Over the next 17 years, Archbishop Ryan founded six more Polish parishes in the city, and each had a parish school. The parish of Saint Josaphat in Manayunk also had a mission church, Saint Mary's Church in Conshohocken. Many of the Polish speaking people moved beyond the city limits to the northern and western suburbs,

where Archbishop Ryan opened a dozen parishes to respond to their spiritual needs.

To provide social assistance to immigrants, different types of lay organizations were established. The public almshouse was falling into disfavor as a place of care for dependent and neglected children, and Protestant "child savers" worked to "rescue" poor children from what they considered the anti-democratic control of the Catholic Church. In response, Catholic lay groups created large institutions which combined religious formation, material assistance and education to help improve the situation of orphans and poor children. The 1880s saw the foundation of Saint Joseph's House for Homeless Industrious Boys, on Pine Street between Seventh and Eighth Streets; Gonzaga Memorial House in Germantown; and Saint Vincent's Home and Maternity Hospital in West Philadelphia. Miss Elizabeth Drexel donated 200 acres of land in Bensalem for Saint Francis de Sales Industrial School, which opened in 1888. The Catholic Protectory for Boys was established near present-day Audubon, Montgomery County. Later called Saint Gabriel's Hall, it became the flagship of the Saint Gabriel's System for adjudicated delinquents.

**Large numbers of Italian immigrants arrived in Philadelphia and other U.S. cities in the 1880s and 1890s.**

**Some of the boys in the care of Saint Joseph's House for Homeless Industrious Boys**

**Saint Vincent's Home and Maternity Hospital, at 69th Street and Woodland Avenue**

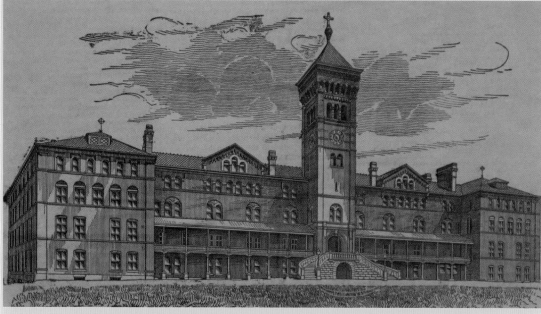

Saint Francis de Sales Industrial School was built in Bensalem in 1888,
on land that was a gift of Miss Elizabeth Drexel, Katharine's sister.

Archbishop Ryan's activities on behalf of African Americans did not end with this collection. He worked diligently to educate and evangelize African Americans in the Archdiocese of Philadelphia. In 1886 Archbishop Ryan founded a school for African American children at Ninth and Pine Streets, and under the care of the Oblate Sisters of Providence, who were succeeded by the School Sisters of Notre Dame. Three years later the Sisters and the girls from the school moved to a new location at Eleventh and Pine, and the Holy Ghost Fathers took over the original building as a school for boys. The Fathers also operated a night school attended by over 100 working adults. Two Masses were celebrated every Sunday morning in the school hall, and Vespers and Benediction were celebrated on Sunday evenings. Additionally, there was an orphanage to care for boys over the age of ten, in what local newspapers called "The Colored Mission."

Care of the sick was another element of Catholic charitable activities. Hospitals grew at a rapid rate following the Civil War, due in large part to the willingness of women's religious orders to assume administrative and nursing responsibilities. Saint Joseph's Hospital on Girard Avenue had opened in 1849, and Saint Mary's Hospital, founded in 1860 on Frankford Avenue, cared for patients in the northern parts of the city. In 1888, Saint Agnes Hospital was founded by the Sisters of Saint Francis of Philadelphia on South Broad Street. Elizabeth Drexel and her sisters made a sizable donation to Saint Agnes Hospital with the specific condition that beds be set aside for African American patients.

## Ministry to African Americans and Native Americans

In 1884, the Third Plenary Council of Baltimore established an annual collection for the "Black and Indian Missions," and also created a board of bishops called the "Commission for Catholic Missions among the Colored People and the Indians" to supervise the collection and distribute the funds. The commission received annual reports from these missions describing the number of people served and the number who had been baptized. These reports were collated and distributed nationally. Archbishop Ryan was among the first three bishops named to this commission, and served in this capacity until his death. When the first collection was taken up in 1887, Philadelphia led all the other archdioceses and dioceses in the country in supporting these two apostolates.

Members of the "Catholic Board for Mission Work among the Colored Peoples"
Archbishop Ryan is pictured in the top row, second from left.

In 1892, this Mission was elevated to the status of a parish, named for Saint Peter Claver, a Spanish Jesuit missionary who ministered for 44 years to African slaves arriving in the port of Cartagena, Colombia. Saint Peter Claver Church was dedicated on January 3, 1893. Later that year, Archbishop Ryan addressed the annual meeting of the National Congress of Colored Catholics, meeting at Saint Peter Claver Church. He told the delegates that he hoped and prayed for the economic, social, and educational improvement of the African American community, since the Incarnation of Jesus Christ was for people of all races.

Archbishop Ryan served as a member of the Bureau of Catholic Indian Missions, a responsibility that belonged to him *ex officio* as the Archbishop of Philadelphia. The Bureau worked with the federal government's Bureau of Indian Affairs to supervise the care and education of Native Americans who lived on government-owned reservations. Archbishop Ryan testified before Congress in 1898, and sought federal money for Catholic schools serving Native Americans. He also asked for Catholic representation in the federal government's supervision of reservations. President Theodore Roosevelt agreed, and on April 19, 1902, he appointed Archbishop Ryan as the first Catholic to sit on the Federal Board of Indian Commissioners, a position he held until his death.

## Mother Katharine Drexel

Katharine Mary Drexel was born on November 26, 1858, the second daughter of the banker Francis Drexel and Hannah Langstroth. Katharine's mother died from compli-cations of childbirth on December 30, one day after her daughter had been baptized by Father Charles Carter in the Church of the Assumption B.V.M. on Spring Garden Street. Her father later married Emma Bouvier, who lovingly raised young Kate (as she was always called) and her two sisters.

Katharine and her sisters, Elizabeth and Louise, learned from Emma that their wealth obliged them to care for the poor. Emma Drexel employed a woman to visit the needy in Philadelphia, and distribute tickets which could be exchanged at the gate of the Drexel home on Moravian Street for food, clothing, or money. It was estimated that Mrs. Drexel's donations amounted to $20,000 a year. This was, of course, an enormous sum in 1860s America.

The death of Emma Drexel in 1883, and Francis Drexel in 1885, left the Drexel sisters as the sole survivors and legatees of an unusual Will. Of Francis Drexel's $15.5 million estate, $1.5 million was divided among 29 charities. The other $14 million was to be held in trust to provide income for his daughters during their lifetimes, and to pass to any children they might have. Both of Katharine's sisters later married, but predeceased Katharine and left no children, so that the entire estate eventually passed to her. She used her income (estimated at nearly $20 million during her lifetime) for work she would undertake as foundress of a new religious community. At her death, the estate reverted to the 29 charities included in the original bequest. Katharine's community had not been founded when her father wrote his Will.

The Bishop of Omaha, Most Rev. James O'Connor, had been Katharine's pastor and spiritual director at Saint Dominic Church in northeast Philadelphia. When she visited him from time to time in Omaha, Nebraska, the bishop would take her on trips to reservations to show her the needs of Native Americans. In 1887, she and her sisters planned an Italian vacation that included a visit to the Vatican, and Bishop O'Connor asked her to plead with Pope Leo XIII to send missionaries to the American West. When she had her audience with the Holy Father, he surprised her by asking "Why not, my child, become a missionary yourself?" After reflecting on the Pope's question, in consultation with Bishop O'Connor, Katharine decided to enter the novitiate of the Sisters of Mercy in Pittsburgh, and then establish a new religious congre-gation dedicated to working with African American and Native American com-munities.

Katharine Drexel, age 21

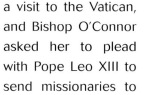

Francis Drexel

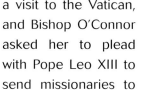

Emma Bouvier Drexel

Katharine was received as a postulant by the Sisters of Mercy on November 7, 1889. When Bishop O'Connor died in 1890 it seemed she would have no help in founding her community. Archbishop Ryan, however, went to Omaha to celebrate Bishop O'Connor's funeral Mass, and on his return journey stopped in Pittsburgh to visit Sister Mary Katharine. He helped to arrange the foundation of the Sisters of the Blessed Sacrament for Indians and Colored People, and, on February 12, 1891, received Sister Mary Katharine's vows as the congregation's first member. In additional to the three vows of poverty, chastity, and obedience, she and her Sisters would also take a fourth vow, namely, to work solely on behalf of Native and African Americans.

Mother Katharine now required a motherhouse. Archbishop Ryan suggested that it be located in the northeast part of the country, so that he could offer his support to Mother Katharine and her vision. The Sisters moved into the Drexel family summer home—"San Michel," in the Torresdale neighborhood of Northeast Philadelphia—as they awaited the completion of a new convent. Designed in the California Mission style, Saint Elizabeth Convent (named in honor of Mother Katharine's sister) opened in 1892 in Cornwells Heights (Bensalem Township), Bucks County. Nearby, Holy Providence Home was the first of 134 institutions opened in the United States by the Sisters of the Blessed Sacrament.

## Development of Archdiocesan High Schools

The establishment of the first tuition-free central diocesan high school for boys in the United States was the result of a bequest made by a wealthy Catholic businessman, Thomas Cahill. As a boy growing up in the Rittenhouse Square neighborhood of Center City, Cahill attended public schools. After a successful career in business, he wanted to provide Catholic boys with the religious education that he had not been able to receive. His Will established the Cahill Trust, which provided funds in February 1884 to purchase a tract of land at Broad and Vine Streets for a Catholic high school for boys. The school, called simply "Catholic High," was opened in 1890 at a cost of $210,000. The faculty of lay teachers was led by a rector, Father Nevin Fisher, appointed by Archbishop Ryan. Admittance to the school, which came to be known as Roman Catholic High School, was based on a competitive examination. The school was supported by an annual grant of $30,000 from the Cahill Trust, and also by private donations.

**Roman Catholic High School, 1890.**
**Inset: Thomas Cahill**

**Sister Mary Katharine Drexel,**
**at the time of her first profession of vows**

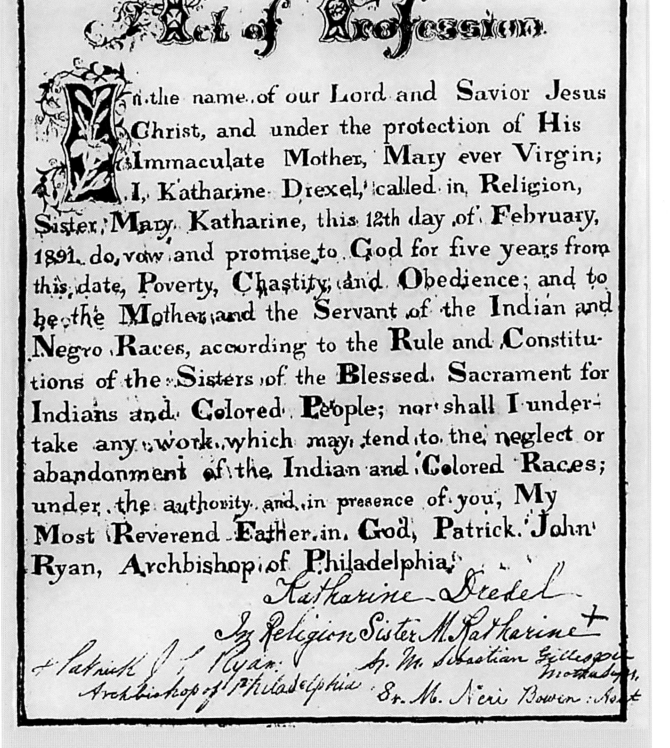

**Sister Mary Katharine's Act of Profession**

In a 1900 editorial, *The Catholic Standard and Times* stated that "Our parochial school system will never realize its grand possibilities until we have... a high school [for girls]. Our girls have as good a right to a thorough and comprehensive education as our boys." When pleas for a donor to build a girls' high school went unanswered, the archdiocese established "Senior Class Centers"—two-year free programs operated in five parish centers where girls could continue their education under the direction of religious Sisters.

In 1905, Father Philip McDevitt, archdiocesan Superintendent of Schools, asked the faithful of the archdiocese to make contributions for a girls' high school to honor the upcoming centennial anniversary of the archdiocese. The largest single contribution—$100,000, the gift of Mrs. Mary Hallahan McMichan—was used to buy a plot of land on 19th Street near Wood Street. Opened in September 1912, and called Catholic Girls High, the school was later renamed John W. Hallahan Catholic High School for Girls, in honor of Mary McMichan's deceased brother.

**Catholic Girls' High School, before it was renamed for John W. Hallahan. Inset: Mary McMichan**

## DEVELOPMENT OF THE ARCHDIOCESAN CATHOLIC HIGH SCHOOL SYSTEM

*P*rivate Catholic secondary schools operated in the Diocese of Philadelphia throughout the nineteenth century, many sponsored and staffed by religious communities of men or women. Parishioners of Saint Matthew Church in Conshohocken founded a parish high school in 1866, and other parishes in the diocese did likewise in the following years.

With the foundation of Roman Catholic High School for Boys and John W. Hallahan Catholic Girls' High School as archdiocesan schools at the turn of the twentieth century, a new era of Catholic secondary education began. The following high schools have been operated by the Archdiocese of Philadelphia. Dates give the year of foundation and, where applicable, of closing.

- Roman Catholic High School for Boys, Philadelphia — 1890
- John W. Hallahan Catholic Girls' High School, Philadelphia — 1911
- West Philadelphia Catholic High School, Philadelphia — 1916/1927
  - West Philadelphia Catholic High School for Boys — 1916–1989
  - West Philadelphia Catholic High School for Girls — 1927–1989
  - Merged as West Philadelphia Catholic High School — 1989
- Northeast Catholic High School for Boys, Philadelphia — 1926
- Saints John Neumann and Maria Goretti High School, Philadelphia
  - Southeast Catholic High School for Boys — 1934–1955
  - Bishop Neumann High School — 1955–1978
  - Saint John Neumann High School for Boys — 1978–2004
  - Saint Maria Goretti High School for Girls — 1955–2004
  - Merged as Ss John Neumann & Maria Goretti High School — 2004
- Notre Dame High School for Girls, Moylan — 1935–1981
- Saint Thomas More High School for Boys, Philadelphia — 1936–1975
- Little Flower Catholic High School for Girls, Philadelphia — 1939
- Saint James Catholic High School for Boys, Chester — 1940–1993
- Saint Hubert Catholic High School for Girls, Philadelphia — 1941
- Lansdale Catholic High School, Lansdale — 1949
- Monsignor Bonner & Archbishop Prendergast Catholic H. S., Drexel Hill — 1953
  - Archbishop Prendergast High School [for Boys] — 1953–1956
  - Archbishop Prendergast High School for Girls — 1956–2006
  - Monsignor Bonner High School for Boys — 1956–2006
  - Restructured as Msgr Bonner and Abp Prendergast Catholic H.S. — 2006

- Father Judge High School for Boys, Philadelphia — 1954
- Kennedy–Kenrick Catholic High School, Norristown — 1955
  - Saint Matthew Parish High School, Conshohocken — 1866–1955
  - Saint Matthew High School, Conshohocken — 1955–1966
  - Archbishop Kennedy High School, Conshohocken — 1966–1993
  - Saint Patrick Parish High School, Norristown — 1941–1955
  - Bishop Kenrick High School, Norristown — 1955–1993
  - Merged as Kennedy-Kenrick Catholic H.S. — 1993
- Saint Pius X, Pottstown — 1955
- Cardinal Dougherty High School (coeducational in 1972) — 1956
- Conwell–Egan Catholic High School, Fairless Hills — 1957/1965
  - Bishop Egan High School, Levittown — 1957–1965
  - Bishop Egan High School for Boys, Fairless Hills — 1965–1993
  - Bishop Conwell High School for Girls, Levittown — 1965–1993
  - Merged as Conwell-Egan Catholic High School — 1993
- Bishop Shanahan High School, Downingtown — 1957
  - Saint Agnes Parish High School, West Chester — 1909–1957
  - Bishop Shanahan High School, West Chester — 1957–1998
  - Bishop Shanahan High School, Downingtown — 1998
- Bishop McDevitt High School, Wyncote — 1958
- Cardinal O'Hara High School, Springfield — 1963
- Archbishop Wood High School, Warminster (coeducational in 1990) — 1964
- Archbishop Ryan High School, Philadelphia (coeducational in 1988) — 1966
- Archbishop John Carroll High School, Radnor (coeducational in 1988) — 1967

## New Bishops from Philadelphia

Almost a quarter of a century had passed since Jeremiah Shanahan and William O'Hara, both Philadelphia priests, had been ordained bishops for the dioceses of Harrisburg and Scranton. At the end of the nineteenth century, several priests of the archdiocese were appointed bishops. In 1892, Father Ignatius Horstmann, a former archdiocesan chancellor, was ordained Bishop of Cleveland. In 1898, Monsignor John Fitzmaurice, pastor of Saint Agatha Church in West Philadelphia, was ordained Bishop of Erie. Father John Shanahan, pastor of Our Mother of Sorrows Church in West Philadelphia, was the brother of Bishop Jeremiah Shanahan, Bishop of Harrisburg, who ordained Father John a priest in 1869. Thirty years later, in 1899, Father John Shanahan succeeded his brother as Bishop of Harrisburg.

In 1897, Father Edmond Prendergast, Archbishop Ryan's vicar general, was ordained as the first auxiliary bishop of Philadelphia. Unlike a coadjutor bishop—the title held by Bishop Kenrick under Bishop Conwell, and by Bishop Wood under Bishop Neumann—an auxiliary bishop does not automatically succeed the diocesan bishop. He does not necessarily take on administrative duties in the diocese, but serves as an advisor and assistant to the diocesan bishop. An auxiliary bishop also assists in the celebration of the sacraments, particularly Confirmation and Holy Orders.

Edmond Francis Prendergast was born in Ireland in 1843, and came to Philadelphia as a teenager. He studied for the priesthood at Saint Charles Seminary, and at the age of 22 was ordained a priest. He served as pastor of three parishes—including Saint Malachy in North Philadelphia, where he served for 37 years—and undertook leadership roles in many archdiocesan projects

In 1903, Father Dennis Dougherty, a professor at Saint Charles Seminary, was appointed the Bishop of Nueva Segovia, in the province of Ilocos Sur in the Philippines Islands. In 1898, the United States had gained control of these islands as a result of the Spanish American War. As the American government assumed administration of the Philippines, the Holy See decided to appoint an American as bishop. Bishop Dougherty asked permission from Archbishop Ryan to take five Philadelphia priests with him to Nueva Segovia. These priests, all volunteers, included two seminary professors—Father James Carroll and Father John MacGinley—and three who were serving parishes as curates—Father James McCloskey, Nativity of the Blessed Virgin Mary Church, Port Richmond;

Father Edgar Cook, Saint Mary Church, Phoenixville; and Father Daniel Gercke, Old Saint Mary Church, Philadelphia. Father Carroll would eventually succeed Bishop Dougherty as Bishop of Nueva Segovia.

Monsignor Thomas Kennedy was born in Conshohocken in 1857, and ordained a priest in 1887. After serving as a professor and administrator at Saint Charles Seminary, he was sent to Rome as the Rector of the North American College, a residence for seminarians and priests from the United States studying at pontifical universities in Rome. In 1907, Monsignor Kennedy was ordained a bishop, and in 1915 was made the titular Archbishop of Seleucia in Isauria. Archbishop Kennedy died on August 28, 1917, and was buried in Rome.

*M*artin I. J. Griffin (pictured in 1911) was born in Philadelphia in 1842. He left his job as a bookkeeper to write for Catholic newspapers, and was the author of a series of pamphlets on Catholic history as well as a chapter on "Catholicity in Philadelphia" in a 19*th*-century history of the city. He edited the Journal of the Irish Catholic Benevolent Union *from 1873 to 1900, renaming it* Griffin's Journal *in 1894. He also published a quarterly magazine,* American Catholic Historical Researches, *devoted entirely to history.*

*On July 22, 1884, Griffin and a friend, John H. Campbell, founded the American Catholic Historical Society of Philadelphia, whose members included newspaper editors, college presidents, professors, pastors and historians. They began to publish the Records of the society, and by 1895 had collected so many books, pamphlets, photographs, and other religious artifacts that the Society needed headquarters for storage. A house on the 700 block of Spruce Street served this purpose until 1967, when the ACHS moved to Fourth and Walnut Streets. In addition to publishing articles on church history—particularly on the Church in Philadelphia—the ACHS has supported the editing and production of numerous books on the history of the archdiocese and Saint Charles Seminary.*

*T*homas Eakins (1844–1916) was born in Philadelphia and studied at the Pennsylvania Academy of Fine Arts, where he became a professor (1876) and later director (1882). He quickly became known in Philadelphia both for his paintings and for his teaching style, which was considered unorthodox by some contemporaries.

From 1900 to 1906, Eakins often bicycled with his friend and student, sculptor Samuel Murray, to Saint Charles Seminary. They visited on Sunday afternoons to hear Vespers chanted by the seminarians. During his visits he painted portraits of several seminary professors, including the rector, Monsignor Patrick Garvey, and Father Dennis Dougherty. A number of his paintings are housed in the Eakins Room at the seminary.

He is pictured here in a self-portrait, done in 1902.

*F*our days in Easter Week 1897 were set aside to celebrate Archbishop Ryan's Silver Jubilee: the 25th anniversary of his ordination as a bishop. The festivities involved people from nearly every parish in the archdiocese, and included a number of events:

*A parade of parochial school boys went from the Philadelphia Baseball Park at Broad and Huntingdon Streets (the Baker Bowl) to the Cathedral. Boys from each parish marched in the order of the parishes' founding, led by the Cathedral parish. Led by mounted officers from the Philadelphia Police Department as well as the marching band from Roman Catholic High School, about 10,000 boys participated.*

*"A Grand Entertainment" was presented at the Academy of Music by girls from parish grade schools. Six groups of girls represented the six largest religious communities which taught in the Catholic schools. Each group presented its own performance of songs, poems, and tableaux. The gala closed with the girls holding canes to which were attached various symbols of Archbishop Ryan: shamrocks (for his Irish heritage), silver keys (for his jubilee), and vine leaves (from his coat of arms)*

*A solemn Pontifical Mass was celebrated in the Cathedral, which was filled to capacity. Twenty-two Bishops from other dioceses attended, and Pope Leo XIII was represented by the Apostolic Delegate, Archbishop Sebastian Martinelli. Archbishop John Hennessey of Dubuque, Iowa—who knew Archbishop Ryan when both were young priests in Saint Louis—preached the sermon.*

*A banquet was given by the priests of the archdiocese at the Academy of Music, which was followed by a torchlight parade for adults on Broad Street. Fifty-seven parishes sent about 27,000 participants for the parade.*

*Receptions were hosted by the school children of the Cathedral parish, and by people with hearing impairment.*

*During a public reception at the Academy of Music, 12,000 people greeted Archbishop Ryan.*

## Last Years of Archbishop Ryan

In 1897, Archbishop Ryan celebrated his Silver Jubilee—the twenty-fifth anniversary of his ordination as bishop—with a solemn Mass and several days of parades and festivities. Six years later came the fiftieth anniversary of his ordination as a priest. At his Golden Jubilee Mass, he noted that the autumn of his life was passing, and that winter was at hand. "In the solitude of the old age of a Christian bishop," he said, "comes the summons, 'Render an account of thy stewardship.'... O friends and brothers in Christ, pray for me that the little time left I may employ in reparation for the past and preparation for the near eternal future." By February 1911 the archbishop was gravely ill, and knowing that the end was near, visitors came from far and wide to ask a last blessing and say farewell. Among them were Edwin Stuart, Governor of Pennsylvania; John Reyburn, Mayor of the City of Philadelphia; and Mother Katharine Drexel.

Archbishop Ryan died on February 11, 1911, and the entire city mourned his passing. Flags were flown at half-staff throughout the area. His funeral Mass was attended by many bishops and priests, Mother Katharine Drexel, members of many religious communities, and parishioners from the 129 parishes that he founded during his years as archbishop. On February 16, his body was entombed in the Cathedral crypt.

In 1911, the Archdiocese of Philadelphia comprised barely a quarter of the territory that had been part of it before the Civil War. The Catholic population of the archdiocese, however, had more than tripled since 1850, as wave after wave of immigrants came to make a new beginning in the United States. The number of parishes and missions increased at the same rate, and included many national parishes and institutions that helped new Americans to worship and work together while maintaining their cherished languages and traditions. Increased diversity brought challenges of its own, but the faithful and their leaders met these challenges by expanding the Church's outreach in nearly every aspect of daily life. The Archdiocese of Philadelphia entered the twentieth century with the resources and commitment to live out the faith that was now a firmly-established part of life in the Philadelphia region.

**The body of Archbishop Ryan lies in state in the Cathedral of Saints Peter and Paul, February 1911.**

# Living the Faith

## (1911–1960)

The Archdiocese of Philadelphia witnessed a great deal of change during the first one hundred years of its existence. From a scattered flock—misunderstood by many and even persecuted by some—it had been transformed into a well-established, highly visible participant in the daily life of Philadelphia and its environs. Sons and daughters of Catholic immigrants had risen to become captains of industry, political leaders, decorated soldiers and respected educators. Consecrated life was flourishing, and religious women and men were dedicating their lives to handing on the faith to a new generation of parishioners. The dawn of the archdiocese's second century brought the promise of an even brighter future in which the living vine of faith would continue to flourish and bear fruit.

### Archbishop Prendergast

Upon Archbishop Ryan's death, Bishop Prendergast became administrator of the Archdiocese of Philadelphia. On May 27, 1911, Bishop Prendergast ordained 24 deacons to the priesthood. This was the largest ordination class from Saint Charles Seminary to that date. Returning to the sacristy after the Mass, he received word that Pope Pius X had named him Archbishop of Philadelphia.

The new archbishop saw to the completion of many projects which Archbishop Ryan

**Archbishop Edmond Francis Prendergast**
**Third Archbishop of Philadelphia, 1911-1918**

had begun. In 1912, he celebrated the opening of Catholic Girls High School (later renamed for John W. Hallahan), and the dedication of the Archbishop Ryan Memorial Library building at Saint Charles Seminary. The following year he opened the Archbishop Ryan Memorial Institute for the Deaf at 18th and Vine Streets, under the direction of the Sisters of Saint Joseph. Archbishop Ryan had fostered a special concern for children with disabilities, and the Institute (which later relocated to 35th and Spring Garden Streets) had long been his dream.

In addition to memorials for his predecessor, Archbishop Prendergast also wished to honor his own patron saint, Saint Edmond of Abingdon, England. In 1912, the archbishop founded Saint Edmond Parish in South Philadelphia, and in 1914, a new residence building for students at Saint Charles Seminary was named Saint Edmond's Hall. He also saw to the founding of Saint Edmond's Home for Children, at 44th Street and Haverford Avenue. This home was under the direction of the Sisters of Bon Secours, and was the first Catholic school in the United States to provide educational opportunities for severely handicapped youth. In its first year, 1916, Saint Edmond's Home admitted 14 boys and 17 girls between the ages of 4 and 14. In 1956, the Home was relocated to Rosemont, Montgomery County.

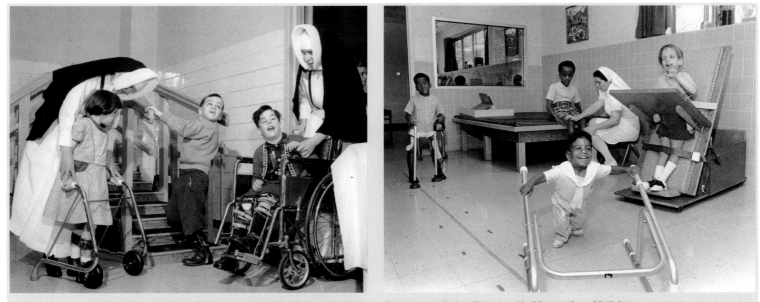

Some of the Sisters of Bon Secours and their charges at Saint Edmond's Home for Children

## Constant Care for Immigrants

Immigration continued steadily in the opening decades of the twentieth century, and especially from Italy. Archbishop Prendergast founded a number of Italian national parishes in the city and other communities: Saint Mary of the Eternal, Mater Dolorosa, Saint Nicholas of Tolentine, Our Lady of Pompeii and Our Lady of Consolation in Philadelphia; Immaculate Conception, Marcus Hook; Saints Cosmas and Damian, Conshohocken; and Our Lady of the Rosary, Coatesville. When Saint Donato School was dedicated in August 1914, the Mass was attended by Mother Frances Xavier Cabrini, whose Missionary Sisters of the Sacred Heart arrived to teach in the parish school. Mother Cabrini, herself an immigrant, worked with Italians in New York City, Chicago and elsewhere. In 1946 she would be the first citizen of the United States to be canonized.

The Italian immigrants brought with them exuberant customs and festivals different from those of the northern Europeans from Ireland and elsewhere. Archbishop Prendergast established the Catholic Mission Society to support several Settlement Houses in the growing Italian communities, including L'Assunta House, Madonna House and L'Annunciata House. In addition to religious instruction, these Settlement Houses offered social activities and educational programs in sewing, music, English, and Italian. In 1912, L'Assunta House prepared 82 children for Confirmation. The Salesian Fathers likewise operated the Don Bosco Institute, to serve Italian young men, who were employed but had no place to live.

Neighborhood processions in honor of the Blessed Mother and the Saints (like this one in 1947) have been part of the tradition of Catholics of Italian descent for generations.

The late nineteenth century also witnessed the growth of the Spanish-speaking community, which included immigrants from Spain as well as from Central and South America. In 1884, Archbishop Ryan invited priests from Arizona to minister to Spanish-speaking Catholics. After the Spanish-American War the United States took possession of Spanish colonies in the Caribbean, and immigration from these islands to the United States increased. In 1909, Archbishop Prendergast invited Father Antonio Casulleras from Barcelona, Spain, to take charge of the apostolate to Philadelphia's Hispanic Catholics. His work included ministry to Spanish sailors in the Port of Philadelphia.

The Chapel of Our Lady of the Miraculous Medal (*La Capilla de Nuestra Señora de la Medalla Milagrosa*), on Spring Garden Street above 19th Street, was one of the first churches in the region specifically dedicated to serve the Hispanic Catholic community. The funds to purchase the building for *La Milagrosa* (as it has come to be called) were a gift of Sor Agueda Quintana, a Mexican Sister of Charity and nurse at Saint Joseph's Hospital, who had received money from an inheritance. *La Milagrosa* opened on April 26, 1912, under the care of Father Antonio Canas.

Once again, large numbers of immigrants called for renewed efforts by Catholic groups and institutions to provide for the needs of the poor. Many initiatives existed on the local level, and in the early decades of the twentieth century, Catholic charity providers sought to consolidate these independent programs under the direction of the archdiocese. The first Catholic Charities Office was created in 1912. In 1919, the Catholic Children's Bureau was incorporated into Catholic Charities. The Missionary Servants of the Blessed Trinity (Trinitarians) assumed a leading role in the organization of charitable works under the Catholic Charities Office.

Centralization and consolidation of services helped to ensure greater accountability and efficiency—especially as archdiocesan charitable institutions looked more and more to professionals rather than volunteers to provide care. The higher visibility that resulted from the creation of this system gave Catholic social workers and health care providers an opportunity to have a greater impact both on the wider community and on public policy.

## Fostering a Life of Prayer

Lay societies played an important role in parish life in the early part of the century. The Holy Name Society, an association for Catholic men, promoted devotion to the Sacred Heart of Jesus and combated blasphemy and profanity in public and private life. Parish-based chapters of the Society boasted more than 32,000 members in 1926. They met for a monthly Communion Mass—usually the earliest parish Mass, because of the requirement to fast from food and drink after midnight—and most

**Children taking part in a celebration at the "Spanish Chapel", La Milagrosa, on Spring Garden Street.**

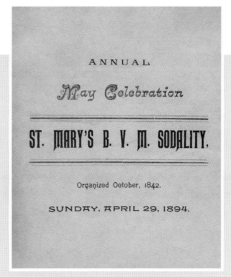

Program for the annual May Devotions held by the Sodality at Old St. Mary's, Philadelphia, 1894

Members of the Holy Name Society of Saint Edward the Confessor parish, Philadelphia, 1913

of the church-going men of the parish were members of the Society. Women of the parish often belonged to the Sodality of the Blessed Virgin Mary, which met frequently to pray the Rosary and offer service to the parish community. Parish missions and novenas, and the annual Forty Hours Devotions, were popular parish events, and helped to foster the devotional life of families and individuals.

In 1915, a group of Sisters Servants of the Holy Spirit of Perpetual Adoration arrived from Steyl, Holland, to take up residence in the Convent of Divine Love, at 22nd and Green Streets. Known as the "Pink Sisters" from the color of their habits, they live a contemplative, cloistered life centered on constant prayer before the Blessed Sacrament. The following year, the Poor Clares established a convent in Philadelphia, and the Discalced Carmelites, who had been in the diocese since 1902, built a new monastery on Old York Road. These communities committed themselves to constant prayer for the needs of the Church, especially in this archdiocese.

## ACTS OF PENANCE IN 1915

*T*he rules of fast and abstinence at the beginning of the twentieth century were much different from those of the twenty-first century:

- *Those over 21 years old—except the sick, nursing mothers, and the elderly—were bound to fast every day in Lent except Sundays.*
- *In the morning a warm drink of tea, coffee or chocolate was permitted, along with bread, not exceeding two ounces.*
- *One full meal could be eaten, usually at midday.*
- *A small meal, not to exceed eight ounces, was permitted in the evening..*
- *All the faithful were bound to abstain from meat on certain days during the whole year.*
- *Fruit and vegetables, bread, milk, butter, cheese and eggs were permitted every day.*
- *Meat was allowed once a day on Monday, Tuesday, Thursday and Saturday. No meat at all was allowed on Wednesday or Friday.*
- *Working men could eat meat any day except Fridays, Ash Wednesday, Holy Saturday and Christmas Eve.*
- *If a meal included meat, fish could not be eaten at the same meal.*

*These regulations bound people "under pain of grievous sin," and were scrupulously observed by most Catholics, including many who were not always faithful to their Sunday Mass obligation. Especially conscientious Catholics agonized over the permissibility of such things as eating Campbell's Pork and Beans on Friday because of the miniscule scrap of meat floating on top of the beans, or eating leftover mince pie on the day after Thanksgiving.*

## The Great War

At the outbreak of war in Europe, President Woodrow Wilson designated October 4, 1914, as a national day of prayer for peace.  This fell on the first Sunday of October, which at the time was celebrated as the feast of Our Lady of the Rosary.  Archbishop Prendergast asked each parish to celebrate a solemn high Mass on that day, and urged the faithful to "say the beads and make many visits to churches . . . to have in mind all day long and to implore the intercession of Our Lady of the Rosary that her Son may take pity on the world."  Twenty-two Philadelphia priests served as military chaplains during World War I, including Father Joseph L.N. Wolfe, later pastor of Saint Barbara Church, Philadelphia, and national chaplain of the newly-formed American Legion.

**Thousands of men and boys gather with members of the police and fire departments and the armed services for a Field Mass at the Philadelphia Navy Yard in May 1916**

**Leaders of the services look on from a reviewing stand**

Dennis Joseph Dougherty was born August 16, 1865, in Homesville, near Ashland, Schuylkill County, in the heart of Pennsylvania's coal-mining region.  As a child he attended Saint Joseph Church in Ashland.  Because there were no Catholic schools in the area, he was educated in public schools in Girardville.  At age 14 he passed the entrance examination for Saint Charles Seminary, but because he was too young to be admitted, he enrolled for a time at Saint Mary College in Montreal, Canada.  Two years later, he was admitted to Saint Charles Seminary.  He completed his philosophy studies in four years, and was sent by Archbishop Ryan to the North American College and the Urban College in Rome.

**Cardinal Dennis Joseph Dougherty
Fourth Archbishop of Philadelphia,
1918-1951**

## Archbishop Dougherty

Archbishop Prendergast died on February 26, 1918, and Auxiliary Bishop John McCort, his vicar general and pastor of Our Mother of Sorrows Church, West Philadelphia, served as administrator of the archdiocese until a successor was named.  On April 30, Bishop Dennis Dougherty, a native of the archdiocese and Bishop of Buffalo, was appointed as Archbishop of Philadelphia.

**Members of the Class of 1902 from Saint Charles Seminary (left) were taught by Father Dennis Dougherty (right, standing at left of photo). Also pictured are Archbishop Ryan (seated, left) and Auxiliary Bishop Prendergast (seated, right).**

Ordained in the Lateran Basilica in 1890, Father Dougherty returned to Philadelphia and was appointed to the faculty of Saint Charles Seminary where he taught for 13 years. In 1903 he was appointed Bishop of Nueva Segovia in the Philippines. After four and a half years as Bishop of Nueva Segovia, Bishop Dougherty was appointed as Bishop of Jaro, a vast diocese centered on the island of Panay. In 1915 he returned to America as Bishop of Buffalo, where he served for three years. When he was appointed as Archbishop of Philadelphia at 52 years of age, Archbishop Dougherty already had fifteen years' experience as a diocesan bishop in three dioceses.

## The Great Influenza Epidemic

Shortly after Archbishop Dougherty's arrival, the nation was hit by the great influenza epidemic of 1918. It started almost unnoticed in March at a U.S. Army encampment—Fort Riley, Kansas—and quickly spread around the world. Inaccurately called "Spanish Flu," the epidemic killed 20 to 40 million world-wide. Ten times as many Americans died from influenza as were killed in World War I. In Philadelphia, 13,000 died in a matter of months. Nearly 300 died on a single day in October 1918. City and suburban health officials ordered churches, schools and places of amusement closed for the duration of the epidemic; however, a number of parishes circumvented the order by holding outdoor Masses.

**The deadly nature of the influenza epidemic that struck Philadelphia in 1918 meant that burials were frequent. Volunteers from Saint Charles Seminary were called upon to assist with the digging of mass graves for those who died from the flu, as contemporary newspaper accounts attest.**

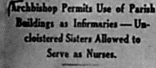

Archbishop Permits Use of Parish Buildings as Infirmaries — Uncloistered Sisters Allowed to Serve as Nurses.

### SEMINARIANS BURY THE DEAD

Students Work in Holy Cross Cemetery — Priests Labor Heroically — Philopatrian Institute Converted into Hospital.

Hastening to the aid of the municipal authorities, confronted with one of the most serious emergencies in the history of Philadelphia and overwhelmed with calls for help, His Grace the Most Reverend Archbishop has placed at the disposal of the Bureau of Health virtually every available diocesan resource in the fight to control and stamp out the influenza epidemic.

Thousands of Sisters of the various uncloistered communities have been

Almost half the dead were Catholics, and archdiocesan and parish cemeteries could not keep up with the number of burials. To make matters worse, in early October overworked cemetery employees went on strike, demanding shorter hours and higher salaries. At the archbishop's request, seminarians from Saint Charles Seminary, members of the Saint Vincent de Paul Society, and Knights of Columbus volunteered to dig graves. Other seminarians ministered to the sick at Saint Mary, Saint Agnes, Saint Joseph and Misericordia hospitals, as well as at emergency facilities set up in Saint Patrick Parish Hall, the Elwyn School and the Catholic Philopatrian Literary Institute. Leo Naylor, a seminarian who worked at Holy Cross Cemetery during the epidemic, died after visiting sick relatives at home.

Sister Florentine, S.S.J., the infirmarian who attended sick students at Saint Charles Seminary, and Mother Marie Aloysius, S.H.C.J., were among the many religious Sisters who died after attending to the sick. A property owned by the Sisters of the Blessed Sacrament at 832 Pine Street was pressed into service as a temporary shelter for orphans of the epidemic, only one of many church facilities put to emergency use. The epidemic abated in November 1918, but less severe outbreaks followed over the next several years.

## Archdiocesan Celebrations

On February 13, 1921, Pope Benedict XV named Archbishop Dougherty a Cardinal of the Roman Church. Cardinals trace their origins to the clergy of the early church in Rome, and today assist the Pope in his world-wide ministry by serving as members of the various congregations and tribunals that make up the administration of the Holy See. Cardinals also meet after the death of a pope—in a solemn convocation called a conclave—to elect a successor. On March 7, 1921, in a ceremony known as a consistory, Cardinal Dougherty and five other archbishops received the red *galero*, a broad-brimmed hat with 30 decorative tassels that formed part of the traditional cardinalatial insignia prior to the Second Vatican Council. Cardinals are also assigned a *titulus* or "title," an honorary link to one of the ancient parish churches in Rome. Cardinal Dougherty was given the titular church of Saints Nereus and Achilleus. Pope Benedict also appointed Cardinal Dougherty a member of the Congregation for the Propagation of the Faith, Congregation of Rites, Congregation for the Discipline of the Sacraments, and Congregation for the Oriental Churches.

In December 1921 the cause for the canonization of Bishop John Neumann advanced to the stage where he was declared "Venerable." This is the first of three major steps in the process of canonization by which a person is formally recognized as a saint. Bishop Neumann's reputation for holiness was marked by humility and great simplicity, and Pope Benedict XV commented on this during the ceremony:

> *Perhaps the very simplicity of these virtues has been misunderstood by those who thought there was no heroic degree in the virtues of the servant of God, because in their minds the good works and holy deeds performed by Neumann are the holy and good deeds which every good religious, every good missionary, every good bishop should perform. We shall not pause to remark that works even the most simple, performed with constant perfection in the midst of inevitable difficulties, spells heroism in any servant of God. Just because of the simplicity of his works we find in them a strong argument in saying to the faithful of whatever age, sex and condition: You are all bound to imitate the Venerable Neumann.*

In the Holy Year 1925, 500 Philadelphians sailed for Europe on the *U.S.S. Ohio* for a 35-day pilgrimage. This was billed as the largest sailing to that date from the Port of Philadelphia. Part of the purpose for the pilgrimage was to attend ceremonies connected with the canonization of Saint Thérèse of Lisieux. The "Little Flower" had caught the imagination of the Catholic world, and was a favorite of Cardinal Dougherty, who had exerted great effort to promote her canonization a mere 28 years after her death. The cardinal's devotion to Thérèse, a special patroness of missionaries, dated back to his days in the Philippine missions when, sorely in need of funds for his poverty-stricken diocese, he entrusted his concerns to her intercession. In later years, Cardinal Dougherty showed his gratitude for the favors received from Saint Thérèse, and personally paid for the altar at her shrine in Lisieux. There he also presided over ceremonies to celebrate her canonization. He encouraged every parish in the archdiocese to place a statue of the Little Flower in the church, and arranged for a shrine of Saint Thérèse in the courtyard of the nuns' cloister at Saint Charles Seminary. In 1939, Cardinal Dougherty used the money he had received as gifts on the fiftieth anniversary of his priestly ordination to build Little Flower High School for Girls, in Northeast Philadelphia.

## New Seminary Building

By 1925 the number of seminarians at Saint Charles Borromeo Seminary required expansion of the facility. In December 1925 ground was broken for a new building for the preparatory seminary and faculty. An E-shaped building nearly 600 feet in length, with three 250-foot wings, was designed by Paul Monaghan and constructed by Matthew H. McCloskey, Jr. Built at

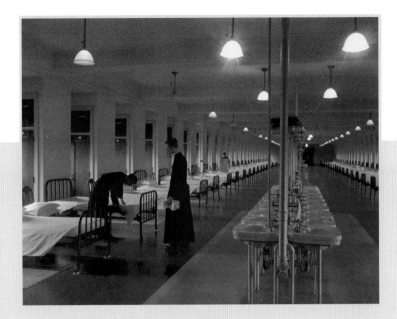

A new building for the preparatory division of Saint Charles Seminary was completed in 1928. The building had room for 400 seminarians, who were housed in large dormitories until single rooms were constructed in 1952.

a cost of $5 million, the building could house 400 seminarians. Much of the money for its construction was raised through the annual seminary collection, which exceeded $300,000 every year from 1924 through 1930.

This new seminary building was dedicated on June 10, 1928, and special railroad, bus and trolley services were provided for the estimated 200,000 people in attendance. This number included nearly 60,000 men from various parishes, led by 25 bands who paraded in a two-hour procession from West Philadelphia to Overbrook. Cardinal Dougherty celebrated a solemn Mass at an outdoor altar for the assembled clergy, religious and laity.

The preparatory division's chapel, dedicated to Saint Martin of Tours, also honors the memory of Martin Maloney, a principal benefactor. Born in Ireland in 1847 in the darkest hour of the terrible potato famine, Maloney's family immigrated to Pennsylvania and settled near Scranton when Martin was about seven years old. After trying his hand at several careers, he invented a gas burner that was an improvement over other available models. This invention led to many contracts in the gas and electrical lighting fields, and made him a multi-millionaire. He devoted much of his fortune to Catholic causes in Europe and the United States. In recognition of his charitable contributions to the Church, he was honored with the title of "Marquis" by the Holy Father.

## Catholic Presence in Civic Life

When the United States celebrated the sesquicentennial anniversary of the Declaration of Independence in 1926, attention naturally focused on Philadelphia, the "cradle of liberty." Civic celebrations were complemented by religious services, including a Mass on October 3 at South Philadelphia's Sesquicentennial Stadium (renamed Municipal Stadium and, later, JFK Stadium). Cardinal Dougherty celebrated Mass for a congregation estimated at 300,000.

In 1928, the Governor of New York, Al Smith, became the Democratic Party candidate for President of the United States. Smith was the first Catholic ever to win the nomination, and anti-Catholic hostility was stirred up nationwide. Officially, the Church took no position on Smith's candidacy. However, Cardinal Dougherty wrote to the superiors of religious congregations in the archdiocese. He usually felt it was inappropriate for religious Sisters to vote, he said, but he would make an exception for this election. Cardinal Dougherty was conservative on most religious and social issues, yet he was vocal in his support for women's rights and the Women's Suffrage movement. He was one of very few American prelates to openly support voting rights for women, and even spoke in favor of an Equal Rights Amendment to the United States Constitution when the matter came up in the 1940s.

John B. Kelly, building tycoon and father of the future actress Grace Kelly, became the first Catholic nominee for Mayor of Philadelphia, running as a Democrat in 1935. Philadelphia voters had supported the Democrat Franklin Delano Roosevelt in 1932 and in 1936; however, Kelly lost this election to Republican Samuel Davis Wilson. When Mayor Wilson died in office, George Connell, the Republican president of Philadelphia City Council, succeeded him as acting mayor. Connell thus became the first Catholic to

*In the 1920s, baseball was big at Ascension of Our Lord Parish in the Kensington section of Philadelphia—so big that even Babe Ruth played on the parish team, at least for one memorable game. On that day the Babe hit the longest double of his career, maybe the longest double in baseball history.*

*Father William Casey, a priest of Ascension parish and an avid baseball fan, was looking for a way to help the semi-pro team at Ascension Catholic Club pay for their new field at "I" and Tioga Streets. As an unofficial chaplain for Connie Mack's Philadelphia Athletics, he persuaded Ruth to play at a benefit for the parish team.*

*The game took place at Ascension's field on September 4, 1923, before a crowd estimated at 10,000. Ascension played a team from the Lit Brothers Department Store on Market Street at 6:00 p.m., after Ruth and the Yankees played the A's at Shibe Park. The bat boy was Thomas Bolton, who would be ordained a priest in Philadelphia in 1938.*

*Wearing an Ascension uniform made especially for him, The Babe hit a towering shot over the fence in the fourth inning, which sent him around the bases. But he was stopped at second base by the umpire. It might have been a home run at Shibe Park or Yankee Stadium, but because Ascension had a short fence on that side of the field, it was ruled a ground-rule double. During other at-bats Ruth popped up and got on base on an error, stealing home for Ascension's only run. The team lost to Lit Brothers 2 to 1, but the parish was a winner that day. The kindness of the most famous member of the Baseball Hall of Fame—and the Knights of Columbus—made baseball history, at least for the Ascension Catholic Club.*

serve as Mayor of Philadelphia, from August 19, 1939, to January 1, 1940. In 1962, James H. J. Tate, a Democrat and President of City Council, became acting mayor when Richardson Dilworth resigned to run for Governor of Pennsylvania. In 1963 Tate became the first Catholic to be elected as Mayor of Philadelphia, and served in the post until 1972.

In 1959, Democrat David Lawrence of Pittsburgh became Pennsylvania's first Catholic governor. The first Catholic to serve as a United States Senator from Pennsylvania was the Philadelphian and former Congressman Francis Myers, a Democrat, elected in 1944.

## The Great Depression

The Great Depression, which began with the stock market crash in 1929, was a difficult time for all Americans. The only parish founded in the archdiocese during the years of hardship was Our Lady of Loreto, an Italian national parish, located near 62nd Street and Grays Ferry Avenue in southwest Philadelphia. Many of the parishes that had been founded in the 1920s were forced to delay construction of their planned churches.

In several cases, a church was never built. Among the very few large-scale projects of the decade was the erection of Fitzgerald Mercy Hospital in Darby. It was constructed through a legacy of Thomas and May Fitzgerald. Opened by the Archdiocese in 1933, it was placed under the direction of the Religious Sisters of Mercy, and eventually deeded to that congregation.

Fifty-four parishes had been founded during the 1920s, and most operated parish elementary schools. Between 1931 and 1937, however, parochial elementary school enrollment fell by nearly 10,000 students. This drop coincided with a decrease in the annual number of infant baptisms, as Catholic young people, facing low wages and unemployment, postponed marrying and starting families.

Cardinal Dougherty insisted that all Catholic parents send their children to Catholic schools, and a statute of the Ninth Archdiocesan Synod in 1934 established the rule that parish schools should not charge tuition. Because the schools were entirely free—except perhaps for a dollar or two annually for books in some parishes—there was no reason for parents

## CATHOLIC PRESENCE IN CIVIC LIFE

Journalist and author Joseph Chandler (1792–1880) was a member of Philadelphia City Council, and served three terms in the United States House of Representatives. In 1855 he delivered a speech in the House on "the temporal power of the Pope." Chandler also served two and a half years as U.S. Ambassador to the Kingdom of the Two Sicilies.

James H.J. Tate, the first Catholic elected Mayor of Philadelphia, seals a document proclaiming Catholic Youth Week in October 1962.

Robert N.C. Nix, Jr. (center), a native Philadelphian and 1950 valedictorian at Villanova University, was the first African American elected to the Pennsylvania Supreme Court, in 1971. He served on the court for 24 years, including 12 years as Chief Justice.

Justice Nix received an honorary degree from Saint Charles Seminary in June 1985. He is pictured here with Father John Shellem, the seminary librarian, and Sister Cor Immaculatum, I.H.M., the assistant dean of the Religious Studies Division.

Genevieve Blatt, "the First Lady of Pennsylvania Politics," addresses the Saint Anne's parish senior citizens in 1972. Judge Blatt was the first woman elected to statewide office, serving as Secretary of Internal Affairs (now known as Auditor General) from 1955 to 1967. She was also the first woman judge of Pennsylvania's Commonwealth Court, serving from 1972 to 1983. A native of East Brady, Clarion County, Judge Blatt was involved with many charitable activities in the archdiocese.

to take the children out of school or to send them to a public school. Even students in the upper secondary grades were now more apt to remain in school because there was no employment available if the students left.

*B*lessed Virgin Mary Church, on Main Street in Darby, Delaware County, was founded in 1913. Father William Fitzgerald, the first pastor, celebrated the first Masses in the parish at the Darby Theater. In 1920, newly-ordained Father Vincent B. Gallagher was assigned to assist Father Fitzgerald at BVM—and never left the parish. He succeeded Father Fitzgerald as pastor in 1934, and served in that position until his retirement in 1972.

*Even as pastor emeritus, Father Gallagher (pictured here in 1979) lived within the territorial boundaries of BVM parish, as a resident at Villa Saint Joseph, on Lansdowne Avenue in Darby. He was made a Prelate of Honor (with the title of Monsignor) shortly before his death on April 26, 1996. His body is buried in Holy Cross Cemetery, Darby—within the boundaries of BVM.*

In 1931, the Archdiocese of Philadelphia was home to 5,120 religious Sisters. Most were relatively young, and many taught in the 288 elementary schools. A veritable army of Sisters working for a very modest stipend was the principal reason parishes could afford to operate schools during this period of severe economic hardship. The average cost to educate a child in a parish elementary school was $12.33 per year in the 1930s ($170 in 2005 values), and $25 per year in the high schools ($345 in 2005 values). A typical classroom might have 60 or more children, and educational tools were largely limited to textbooks and a blackboard. Hardcover textbooks usually remained in school and were recycled many times; however, children might take home disposable, soft-cover spellers and workbooks.

Various religious orders and organizations provided relief for the poor during the Depression. The Catholic Young Men's Association reported that it gave 20,346 nights of free beds during 1934, both at its Arch Street and its North 15th Street locations. The philanthropist Louise Morrell, one of Mother Katharine Drexel's two sisters, sold her family heirloom jewelry to provide coal, shoes and food for the poor.

The 1930s also saw the first closing of a parish in the Archdiocese of Philadelphia. Our Lady of Good Counsel Church, an Italian national parish founded in 1898, was suppressed in 1932. Parishioners barricaded the Augustinian parish clergy in the rectory, and Father Simpliciato Gatti, the

acting pastor, was held a virtual prisoner for five months while the archdiocese addressed the matter in court.

In a letter to Judge Eugene Alessandroni, Philadelphia's leading Italian American layman, Cardinal Dougherty explained that he closed the parish because the surrounding territorial parishes—Annunciation B.V.M. Church and Saint Paul Church—had virtually become Italian parishes after Irish parishioners moved away. He also noted that the densely populated area had other Italian national parishes. By closing Our Lady of Good Counsel Church, he said, Italian ministry could be strengthened at the two territorial parishes and at Saint Nicholas of Tolentine Church, another area Italian parish.

## Devotional Life

Eucharistic adoration in the Archdiocese blossomed in the 1930s. In 1932, a Men's Perpetual Adoration Society was established at the Cathedral. Adoration was held in the Cathedral chapel from First Friday morning until Sunday afternoon. In 1934, Mary Lowery, a leader of the Alliance for Catholic Women, asked Cardinal Dougherty's permission to form an "Hour of Adoration Society." She planned to recruit 100 women as "promoters," and each of them would be responsible for finding another ten women to adore the Blessed Sacrament on a regular basis. Adoration was to be conducted in daylight hours, on the Friday and Saturday following the first Friday of the month.

Members of the Archdiocesan Holy Name Society participate in a Eucharistic Procession on the Benjamin Franklin Parkway in Philadelphia, October 10, 1948.

**Catholic members of the Philadelphia Police Department and the Philadelphia Fire Department often joined the League of the Sacred Heart. Pictured here are scenes from a parade and Mass celebrated on Logan Circle, circa 1930.**

With 500 registered members, the Society first met at the chapel of the Sisters of the Assumption at Ravenhill Academy. By 1943, the Adorers were meeting at 27 centers around the archdiocese. Recruiting both adult women and students at elementary and high schools, the Society listed 632,212 hours of adoration undertaken by its members in 1949. In addition to their purely spiritual work, the Adorers raised large sums of money for foreign relief in the years following World War II.

**Representatives of the police officers and fire fighters kneel to receive Holy Communion at the Mass.**

Cardinal Dougherty convoked the Ninth Archdiocesan Synod in 1934, to address a variety of topics including clerical conduct, annual parish visitations, and the necessity for sermons to be preached against alcohol abuse, improper music and the evils of mixed marriages and divorce. One decree of the synod directed priests to read the Gospel in the vernacular at every Mass, and to give a five-minute sermon from memory. At the last Mass of Sunday, the sermon was to be at least twenty minutes long. Parishes were required to celebrate Sunday Vespers every week, but could substitute another devotion, usually Benediction or a novena. Most parishes had a special "children's Mass" around 9:00 a.m., and the children were watched over by school Sisters who might question absences. First Communion liturgies and May processions remained important liturgical and social events in the lives of the children and their families.

## Legion of Decency

Before the advent of television, motion pictures were America's most popular year-round form of amusement. American bishops were concerned about sexual content and violence in film. Cardinal Dougherty went further than most bishops, and in May 1934 he issued a pastoral letter forbidding Catholics, on pain of serious sin, to attend any movies at all. The immediate effect was a dramatic fall-off in attendance at

Philadelphia theaters. In cooperation with the National Catholic Welfare Conference's "Legion of Decency," Hollywood eventually responded by toning down the content of motion pictures. Cardinal Dougherty reiterated his ban against movies in subsequent years, but Catholics gradually made their way back to weekly or semi-weekly films. The ban was never revoked, but was not really enforced.

For most of this era, *The Catholic Standard and Times* published Legion of Decency ratings weekly. Films could not be shown in schools during class hours; however, child care institutions conducted by the Archdiocese showed movies to children on a regular basis. Cardinal Dougherty himself had viewed the first film shown to the boys of Saint Francis Industrial School. The film was a 1922 silent movie called "The Bachelor Daddy."

*Although Cardinal Dougherty forbade Catholics to watch secular movies, exceptions were made for children in Catholic institutions. On one occasion, the cardinal made an exception for another child, Grace, the daughter of Olympic gold medal-winner John B. Kelly, who wanted to go with her father to see a movie by Walt Disney.*

*A native of Saint Bridget parish in East Falls and an alumna of Ravenhill Academy, Grace Kelly became an actress and starred in eleven feature films. She won the Academy Award for Best Actress for The Country Girl in 1955.*
*Grace Kelly married Prince Rainier III of Monaco on April 19, 1956. Princess Grace of Monaco, as she was known, was the mother of three children, including the reigning Prince, Albert II.*

*Princess Grace had a stroke while driving and crashed her car on September 13, 1982. She died the next day at the age of 52.*

**Princess Grace, Prince Rainier III and their children
visit with Archbishop Krol in 1963.**

## Ministry to African Americans in the 1930s and 1940s

By the 1930s, Philadelphia had four parishes dedicated to ministry among African Americans: Saint Peter Claver, Twelfth and Lombard Streets; Our Lady of the Blessed Sacrament, Broad Street and Fairmount Avenue; Saint Catherine of Siena, on Penn Street in Germantown; and Saint Ignatius of Loyola, 43rd and Wallace Streets in West Philadelphia. The first three were funded at their foundation primarily by Mother Katharine Drexel; Saint Ignatius had been a German parish. Father Vincent Dever, ordained in 1902, was a pioneer in ministry in predominantly African American neighborhoods, and Holy Ghost Fathers and many Sisters of various religious communities dedicated their lives to this work.

In these parishes, congregants were more likely to be converts, and the parishes were established primarily because racial prejudice made African American people feel unwelcome at the neighborhood territorial parish. In many cases, white families would move away from a neighborhood simply because African Americans moved in. There are even a few documented cases of pastors quietly buying up vacant houses to rent them only to whites.

Cardinal Dougherty, a former missionary, was strongly opposed to racial discrimination in any form, and strictly forbade pastors to refuse to accept African American Catholics as parishioners or students in their schools. Any complaint to the chancery alleging such treatment would result in a pointed inquiry from the Cardinal asking for an explanation. When a neighborhood group—the "Gesu Parish Neighborhood Improvement Association"— tried to prevent a local African American organization from acquiring a neighborhood property and converting it into a health clinic, the leadership sought the support of the cardinal. Cardinal Dougherty refused to meet with them, saying, "I do not wish to create an impression of discriminating against the poor colored race who, through no fault of their own, have been persecuted ever since they were dragged here in chains." He informed Father Thomas Love, S.J., pastor of the Church of the Gesu, of his great devotion to Saint Peter Claver, and of his admiration for Mother Katharine Drexel.

Saint Peter Claver Church, Twelfth and Lombard Streets, Philadelphia

## Orphanages and Other Institutions

In 1922 there were 15 child care institutions in the archdiocese, under the direction of various religious congregations. By 1950 there were 2,950 children in Catholic institutions, and another 1,326 in foster homes supervised by the Catholic Children's Bureau. At first the orphanages were funded through donations by benevolent Catholics; however, over time, although some buildings were built by donations from the faithful, most operating expenses were met through county funding.

Once children entered the system, they usually stayed until they were deemed old enough to go out on their own. If there was family in the child's life, limited family visitation and home visits were permitted. In cases where multiple children of one family were in the system, they were often placed in separate institutions or foster homes because of institutional policies. A number of the religious congregations were bound by their rules to care only for girls or only for boys, and sometimes only for children up to a certain age.

A boy who entered the system at or near birth might start at Saint Vincent's Home, Drexel Hill, conducted by the Daughters of Charity to care for infants and toddlers of both sexes. When a boy was old enough for school he would move to Saint John's Orphan Asylum in West Philadelphia. This orphanage, conducted by the Sisters of Saint Joseph, was home to 500 boys. From Saint John's, an adolescent boy might be placed with the Holy Ghost Fathers at Saint Joseph's House or the Christian Brothers at Saint Francis Industrial School. A girl might remain at Saint Vincent's, or move on to the Catholic Home for Girls or Saint Margaret's Industrial School.

Children who entered the system at a later age would begin at the age-appropriate institution. If children were of a non-English-speaking heritage, they might be assigned to other institutions which served particular ethnic groups, such as Saint Vincent's Orphanage in Tacony for German children, or Saint Mary's Villa in Ambler for Polish orphans.

All of the 4,000 Catholic children from institutions and foster homes came together twice a year. When the Ringling Brothers Circus came to town, the children would be treated to the show by department store owner Ellis Gimbel, or by restaurateur Frank Palumbo. Each June, the Knights of Columbus hosted an annual picnic, at Woodside Park or Willow Grove Park—the only two area amusement parks of sufficient size for so large a crowd. For those unfortunate children who had siblings but not a parent in their life, this day was sometimes the only day in the entire year when they might see brothers and sisters.

In 1913, Saint Francis Country House, on Lansdowne Avenue in Darby, opened as a home for mothers convalescing after childbirth. Located on property once owned by the colonial-era American botanist John Bartram, Saint Francis soon evolved into the first archdiocesan nursing home. Construction projects in 1948 and 1954 added two wings and a total of 224 beds to the facility which also houses a beautiful chapel. The Saint Francis Country House Women's Auxiliary, chartered in 1914, continues to spearhead renovations and improvements.

Tommy Loughran was the undefeated light heavyweight boxing champion of the world from 1927 to 1929. He was also a parishioner of Saint Monica Parish in Philadelphia, where he attended Mass and received Holy Communion every day.

**Saint Francis Country House in 1913**

**Saint Francis Country House in 2005**

**Sister Anne Lutz, C.B.S., and Mr. John McShain with Cardinal Krol at the groundbreaking for the McShain Pavilion at Saint Francis Country House, 1978**

# World War II

In 1936, Philadelphia welcomed Cardinal Eugenio Pacelli, the Secretary of State of the Holy See, during his tour of the United States. Accompanied by Cardinal Dougherty on October 20 and 21, Cardinal Pacelli visited Saint Charles Borromeo Seminary, Ravenhill Academy, Rosemont College, Fitzgerald Mercy Hospital, West Catholic High School for Girls, the Church of the Holy Child and the Cathedral of Saints Peter and Paul. He also made the almost-obligatory visits to Independence Hall and the Liberty Bell. Three years later, Cardinal Dougherty would participate in the conclave which elected Cardinal Pacelli as Pope Pius XII.

**A military chaplain celebrates Mass on a battlefield during World War II**

Only six months later, on September 1, 1939, the invasion of Poland by Nazi Germany marked the beginning of the Second World War. Isolated at first, the United States joined the Allied Forces of the United Kingdom, France and the Soviet Union after the Japanese attack on Pearl Harbor on December 7, 1941. Philadelphia's Catholics faced the same grim realities of wartime as the rest of Americans. Many young fathers were called into the service; Saint Adalbert Parish in Port Richmond sent more than 2,000 young men off to war. Many houses displayed on a prominent window or door a small silk banner, white with a red border. Blue stars on the banner represented members of the household serving in the military; silver stars symbolized those missing in action; and gold stars stood for those who gave their lives for their country.

Those at home faced food, cigarette and gasoline rationing, as well as restrictions on new automobiles, household appliances and construction materials. No new churches or schools could be built or expanded, and often classroom space was very crowded. Some schools, such as Saint Bernard's in Mayfair, resorted to shifts: for the war's duration half the children in the lower grades of the school attended in the morning, and the other half in the afternoon.

Devotions of all kind saw an increase in attendance, and often the only church organization to have depleted ranks was the Holy Name Society because so many members were in the service. Bond drives, victory gardens, scrap metal drives and USO fundraisers became a temporary part of parish life and air raid drills a matter of course in parish schools.

Seventy-six graduates of Saint Charles Seminary served as Army, Navy and Marine chaplains during World War II. Several priests, including Father Peter Bonner and Father Anthony Conway were killed in action. Father Charles Gorman, Father Joseph Wolfe and Father Garrett Murphy served in both World Wars, and seven World War II chaplains would also serve during the Korean War (1950–53).

**Cardinal Dougherty and Cardinal Thomas Tien Kin-sin, S.V.D., Archbishop of Beijing, visit Holy Redeemer Parish, April 9, 1946.**

The only city churches founded in the 1940s were Saint Raymond of Peñafort Church and Holy Redeemer Church, both established in 1941 during the post-Depression, pre-war period. Holy Redeemer Church, under the direction of Saint John the Evangelist Church, was founded specifically to serve Chinese Catholics in Philadelphia's Chinatown and elsewhere. Cardinal Dougherty founded seven more parishes in the post-war period. All but one of these were in suburban communities. Many parishes which had delayed building plans during the Depression and war years now erected new churches and schools. Perhaps the largest of the post-war churches was the imposing edifice built by already-established Saint Martin of Tours Parish. Construction began in September 1948, and cost $2 million. The interior of the church was surfaced with marble— reportedly the largest shipment of stone ever received in the Port of Philadelphia.

## Last Days of Cardinal Dougherty

General Alfred Jodl signed an unconditional surrender of all German forces on May 7, 1945, and the Allied nations celebrated Victory in Europe (V-E) Day on May 8. One hundred days after the German surrender, Japanese Emperor Hirohito accepted the Allies' terms of surrender on August 15, bringing an end to the Second World War. The following day, August 16, Cardinal Dougherty celebrated his 80th birthday.

Two years earlier, in a letter to his vicar general, Bishop Hugh Lamb, Cardinal Dougherty mentioned that his ordination class of 1890 was then the oldest in the diocese, and that of this class only he and Monsignor Henry Gantert —the only priest older than the cardinal—were still living. He asked Bishop Lamb to take on additional responsibilities, including most ordinations and other liturgical celebrations.

On May 23, 1951, Bishop Lamb was appointed by Pope Pius XII as the first bishop of the newly-established Diocese of Greensburg. This diocese had been created from territory belonging to the Dioceses of Pittsburgh and Altoona-Johnstown in western Pennsylvania. Only a few days after this announcement, Cardinal Dougherty died of a cerebral hemorrhage at his residence. His death—at about 9:30 in the morning of May 31, 1951— occurred a few hours after he had celebrated Mass of thanksgiving to mark the sixty-first anniversary of his ordination as a priest of the Archdiocese of Philadelphia.

That afternoon, Cardinal Dougherty's body was taken to Saint Martin's Chapel at Saint Charles Borromeo Seminary. Here he lay in state for two days. Seminarians were appointed to keep vigil around the clock. Thousands of mourners passed in a quiet procession through the chapel. On Saturday, June 2, Archbishop Gerald O'Hara—the Bishop of Savannah, Georgia, who had been an auxiliary bishop to Cardinal Dougherty from 1929 to 1935 — celebrated a solemn Requiem Mass in Saint Martin's Chapel. The Cardinal's body was taken in procession to the Cathedral to lie in state for several more days. Cardinal Dougherty's nephew, Auxiliary Bishop J. Carroll McCormick, celebrated the Funeral Mass in the Cathedral on June 7, 1951, and then entombed his uncle's body in the Cathedral crypt.

Although Bishop Lamb had already been appointed Bishop of Greensburg, he was elected by the archdiocesan College of Consultors as Administrator of the Archdiocese of Philadelphia. He remained in this post until the arrival in November 1951 of Archbishop John O'Hara.

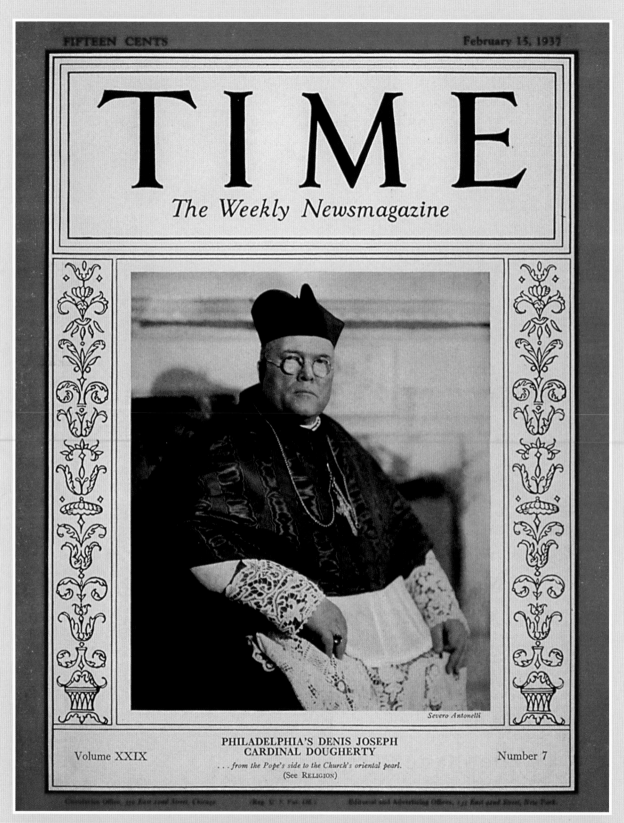

Cardinal Dougherty was appointed as the representative or legate of Pope Pius XI to the 33rd International Eucharistic Congress in Manila, Philippines, in 1937. As papal legate he celebrated the Mass that closed the Congress, known as the *statio orbis* Mass. The cardinal's photo appeared on the cover of *Time* magazine on February 15, 1937, accompanying an article on Eucharistic Congresses.

# Archbishop O'Hara

Born May 1, 1888, in Ann Arbor, Michigan, John Francis O'Hara was raised in the city of Peru in north-central Indiana, and also in Uruguay and Brazil where his father was a United States Consul. At age 20 he returned to Indiana, and enrolled at the University of Notre Dame. During his college years, and for a brief time after college, he taught Spanish at the University, and in 1912 entered the novitiate of the Holy Cross Fathers, the congregation which conducts Notre Dame. Ordained on September 9, 1916, he studied briefly at the Catholic University of America before returning to Notre Dame. A popular teacher, he was named Vice President of Notre Dame in 1933, and President in 1935.

In 1940 Father O'Hara was named an auxiliary bishop of the Archdiocese of New York, and Vicar Delegate for the Military Ordinariate. He was now responsible for supervising more than 1,800 Catholic military chaplains who provided pastoral care for servicemen and servicewomen and their families. In March 1945, as World War II was coming to a close, Bishop O'Hara was appointed Bishop of Buffalo, New York, where he served for six years.

Archbishop O'Hara arrived in Philadelphia on January 8, 1952. In February, on an early visit to Saint Charles Borromeo Seminary, he gave the seminarians cause for cheer. A heavy smoker himself, Archbishop O'Hara lifted Cardinal Dougherty's ban on tobacco in the seminary, and also allowed seminarians to drive automobiles and to take summer employment. In 1953 the archbishop, an avid swimmer, saw to the construction of a swimming pool on the seminary campus. Additionally, Archbishop O'Hara permitted the rector of the seminary to accept candidates for the priesthood from other dioceses.

**Guidance from the Sisters of Mercy made it possible for women inmates of Moyamensing Prison to celebrate a May Procession during the Marian Year, on May 8, 1954. This was the first time that such an event took place in the prison.**

**Cardinal John Francis O'Hara, C.S.C.
Fifth Archbishop of Philadelphia, 1951-1960**

**The installation of Bishop John F. O'Hara, C.S.C., as Archbishop of Philadelphia in 1952**

Scenes from a procession on the Benjamin Franklin Parkway led
by Archbishop O'Hara, to celebrate the Marian Year in 1954

Casa del Carmen, Seventh and Jefferson Streets, Philadelphia, opened in 1954, and provided a full range of social and educational services to the Hispanic community in North Philadelphia.

In 1952, during a visit to Barcelona with Cardinal Spellman to attend the Thirty-fifth International Eucharistic Congress, Archbishop O'Hara made a side trip to Fatima to dedicate the Archdiocese of Philadelphia to the Immaculate Heart of Mary. The archbishop was known for his lifelong devotion to Our Lady, which he expressed in the motto he chose for his episcopal coat of arms: *Ipsam sequens non devias*—"Following her [Mary] you shall not go astray."

Pope Pius XII declared a special Marian Year in 1954 to commemorate the 100th anniversary of the solemn definition of the dogma of the Immaculate Conception of the Blessed Virgin Mary. The ten parishes that Archbishop O'Hara founded during the Marian Year were all named in honor of the

Activities at Casa del Carmen included after-school child care and parent education programs, catechesis and training for neighborhood evangelization and outreach, and social gatherings like the Puerto Rican festival.

Blessed Mother, under various titles and mysteries of her life. At the same time, a newly-constructed and larger chapel was opened adjacent to the Cathedral, and dedicated under the title of "Our Lady of the Blessed Sacrament."

## Addressing Immigration and Racism

As development of new communities continued in the 1950s, most new parishes were founded in counties other than Philadelphia. Only five of the thirty-two parishes founded by Archbishop O'Hara were in the City of Philadelphia, and this number included no new national parishes. Philadelphia continued to welcome large numbers of immigrants, particularly Spanish-speaking Catholics from Central and South America and the Caribbean—especially from Puerto Rico. Many of these Hispanic immigrants settled in the Spring Garden neighborhood of Philadelphia. In later years they moved to North Philadelphia, and the territorial parishes in that neighborhood made efforts to provide religious and social services in Spanish. An Office for Hispanic Catholics—one of the first of its kind in the northeastern United States—opened in 1954, under the direction of Auxiliary Bishop Joseph McShea. The same year saw the foundation of Casa del Carmen, an outreach center at Seventh and Jefferson Streets, to attend to the needs of immigrants in the neighborhood.

Archbishop O'Hara's own view of America as a melting pot is revealed in a 1953 letter to a member of the Bucks County Human Relations Council:

*If we fulfill our duty to immigrants, we welcome them as brothers. If they cannot speak our language we provide them with a church of their own and a priest who speaks their language. But we encourage them to learn English, adapt to American ways and become good citizens… Those of us who have been around long enough to have observed the assimilation of immigrants from European nations whose traditional hostility have kept their people from natural understanding and satisfaction have seen that intermarriage of children in the second and third generation has wiped out age-old animosities to a surprising degree.*

Archbishop O'Hara was committed to promoting unity in the Church and society, and worked for full integration of African Americans into the life of the archdiocese. The 1950s saw the migration of large numbers of African Americans from Southern states to the Northeast, and in March 1953, Archbishop O'Hara exhorted his priests to welcome newly-arrived African Americans to their parishes. "If in the Providence of God the present migration from the South gives us the opportunity to bring the truths of our religion, and the graces of our sacramental life, to these good people who have never before had contact with Catholics, we must not be wanting in any particular," he wrote. He instructed that the designation "Colored" was no longer to be used to refer to the parishes of Saint Ignatius, Saint Peter Claver, Saint Catherine of Siena, and Our Lady of the Blessed Sacrament. These parishes traditionally served the African American community.

The Philadelphia Catholic Interracial Council sponsored a Communion breakfast in November 1956 and a training day for teachers in March 1957, both at Saint Elizabeth Parish, Philadelphia.

## Education Expansion

By 1952, more than 135,000 children were attending parish elementary schools in the archdiocese, and another 28,000 students were enrolled in archdiocesan high schools. Because the high schools were severely overcrowded, the archbishop began an ambitious high school building and expansion program. Eleven high schools were built, including eight in suburban areas, at a total cost of $28 million. Cardinal Dougherty High School opened in 1956 with 2,883 students, and quickly built up to its capacity of 6,000, thus replacing Northeast Catholic High School as the largest enrollment in the archdiocese. Mercy Technical School was founded by the Sisters of Mercy in 1950 at Broad Street and Columbia Avenue. Now located on West Hunting Park Avenue and known as Mercy Vocational High School, it is the only four-year coeducational Catholic vocational high school in the United States.

Meanwhile, Catholic colleges continued to grow, and new institutions were springing up. Gwynedd Mercy College, conducted by the Sisters of Mercy, was founded in 1948; Holy Family College, by the Sisters of the Holy Family of Nazareth, in 1954; and Cabrini College, by the Missionary Sisters of the Sacred Heart, in 1957. Originally all three colleges were exclusively for women.

## Death of Mother Katharine

Mother Mary Katharine Drexel had suffered a heart attack in 1935, and after 34 years of service retired as Superior General of the Sisters of the Blessed Sacrament. She continued to spend her days in quiet prayer at the motherhouse until her death on March 3, 1955, when she was 96 years of age. Sisters from missions around the country returned to the motherhouse for her funeral. Mother Katharine's body lay in state in the motherhouse chapel for two days, as people young and old, of all races, came to pay their respects and, often, to touch religious articles to her body.

On March 8, Archbishop O'Hara celebrated Mother Katharine's funeral in the Cathedral. Seven other bishops and hundreds of priests and religious were present, and thousands of the faithful filled the Cathedral and overflowed into the street. After her funeral Mass, Mother Katharine's body was taken in procession back to the motherhouse, and was entombed in a small chapel which had been built in 1949.

The next day saw a new beginning in the flowering of Mother Katharine's work. Several years earlier, the Sisters had reversed their long-standing policy of not accepting vocations from among the communities they served. In 1952, Rose Haynes had entered the Sisters of the Blessed Sacrament, and on March 9, 1955, she became the first African American woman to profess vows in Mother Katharine's congregation.

The trust fund that Mother Katharine had inherited from her father, which for decades had provided a steady income for her community and funded schools and institutions across the United States, ended at her death. Her father's fortune was now divided among dozens of charities as specified in his Will. Mother Katharine's congregation, the founding of which Francis

*In October 1956, the Society for the Propagation of the Faith sponsored Vistarama, the largest American exhibition to date of Catholic missionary activity.*

*More than 330 religious communities and Catholic lay organizations took part, setting up displays to inform visitors of their work in the mission of evangelization.*

*Vistarama drew national and international attention. The Apostolic Delegate, Archbishop Cicognani, the Secretary of the Congregation for the Propagation of the Faith, Archbishop Sigismondi, Cardinal Tien, the Archbishop of Beijing, and Bishop Fulton J. Sheen all visited the exhibit.*

Drexel had not lived to see, now received no support from the trust. Archbishop O'Hara, sensing an unintended injustice, prevailed upon some of the charities and institutions to share their legacies with the Sisters of the Blessed Sacrament.

## Care for Children and Families

Archbishop O'Hara established a Committee for Christian Home and Family, directed by Monsignor Thomas McNally, to assist parents in fostering the spiritual development of their children. Volunteers would give the parents a card with a personal message from the archbishop, and follow up with periodic home visits. Often these volunteers gave the child a religious medal, and provided catechetical pamphlets and spiritual encouragement to the family. At times, volunteers would extend their efforts to more corporal works: for example, assisting harried mothers by taking children to dental appointments. Holy Child Sunday was set aside as a time for receiving Holy Communion as a family, and each May the archbishop and his auxiliaries visited specific large churches for joyful ceremonies to bless infants and children.

In December 1956, Archbishop O'Hara hosted a Christmas Party at the Benjamin Franklin Hotel for children from institutions and for children with disabilities. This widely-publicized event, a fundraiser to highlight the needs of this vital ministry, was such a success that it became an annual tradition. It has become an important source of funds for the Children's Services Division of Catholic Social Services.

Another lasting innovation was the establishment of the Catholic Charities Appeal in 1958. A single major appeal for donations for the archdiocese's 53 charitable institutions replaced a number of smaller collections. A set goal would be announced, with particular projects as an annual focus. After a huge rally at Philadelphia's Convention Hall, lay volunteers went door-to-door on Sunday, May 4, to ask for pledges. The final result, more than $2 million, was $400,000 over the goal.

## Going Home

Pope Pius XII died on October 9, 1958, and was succeeded by Pope John XXIII. One of the first acts of the new pope was to create 23 new cardinals, including Archbishop O'Hara, who was given the titular church of Saints Andrew and Gregory on the Celian Hill. This church, on the site of a monastery built by Pope Gregory the Great, is a short walk from the church of Saints Nereus and Achilleus, which had been Cardinal Dougherty's titular church. The consistory was held on December 18, 1958, and although Cardinal O'Hara was ill during most of his trip to Rome, he was well enough to attend.

On June 9, 1960, Cardinal Giovanni Battista Montini, Archbishop of Milan and the future Pope Paul VI, traveled to Philadelphia. After visiting Bishop Neumann High School, Rosemont College, the Cathedral and Saint Charles Seminary, he stopped to see Cardinal O'Hara in Misericordia Hospital. He may have heard the cardinal's secretary, Monsignor Joseph McGlinn, remark that "the poor fellow had [every disease] in the books," for the 72-year-old cardinal was very seriously ill. A few weeks later, Cardinal O'Hara remarked to his sister, "I want to go home and rest." She assured him that the doctors would probably allow him to return to his residence soon; however, he corrected her. "No," he said, "I want to go to heaven."

Cardinal O'Hara died on August 28, 1960. Cardinal Francis Spellman, the Archbishop of New York, with whom Cardinal O'Hara had served in the Military Ordinariate, celebrated the funeral Mass at the Cathedral. However, Cardinal O'Hara was not buried in the Cathedral crypt. Instead, his body was taken to the campus of the University of Notre Dame, and entombed in a chapel in the Basilica of the Sacred Heart of Jesus.

Fifteen years of economic hardship and the grim realities of war had given way in the United States to more than a decade of post-war prosperity and growth. The archdiocese that Cardinal O'Hara left at his death was on a solid footing spiritually and materially, and was breaking new ground throughout the region to serve growing suburban neighborhoods, now being rapidly populated by the parents of the "Baby Boom" generation. At the same time, archdiocesan leaders were adapting to meet the new realities of life in the inner city, and to welcome and care for diverse groups of people who were all too often marginalized by the larger society. New educational and charitable institutions were organized, and parishioners were taking more active roles in both civic and spiritual affairs.

Most important, however, was the quiet, persevering faith that lay at the heart of Catholic families and homes, and which formed the living center of Catholic neighborhoods. This steady piety had been the solid foundation of the way that the "greatest generation" lived the Catholic faith in the first half of the twentieth century. This same faith would become the rock on which they and their children would weather the cultural storms that were about to challenge the Church in the modern world.

# Renewing the Faith

## (1960–2008)

When Pope John XXIII convoked the Second Vatican Ecumenical Council on January 25, 1959, the announcement came as a surprise to many within and outside the Catholic Church. Many people speculated about how the Council would respond to the needs of the faithful in a world changing at a seemingly impossible pace. Few, perhaps, could foresee just how rapidly and how radically society was about to change.

This would not be the first time that the Church in Philadelphia had to defend the faith against misunderstanding and criticism. But the questions and demands that the modern world were bringing to bear on so many aspects of the Church's life—moral teachings, pastoral service, and even material resources—would not be answered by defensiveness or isolation. The new situation in which the faithful and their leaders were about to find themselves called for a new commitment to preserving and renewing the heritage of faith that lay at the heart of this local Church.

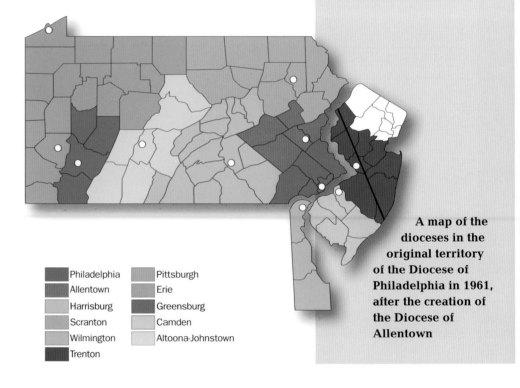

| | |
|---|---|
| ■ Philadelphia | ■ Pittsburgh |
| ■ Allentown | ■ Erie |
| ■ Harrisburg | ■ Greensburg |
| ■ Scranton | ■ Camden |
| ■ Wilmington | ■ Altoona-Johnstown |
| ■ Trenton | |

**A map of the dioceses in the original territory of the Diocese of Philadelphia in 1961, after the creation of the Diocese of Allentown**

## Archbishop Krol

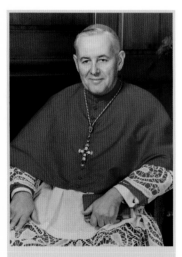

**Bishop Joseph M. McShea First Bishop of Allentown, 1961–1983**

Upon the death of Cardinal O'Hara, Auxiliary Bishop Joseph McShea was chosen to be the Administrator of the Archdiocese of Philadelphia. On January 28, 1961, Pope John XXIII created the new Diocese of Allentown, comprising the five northern counties of the Archdiocese of Philadelphia, and appointed Bishop McShea as founding Bishop of Allentown. Two weeks later, on February 11, the Holy Father named an auxiliary bishop of the Diocese of Cleveland, Bishop John Krol, as Archbishop of Philadelphia.

John Joseph Krol was born in Cleveland, Ohio, on October 26, 1910. The economic needs of his large family—he was the fourth of eight children—meant that he spent much of his youth as a laborer in various trades, and by the age of eighteen he had become the manager of the meat department of a large grocery store. He resigned this job to attend Saint Mary's College in Orchard Lake, Michigan, and then Saint Mary's Seminary in Cleveland. He was ordained for the Diocese of Cleveland in 1937 and served as assistant pastor at Immaculate Heart Church in Cleveland.

In 1938, Father Krol was sent to Rome to study canon law. He earned his licentiate there, but the outbreak of World War II forced him to continue his studies at the Catholic University of America where he received a doctorate in 1942. He taught canon law at Saint Mary's Seminary for two years, and was then appointed to various posts in the office of the diocesan tribunal. In April 1951 he became the chancellor of the diocese, and on September 2, 1953, he was ordained as an auxiliary bishop. The following year Bishop Krol was appointed Vicar General of the Diocese of Cleveland, and served in that position until becoming Archbishop of Philadelphia in 1961.

Accompanied by Archbishop Edward Hoban of Cleveland, Auxiliary Bishop Floyd Begin and a large group of Cleveland clergy, Archbishop Krol arrived at the Pennsylvania Railroad's 30th Street Station on the morning of March 21, 1961. He was met by Bishop McShea and the two auxiliary bishops, Bishop Cletus Benjamin and Bishop Francis Furey, and went with them to present his letters of appointment to the College of Consultors. The next morning, he was formally installed as Archbishop of Philadelphia by the Apostolic Delegate, Archbishop Egidio Vagnozzi. At his installation, Archbishop Krol declared, "I come to minister and to serve wholeheartedly and unreservedly."

**A view of the bishops gathered in Saint Peter's Basilica for the Second Vatican Council, 1962–65**

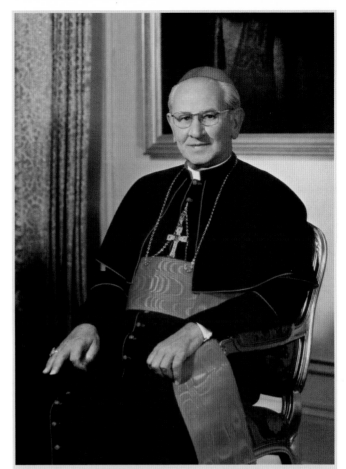

**Cardinal John Joseph Krol**
**Sixth Archbishop of Philadelphia, 1961-1988**

## Preparing for the Second Vatican Council

Archbishop Krol faced busy days before the scheduled opening of the Council in October 1962. He blessed the new Saint Dorothy Church, Drexel Hill, on May 6, 1961, and ordained his first priests for the archdiocese on May 13. He established several archdiocesan commissions with responsibilities for the sacred liturgy, parish sites and boundaries, and cemeteries. To stimulate vocations, the archbishop invited Serra International to hold their twentieth annual convention in Philadelphia in June 1962. Here he addressed the 2,500 delegates who had assembled from the United States and from around the world.

While Bishop Krol was an auxiliary bishop in Cleveland, he had taken an active role in preparatory work for the Second Vatican Council. Now, as the opening of the Council approached, Archbishop Krol called on the faithful to pray for its success. He celebrated Mass at the Cathedral on September 30, 1962, to begin a special period of preparation. He and Bishop Gerald McDevitt—who had been ordained as auxiliary bishop in Philadelphia on August 1, 1962—left for the Council on October 9. Pope John XXIII appointed Archbishop Krol as one of the five under-secretaries of the Council, and he was later appointed to serve on the Central Coordinating Committee. Bishop Furey served on the Administrative

Tribunal of the Council and the U.S. Bishops' Study Committee, while Bishop McDevitt became a member of the Study Committee on the Liturgy and the Conciliar Commission for Religious.

Each time Archbishop Krol returned from Rome, he held a press conference, including a special session with young people of the archdiocese. When he returned from the Council's second session in 1963, he told 150 editors of high school and college journals what he had seen of the Council's "great progress and historic accomplishment."

Father Thomas Falls, pastor of Sacred Heart Parish in Manoa, was invited to the Council as one of five American parish priests to attend sessions dealing with parish priests and the care of souls. He spoke in Latin in favor of the document on the Ministry and Life of Priests, and concluded by saying, "After this ecumenical council has ended, it will be the task of the Bishops to implement its decrees and constitutions. In carrying out this work, all of us, pastors and other priests, will have to be of great help to our Bishops, by making clear to the people the true meaning of the Council's promises."

## Archdiocesan Celebrations

Bishop John Nepomucene Neumann was beatified on Sunday, October 13, 1963, during the second session of the Council. Pope Paul VI invited Archbishop Krol to celebrate the Mass of Beatification at the Altar of the Chair in Saint Peter's Basilica. Twenty thousand people were present, including Eva Benassi, a young woman from Sassuolo, Italy, and J. Kent Lenahan, Jr. of Villanova. Both had been miraculously cured through Bishop Neumann's intercession. The Holy Father captured the feeling of the day when he said, "This is a day of rejoicing for the great Archdiocese of Philadelphia."

**Archbishop Krol (standing in front of altar at right) celebrates Mass for the Beatification of Blessed John Neumann, October 13, 1963, in the presence of Pope Paul VI (kneeling at left).**

Four years later, Pope Paul VI named Archbishop Krol a cardinal. The consistory, on June 26, 1967, was televised live in Philadelphia on Channel 6, WFIL (since 1971, WPVI). It was the first live transatlantic broadcast to use new communications satellite technology. Cardinal Krol was given the titular church of Our Lady of Mercy and Saint Hadrian, the mother church of the Order of Our Lady of Mercy (Mercedarians), some of whose members accompanied Christopher Columbus to the New World.

Another priest of the archdiocese was also named a cardinal in the same consistory. Monsignor Francis Brennan, of Shenandoah, Schuylkill County, was professor of moral theology at Saint Charles Borromeo Seminary from 1928 to 1940. He was appointed an official of the Sacred Roman Rota—the ecclesiastical court of appeals of the Apostolic See—in 1940, the first American to serve on the Rota. He was appointed Dean of the Rota in 1959, and Prefect of the Sacred Congregation of the Discipline of the Sacraments in 1967. He died in 1968.

## Response to Difficult Times

While the Council's work proceeded in Rome, the Catholic Church in the United States experienced difficult times. Our nation mourned the death of President John F. Kennedy in 1963, and would soon be shocked by the assassinations of Robert F. Kennedy and Martin Luther King, Jr. Both were outspoken advocates for Civil Rights and ending racial discrimination. The 1960s saw turmoil and tension, including race riots in Philadelphia and other major American cities—Detroit, Los Angeles, Washington, D.C., and Newark, New Jersey. The archdiocese was challenged to respond to this crisis and give witness to the importance of human and civil rights.

In 1964, the archbishop established the Commission on Human Relations, under the direction of Auxiliary Bishop John Graham. The purpose of the Commission was to provide positive and constructive programs, and to formulate particular proposals and guidelines to promote racial harmony and ecumenical understanding. The Commission would also serve as a Catholic liaison for interfaith and ecumenical activities.

At Mass in the Cathedral on May 14, 1964, Archbishop Krol emphasized "the crusade of prayer, which is the dynamic source of all that we hope to accomplish toward religious unity and the elimination of prejudice." That evening in the Cathedral, religious leaders of the many churches and faiths in the Philadelphia metropolitan area committed themselves to an unprecedented crusade for racial harmony. This prayer service was the first time in local history that Catholic, Protestant and Jewish leaders united in a joint pronouncement on a major social issue, condemning as "immoral anyone who refuses to associate with other persons solely because of race."

The Commission was one of the first agencies to join the "Philadelphia Plan," lending moral influence and the purchasing power of the archdiocese to promote fair employment practices. The Commission also established the Interparochial Cooperating Committee of pastors, the nation's first diocesan commission designed to bring financial aid from more affluent parishes to needy inner-city and rural parishes. On one occasion, the Archbishop invited the members of the Commission to his home, remarking "Your task is not to make headlines but to make history."

Although the military action in Korea ended with a cease-fire in 1953, the 1960s and early 1970s saw the beginning and escalation of war in Vietnam. As the conflict intensified, protests for peace and against the draft were common in every large American city, including Philadelphia. Catholics who objected to military service on moral grounds were typically denied "conscientious objector" status, since the policy of the armed forces for most of the century had been to extend this status only to members of the historic "peace churches"—Mennonites, Church of the Brethren, and Society of Friends (Quakers)—which rejected violence in all circumstances. Several Supreme Court decisions in the 1960s struck down this policy, but some Catholics had taken steps to avoid the draft by breaking the law.

Conscientious objection to taking part in armed combat, while serving society in some other way, was consistent with Church teaching—something that would be reiterated by Vatican II in its 1965 "Pastoral Constitution on the Church in the Modern World" (*Gaudium et Spes*), and by Pope Paul VI in his 1968 encyclical *Humanae Vitae*. Cardinal Krol often acknowledged this right to conscientious objection—which was supported by the United States Catholic Conference in 1969, and by the Pontifical Commission on Justice and Peace in 1971—and as President of the National Conference of Catholic Bishops from 1971 to 1974, he spoke in support of young men "who for reason of sincere conscientious belief

George Nakashima (1905–1990) moved to New Hope, Bucks County, in 1943, after being released from a internment camp in Idaho which housed Americans of Japanese descent during World War II. He became known for woodworking which combined traditional Japanese and American craft styles, and his work has been displayed at the Smithsonian Institution. He designed furnishings for a number of Philadelphia churches, including Immaculate Conception Chapel at Saint Charles Seminary, Saint Rose of Lima, Philadelphia, and his parish church, Saint Martin of Tours, New Hope. He is pictured here at Holy Family College, Philadelphia, in February 1985.

refused to participate in the war." He encouraged their fair treatment and sought pardon for those who broke the law. The cardinal often led public prayers for peace, and spoke in favor of disarmament at the 1971 Synod of Bishops in Rome.

At the same time, Cardinal Krol frequently wrote to the Philadelphia priests who were serving as military chaplains in Vietnam, and visited wounded soldiers at the Veterans' Administration Hospital in Valley Forge. He blessed aircraft carriers at the Philadelphia Navy Yard, and administered the sacrament of Confirmation at the Marine Corps Officers School in Quantico, Virginia. He also took a personal interest in the condition of the Catholic Church in Vietnam and the faithful living there in the midst of war. Cardinal Krol paid from his own funds for the building of the parish church of Saint John in Phu Tong Hóa in North Vietnam.

Bishop Fred Pierce Corson, President of the World Methodist Church and head of the Methodist Church in Philadelphia, was one of the first non-Catholic observers at the Second Vatican Council. He joined Archbishop Krol in 1963 and 1964 for a number of televised discussions of the work of the Council. Bishop Corson also participated in the interfaith gathering on the feast of the Sacred Heart in 1964 to promote racial harmony.

## Implementation of Vatican II

After more than three years of deliberation, the Second Vatican Council was formally concluded on December 8, 1965. Archbishop Krol remarked that the Council had "far surpassed even the fondest expectations of Pope John XXIII," who had died on June 3, 1963. It had stimulated social, moral, religious and theological changes which would affect Catholic life in the Archdiocese of Philadelphia and throughout the world. The Church in Philadelphia would expend much effort during the next decade to respond to the Council's mandate and implement its decrees.

The "Constitution on the Sacred Liturgy" (*Sacrosanctum Concilium*) of 1963 dramatically emphasized the importance of the liturgy as "the summit toward which the activity of the Church is directed" and "the font from which all her power flows." Archbishop Krol issued a pastoral letter outlining the liturgical norms set forth by Pope Paul VI in the apostolic letter *Sacram Liturgiam* (1964), and directed that they be immediately implemented in parishes.

The liturgical renewal that led to the Council's constitution on the liturgy included the restoration of the rites of Holy Week. Here, parishioners from Saint Charles Borromeo Church, Philadelphia, take part in the blessing of palms and procession at the beginning of Mass on Palm Sunday, March 30, 1958.

Cardinal Krol and auxiliary bishops with the members of the second ordination class of Permanent Deacons and some of the deacons' wives, November 7, 1982

The Archbishop celebrated the first solemn Mass in English in the Cathedral on the First Sunday of Advent, November 29, 1964. The Mass was televised locally, and also celebrated the 100th anniversary of the official opening of the Cathedral. At the same time, English was introduced into the liturgy. The Archdiocesan Liturgical Commission provided both detailed written instructions and seminars to explain the changes in liturgical rubrics.

In the Constitution on the Liturgy, the Council also called for the restoration of the catechumenate—the period of preparation for adult candidates for Baptism—and for a revision of the rites of Catholic initiation for adults. After the Council, the Congregation for Divine Worship prepared a new Rite of Christian Initiation of Adults (RCIA), outlining the various stages and ceremonies of the catechumenate. The RCIA was translated and adapted for use in the United States, and received official approval in 1988.

In the "Dogmatic Constitution on the Church" *(Lumen Gentium)* in 1964, the Council spoke of the ministry of permanent deacons—that is, men who would be ordained deacons but would not seek ordination to the priesthood. In 1967, Pope Paul VI issued an Apostolic Letter *(Sacrum Diaconatus Ordinem)* which officially restored the permanent diaconate.

In 1971 the bishops of the United States issued guidelines for the formation of candidates—who included married men—for ordination as deacons.

In 1977, the Permanent Diaconate Office began to prepare men for service as deacons in the Archdiocese of Philadelphia. The first candidates were drawn from Hispanic and African American neighborhoods, with the hope that the presence of deacons would further enrich the faith and apostolic zeal in these communities. Sixteen Hispanic men were ordained deacons in 1981, and seven African American deacons were ordained in 1982. Since 1986 the program has been open to candidates of any ethnic background.

In 1963 the "Decree on the Means of Social Communication" *(Inter Mirifica)* urged church leaders to make extensive use of the communications media to carry out the Church's mission of evangelization. As the archdiocesan newspaper, The Catholic Standard and Times, approached its 80th anniversary, Cardinal Krol augmented the archdiocesan communications effort by establishing the Delaware Valley Catholic Office for Radio and Television, a joint effort with the bishops of neighboring dioceses. Two radio studios were set up in the Archdiocesan

Office Center, broadcasting four times a week via Armed Forces Radio and producing Catholic radio programs like "As the Spirit Leads." The weekly television program "Real to Reel" aired on Channel 17 (WPHL) from 1981 to 1992, and was succeeded by "Catholic Magazine" from 1992 to 1994. Television viewers, especially the elderly and infirm, were also able to watch a broadcast of Mass early each Sunday on Channel 6 (WPVI).

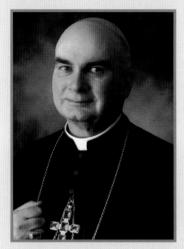

*In 1948, the Holy Father established an office in the Roman Curia to respond to the latest development in the media: motion pictures. Originally called the Pontifical Commission for Educational and Religious Films, and later the Pontifical Commission for Cinema, this office had a major role in preparing the Council's decree on the means of social communication. In April 1964, Pope Paul VI reorganized the commission into the Pontifical Commission for Social Communications, giving it the responsibility of implementing Inter Mirifica and of overseeing the Vatican Press Office.*

*Two decades later, a Philadelphia priest would be appointed to lead the commission. Monsignor John Foley—a professor of philosophy at Saint Charles Seminary and Editor-in-Chief of The Catholic Standard and Times—was appointed titular Archbishop of Neapolis in Proconsulari and President of the Pontifical Commission for Social Communications. His appointment was made on April 5, 1984, when Monsignor Foley was 48 years of age. He was ordained a bishop at the Cathedral on May 8 by Cardinal Krol, who had ordained Archbishop Foley a priest in May 1962.*

*In 2006, Archbishop Foley still holds the position of President of the Pontifical Council for Social Communications, and he is the longest-serving head of any of the dicasteries of the Roman Curia.*

In the "Declaration on Christian Education" *(Gravissimum Educationis)*, the Council declared that "all those who, having been reborn in water and the Holy Spirit, are called and in fact are children of God, have a right to a Christian education." To implement this declaration, and continue a long tradition in the archdiocese, Cardinal Krol announced a new expansion program in 1967—at a cost of more than $20 million—which was designed to increase high school capacity by 16,000 students. In addition, he reorganized the archdiocesan Board of Education, with fifteen members, five of whom were lay people. One of its first recommendations was to establish a Home and School Association in each parish.

*John Connelly was born in North Philadelphia in 1905. In 1945 he founded Connelly Containers, and in 1956 became Chairman and CEO of Crown Cork and Seal, Inc. In 1955, he and his wife, Josephine C. Connelly, established the Connelly Foundation to provide grants for organizations in the Philadelphia region.*

*For more than fifty years the Connelly Foundation has supported the work of Catholic education in the Archdiocese of Philadelphia. Grants from the foundation include assistance for capital projects, technology, and curriculum enhancements in parish and archdiocesan schools. Each year the Foundation awards Neumann Scholarships—full tuition grants to archdiocesan high schools—to graduates of parish elementary schools who demonstrate academic excellence.*

Matthew H. McCloskey, Jr., established an endowment for the Catholic high schools—the Archdiocesan Educational Fund—with a personal donation of $500,000. Still, the financial situation in the high schools required them to begin charging tuition in the early 1970s. Parish elementary schools would soon do the same. In 1972, as costs increased and enrollment declined, the Advisory Committee on the Archdiocesan Schools released a 200-page report on the "Financial Crisis of Catholic Schools in Philadelphia and Surrounding Communities." The report estimated a deficit of $4 million that year, and $55.4 million by 1975.

Cardinal Krol asked for support from the faithful for the Catholic school system. "Given the materialism and moral confusion of our times," he wrote, "I urge you to share my deep conviction that the Catholic school remains the best instrument to assist parents in meeting their heavy responsibilities to their children. I urge our Catholic people to translate their convictions into active support… We can no longer take our Catholic schools for granted."

Declining enrollment and prohibitive costs of repairs led to the closing of Saint Thomas More High School, West Philadelphia, in 1975; as well as Notre Dame High School for Girls, Moylan, Delaware County, in 1981. Despite this and other difficult decisions, Cardinal Krol's commitment to Catholic education remained firm. "We stand as fully committed to private education as ever before," he said at the time, "and we remain staunchly committed to keeping the doors of our schools open, especially to the underprivileged. We will make every effort, every sacrifice possible to

Cardinal Krol with Daniel J. Keating, Jr. (center) and Matthew H. McCloskey, Jr., members of the seminary Board of Trustees, in 1986. In the 1970s Mr. McCloskey was instrumental in establishing the Archdiocesan Educational Fund, an endowment for the archdiocesan high school system.

continue Christian education at a time when it is needed more than ever in the history of our country."

In 1965 the "Decree on the Pastoral Office of Bishops in the Church" (*Christus Dominus*) highlighted the pastoral challenge of catechesis as an essential part of a bishop's role as teacher. With the approval of Pope Paul VI, the General Catechetical Directory was issued in 1971. The Directory advocated new teaching methods quite different from those used with preceding generations; however, some Catholics questioned its methodology and orthodoxy. A group established in Philadelphia in 1969, "Parents for Orthodoxy in Parochial Education" (POPE), claimed "to

---

*The Declaration on the Relation of the Church to Non-Christian Religions* (Nostra aetate, 1965) *condemned anti-Semitism and highlighted the "common spiritual heritage" that unites Jews and Christians. The declaration was followed in 1974 by* Guidelines on Religious Relations with the Jews, *which encouraged dialogue, shared prayer, and catechesis to strengthen relationships between Catholics and Jews.*

*In 1979, the archdiocese issued a teachers' guide for presenting Judaism in the Catholic school curriculum.* Abraham, Our Father In Faith *was designed to provide basic knowledge of the beliefs and practices of Judaism, and to help students to understand how the Jewish people view their religious experience. The guidelines (which were updated in 1990) were well received, and were distributed nationally by the Anti-Defamation League. The Bishops' Conference of Latin America (CELAM) translated the program into Spanish and distributed it in dioceses throughout Central and South America.*

---

safeguard and transmit to posterity ...true, orthodox Roman Catholicism," and argued against the orthodoxy of some religion textbooks being used in Catholic schools.

Cardinal Krol warned against "broad sweeping condemnations of teachers, programs methods and materials," and in 1975 directed the archdiocese to issue guidelines for parish catechetical programs. As the number of parish directors and coordinators of religious education increased, they formed an Association with the support of the Office for Catholic Education, to provide ongoing training and formation for parish catechists. Parish catechists were also assisted by the foundation in 1969 of the Religious Studies Division of Saint Charles Seminary, which grants undergraduate and graduate degrees in theology, as well as the "Roman Diploma"—a certificate in catechetics granted in conjunction with the Holy See's Congregation for Clergy.

Misunderstanding was not limited to parents of school-aged children in the years following the Council. On March 7, 1966, 30 students at Saint Charles Seminary walked out of one scripture class to protest teaching methods that the seminarians considered ineffective. In response, Archbishop Krol ordered a canonical visitation of the Seminary, from March 26 to 30, "to secure information that proves helpful in implementing the Conciliar Decree and Post-Conciliar Instructions on Priestly Training."

Students and faculty were invited to submit reports to the Canonical Visitors, and these reports were to remain confidential. One of these reports—a 51-page document written by a group of students and referred to as the "White Paper" —was leaked to The Philadelphia Bulletin and published without any mention that it had been prepared at the request of the Visitors. A week later, after Sunday Vespers, Archbishop Krol addressed the seminarians in Saint Martin's Chapel. He told them that the publication of the White Paper had caused resentment, disunity and scandal among the faithful. He called on them all to work together with him to implement the "authorized directives of renewal."

As a result of the canonical visitation, the reforms which were ultimately suggested and implemented helped Saint Charles Borromeo Seminary to avoid unorthodox teaching and mass departures of students and faculty that other seminaries in the United States experienced during the 1960s and 1970s. Under the leadership of the rector, Monsignor Thomas Welsh, the seminary received its first professional and academic accreditation from the American Association of Theological Schools in June 1970, and the Middle States Association of Colleges and Secondary Schools in December 1971. Monsignor Welsh was ordained an auxiliary bishop on April 2, 1970, and was later appointed Bishop of Arlington, Virginia (1974–1983), and Bishop of Allentown (1983–1997).

## Archdiocesan Outreach

In the 1960s Cardinal Krol directed an administrative reorganization of the departments which assist the archbishop in meeting needs of parishes and institutions in the archdiocese. One notable change was the restructuring of the Catholic Youth Organization (CYO), and the foundation, in November 1965, of the Community Service Corps (CSC). Designed in the spirit of President Kennedy's Peace Corps initiatives, by 1967 the CSC counted more than 2,000 student members, under the leadership of a Student Senate. The same year saw the beginning of the annual Christmas toy drive called "Operation Santa Claus."

Camp Neumann, in Jamison, Bucks County, opened in 1966 as a summer camp for children from inner-city neighborhoods, and also served as a conference and retreat center for youth groups. Camp Overbrook, established in 1968, brought children from the inner city to a day camp on the grounds of Saint Charles Seminary. "Operation Discovery" was designed to develop leadership skills and personal responsibility among inner-city youth. This program also provided leadership training for more than 1,000 participants. In 1971, these and other programs for young people were united under the Department of Youth Activities.

**Participants in "Operation Discovery"
in 1971 learn leadership skills by taking part in a student "senate".**

**Cardinal Krol with children from "Camp Overbrook",
at Saint Charles Seminary, 1971**

The 1970s also saw a dramatic expansion in social and human services. Administrative staff of Catholic Social Services had grown to more than 400 full-time religious and lay members, making it the largest multi-purpose social service agency in southeastern Pennsylvania. Programs were developed to provide care and support for those suffering from physical, emotional and social distress.

The Committee on Research and Development of Urban Ministry (CORDUM) was established in September 1971, to find ways to expand evangelization efforts in neighborhoods that had experienced social, economic and cultural distress. With the help of the Academy of Food Marketing of Saint Joseph's College, the Cardinal's Commission on Human Relations started a successful breakfast and lunch program for children in 25 inner-city parochial schools. This program was expanded to include not only 35 additional schools but also food programs for needy families and elderly persons. Eventually the program became a distinct archdiocesan agency, Nutritional Development Services.

Such programs relied heavily on the annual Catholic Charities Appeal, which also funded the expansion and renovation of Saint Joseph's Hall

Special programs for migrants and refugees, like this "Heritage Day" procession in 1979, are a reminder of the ethnic and cultural diversity that has long been characteristic of the Church in Philadelphia.

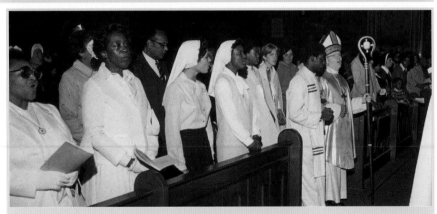

Auxiliary Bishop Francis Schulte (later Archbishop of New Orleans) celebrates a Mass for Vocations from the African American Community at Immaculate Conception Church, Philadelphia, in November 1981.

for Girls, Philadelphia, and Saint Gabriel's Hall for Adjudicated Delinquents, Audubon, Montgomery County. The appeal also made possible the building of a new school for Saint Francis Vocational School in Bensalem, Bucks County.

Senior members of the Catholic community were served by several facilities. Saint Ignatius Nursing Home, initiated by Monsignor John Mitchell and located in West Philadelphia, was replaced with a new facility. Several new nursing homes were opened in 1965, including Saint Mary Manor, Lansdale, and Saint John Neumann Nursing Home on Roosevelt Boulevard. Immaculate Mary Home, founded in 1976 on Holme Circle in Northeast Philadelphia, provided 300 nursing beds and was a special project of Cardinal Krol and Mr. and Mrs. John Connelly.

Developmentally challenged people had a special place in Cardinal Krol's affections. The cardinal invited communities of men and women religious —the Servants of Charity and the Daughters of Saint Mary of Providence— to exercise their special ministry of care for the developmentally disabled in the archdiocese. Both communities had been founded by an Italian priest, Blessed Luigi Guanella. Using funds generated by the Catholic Charities Appeal, two centers were constructed in Springfield, Delaware County. The Daughters of Saint Mary of Providence care for adolescent girls and young women at Divine Providence Village. The Servants of Charity work a short distance away at Don Guanella School, to serve young children, and the Cardinal Krol Center, to assist adult men.

## Advocacy in Defense of Human Life

On July 25, 1968, Pope Paul VI issued the encyclical *Humanae Vitae*, which explained the immorality of contraception and promoted Natural Family Planning as a morally upright method of regulating the conception and birth of children. In the face of sharp criticism of the pope's letter and the Church's teaching, Cardinal Krol repeatedly reaffirmed the teaching expressed in the encyclical. He asked that prayers and catechesis on the necessary respect for human life be a central part of Masses on "Human Life Sunday," September 29, 1970.

The Supreme Court of the United States issued its ruling on the case of *Roe v. Wade* in 1973, thus legalizing abortion on demand throughout the United States. This decision made the Church's efforts to protect the dignity of human life more urgent than ever. The Respect Life Office was founded to coordinate advocacy in defense of life throughout the archdiocese. This office works to ensure significant participation by the faithful and members of institutions from all five counties of the archdiocese in the annual March for Life, held each year in Washington, D.C., on January 22, the anniversary of the *Roe* decision.

Pro-Life demonstrators picket the Women's Medical Center, Bridgeport, Montgomery County, in March 1985.

The Cold War, which had been creating tension between the United States and the Soviet Union since the 1950s, led to an escalation of federal spending on nuclear weapons in the 1970s and 1980s. Cardinal Krol was outspoken in his opposition to this arms race, arguing that it "violates the rights of the world's poor in a way that is fruitless and intolerable." In 1979 he testified before the Senate Foreign Relations Committee, speaking against the notion of nuclear deterrence. To threaten nuclear war against a civilian population, he said, "runs directly counter to the central moral affirmation of the Christian teaching that innocent lives are not open to direct attack."

## Holy Year and Bicentennial

In preparation for the Holy Year, decreed by Pope Paul VI for 1975, Cardinal Krol organized a local year of prayer from mid-1973 to 1974, with numerous pilgrimages and projects coordinated by Father Walter Conway. The faithful gathered for a special Mass for Vocations at the Cathedral, and were addressed by Mother Teresa of Calcutta. In 1950, Mother Teresa had founded the Missionaries of Charity, a religious congregation of women dedicated to serving the poorest of the poor. She had received the first Pope John XXIII Peace Prize in 1971, and would be awarded the Nobel Peace Prize in 1979. Following the Mass, Mother Teresa and Cardinal Krol led 5,000 people to the steps of the Philadelphia

**Auxiliary Bishop Martin N. Lohmueller (front row, third from right) participates in an interfaith prayer service at Independence Hall, on the Bicentennial of American Independence, July 4, 1976.**

Museum of Art on an interfaith "Pilgrimage of Hope." Mother Teresa spoke to those gathered about finding hope for humanity in the world's poor.

During the Bicentennial year, the archdiocese hosted the Forty-first International Eucharistic Congress, from August 1 to 8, 1976. It was only the second time in history that such an event had been held in the United States. Two years of renewal and preparation were observed in the Archdiocese of Philadelphia—and in dioceses around the country—centered

**Mother Teresa of Calcutta spoke to the faithful gathered at the Cathedral for a Mass for Vocations in 1974. Later that day she told participants in an inter-faith Pilgrimage of Hope that the hope of the world is found in the poor.**

on a theme suggested by Archbishop Fulton Sheen: "The Eucharist and the Hungers of the Human Family." Once again, Father Conway took a leading role in the preparations for this important event. He was named a Prelate of Honor with the title of Monsignor in January 1976.

The Eucharistic Congress was officially opened at a Mass in the Cathedral on the first of August, attended by 31 cardinals and more than 160 bishops, as well as an international congregation of more than 2,000 worshippers, including the royal family of Monaco. After the Mass, Cardinal James Knox, the Archbishop of Sydney, Australia, and the official representative of the Holy Father, enthroned the Blessed Sacrament on the main altar, in the same monstrance used in the 1926 International Eucharistic Congress in Chicago.

That evening, 350,000 area Catholics and visitors joined in a solemn Eucharistic procession from Independence Hall to the Philadelphia Museum of Art. Here Benediction was celebrated by Cardinal Knox. Over the following week participants were addressed by many leaders in the Church's work of social ministry, including Mother Teresa of Calcutta; Dorothy Day, author and co-founder of the Catholic Worker Movement; Father Pedro Arrupe, S.J., the Superior General of the Society of Jesus; Dom Hélder Câmara, theologian and Archbishop of Olinda e Recife, Brazil; and the Archbishop of Krakow, Cardinal Karol Wojtyła. The magnificent

**Pilgrims from the archdiocese take part in the offertory procession at the Mass of Canonization for Saint John Neumann in Saint Peter's Square, June 19, 1977.**

Statio Orbis Mass closed the Congress a week later. President Gerald Ford addressed the 100,000 worshippers who, despite a driving rain, packed JFK Stadium. The faithful also viewed a videotaped message from Pope Paul VI.

Less than a year after the Eucharistic Congress, Cardinal Krol led 1,800 pilgrims, including Philadelphia Mayor Frank Rizzo, to Rome for the canonization of Saint John Neumann on June 19, 1977. The pilgrimage also included Michael Flanigan, a young West Philadelphia man who had been cured of cancer through Saint John's intercession in 1963, when Michael was six years old. In his homily, Pope Paul VI said, "The man we are honoring today was an immigrant who came not to find gold in the earth, but rather to spread throughout America, fabled for its riches, a gold which is more valuable—the gold of charity."

On the day of the canonization, Masses were celebrated in the Archdiocese of Philadelphia as well. Notable celebrations took place at the Glen Riddle motherhouse of the Sisters of Saint Francis of Philadelphia—which Saint John had founded in 1855—the Saint John Neumann Shrine in Saint Peter the Apostle Church, and the Cathedral. When the pilgrims returned from Rome on June 26, Cardinal Krol celebrated a Mass on the Parkway attended by 30,000 people.

## Papal Visit

Cardinal Karol Wojtyła, the Archbishop of Krakow, Poland, had visited Philadelphia during the Eucharistic Congress in 1976. Three years later he returned, with a new name: Pope John Paul II. He arrived on October 3, 1979, to spend two days in the city he called "a symbol of freedom and fraternal relations."

On that beautiful autumn afternoon, over a million people attended the papal Mass celebrated on Logan Square. That evening the Holy Father visited the students and faculty at Saint Charles Borromeo Seminary. The next morning the Pope visited the shrine of Saint John Neumann—where he spoke both in English and in Spanish—and the Cathedral of the Immaculate Conception of the Ukrainian Catholic Archdiocese of Philadelphia. Finally, he celebrated Mass at the Philadelphia Civic Center for clergy, seminarians and members of religious communities. By 12:30 on the afternoon of October 4, he was on his way to Des Moines, Iowa, to continue his first papal visit to the Church in the United States.

## KEYNOTE SPEAKERS AT THE EUCHARISTIC CONGRESS

*Mother Teresa of Calcutta founded the Missionaries of Charity in 1950 to care for the poorest of the poor.*

*She became famous for her work with lepers in Calcutta, and was awarded the Nobel Peace Prize in 1979. She was beatified by Pope John Paul II in 2003.*

*Dom Hélder Câmara was Bishop of Olinda e Recife in Brazil, and an outspoken advocate for the rights of the poor.*

*He took an active role in national and international bodies dedicated to working for human rights and the liberation of the poor from oppression.*

### THEMES OF THE 41st INTERNATIONAL EUCHARISTIC CONGRESS

*Philadelphia, August 1–8, 1976*

| | | |
|---|---|---|
| Sunday | Opening Day | "Hunger for God" |
| Monday | Family Day | "The Eucharist and the Hunger for Bread" |
| Tuesday | Suffering People Day | "Hunger for Freedom and Justice" |
| Wednesday | Clergy and Religious Day | "Hunger for the Spirit" |
| Thursday | Pilgrim People Day | "Hunger for Truth" |
| Friday | Youth Day | "Hunger for Understanding" |
| Saturday | Peoples of the World Day | "Hunger for Peace" |
| Sunday | Day of Thanksgiving | "Hunger for Jesus, the Bread of Life" |

*Father Pedro Arrupe, S.J. was Father General of the Society of Jesus from 1965 to 1983. After his election he called on the Jesuits to take action for social justice, especially in Latin America.*

*He died in Rome in 1991.*

*Dorothy Day was a journalist and author, who in 1933 cofounded (with Peter Maurin) the Catholic Worker Movement.*

*She used articles in The Catholic Worker as well as social activism to spread a message of peace and justice. She died in New York in 1980, and her cause for canonization was opened in 2000.*

During his visit to Philadelphia in October 1979, Pope John Paul II celebrated Mass on Logan Circle and in the Philadelphia Civic Center.

He also visited the Cathedral of the Immaculate Conception, of the Byzantine-Ukrainian Archdiocese of Philadelphia, and Saint Martin's Chapel at Saint Charles Borromeo Seminary.

## Retirement of Cardinal Krol

The revised Code of Canon Law, which came into effect in 1983, requires that bishops submit a letter of resignation to the Holy Father when they reach their 75th birthday. Cardinal Krol retired on February 11, 1988, after exactly 27 years as archbishop, and became the first Archbishop Emeritus of Philadelphia. He continued to serve the Church in retirement by celebrating Confirmation in several parishes each year, and by organizing the Papal Foundation to raise an endowment to ease the financial burden of the Holy See. After several struggles with illness, Cardinal Krol died in the early morning of March 3, 1996, the feast of Blessed Katharine Drexel. His body was entombed in the Cathedral crypt behind a marble panel of his own design. In contrast to the ornate Latin inscriptions of some of his predecessors, his tomb is marked, in English, simply with his name, and dates of his birth, ordinations and death.

## Arrival of Archbishop Bevilacqua

Anthony Joseph Bevilacqua was born in Brooklyn, New York, on June 17, 1923, one of eleven children of Italian immigrants. He studied for the priesthood at Cathedral College in Brooklyn and Immaculate Conception Seminary in Huntingdon, New York, and was ordained a priest on June 11, 1949. Father Bevilacqua obtained a doctorate in canon law at the Gregorian University in Rome in 1956, and a doctorate in civil law from Saint John's University in Queens in 1975. He was ordained an auxiliary bishop in Brooklyn on November 24, 1980, and appointed Bishop of Pittsburgh in 1983. In December 1987, Bishop Bevilacqua was appointed to succeed Cardinal Krol as Archbishop of Philadelphia. When he arrived in Philadelphia for his installation on February 11, 1988, the new archbishop said that he wanted to be a "face of Christ" to all, particularly "the disadvantaged, the young, all those who have a special

**Cardinal Bevilacqua and Cardinal Krol at a reception at the North American College, Rome, in July 1991**

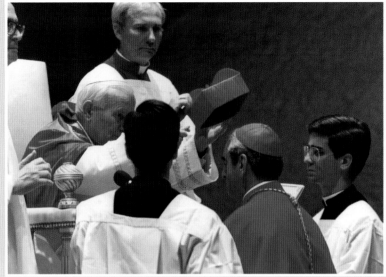

**Pope John Paul II places a red biretta—a symbol of the office of Cardinal—on the head of Cardinal Bevilacqua at the consistory on June 28, 1991.**

need for our support, the homeless, the new-comers, the poor."

Archbishop Bevilacqua soon began a reorganization of the administrative offices of the archdiocese, appointing Monsignor Edward Cullen as Vicar for Administration in 1988, and designating five Secretaries in 1989 to oversee various categories of archdiocesan activities. That April, he appointed six Regional Vicars, each with responsibility to assist the archbishop in caring for the priests and people of a particular geographic region of the arch-diocese.

In 1991, Pope John Paul II named Archbishop Bevilacqua a cardinal. In the consistory on June 28, he received the titular church of the Holy Redeemer and Saint Alphonsus, the mother church of the Congregation of the Most Holy Redeemer—the Redemptorists—in Rome. The choice of his titular church, the new cardinal said, "brings to mind the life and example of the great Saint John Neumann, the first Redemptorist to be professed in America." In the early years of his tenure, Cardinal

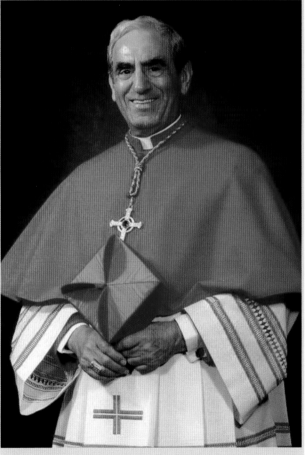

**Cardinal Anthony Joseph Bevilacqua**
**Seventh Archbishop of Philadelphia,**
**1988–2003**

Bevilacqua was assisted by two auxiliary bishops—Bishop Martin Lohmueller, who had been ordained bishop in 1970, and Bishop Louis DeSimone, ordained bishop in 1981. In the following years, Pope John Paul II appointed three more auxiliary bishops for the Archdiocese of Philadelphia. Bishop Edward Cullen, the Vicar for Administration, was ordained an auxiliary bishop in April 1994, and would be appointed as Bishop of Allentown in 1998. Only a few days after the funeral of Cardinal Krol, on March 11, 1996, Bishop Robert Maginnis and Bishop Joseph Martino were ordained auxiliary bishops. Bishop Martino would be appointed the Bishop of Scranton in 2003.

## Catholic Faith and Life 2000

Cardinal Bevilacqua inaugurated a plan for spiritual and pastoral renewal in preparation for the Great Jubilee of the Year 2000, the beginning of the Third Millennium of Christianity. On Holy Thursday in 1991, he announced a "new spring," and invited the faithful to take part in "Catholic Faith and Life 2000." The process of renewal, he said, would enliven faith, engage people in the mission of evangelization, and revitalize parish and family life. The program officially opened with a Holy Hour at the Seminary on December 1, 1991, attended by approximately 600 priests and televised on Channel 57 (WGBS).

A "Year of Listening" included the formation of Parish Pastoral Councils, to foster full participation in the mission of the parish and universal Church. These councils developed pastoral plans for the parish, and later worked with neighboring parishes to develop pastoral plans for each "cluster" or regional group.

Major liturgical events marked important stages in the renewal. Cardinal Bevilacqua and the auxiliary bishops celebrated the Sacrament of Confirmation for 6,500 people at Villanova University on Pentecost Sunday in 1998. "Reconciliation Weekend" during Lent 1999 encouraged Catholics to come to the Sacrament of Reconciliation in preparation for the Jubilee. During the Holy Year itself, each parish exposed the Blessed Sacrament for adoration at least one day a week. In April, five thousand people attended a three-day Eucharistic Convocation at the Liacouras Center at Temple University. They were addressed by Francis Cardinal Arinze, President of the Pontifical Council for Inter-Religious Dialogue, and the Papal Nuncio to the United States, Archbishop Gabriel Montalvo. On October 22, 2000, tens of thousands of the faithful from throughout the archdiocese gathered for a solemn Eucharistic

Auxiliary Bishop Joseph Martino administers the Sacrament of Confirmation to 14-year-old Thao Nguyen, on Pentecost 1998 at Villanova University.

Procession on the Benjamin Franklin Parkway. A solemn Mass at the Cathedral on January 1, 2001, concluded the Holy Year celebrations.

Part of the plan for renewal was a major capital campaign. Named "Catholic Life 2000," the campaign sought to raise $100 million over three years, to create an endowment that would generate funds for archdiocesan high schools, improvements and repairs at the Seminary and in needy parishes, necessary renovations for the archdiocesan archives, and a spirituality center for youth. Much of the fundraising was done at the parish level by priests and parishioners. A percentage of the funds raised in each parish remained under the control of the pastor, to be used to make repairs and improvements to parish churches and schools.

## Social Advocacy

For much of the 1990s Cardinal Bevilacqua chaired the National Conference of Catholic Bishops' Committee for Pro-Life Activities. In that capacity he was an ardent advocate at the local and national levels for the need to respect the dignity of human life. He often led the archdiocesan contingent at the annual March for Life, and addressed issues as varied as the death penalty, HIV-AIDS, persons with disabilities, migrants and refugees, benefits to same-sex partners, homosexuality, embryonic stem cell research, healthcare, violence and co-habitation.

The Archdiocesan Catholic Institute for Evangelization was created in November 1993, to provide a program of religious education and continuing formation for Spanish-speaking lay adults. In 1999, the Archdiocese took responsibility for pastoral care in the parish of Nuestra Señora del Carmen (Our Lady of Mt Carmel) in Barceloneta, Arecibo, Puerto Rico. A goal of this ministry was to train priests and seminarians for ministry among Spanish-speaking Catholics.

Cardinal Bevilacqua blesses the Holy Door at the Cathedral to open the Holy Year of the Great Jubilee 2000, on Christmas Eve 1999.

Casa Del Carmen, which relocated to Reese Street in North Philadelphia, continues to serve as a center for social services and outreach to the Hispanic community. La Misión Santa Maria, Madre de Dios, was founded in 1992 in Avondale, Chester County. A priest chaplain at the Mission, assisted by the Sisters, Servants of the Lord and the Virgin of Matara, attends to the spiritual needs of the Spanish-speaking community in Chester County.

Thousands of parishioners from the Archdiocese of Philadelphia—including hundreds of school-age children—attend the 1998 March for Life in Washington, D.C.

The Philadelphia chapter of "Helpers of God's Precious Infants" (pictured here in 1999) holds prayers vigils twice each month. Participants gather for Mass and then proceed to a local abortion facility to pray quietly and demonstrate peacefully.

The archdiocese sponsored a Spanish-language radio broadcast, "Un Poco Más", during the 1980s. A new radio program, "La Voz de Dios en Las Voces de Nuestros Pueblos," ("The Voice of God in the Voices of Our People") was begun in the late 1990s to extend evangelization and catechetical efforts for Hispanic Catholics.

In January 1998, Cardinal Bevilacqua wrote a pastoral letter, "Healing Racism through Faith and Truth," to address the evils of racism. "It must be clearly stated that racism is a sin, an evil that can never be justified," he said, calling on "the faithful to end the evil of racism in their own lives through prayer, forgiveness and reconciliation." The letter was distributed to all parishes, schools and institutions. Saint Peter Claver Evangelization Center, founded in 1995, provides support and formation for the work of evangelization, liturgical inculturation and outreach in the African-American community.

The staff of the Spanish-language Catholic radio program "Un Poco Más" in 1987: (from left) Vicky Morales, Apolonio Collazo and Jávier Suarez

## Parish and School Closings

Population shifts necessitated the closing of several inner-city parishes in 1992 and 1993. Six parishes in the City of Chester were suppressed, and one new parish—Blessed Katharine Drexel—was founded, at the site of the former Saint Robert's church and school. Eight parishes in North Philadelphia were also closed. Boundaries of neighboring parishes were redrawn to incorporate parishioners from those that were closed, and two new parishes were established: Our Lady of Hope, at the site of the former Holy Child Church, Broad and Duncannon Streets; and Saint Martin de Porres, at the former Saint Columba Church, 24th Street and Lehigh Avenue.

In 1993, declining enrollment and rising costs caused the closing of Saint James Catholic High School for Boys in Chester. At the same time, Bishop Conwell and Bishop Egan High Schools, in Bucks County, merged to form Conwell–Egan Catholic High School. Archbishop Kennedy and Bishop Kenrick High Schools—in Conshohocken and Norristown, Montgomery County—were consolidated as Kennedy–Kenrick Catholic High School. Although Cardinal Bevilacqua made efforts to consult with community, parish and alumni groups before making these difficult decisions, they were obviously painful for many people. In certain areas parishioners responded with written and vocal protests, picket lines and lawsuits to block closures and consolidations.

A choir member at Our Lady of Hope, the new parish founded at the site of the former Holy Child Church at Broad and Duncannon Streets, at a parish celebration in March 1994

In the 1990s, continued concern for children with special needs led to the creation of "a school within a school" at Cardinal Dougherty High School in Philadelphia. The older students of Our Lady of Confidence Day School attended Cardinal Dougherty High School. There they followed their own academic program; however, they shared activities, assemblies, lunch periods and liturgies with the larger school community. Every Thursday, students from both schools— "best buddies"—spent an hour together doing normal teenage things in an age-appropriate setting. Success in this pilot program led to a similar program at Archbishop Carroll High School for students from Saint Katherine Day School.

## Canonization of Mother Katharine

On November 20, 1988, Pope John Paul II beatified Mother Katharine Drexel, calling her a woman of lively faith "who stood courageously for the rights of the oppressed." The Holy Father canonized Mother Katharine on October 1, 2000, making her only the second native-born citizen of the United States to be so honored. Present for the canonization were more than 1,300 pilgrims led by Cardinal Bevilacqua, and including 120 Sisters of the Blessed Sacrament. Robert Gutherman, of Bristol Township, and

eight-year old Amy Wall, of Bensalem, who received miraculous cures through Mother Katharine's intercession—both were healed of deafness—also attended the canonization.

Robert Gutherman of Bristol Township, Bucks County, lost his hearing in February 1974 due to an acute ear infection. After several unsuccessful operations, doctors gave up hope of curing him. However, the Sisters of the Blessed Sacrament at the motherhouse, where Robert and his brothers often served Mass, prayed for a miracle, and Robert's hearing was restored. This miracle was approved as part of the process of Mother Katharine's beatification in 1988. The parents of Amy Wall—a one-year old girl from Bensalem, also in Bucks County, who was born with severe

Pope John Paul II canonized Saint Katharine Drexel on October 1, 2000.

deafness—heard Gutherman's story, and prayed for a miracle for their daughter. Her mother touched a relic—a piece of a religious habit that Mother Katharine had worn—to Amy's ear, and her hearing was restored within four months.

At the Mass of Thanksgiving on October 3, in the Roman Basilica of Saint Paul Outside-the-Walls, Cardinal Bevilacqua expressed what many were thinking. "We are grateful today that God chose Saint Katharine Drexel to do His work on earth. She became poor to help others become rich, rich in Christ. Let us go forth from this basilica and do the same."

Amy Wall (on her father's lap at left) and Robert Gutherman (seated at right)—who both received miraculous healings through Saint Katharine's intercession—attend a celebratory concert on October 9, 2000, in Bensalem.

Eagle Dancers at the Thanksgiving liturgy at the Basilica of Saint Paul Outside the Walls, the day after the canonization.

Renovations to the shrine of Saint Katharine Drexel at the Motherhouse of the Sisters of the Blessed Sacrament—including the construction of a Mission Center to educate the public about the Sisters' work—were completed in 2005.

## Ensuring a Safe Environment

Criminal prosecution and civil lawsuits against several priests in the Archdiocese of Boston in 2002 brought to national attention the issue of sexual abuse of minors by clergy. Sadly, the issue was not a new one, and Cardinal Bevilacqua had addressed it at meetings of the United States Conference of Catholic Bishops as early as November 1993. But media attention helped to uncover the actual extent of abuse in dioceses around the country. The number of offenders far exceeded all previous estimates. The Holy Father summoned the cardinals of the United States, along with the President and Vice President of the United States Conference of Catholic Bishops, to Rome in late April 2002 to discuss the crisis. Meeting in Dallas in June 2002, the bishops of the United States adopted a "Charter for the Protection of Children and Young People" which instituted a "zero tolerance" policy for clergy who committed such crimes against children and youth.

In April 2002, Cardinal Bevilacqua established a "Commission for the Protection of Children and Clerical Conduct" headed by Helen Alvaré, a professor of law at the Catholic University of America. The Commission, which included experts in all aspects of child sexual abuse, reviewed archdiocesan policies and issued a report in January 2003. The report outlined the state of the problem in the archdiocese, and made numerous recommendations.

In June 2002, the archdiocese established an Office for Victims Assistance, as the first point of contact for those making reports of sexual abuse by clergy, religious, and other archdiocesan employees and volunteers. The Office employs licensed social workers who work with victims and their families to assist in obtaining outpatient counseling and spiritual and mental health support services. These social workers also assist the victim and his or her family to file a report of sexual abuse with civil authorities.

The Safe Environment Office was established to provide training for clergy, religious and lay employees and volunteers who have regular contact with children. Mandatory sessions included instructions on recognizing signs of abuse, and understanding appropriate professional boundaries and standards of ministerial behavior. The Office also implemented programs to provide Catholic school students with age-appropriate training to recognize and report sexual abuse.

In April 2002, the District Attorney of the City of Philadelphia initiated a special Grand Jury investigation into the issue of sexual abuse in the archdiocese. The Grand Jury completed its investigation and issued a 671-page report in September 2005 which detailed allegations of sexual abuse against 63 priests of the Archdiocese of Philadelphia from the 1950s through the 1990s. The report was highly critical of the handling of these allegations by archdiocesan leaders and administrators. No criminal charges were filed as a result of the report, in part because of the Pennsylvania statute of limitations on such crimes. By the time the report was published, all the accused priests either were deceased or had been removed from active ministry.

## Leading in the Third Millennium

On June 17, 1998, Cardinal Bevilacqua reached the age of 75, the point at which he was required by Canon Law to submit his resignation to the Holy Father. The Pope allowed him to remain Archbishop of Philadelphia, however, for several more years. Like Pope John Paul II, Cardinal Bevilacqua would lead the Church in Philadelphia into the Third Millennium of Christianity.

Towards the end of the Jubilee Year, on December 8, 2000, Cardinal Bevilacqua announced his plans for the Tenth Archdiocesan Synod, the first synod in the Archdiocese of Philadelphia since 1934. During a synod—a word which comes from Greek and means "on the road together"—the clergy, religious and faithful of a diocese or archdiocese meet to advise the diocesan bishop on topics of pastoral concern. For the first time in the history of the archdiocese, the 200 elected and appointed members of the Tenth Synod included priests and deacons, men and women in consecrated life, and representatives of the lay faithful.

After more than a year of catechetical formation and consultation with the faithful, nine broad topics were chosen for discussion. Papers were prepared on each topic and distributed to Synod members. The Tenth Synod opened with the celebration of Mass in the Cathedral on September 15, 2002. Members met in three weekend sessions from September to November to propose and discuss recommendations to the cardinal on each of the nine synod topics. Cardinal Bevilacqua formally closed the synod with Mass on December 8, 2002. After reviewing the recommendations of the Synod, the cardinal promulgated a number of declarations and decrees to implement the proposals of the Synod members. These decrees took effect on June 29, 2003.

THE CHURCH • PRAYING  •  LISTENING • PLANNING

2002

Tenth Synod
ARCHDIOCESE OF PHILADELPHIA

One of the challenges facing the archdiocese at the beginning of the new millennium was a decrease in the number of priests in active ministry. Pastoral planning had also identified several city and suburban areas where the Catholic population, though strong in faith, was becoming increasingly small in number. Cardinal Bevilacqua appointed several priests as pastors

Clergy, religious and lay members of the Tenth Archdiocesan Synod met in three sessions to consider draft declarations on pastoral topics, and to make recommendations to Cardinal Bevilacqua.

of "twinned" parishes—that is, one priest with responsibility for two parishes. Each parish retained its own church, pastoral council and parish organizations, but in many cases the two communities worked together on matters such as religious education and celebration of the sacraments. The experience of many of these twinned parishes showed the willingness of the faithful and their pastors to work together to maintain solid parish communities.

At the same time, growth in several suburban communities led Cardinal Bevilacqua to found two new parishes, the first in the archdiocese since 1993. Our Lady of Guadalupe Church, Buckingham, Bucks County, and Saint Elizabeth Parish, Upper Uwchlan Township, Chester County, were both founded on July 1, 2000.

Monsignor Michael Burbidge served as Cardinal Bevilacqua's administrative secretary from 1992 to 1999, until he was appointed Rector of Saint Charles Seminary. On September 5, 2002, he was ordained an auxiliary bishop for the Archdiocese of Philadelphia, and continued as rector until 2004. On August 4, 2006, Bishop Burbidge was installed as the fifth Bishop of Raleigh, North Carolina.

## Cardinal Rigali

Cardinal Bevilacqua turned 80 years of age on June 17, 2003, and the Holy Father accepted his request to resign his duties as archbishop. On July 15, 2003, Cardinal Bevilacqua became Archbishop Emeritus of Philadelphia, and was appointed as Apostolic Administrator of the archdiocese. At the same time, Pope John Paul II appointed the Archbishop of St. Louis, Archbishop Justin Rigali, as the eighth Archbishop of Philadelphia.

Justin Francis Rigali was born in Los Angeles, California, on April 19, 1935, one of seven children. He studied for the priesthood at Los Angeles College; Our Lady Queen of Angels Seminary in San Fernando, California; and Saint John's Seminary in Camarillo, California. He was ordained a priest on April 25, 1961, and in October of that year began graduate studies in Canon Law at the Gregorian University. After obtaining his doctorate in 1964, he attended the Pontifical Ecclesiastical Academy in Rome, and worked in the Secretariat of State of the Holy See until 1966.

After serving the diplomatic mission in Madagascar—which included the Indian Ocean islands of Mauritius and La Reunión—Monsignor Rigali returned to Rome in 1970 and was appointed Director of the English-language section of the Secretariat of State. At the same time he served as an English-language interpreter for Pope Paul VI. Between 1979 and 1987 he accompanied Pope John Paul II on many pastoral visits to

### DECREES
### CHAPTER I
#### GENERAL NORMS

NORM 1    These decrees, or norms, are based on the recommendations proposed by the Tenth Synod of the Archdiocese of Philadelphia and accepted by the Archbishop, constitute archdiocesan particular law issued by him in accord with canon 29 of the *Code of Canon Law*, and bind, according to their subject matter, all members of the Christian faithful of the Archdiocese of Philadelphia.

NORM 2    By virtue of these decrees, the Archbishop of Philadelphia intends: to promote and to foster the observance of those canonical norms which are especially required by the circumstances of archdiocesan life; to regulate certain of those matters which the universal law of the Church entrusts to his competence and that of his successors; and, to apply the discipline which is common to all the particular Churches.

NORM 3    These decrees obtain the force of law on June 29, 2003, one month after their promulgation by the Archbishop of Philadelphia, in accord with the Decree of Promulgation issued by him.

**After the Synod was closed in December 2002, Cardinal Bevilacqua considered the recommendations of the Synod members, and issued a number of declarations and decrees, which took effect on June 29, 2003.**

English-speaking countries, including his two major visits to the United States. Monsignor Rigali had been a professor at the Pontifical Ecclesiastical Academy in 1972 and 1973, and was appointed President of the Academy on June 8, 1985. He was ordained titular Archbishop of Bolsena on September 14, 1985.

During his tenure as President of the Pontifical Ecclesiastical Academy from 1985 to 1990, Archbishop Rigali held a number of positions in the Vatican, serving the Secretariat of State, the Council for Public Affairs of the Church, the Congregation for Bishops and the Pontifical Council for the Laity. On December 21, 1989, he was named Secretary of the Congregation for Bishops, and on January 2, 1990 he became the Secretary of the College of Cardinals. He was likewise a member of the Permanent Interdicasterial Commission of the Holy See and served as a consultant to the Pontifical Commission for Latin America and the Congregation for the Doctrine of the Faith. On January 25, 1994, he was appointed the seventh Archbishop of St. Louis, where he served for more than nine years.

Archbishop Rigali's appointment as Archbishop of Philadelphia in 2003 was not his first connection with the archdiocese. He had been present at the Mass of Canonization of Saint John Neumann on June 19, 1977, and at the special audience with Pope Paul VI that Philadelphia pilgrims attended the following day. He had also accompanied Pope John Paul II on his visit to Philadelphia on October 3 and 4, 1979. When Archbishop Rigali came to Philadelphia for his installation as archbishop on October 7, 2003, he

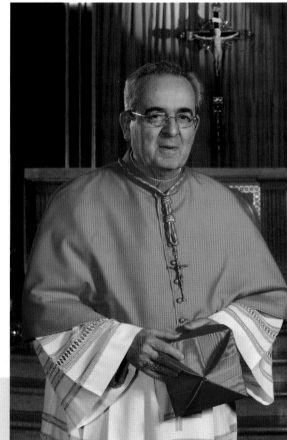

**Cardinal Justin Francis Rigali**
**Eighth Archbishop of Philadelphia**
**since 2003**

Cardinal-designate Rigali on the morning of his installation as Archbishop of Philadelphia, October 7, 2003. Also pictured are (from left): Cardinal Theodore McCarrick, Archbishop of Washington; Cardinal William Keeler, Archbishop of Baltimore; Archbishop Gabriel Montalvo, Apostolic Nuncio to the United States; and Cardinal Bevilacqua.

As Archbishop of St. Louis from 1994 to 2003, Archbishop Rigali was a successor of Archbishop Peter Richard Kenrick, a Philadelphia priest and former rector of Saint Charles Seminary, who led the Archdiocese of St. Louis from 1841 to 1896.

was the second archbishop from Saint Louis to make that journey. One of his predecessors, Archbishop Patrick Ryan, had been coadjutor Archbishop of St. Louis at the time of his appointment as Archbishop of Philadelphia in 1884.

Before leaving St. Louis, Archbishop Rigali had already been informed of the Holy Father's intention to create him a cardinal. The consistory took place on October 21, 2003, two weeks after his installation. Cardinal Rigali was assigned the titular church of Santa Prisca on the Aventine Hill in Rome, named for one of Saint Paul's co-workers during his missionary journeys. "We should be filled with enthusiasm as we confront the challenges and problems," he told the Philadelphians who journeyed with him on the occasion, "but also as we live the Gospel and as we enjoy the satisfactions, the fulfillment and the happiness of being followers of Jesus Christ."

To assist the Holy Father, Cardinal Rigali was made a member of the Congregation for Divine Worship and the Discipline of the Sacraments. He also was appointed a member of the Administration of the Patrimony of the Holy See. Returning to Philadelphia, the cardinal made a number of pastoral visits to parishes and institutions throughout the archdiocese. As he met with the clergy, religious and laity in each vicariate, he repeated the commitment he had made at his installation "to proclaim Jesus Christ

When Archbishop Rigali became the Archbishop of Philadelphia in 2003, he succeeded Bishop Peter Richard Kenrick's brother, Bishop Francis Patrick Kenrick, the third Bishop of Philadelphia from 1830 to 1851.

**Cardinal Rigali offers a sign of reverence to Pope John Paul II during the public consistory, October 21, 2003.**

auxiliary bishops designated geographical regions of the archdiocese, with responsibility for canonical visitation of parishes, installation of new pastors and specific responsibilities in the archdiocesan administration.

In September 2005, Cardinal Rigali appointed Monsignor Hugh Shields, pastor of Visitation B.V.M. parish in North Philadelphia, as the archdiocese's first Vicar for Hispanic Catholics. Monsignor Shields had spent twelve years—including nine years in Peru—working with the Missionary Society of Saint James the Apostle, a group of diocesan priests who are released by their dioceses to minister in South America. As Vicar, Monsignor Shields became the cardinal's direct representative to Spanish-speaking Catholics from more than 20 nations who live in the archdiocese.

as the Son of God and Savior of the world... to proclaim His liberating and uplifting Gospel of merciful love, and to serve in His name."

In 2004, Pope John Paul II appointed Monsignor Joseph Cistone, Vicar for Administration, and Monsignor Joseph McFadden, pastor of Saint Joseph Church in Downingtown, as auxiliary bishops in Philadelphia. Cardinal Rigali used the occasion of their ordination on July 28, 2004, to restructure the archdiocesan administration. He assigned each of the

When Bishop Burbidge was appointed Bishop of Raleigh in 2006, Monsignor Daniel Thomas—the pastor of Our Lady of the Assumption Church in Strafford, who had worked in the Congregation for Bishops in Rome for fifteen years—was appointed an auxiliary bishop and ordained on July 26, 2006. Auxiliary bishops are traditionally given honorary titles derived from dioceses and archdioceses that are presently defunct—either because the Church was expelled from a certain territory by a hostile ruler or government, or because the area of the former diocese has been divided or combined to create new dioceses. Bishop Thomas was appointed the titular Bishop of Bardstown, a former diocese in Kentucky that was established on April 8, 1808—the same day as the Diocese of Philadelphia. (The Diocese of Bardstown was renamed the Diocese of Louisville in 1841.)

**Cardinal Rigali preaches the homily and celebrates Benediction at "Prayer on the Parkway," the closing event of the archdiocesan observance of the Year of the Eucharist, September 18, 2005. Tens of thousands of the faithful attended the event on Logan Circle.**

Pope John Paul II designated the twenty-seventh year of his pontificate, October 2004 to October 2005, as the Year of the Eucharist. He called on the faithful throughout the world to focus their attention and prayer on the mystery of the Most Holy Eucharist in the life and mission of the Church. Cardinal Rigali encouraged the faithful to participate faithfully at Mass and to make a special effort to spend time in prayer before the Blessed Sacrament. He celebrated Holy Hours in each vicariate to pray for vocations to the priesthood and religious life, and led a "Reconciliation Weekend" on February 25 and 26, 2005. The highlight of the Year of the Eucharist came on September 18, 2005, when tens of thousands of the faithful attended a public Eucharistic Procession from the Cathedral to an outdoor altar constructed on Logan Circle.

## Death of Pope John Paul II

Pope John Paul II made his last public appearance at the window of his apartment overlooking Saint Peter's Square on Easter Sunday, March 27, 2005. However, he was unable to speak to the crowds of well-wishers and pilgrims assembled there. The following Saturday, April 2, the Holy Father died at 9:37 p.m., Rome time. It was the vigil of the Feast of Divine Mercy, which he had added to the Church's calendar several years before.

Before Cardinal Rigali left for Rome to take part in the various ceremonies surrounding the funeral of the Holy Father, he and the auxiliary bishops celebrated Mass in the Cathedral for the repose of the soul of the man

crowds were already calling "John Paul the Great." Television viewers around the world watched as crowds in Saint Peter's Square held up signs that read *"Santo Subito!"*—"A saint right away!" English-speaking viewers heard the voice of Philadelphia native Archbishop John Foley, who provided English translations and commentary during the funeral of the Holy Father.

Following the funeral and the traditional *Novendiales* or nine days of mourning, Cardinal Rigali and the other cardinals eligible to vote for the new pope entered the Sistine Chapel for the conclave to elect the next successor of Saint Peter. On April 19, 2005, the second day of voting, the cardinals elected Cardinal Joseph Ratzinger—who was the Dean of the College of Cardinals and Prefect of the Congregation for the Doctrine of the Faith—as Pope Benedict XVI. Cardinal Rigali participated in the Mass that marked the beginning of Pope Benedict's Petrine ministry, and then returned to Philadelphia to gather the faithful to pray for the Holy Father. "It is in the unity of faith and love," he said during his homily at the Mass of Thanksgiving at the Cathedral, "that we make our prayer today that God will sustain and give strength to Pope Benedict."

"The Church is alive… She holds within herself the future of the world, and therefore shows each of us the way toward the future. The Church is alive, and we are seeing it." This was the heart of the message of Pope Benedict XVI to the world, proclaimed in the homily he gave at his Mass of Installation on April 24, 2005. Those words from Saint Peter's Square direct the Church in Philadelphia to consider most carefully the living

heritage of faith that has sustained her for more than two hundred years. Tribulations will come. The example of courageous ancestors in the midst of turmoil provides a reason for courage and a foundation for hope. Important lessons have been learned, sometimes at the cost of misunderstanding and error. These lessons must be remembered and renewed in each generation, and applied afresh to the questions posed by modern life. Heroes and leaders have emerged in unexpected places. Their example continues to challenge ordinary people to live extraordinary lives. "The Church is alive, and we are seeing it." This truth impels the sons and daughters of the Church to recognize and cherish their faith-filled heritage, as they follow Christ into a new century of Catholic life in the Archdiocese of Philadelphia.

Cardinal Rigali took part in the conclave which elected Cardinal Joseph Ratzinger, the Prefect of the Congregation of the Doctrine of the Faith, as Pope Benedict XVI. Cardinal Ratzinger had visited Saint Charles Seminary in 1991.

# Part II

# The Fruits of Faith:
## The Parishes of the Archdiocese of Philadelphia

*I rejoiced when I heard them say,*
*"Let us go to God's house."…*
*For Israel's law it is*
*there to praise the Lord's name*

*Psalm 122:1,4b.*

So often, Catholic people have an abiding commitment to particular parishes that have been significant in their lives. Time and distance do little to diminish loyalty and affection for the church in which a person received the sacraments and worshipped each Sunday. Catholic schools and parish organizations provide memories to be cherished for a lifetime.

Catholics who have grown up in the Archdiocese of Philadelphia readily identify themselves by their parishes, past and present. "I grew up in Saint Anne's parish", "I'm from Holy Saviour," "I belong to The Epiphany"—these are more common responses to the question, "Where are you from?" than place names like Port Richmond, Norristown or South Philadelphia.

In Part I, this commemorative book set forth a broad view of the history of the Archdiocese of Philadelphia, and focused chiefly on the work of the archbishop and the archdiocese as an institution. In Part II, the reader will find stories of more than 330 parishes and missions that have been established in the five counties that make up the area of the present Archdiocese. The parishes are arranged first by county, and then by general area or neighborhood within the county. Within each area, the parishes are presented in the order of their foundation. In this way, the authors hope to show how the development of local communities has impacted decisions about when and where parishes have been established.

Generally speaking, parishes fall into two categories. The majority of parishes can be described as *territorial parishes.* That is, almost all Catholics living within specified geographical boundaries belong to a particular parish. Most of the time these boundaries are county lines and major roads; however, borders may also follow railroad tracks, creeks, rivers or "air lines" connecting certain points. Other parishes are commonly called *national parishes,* because they were established to provide pastoral care for a particular nationality and language. A national parish includes all people who speak that language or claim that nationality, and live within a particular area, usually much wider than that of a territorial parish. National parishes are more exactly called *personal parishes,* since membership in them depends on the ethnic background of the particular person.

The following pages illustrate that the parishes of the archdiocese have been established in a variety of ways. In some cases, the Catholics of a particular area petitioned the bishop or archbishop to found a parish in their community. At other times, the need for a new parish was recognized by the archbishop, or by advisors responsible for planning parish sites and boundaries. From time to time, the population of a territorial parish either outgrew parish facilities or exceeded the ability of parish priests to care for all of their parishioners. In such cases, the territory of a parish—or of several neighboring parishes—was divided in order to form a new parish.

A number of parishes had their origins as *missions.* An established parish would identify locations in which parish priests could celebrate Mass for people living in remote parts of the parish territory. Often these missions started in parishioners' homes, or in local hotels or social halls. Over time, chapels were built in many locations. Once the community grew large enough to warrant a resident priest, the mission chapel was canonically established as a separate parish.

Most parishes opened parish elementary schools shortly after the foundation of the parish itself. In nearly every parish established in the nineteenth and twentieth centuries, the parish school was founded and staffed by women religious. An effort has been made in this section to identify the religious Congregation that opened each parish school. Many parishes still benefit greatly from the presence of these consecrated women, who are now joined by dedicated lay men and women. As the number of women religious available for ministry in parochial schools has declined in recent decades, more and more schools have made the transition to a faculty and administration composed entirely of lay persons.

It is important to remember that, although it is the Archbishop of Philadelphia who canonically establishes a parish, the parishioners themselves are responsible for constructing and operating the church, school and other necessary facilities. Many parish histories contain stories of ordinary parishioners making great sacrifices to build, adorn and maintain their parish buildings. Unfortunately, various factors can make it difficult for a particular community to support the needs of its parish. This difficulty occurs when large numbers of practicing Catholics move out of a certain neighborhood, and are replaced by residents who are not Catholic. Moreover, it sometimes

happens that, with a dwindling number of priests available for parish ministry, it becomes impractical to assign a priest as pastor of a very small parish.

In such cases, good stewardship of parish and archdiocesan resources requires that parishes be reorganized. This can happen in several ways. The arrangement known as *twinning* gives pastoral responsibility for two parishes to one priest. Each parish retains its own identity, buildings and organizations, while cooperating with each other in various ways. At times, two or more parishes are consolidated to form one new parish. Occasionally the *consolidated* parish is given the name of both former parishes; however, it is more common for the new parish to be given a new name. In some cases, a struggling parish is simply *suppressed,* its territory reassigned, and parishioners welcomed into other parishes in the vicinity.

Sometimes when a parish is closed or consolidated, its church is maintained as an alternative *worship site.* Sunday Mass may be celebrated there, and parishioners may arrange for funeral Masses in their former parish church. This arrangement is not always feasible, however, and in some cases the real estate, church furnishings and other property of a parish are sold. In the Archdiocese of Philadelphia, the disposition of this property is handled by the Office for Closures through the *Ecclesiastical Exchange.* The Exchange removes items from closed churches, arranges for storage and sale, and distributes the proceeds to the parish or parishes currently responsible for the former parishioners of the

suppressed parish. Although it can be very sad to witness the closure of a beloved parish church, the work of the Exchange ensures that objects of art and devotion donated by preceding generations live on in newly-constructed churches both in the Archdiocese of Philadelphia and around the country.

The last few decades have witnessed many changes in parish life in the Archdiocese of Philadelphia. Demographic shifts prompt closures in some neighborhoods while at the same time new foundations are being made in other areas. Parochial schools are adapting to changing technology, and finding ways to collaborate with one another to make the best use of available resources. Parish facilities have been made more accessible to people with disabilities, and in a number of churches Mass is translated or celebrated in sign language. New generations of immigrants enrich their parishes with languages, music and traditions from many cultures, and in various locations Mass is celebrated in more than a dozen languages. In the midst of these and other changes, however, the parish still remains the focal point for Catholic faith, worship and identity.

The number of parishes that have been part of the Archdiocese of Philadelphia means that the sketches on the following pages are necessarily quite brief. The authors hope, however, that the information presented here will encourage the reader to become better acquainted with the parishes—so many and so varied—that shape and structure the faith-filled heritage entrusted to this local Church.

# CITY OF PHILADELPHIA

# Center City

Covering an area of about 142 square miles, the City of Philadelphia has long been one of the largest cities on the East Coast of the United States. The present city limits, however, date only from 1854, when the Act of Consolidation incorporated the many districts, boroughs and townships of Philadelphia County into one city. Between 1682—when the city was founded and planned by William Penn, the proprietor of the Colony of Pennsylvania—and 1854, the City of Philadelphia comprised a much smaller area, bounded by Vine Street and South Street, the Schuylkill River and the Delaware River. Today, this neighborhood is often referred to as "Center City" Philadelphia. It was in this area that most of the early settlement of the city took place, and it was here that Philadelphia's first Catholic churches were built.

The Jesuit mission of Bohemia Manor, on the Chesapeake Bay in Maryland, was founded in 1706. Missionary priests traveled from there to various locations in Pennsylvania, New Jersey and New York, and often stopped in Philadelphia. These pioneer priests would celebrate Mass and administer the sacraments in the homes of local Catholics like John Tatham, Lionel Britten and Peter Dubuc. As the Catholic population increased in the 1720s, the need for a permanent mission in Philadelphia became apparent. In 1729, Father Joseph Greaton, S.J., was appointed the first resident pastor in Philadelphia.

Father Greaton lodged with a Catholic surgeon-barber, John Dixon, at Second and Chestnut Streets, and with Mr. Dixon's help, the priest began the search for a suitable plot of land for a church. On February 22, 1732, Father Greaton gathered eleven members of the Catholic community for the first Mass in a new little chapel dedicated to SAINT JOSEPH. Located on Willings Alley, near Fourth and Walnut Streets, it was the first public chapel in the British North American colonies, and the oldest foundation of the Jesuits in the City of Philadelphia.

**Old Saint Joseph's**

As the small Catholic population continued to grow in the 1740s and 1750s—largely due to the arrival of Irish and German immigrants to the city—the congregation at Saint Joseph's often faced suspicion and hostility from Philadelphia's non-Catholics. In 1740, and again in 1755, axe-wielding mobs attempted to destroy Saint Joseph's Church, and it took the intervention of local Quakers to fend off the attacks. Nevertheless, the congregation continued to grow, and in 1757 a new church—nearly five times as large as the original chapel—was built on the same site. The present church of Saint Joseph was dedicated in 1839. Sisters of Saint Joseph arrived in 1851 to teach in the parish school.

When Saint Joseph's was rebuilt in 1757, the expansion occupied much of the land that the Catholic community hoped to use for a cemetery. Father Robert Harding, S.J., who had become pastor in 1749, collected money from local Catholic merchants and craftsmen to purchase another plot at Fourth and Walnut Streets. Once in possession of this property, Father Harding and his parishioners began to plan not only for a burial ground, but also for a new, larger church.

The parish church of SAINT MARY was dedicated in 1763, and measuring 50 feet by 80 feet it was nearly eight times as large as the original Saint Joseph's. One priest served both churches, celebrating solemn Sunday Mass at Saint Mary's, and other Masses at

**Old Saint Mary's**

Saint Joseph's. Saint Mary's was also the site of many public celebrations during the American Revolution, including the first public religious commemoration of the signing of the Declaration of Independence. The celebration took place on July 4, 1779. The Continental Congress worshipped here four times, and on several occasions, members of Congress attended funeral Masses for Catholic diplomats from France and Spain.

When Bishop Michael Egan was ordained the first Bishop of Philadelphia in 1810, Saint Mary's became the pro-cathedral of the new diocese, and the church was enlarged and redecorated that same year. Much of the history of the parish through the 1820s was marred by unfortunate conflicts between the Bishops of Philadelphia and members of the parish Board of Trustees—conflicts which were

finally resolved by Bishop Kenrick in 1831. The parish, however, was also home to many outstanding members of the Philadelphia Catholic community. Military heroes like Commodore John Barry and General Stephen Moylan, civic leaders like Matthew Carey, and patriots like Thomas FitzSimons—one of two Catholic signers of the United States Constitution—were parishioners of Saint Mary's. It is also the site of the oldest parish school in Philadelphia. In operation from at least 1782, Saint Mary's School continues to educate Catholic children in the Center City area as Saint Mary's Interparochial School.

The 1700s saw a significant number of Catholic immigrants arrive in Philadelphia. In addition to the Irish, many Catholics arrived from Germany. For decades they were served by German "circuit riders" from Bohemia Manor—including Father Theodore Schneider and Father Ferdinand Steinmeyer, known as Father Farmer—who also attended missions in Lancaster and Goshenhoppen (Bally), Pennsylvania. By the 1780s, the German Catholic community in Philadelphia was large enough to support a resident priest, and the efforts of local businessman Adam Premir made it possible to buy land for the first German national parish in the city. Located at Sixth and Spruce Streets, the church was dedicated to the HOLY TRINITY.

Holy Trinity parish also struggled at various points in its early history with conflicts between the parish Board of Trustees and the diocesan bishops. Such conflicts continued until the time of Bishop Neumann in the 1850s. Nevertheless, the parish was often at the center of projects to care for those in need. French Catholics took refuge here after the French Revolution in 1789, and parishioners cared for the victims of the yellow fever epidemics throughout the 1790s. A parish school was in operation by 1787, and later staffed by the School Sisters of Notre Dame. In the 1830s and 1850s, pastors and parishioners of Holy Trinity were instrumental in founding several orphanages for boys. Although Holy Trinity is still officially the parish of German-speaking Catholics in Center City, Sunday Mass is celebrated here only once a month. The pastor of Saint Mary's serves as the parochial administrator of Holy Trinity.

**Holy Trinity**

These three parishes were all located close to one another in the southern part of the city. In the 1790s, the Catholic population in the northern areas of Center City was gaining in numbers, and a new parish was needed. Father Matthew Carr, O.S.A., a member of the first group of Augustinians from Ireland to settle in Philadelphia, raised donations to build SAINT AUGUSTINE Church on Fourth Street south of Vine Street. Founded in 1796 and dedicated in 1801, it was the first permanent establishment of the Augustinians in the United States.

In 1803, Market Street was established as the official boundary between Saint Augustine's and Saint Mary's, and the Augustinian parish also took in much of the area north and east of the city. Saint Augustine's Academy was founded here in 1811, and was the forerunner of what became Villanova University. The parish continued to grow—comprising 3,000 members by the late 1830s—and its prominence in the northern part of the city made it a target of the Nativist riots in May 1844. Over three days, the church was repeatedly attacked by mobs, and on May 8, 1844, was burned beyond repair. The present church, dedicated in 1847, was designed by Philadelphia architect Napoleon LeBrun. Sisters of Saint Joseph began their ministry in the parish school in 1865.

The area of Center City west of Seventh Street was developed in the late 1820s, and soon after his arrival in Philadelphia, Bishop Kenrick announced plans for a new parish in the western part of the city. On December 27, 1830, he founded the church of SAINT JOHN THE EVANGELIST (whose feast day is celebrated on that date), and appointed Father John Hughes, the future Bishop of New York, as the first pastor. Saint John's was the first Philadelphia parish without trustees, and the church was built with donations from prominent Philadelphians as well as from Catholics in foreign countries, including Joseph Bonaparte, the exiled King of Spain. Two fires in 1899 destroyed the interior of the church, which was rebuilt in 1900 and faced with granite in 1907.

Saint John's served as the pro-cathedral from 1838 through 1864, and was the site of the first collection for Saint Charles Seminary

**Saint John the Evangelist**

(1840) as well as the Second Diocesan Synod (1842). Bishop Kenrick had his residence at Saint John's from 1838 to 1847, Saint John Neumann was installed here as Bishop of Philadelphia in 1852, and his funeral Mass was celebrated here in 1860. In her youth, Saint Katharine Drexel frequently attended Mass at Saint John's, and prayed in the parish church before leaving Philadelphia to enter religious life. The parish school was founded in 1834, and was staffed by the Sisters of Saint Joseph in 1889. The parish was entrusted to the Jesuits from 1855, when pastor Father Edward Sourin joined the Society, until 1860. It is now served by the Capuchin Franciscan Friars.

**Saint Augustine**

**Cathedral-Basilica of Saints Peter and Paul**

The construction of the Schuylkill Canal—which brought coal from mines near Reading, Berks County, to Philadelphia—attracted large numbers of Irish immigrants to the coal wharves being constructed along the Schuylkill River. In 1839, Bishop Kenrick established the parish of SAINT PATRICK to tend to the pastoral needs of these Irish men and women. The first Masses were celebrated in a rented house (a former carpenter shop and vinegar factory) until the first church was built at Twentieth and Rittenhouse Streets in 1841. The original parish boundaries included large areas of western Philadelphia County, Delaware County and regions of southern New Jersey. Eventually the parish also established a mission in the Port Richmond neighborhood. The parish school was founded in 1839, and Sisters of Saint Joseph took responsibility for the school in 1857.

Saint Patrick's survived various periods of anti-Catholic hostility in the nineteenth century, and posted a 24-hour watch to protect the church during the Nativist riots of 1844. In the late 1800s, the Catholic population showed a marked increase, and when a new church was built in 1910 it reflected the Irish heritage of many parishioners. An ornate cornerstone of Irish marble was given by Cardinal Michael Logue, the Archbishop of Armagh and Primate of All Ireland from 1887 to 1924. In 1862, Pope Pius IX had granted a plenary indulgence to all who came to the church to celebrate the feast of Saint Patrick on March 17. The church is still the site of the annual Mass celebrated before the Philadelphia Saint Patrick's Day Parade.

On June 29, 1844, Bishop Kenrick issued a pastoral letter to solicit funds for the construction of the CATHEDRAL OF SAINTS PETER AND PAUL, the two great apostles whose feast is celebrated on that day. Eight thousand people

**Saint Patrick**

attended the laying of the cornerstone on September 6, 1846, on a plot adjoining the diocesan seminary and fronting Logan Square. Work on the Cathedral—designed by Philadelphia architects Napoleon LeBrun and John Notman—was conducted in stages as funds became available. This meant that on a number of occasions construction was delayed, and the Cathedral was not completed until 1864.

A chapel adjoining the Cathedral, named for Our Lady of the Blessed Sacrament, was constructed in 1955, and remains the site of daily Mass and other devotions. The Cathedral itself underwent an extensive renovation during 1956 and 1957, at which time a semi-circular apse was constructed which extended the sanctuary to its present depth of more than 90 feet. The sanctuary is the home of the *cathedra* or throne of the bishop of a diocese, and this fact gives the church its special title. A cathedral is considered the bishop's own church and the "mother church" of a diocese or archdiocese. The Archbishop of Philadelphia celebrates the major feasts of the liturgical year in the Cathedral, as well as special archdiocesan liturgies such as the ordinations of deacons, priests and bishops, and jubilees of marriage and religious profession. The late Bishops and Archbishops of Philadelphia are entombed in the Cathedral crypt—with the exceptions of Bishop Kenrick, Saint John Neumann and Cardinal O'Hara. Following the celebration of the 41st International Eucharistic Congress in Philadelphia in 1976, Pope Paul VI bestowed the dignity of a "minor basilica" on the Cathedral of Saints Peter and Paul. This honorary distinction shows both the connection between the local Church and the universal Church, and also the special concern of the Holy Father for the faithful of every land.

The African American community in Center City grew during and after the Civil War and the emancipation of slaves in the South. In 1883, the Oblate Sisters of Providence opened a school at Seventh and Pine Streets to educate African American children. The school was later administered by the School Sisters of Notre Dame. During these years, African American families attended Mass at Holy Trinity church, where Mass was celebrated for "colored" people at 9:00 on Sunday morning.

In 1886, this growing community founded the Peter Claver Union to raise funds for a church of their own. Mother Katharine Drexel bought a house at 832 Pine Street to serve as a school for boys, and girls were taught in the original school building by Immaculate Heart Sisters.

The boys' school also housed a chapel, named for SAINT PETER CLAVER, the Jesuit missionary who baptized and ministered to hundreds of thousands of African slaves in Cartagena, Colombia, from 1610 until his death in 1654. The girls' school was later moved to Eleventh and Pine Streets, and the two schools were consolidated in 1947.

**Holy Redeemer**

In 1891, the congregation of the Fourth Presbyterian Church at Twelfth and Lombard Streets decided to sell its building, and Father James Nolan, C.S.Sp., who was responsible for Saint Peter Claver chapel, made the purchase. The church was renovated and dedicated the

following year as the parish church. In the 1950s, as the African American community moved to other areas of the city—particularly North Philadelphia—members of Saint Peter Claver pioneered racial integration in many other parishes. However, the migration of African American Catholic families out of Center City led to the closing in 1985 of what had come to be known as the "Mother Church of Black Catholics" in Philadelphia.

Following the invasion of China by Japanese forces in 1937, Bishop Paul Yu-Pin, Vicar Apostolic of Nanking, made several tours of the United States to ask for support for the Catholic Church in China. During his visit to Philadelphia in 1939, he spoke to Cardinal Dennis Dougherty about pastoral care for Chinese-speaking Catholics in Philadelphia's Chinatown. In 1941, Monsignor William Kavanagh of Saint John the Evangelist Church was given responsibility for a chapel located in Chinatown and dedicated to the HOLY REDEEMER. With the assistance of the Trinitarian Sisters, the priests of Saint John's made many converts among Chinese residents, and by 1955, Holy Redeemer was home to the largest Chinese Catholic community east of the Mississippi River. The subsequent construction of the Vine Street Expressway necessitated the removal of the chapel to its present location at 915 Vine Street. Holy Redeemer chapel and school are still cared for by the priests of Saint John the Evangelist parish.

# Germantown, Chestnut Hill and Mount Airy

In 1681, William Penn published an appeal in German, inviting settlers to his newly-formed colony of Pennsylvania. Quakers and Mennonites from the Rhine Valley town of Krefeld arrived on the *Concord* in 1683, and established homes in Philadelphia. By 1685, many Germans had moved about six miles northwest of present-day Center City, and under the leadership of Francis Daniel Pastorius established German Township, the forerunner of the Borough of Germantown.

In 1683, a "Romanist" servant of Mr. Pastorius is mentioned in the records of missionary priests, and may have been the first Catholic resident of what is today the City of Philadelphia. Catholic families in Germantown—who were few in the eighteenth and early nineteenth centuries—had to travel into the city or, after 1843, to Saint Stephen's in Nicetown for Mass and the sacraments.

Vincentian priests had come to Philadelphia in 1841 at the invitation of Bishop Kenrick to take on the responsibility of the new diocesan seminary. In 1849, the Congregation purchased a plot of land on Price Street east of Main Street, where they laid the cornerstone for a new parish church. Named for their founder, SAINT VINCENT DE PAUL, the church was completed in 1851; however, financial problems delayed the dedication of the building until 1859. The young parish faced hostility from non-Catholic neighbors, some of whom threw rocks at Bishop Kenrick when he arrived for the dedication.

**Saint Vincent de Paul**

Early on, parishioners established a Sunday school, and by 1865 the parish school was in operation. It was founded by the Daughters of Charity, the sister congregation to the Vincentians; these Sisters were succeeded by the Sisters of Saint Joseph in 1867. In 1868, the novitiate and seminary of the Vincentian province were moved from Saint Louis, Missouri, to Germantown, where Saint Vincent's Seminary was built on Chelten Avenue.

The Vincentians still provide pastoral care for Saint Vincent de Paul parish, and continue to operate the novitiate, Saint Catherine's Infirmary, and the nearby Central Shrine of Our Lady of the Miraculous Medal. In recent decades the parish community has organized many efforts to reach out to the poor and disadvantaged of the surrounding neighborhoods—including educational and job-placement programs, food cupboards and thrift shops, and community and economic development.

The farming village of Chestnut Hill, in the northwest corner of Germantown, was a popular country vacation spot for prosperous families during the eighteenth century. Here, Augustinians from Saint Augustine's parish in Center City established a mission in 1855. The chapel of OUR MOTHER OF CONSOLATION was dedicated by Saint John Neumann in November of that year. The founding pastor, Father Patrick Moriarity, O.S.A., had been pastor of Saint Augustine's when that church was attacked by Nativist mobs in 1844.

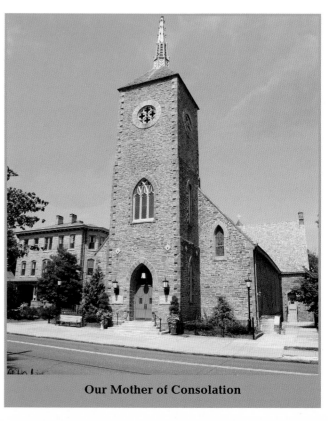

**Our Mother of Consolation**

Through the generosity of wealthy parishioners like Joseph Middleton, a former Quaker, the church was enlarged and renovated in 1880, and a spire added in 1885. The parish school was founded in 1881 by the Sisters of Saint Joseph, whose Motherhouse was located nearby. The school was first housed in a rented home on a neighborhood estate, until a school building opened in 1916. Augustinians continued to staff the parish until 1999, when it was entrusted to the Oblates of Saint Francis de Sales.

**Holy Cross**

The neighborhood of Mount Airy, situated between Chestnut Hill and Germantown, was developed in the 1880s and 1890s, when extended service on both the Germantown

**Saint Francis of Assisi**

Avenue Trolley and the Philadelphia, Germantown and Chestnut Hill Railroad connected the area with other parts of the city. The parish of HOLY CROSS was founded in 1890, and utilized the former Grace Episcopal Church. A parish school opened in 1910, staffed by the Sisters of Saint Joseph. The present church, at Mount Airy Avenue and Boyer Street, was dedicated in 1929.

In 1899, continued residential development prompted the foundation of SAINT FRANCIS OF ASSISI parish on Greene Street in Southwest Germantown. The original rectory, on the 300 block of West Logan Street, was the site of parish Masses until a church/school building was dedicated in 1900. The school, conducted by the Sisters of Saint Joseph, included a two-year high school for girls and a four-year program for boys. New school buildings were erected in 1968, and in 1986 the school was renamed Saint Martin de Porres Interparochial School. The present church was dedicated in 1928, and is entrusted to the Vincentians.

A third Vincentian parish was founded in 1902. Father James Hayden, C.M., the rector of Saint Vincent Seminary, built the first chapel of the IMMACULATE CONCEPTION on Chelten Avenue in that same year. This chapel would later be established as the Central Shrine of Our Lady of the Miraculous Medal—still a popular place of pilgrimage for local Catholics—and the present church was built at Price and Ardleigh Streets in 1905. The large upper church, dedicated in 1930, can seat more than 1,300 people, and in the late 1950s it was the site of the ordination of archdiocesan priests when the Cathedral was being renovated. Immaculate Heart Sisters founded the parish school in 1904. Since 1989, the parish community has operated the Ghebre Michael Inn (named for an African convert and associate

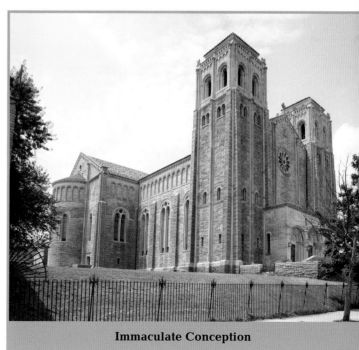

**Immaculate Conception**

of the Vincentians who was beatified as a martyr in 1926), to provide services for homeless and unemployed members of the community.

Several parishes were founded in the early 1900s to care for particular ethnic groups in Germantown. In 1910, Father Jeremiah Hartnett, C.M., of Saint Vincent parish, founded SAINT CATHERINE OF SIENA church on West Penn Street as a place of worship for the African American community. The church was paid for by Mother Katharine Drexel and named for her patron saint—although the title was not spelled with a "K" as was the case in other parishes connected with Mother Katharine and her family. Mother Katharine's Sisters of the Blessed Sacrament established the parish school in 1915. The parish was closed in 1972.

In 1924, SAINT MICHAEL OF THE SAINTS parish, at 4811 Germantown Avenue, cared for local Italian Catholics, although the patron saint of the parish was actually a Trinitarian priest from Catalonia, Spain. Sisters of Saint Joseph were invited to staff the parish school in 1944. A decline in the number of Italian-speaking families in the area prompted the closing of Saint Michael's in 1982.

When a new parish was founded on Manheim Street in 1925, it was named for the sixth-century Irish monk SAINT BRENDAN, also known as "Saint Brendan the Navigator." There is speculation the saint may have sailed to North America from County Kerry, Ireland, around A.D. 530, and the name of the parish would have appealed to Irish immigrants who

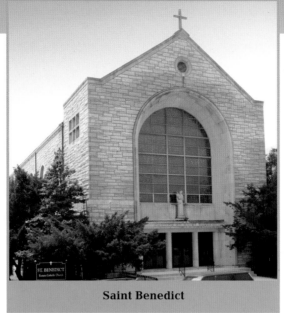
**Saint Benedict**

worked as domestic staff on Germantown estates. About 65 families founded the parish during a period of increasing population in the area; by 1934, however, the parish only numbered 116 families. The Atwater Kent Radio Company and the Germantown Cricket Club owned most of the open land within the parish boundaries, and there was little room for further residential development. In 1934, the parish was suppressed, and parishioners returned to the parishes to which they had belonged in 1925.

In the 1920s, residential development of the area necessitated the establishment of five new parishes. The first Masses of SAINT BENEDICT parish were celebrated in a movie theater at Chelten and Anderson Avenues, until a church/school building was completed in 1925. The present church, at Chelten Avenue and Garnet Street, was dedicated in 1953. The school was founded by the Franciscan Sisters of Glen Riddle.

Mount Airy was given two new parishes in 1925, and both were named for women who had been canonized by Pope Pius XI in May of

that year. The chapel of SAINT THERESE OF THE CHILD JESUS was founded on the day of her canonization, May 17, 1925, and established as a shrine church in honor of the saint to whom Cardinal Dougherty—like many Philadelphia Catholics—was so devoted. The first church, built in 1927, was a reconstructed barracks from the Hog Island shipyard in South Philadelphia. The parish school was founded in a converted stable by the Sisters of Saint Joseph, and moved into its own building in 1927. The auditorium of the new school, built in 1951, was converted in 1971 as the parish church.

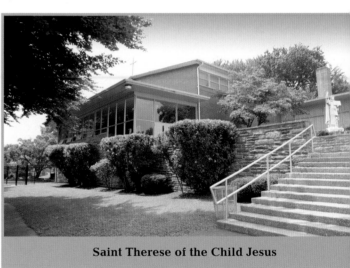
**Saint Therese of the Child Jesus**

SAINT MADELINE SOPHIE Barat, foundress of the Society of the Sacred Heart in 1801, was canonized by Pope Pius XI on May 24, 1925. The West Mount Airy parish that bears her name had its first home in the former Pelham Theatre, at Germantown Avenue and Cliveden Street. The parish site was moved in 1927 to the estate of Thouron Crane, in the 6400 block of Greene Street. A church/school building was dedicated in 1930. It was designed in the

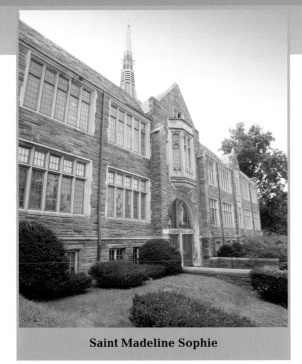

**Saint Madeline Sophie**

English Collegiate Gothic style to blend with the large houses and luxury apartment buildings of the Pelham and Upsal Gardens neighborhoods.

In 1954, the West Mount Airy Neighbors Association worked to overcome racial tensions in the neighborhood, and was a driving force in the integration of Saint Madeline Sophie School. In recent years, the parish has been home to a dynamic African American community, and prominent parishioners have included Chief Justice Robert Nix, the first African American elected to the Pennsylvania Supreme Court, and its first African American Chief Justice. However, since many members of the local community are not Catholic, parish membership has declined both at Saint Madeline Sophie and at Holy Cross. These parishes were twinned in 2000.

The parish of OUR LADY OF THE ROSARY was founded on East Haines Street—about a mile southwest of Immaculate Conception parish—in 1928, in the midst of continued growth in Germantown. The parish school was staffed by the Franciscan Missionaries of the Sacred

Heart. The same changes that affected the other Mount Airy parishes prompted the closing of Our Lady of the Rosary in 1977.

SAINT ATHANASIUS parish, in the West Oak Lane neighborhood, northeast of Germantown, was also founded in 1928, and had a temporary home in a storefront on Ogontz Avenue. A church/school building was constructed near the intersection of Limekiln Pike and Middleton Street in 1930, and the Sisters of Saint Joseph staffed the parish school. The lower portion of the present church was completed in 1943, and the large upper church was dedicated in 1955.

**Saint Athanasius**

In the late 1960s, the local population was made up predominantly of African-Americans, many of whom were not Catholic. The upper church was closed from 1973 to 1995, and the parish school was consolidated with Immaculate Conception School in 1987. Recent decades have seen a resurgence in parish life at Saint Athanasius, and each year the parish Easter Vigil witnesses the Baptism or reception into the Catholic Church of many members of the local community. Prompted by the pastor, Monsignor Herbert Bevard, parishioners have taken to honoring not only the parish's original patron, Saint Athanasius of

Alexandria (d. 373), but also Saint Athanasius Badsekukuttu, one of the 21 companions of Saint Charles Lwanga martyred in Uganda in 1886 and canonized in 1964.

The youngest parish in Mount Airy is named for SAINT RAYMOND of Peñafort, a thirteenth-century Dominican priest and canon lawyer. It was founded in early December 1941, just before the United States entered World War II, and the constraints of war-time meant that plans to build a church and school were delayed for several years. The first parish Masses were celebrated in a barn belonging to the Nolan family, non-Catholic residents of the neighborhood. The "Hatchet and Saw Club"—as parish volunteers called themselves—renovated the barn in 1942 and 1943, using lumber and supplies that were left over from army projects. The barn chapel served as both worship site and school until the parish buildings were completed in 1949. In that year, the Sisters of Mercy were invited to staff Saint Raymond School.

**Saint Raymond**

# Roxborough and Manayunk

Around the time of the founding of Philadelphia, a well-established Native American trail led northwest on the high ground above the Schuylkill River. The road became known as Ridge Road (later Ridge Avenue), and the farms and homesteads which had grown up along it were incorporated as the Township of Roxborough by 1707.

The development of dams, locks and canals by the Schuylkill Navigation Company attracted many settlers to the area during the 1820s, including many Irish immigrants. To provide for their spiritual needs, the parish of SAINT JOHN THE BAPTIST was established in 1831 on property donated by parishioner Jerome Keating. The parish school was established in the rectory in 1840, the same year that the surrounding neighborhood was incorporated as the Borough of Manayunk, distinct from Roxborough Township. Both municipalities were consolidated into the City of Philadelphia in 1854.

Immaculate Heart Sisters began teaching parish children in 1863, and a school building was erected in 1878. The present parish church was begun in 1886, with grants from parishioners Bernard McCane and Patrick Loughery, and dedicated in 1894.

In the 1840s, nearly a quarter of foreign-born inhabitants of the United States were of German origin. This number included many Catholics, and at this time about forty German-speaking families in Manayunk attended Mass at Saint John the Baptist. They might travel to Holy Trinity in Center City to attend Mass in a German-speaking community, and Saint Peter's Church on Girard Avenue sent priests once a month to hear confessions in German at Saint John's. In 1849, Manayunk German-speaking families raised funds among themselves to construct their own church,

**Saint Mary of the Assumption**

which was established as the German national parish of SAINT MARY OF THE ASSUMPTION. The church on Connaroe Street was designed to resemble the hillside churches of the parishioners' homeland; this church was enlarged in 1872 and again in 1881. The parish school, founded in 1851, received its own buildings in 1862 and 1892, and after 1868 was staffed by Franciscan Sisters from Glen Riddle.

Priests from Saint Stephen's parish in Nicetown established a mission in the neighborhood of

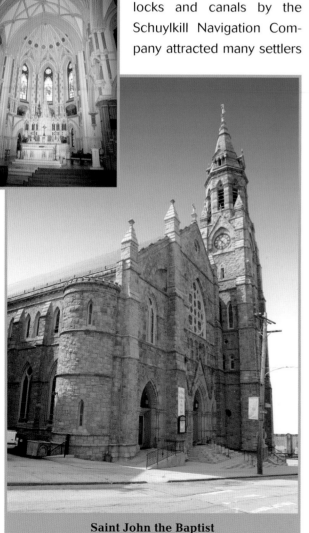

**Saint John the Baptist**

**Saint Bridget**

the Falls of Schuylkill—now East Falls—in the 1840s. They celebrated Mass for the twenty Catholic families in the area at the Village Hall, which had been used by several religious denominations; however, local residents resented its being made available to Catholics. In the summer of 1853, plans were drawn up for a new mission church, which later that year became the parish of SAINT BRIDGET. The parish was named for one of the patron saints of Ireland, the homeland of many local Catholic families. A parish school was erected in 1887, under the direction of the Sisters of Saint Joseph. The present parish church was dedicated in 1927, and a new school building opened in 1949.

Among parishioners of Saint Bridget, the most famous were the family of John B. Kelly, Sr. (1889–1960), one of the most accomplished rowers in United States history. Mr. Kelly won 126 straight single-scull races and three Olympic gold medals, and later became a leader in Philadelphia civic and political affairs, running for Mayor of Philadelphia in 1935. Mr. Kelly's daughter, Grace (1929–1982), became a famous movie actress, starring in eleven feature films and winning the Academy Award for Best Actress in 1955. In 1956, she married Prince Rainier III of Monaco, with whom she had three children, including the reigning Prince Albert II.

The Reading Railroad, developed in the 1830s, provided cheap transportation for coal and manufactured goods between Philadelphia and Reading by way of Norristown and other communities along the Schuylkill River. As the railroad developed passenger service, neighborhoods like Manayunk and Roxborough became more attractive to people who wanted to work in Center City but live outside the urban area. A growing community of Catholics in the area of North Manayunk became the first parishioners of HOLY FAMILY parish in 1885. A small chapel was soon replaced with a larger, permanent church. At its dedication in 1898, Archbishop Ryan told parishioners, "The house of the Holy Family of Nazareth was the first church; your church is for the sanctification of your parish family." Early Mass was celebrated here at 8:10 a.m.—rather than the more common 8:00—to accommodate the train schedule. Immaculate Heart Sisters opened Holy Family School in 1906, and a new building was erected in 1911.

In 1898, the year Holy Family church was dedicated, the Fourth Presbyterian Church was purchased and remodeled by the growing community of Polish Catholics in Manayunk. These immigrants had come to Philadelphia in search of the political and religious freedom they were denied in their homeland, and were attracted to Manayunk by ready employment offered by river- and canal-based industries like the Pencoyd Iron

**Holy Family**

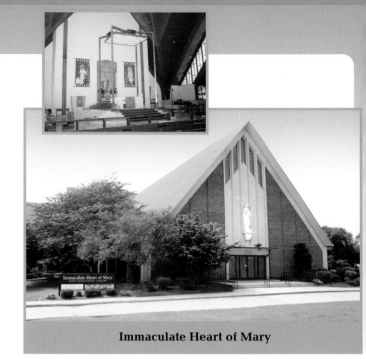

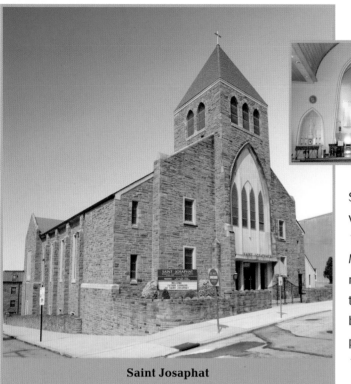

**Saint Josaphat**

Manayunk in Saint John the Baptist Church. In 1906, Father Orlando established a mission chapel at Jefferson and Price Streets in West Manayunk, at a cost of $3,000 (about $65,000 in 2005). This chapel was succeeded by the first parish church in 1927, when the parish purchased the former Mount Zion Methodist Church on Green Lane, renovating and rededicating the building as the church of SAINT LUCY. When this church became too small for an increasing parish population, the present church was built in 1967 at Smick Street and Green Lane.

**Immaculate Heart of Mary**

the new parish of the IMMACULATE HEART OF MARY experienced rapid growth, with the parish population increasing more than 10 times over in the first forty years.

Works. The people faced a six-mile journey to attend the Polish national parish of Saint Laurentius in Fishtown, and so asked for a national parish of their own. The new church at Cotton and Silverwood Streets was named for SAINT JOSAPHAT Kuncevyc, a Polish bishop and martyr of the sixteenth century who worked tirelessly to rebuild unity in the Church in Poland and Ukraine.

The parish school was founded in 1911 by Sisters of the Holy Family of Nazareth, and expanded in 1927. A new parish church was begun in 1956 and dedicated in 1958. The parish now has territorial boundaries, but Mass is still celebrated in Polish on Sundays and holy days of obligation.

In 1905, Father Antonio Orlando began celebrating Mass and the sacraments for the Italian immigrants of Roxborough and

When the Henry Howard Houston estate was subdivided for housing in the 1950s, the area of Andorra, at the northwest end of Roxborough, was almost entirely open country. Some questioned the need to establish a new parish from the territory of Holy Family for the 250 families who lived in Andorra. However,

The first Masses in Immaculate Heart of Mary parish were celebrated in a former public school building near the parish property on Cathedral Road. A church/school building was built in 1953, and Sisters of Saint Joseph were invited to staff the school. The present parish church was dedicated in 1965.

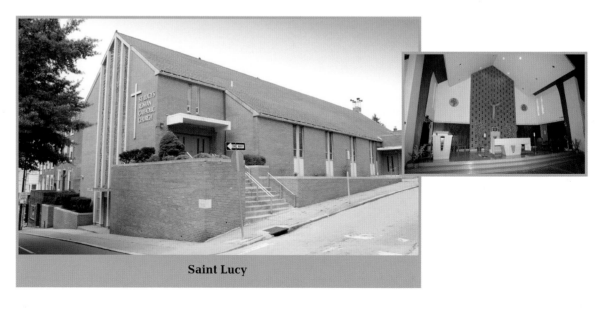

**Saint Lucy**

# Kensington

When Philadelphia merchant Anthony Palmer laid out the district of Kensington in the 1730s, this area along the Delaware River north of the city limits was an attractive alternative to crowded conditions in Center City. Part of the "liberty lands" established by William Penn, Kensington and Northern Liberties fell outside the jurisdiction of city authorities prior to 1854. Palmer sold lots along the river to Philadelphia shipbuilders seeking to expand their businesses, and residences grew up alongside the shipbuilding industry. By the 1820s, Kensington had become a center of manufacturing and shipping, and many immigrants, especially Irish, were attracted to the

Saint Michael

area by the ready availability of jobs in factories and on the wharves.

The parish of SAINT MICHAEL was founded at Second and Jefferson Streets in 1831—the first Philadelphia County parish outside the original city limits. Trustees of the parish mortgaged their own homes to secure funds for the building of the first church, dedicated in 1834. As in many churches of the time, parishioners paid a bi-annual pew rent of $2.50 (about $48.00 in 2005). The Catholic population of the area grew steadily with the arrival of numerous Irish immigrants in the 1840s, and the parish established a mission chapel, Saint Stephen's in Nicetown, in 1844. The Sisters of Charity of the Blessed Virgin Mary were founded in the parish in 1833 by Mary Frances Clarke and the pastor, Father Terence Donaghoe. These Sisters operated a private school here until 1843, when their congregation moved to Dubuque, Iowa. Sisters of Saint Joseph arrived in 1859 to staff the parish school.

In 1844, growing suspicion of Catholic immigrants and the controversy over the opposition by Catholics to reading the King James Version of the Bible in public schools combined to spark violent reactions against Catholic people and institutions in Philadelphia. Rallies in Kensington, organized by the Native American Party over several days in early May, erupted in violence, and Saint Michael's church, rectory and convent were destroyed by fire on May 8.

A new church was dedicated in 1847, after the parish successfully sued the County of Philadelphia for damages. The lawsuit—which highlighted the county's inability to stop the violence—was a driving force behind the decision to consolidate the many municipalities of Philadelphia County under one city government. The Act of Consolidation of 1854 made the City of Philadelphia coterminous with Philadelphia County.

The church of SAINT PETER THE APOSTLE was founded at Fifth Street and Girard Avenue in 1842. Redemptorist priests served the German-speaking immigrants of the neighborhood, who found the trip to Holy Trinity in Center City difficult. The red brick church, constructed in 1842, was paid off in only five years thanks to the industriousness and generosity of parishioners. In the early 1900s the church was refaced with granite, as it appears today.

Saint Peter the Apostle

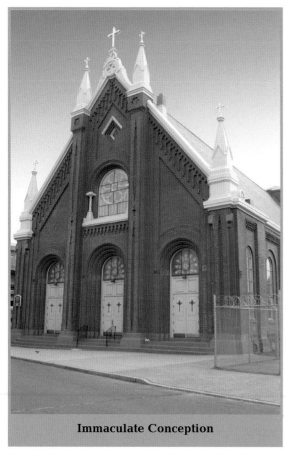

**Immaculate Conception**

The parish school was staffed by School Sisters of Notre Dame, who also taught German-speaking children at Holy Trinity.

A Redemptorist priest, Father John Nepomucene Neumann, was appointed Bishop of Philadelphia in 1852. When Bishop Neumann died in 1860, his successor, Bishop Wood, honored his request to be buried in his Congregation's church of Saint Peter. Bishop Neumann was beatified in 1963, and canonized in 1977. His remains, clothed in a bishop's vestments, now rest in a crystal casket under the altar in Saint Peter's lower church. The Redemptorists welcome thousands of pilgrims every year to this shrine and museum dedicated to Philadelphia's "Little Bishop." The priests here also minister to the local community, where the predominant language is no longer German, but Spanish.

In 1869, as the Kensington area continued to develop, a new chapel was built to serve the neighborhood between Saint Michael's and Saint Augustine's. Named for the IMMACULATE CONCEPTION of the Blessed Virgin Mary, the chapel was succeeded by a larger church at Front and Allen Streets, dedicated in 1872. The original chapel was converted to a school, which opened in 1880 and was staffed by Sisters of Saint Joseph. The church was renovated in 1895, and again in 1907. The development of Interstate 95 in the 1960s displaced many parishioners. Consequently, faced with declining school enrollment and parish membership, Immaculate Conception School closed in 1976, and the parish was twinned with Saint Michael's in 2000.

As Polish immigrants moved to the Fishtown neighborhood in the 1870s and 1880s, they desired a parish where the priests could preach and provide pastoral care in their own language. The congregation first gathered in 1882 in Friendship Hall, at Norris and Sepviva Streets. By 1885, parishioners had built a lower church at Berks and Memphis Streets. Originally called Holy Cross, the church was soon renamed for the 14th-century Polish priest SAINT LAURENTIUS. The parish school, staffed by Felician Sisters, opened in 1888. The upper church was dedicated in 1890.

In October 1899, a vacant store at 3018 Kensington Avenue was the site of the first Mass celebrated in the parish of the ASCENSION OF OUR LORD. Ground was broken for a church/school building at Westmoreland and F Streets in 1899, and the parish school opened in the following year. Sisters of Saint Joseph composed the founding faculty. Mass was celebrated in this building until the completion of the lower church in 1914. The upper church was dedicated in 1928. Presently, the parish is home to a significant number of parishioners of Hispanic origin, and Masses are offered in English and in Spanish.

In 1905, the first building of the parish of the HOLY NAME OF JESUS was built at 1832 Frankford Avenue. The first floor of the building

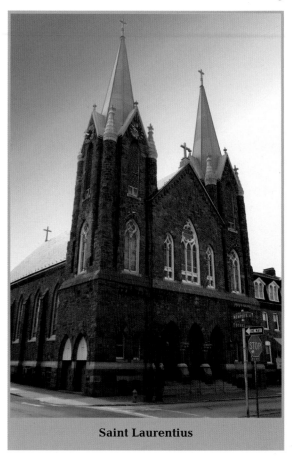

**Saint Laurentius**

**Ascension of Our Lord**

**Saint Agnes—Saint John Nepomucene**

different regions of Slovakia, prompted the community to seek a national parish in their Kensington neighborhood. The parish of SAINT AGNES was established at Fourth and Brown Streets in 1907, and grew steadily until the late 1930s. The parish school was established under the Sisters of Saints Cyril and Methodius in 1926. In 1980, the two Philadelphia Slovak parishes were consolidated to form SAINT AGNES—SAINT JOHN NEPOMUCENE parish at Fourth and Brown Streets.

Religious oppression also led many Hungarian Catholics to emigrate to the United States, and in 1913 the parish of the SACRED HEART was founded at Mascher and Master Streets as a national parish for this community. Most Hungarian-speaking families moved out of the neighborhood in the mid-twentieth century, and the parish was closed in 1977.

was a chapel. The upper floors housed the parish school, conducted by Immaculate Heart Sisters since 1907. Ground was broken in 1906 for a new church and school at Gaul and Hewson Streets, and the present church was dedicated in 1923. In 1912, the parish was entrusted to Dominican priests, who staffed the parish until 1998. In that year, an archdiocesan priest was assigned to Holy Name.

In the early twentieth century, Catholics in the Eastern European nation of Slovakia were oppressed by the rulers of the Kingdom of Hungary, who tried to assimilate the Slovaks into the larger population. By 1914, over half a million Slovaks—one-fifth of the entire population—had emigrated to the United States. Those who settled in the Kensington area traveled south for Mass to Saint John Nepomucene Church, but the long distance, combined with tensions between groups from

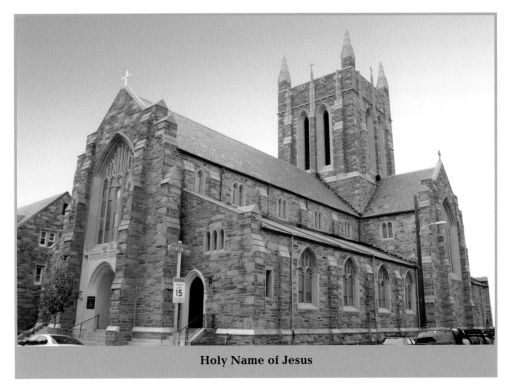

**Holy Name of Jesus**

# Frankford, Bridesburg and Port Richmond

The area northeast of Kensington along the Delaware River was the site of several small municipalities before the Act of Consolidation in 1854. The Borough of Frankford, the Borough of Bridesburg, and the Richmond District were largely settled by German farmers. However, the development of industry and commerce along the river attracted many immigrants throughout the second half of the nineteenth century.

A number of Irish immigrants, who had found work on the coal wharves along the Schuylkill River, moved to Port Richmond in the early 1840s. Their parish priests at Saint Patrick's established a mission chapel here in 1842, but the five-mile distance between the two churches made this arrangement impractical. A new parish was established in 1845, and was named in honor of SAINT ANNE, the mother of the Blessed Virgin Mary. Napoleon LeBrun, the architect of the Cathedral, designed the church, dedicated in 1846. The parish school opened

in 1855 under the direction of Sisters of Saint Joseph, and numbers three former United States Congressmen among its alumni. Parishioners dug the foundation of a new church, dedicated in 1870. Since 1928, this church has been the site of an annual novena in honor of Saint Anne, celebrated on the nine days preceding her feast day, July 26. A relic of Saint Anne is venerated at the novena, and housed in a reliquary crafted from gold jewelry donated by parishioners.

In Frankford, about three miles northeast of Saint Anne's, a second parish was founded in 1845, named for SAINT JOACHIM, the husband of Saint Anne and father of the Blessed Virgin Mary. Founded from territory belonging to Saint Michael's and Saint Stephen's, the original boundaries of the parish stretched well beyond the boundaries of Philadelphia County, as far as Cornwells Heights to the north, and Jenkintown and Fox Chase to the northwest. The first parish church was dedicated in 1845, and enlarged in the 1870s. The parish school was founded by Immaculate Heart Sisters in 1864. Following a fire in 1979, the present church was dedicated in 1981. The parish is entrusted to the care of the Oblates of Saint Francis de Sales.

The area of Port Richmond and Bridesburg was home to many German Catholics in the nineteenth century, and several parishes in the neighborhood began as missions to the German-speaking community. The first church of ALL SAINTS, on Buckius Street in Bridesburg, was built in 1860. Another church was built in 1889 and dedicated in 1903; a steeple was added in 1954. The parish school welcomed its first students in 1864, staffed by the Franciscan Sisters of Glen Riddle, and a new building was constructed in 1922.

**Saint Joachim**

In 1877, Redemptorist priests from Saint Boniface parish, which had been established ten years earlier, saw to the construction of a school for German children in Port Richmond, staffed by Sisters of Christian Charity. In 1882, the Redemptorists established the mission chapel of the NATIVITY OF THE BLESSED VIRGIN MARY at Belgrade Street and

**Saint Anne**

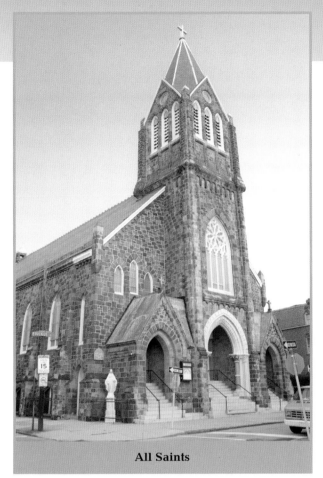

**All Saints**

roughly the amount the German parishioners had contributed in the first years of Nativity's existence. A frame chapel at Allegheny Avenue and Gaul Street was built in 1885, and had room in the rear of the building for a parish school, staffed by Sisters of Christian Charity. This church attracted additional German

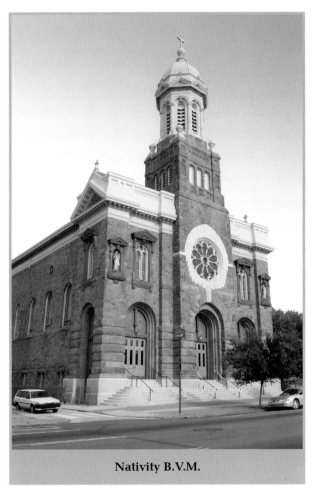

**Nativity B.V.M.**

completed in 1898, and the upper church was dedicated in 1905. Restrictions placed on Catholics in the Prussian sector of Poland in the 1870s led many of them to emigrate to the United States. The 90 Polish families who had settled in Bridesburg by 1890 traveled by horse-drawn trolley to Saint Laurentius in Fishtown, until a new national parish was established in Bridesburg in 1892. The original chapel of All Saints parish, built in 1860 at Edgemont and Buckius Streets, was the first worship site for parishioners of SAINT JOHN

Allegheny Avenue. The parish population soon changed from German to predominantly Irish, however, and an archdiocesan priest, Father Francis Quinn, was given charge of the parish in 1885. In that year, parishioners helped build a new parish church, dedicated in 1891, and Sisters of Saint Joseph arrived to staff the school. A storm knocked down the original church in 1893, and the present church was built in 1896.

As the German population of Nativity B.V.M. was outnumbered by their Irish neighbors, a new German national parish, OUR LADY HELP OF CHRISTIANS, was founded in 1885. Nativity B.V.M. donated $10,000 to the new parish (about $217,000 in 2005 values)—

families to the area, and in 1887, the growing community erected a church/school building at Allegheny Avenue and Chatham Street. The lower portion of the present church was

**Our Lady Help of Christians**

CANTIUS, until a church/school building was constructed in 1893. Sisters of the Holy Family of Nazareth arrived in 1911 to assume responsibility for the parish school. The present church was dedicated in 1899.

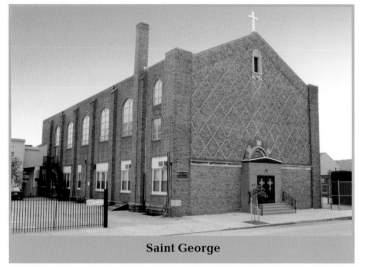
**Saint George**

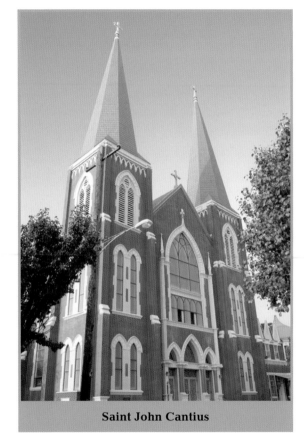
**Saint John Cantius**

Poverty in their homeland led many Lithuanians to emigrate in the 1890s. Before the national parish of SAINT GEORGE was founded in Port Richmond in 1902, the Lithuanian community faced a long journey to Saint Casimir in South Philadelphia. The parish church was built in 1902 on Venango Street, and the parish school opened its doors in 1910, with classes conducted in the rectory. A church/school building was dedicated in the early 1920s, and in 1923 Sisters of Saint Francis of the Providence of God were invited to teach in the school.

The intersection of Allegheny Avenue and Richmond Street was the center of Polish settlement in Port Richmond; consequently, the parish of SAINT ADALBERT was founded on Allegheny Avenue in 1904. The first Masses were celebrated in a classroom of Our Lady Help of Christians School, until a church/school

**Saint Adalbert**

building was built in 1905. A large parish church was dedicated in 1909. Sisters of the Holy Family of Nazareth were the founding faculty of the parish school, enlarged in 1923 and 1954.

In 1908, Italian immigrants in Frankford petitioned for a national parish in their neighborhood, and in that year the mission chapel of Saint Peter—later renamed Saint Rocco—was constructed. When the chapel was dedicated in 1911, the mission was established as a parish, and the name was changed to MATER DOLOROSA (Latin for "Sorrowful Mother"). The parish church, on Ruan Street, was dedicated in 1914. The parish school, founded in 1926 on Paul Street, moved

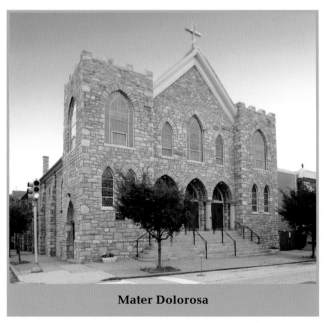
**Mater Dolorosa**

to a new building in 1960. The Franciscan Missionaries of the Sacred Heart staffed the school in the 1940s, and were succeeded by the Immaculate Heart Sisters in 1970.

In 1919, a Chinese laundry on Frankford Avenue became the rectory and chapel for a new parish in the Harrowgate neighborhood. The founding pastor, Monsignor Edward Hawks, had served as a chaplain in World War I, and he named the parish after SAINT JOAN OF ARC, the young French woman who led the army of King Charles VII to victory during the Hundred Years' War. The parish school began in 1920 in a former blacksmith shop, and was administered by Immaculate Heart Sisters. A church/school building was dedicated in 1922.

The Italian national parish of MOTHER OF DIVINE GRACE, founded in Port Richmond in 1926, actually had its first home in a hall belonging to an Irish association—the Ancient Order of Hibernians—at Cambria and Thompson Streets. A church/school building opened in 1947, staffed by Holy Trinity Sisters. A new church was dedicated in 1951, and a new school building in 1964.

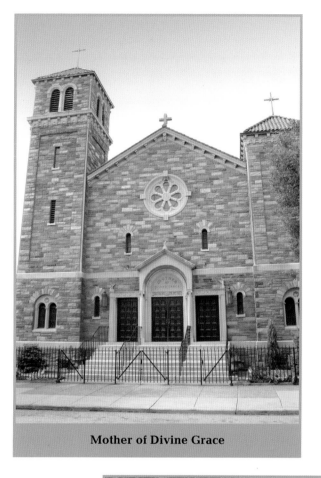
**Mother of Divine Grace**

About 200 Catholics lived in the neighborhood of Juniata Park in 1927, when the boundaries of Saint Joachim, Saint Joan of Arc and Ascension parishes were adjusted to form another parish. The first pastor, Father Martin Lynch, was appointed on December 28, 1927, and named the parish HOLY INNOCENTS, after the feast celebrated on that date. To save parish funds during the Great Depression, Father Lynch did not draw a salary from the parish.

Sunday Mass was celebrated at Northeast Catholic High School until a chapel was built in 1928, using beams from the decommissioned chapel of the Hog Island naval shipyard. The school, staffed by Immaculate Heart Sisters, began in 1929; it now serves as a regional school for several parishes. The present church was dedicated in 1958, and today serves a diverse community, including African American, Hispanic and Vietnamese families.

**Saint Joan of Arc**

**Holy Innocents**

149

# Northeast Philadelphia

The farming village of Tacony was situated about 10 miles northeast of Center City along the Delaware River, and between Frankford and Holmesburg. Tacony was sparsely populated until the 1840s, at which time the Philadelphia and Trenton Railroad was built. The railroad was denied permission to run trains into the city, and inbound passengers were forced to disembark at Tacony and continue their journey to Philadelphia by boat. Several inns grew up around the railroad terminus, and became the center of the new community.

In 1855, the pastors of the German parishes of Holy Trinity and Saint Peter formed the Saint Vincent's Orphan Society, with the goal of

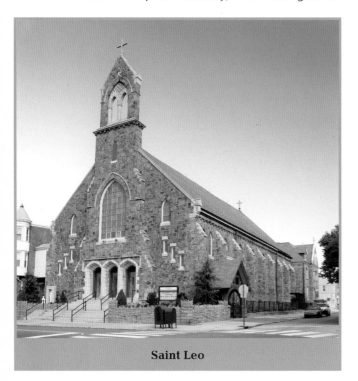

Saint Leo

building in Tacony a home for German-speaking orphans. To raise money for construction and operation of Saint Vincent's orphanage, the two pastors subdivided the land around it for residential development. Catholic residents of the district gathered for Mass in the chapel of the orphanage.

In the early 1860s, the tool manufacturing plant built by Henry Disston attracted large numbers of newly-arrived Irish families to the Tacony area, and Saint Vincent's chapel was no longer of adequate size. As a result, in 1884 a new parish was established at a social hall on State Road. Construction on the parish church began the following year, on lots purchased from Mrs. Mary Disston for $1,500 (about $32,500 in 2005). The church was named for SAINT LEO the Great, pope from 440 to 461, and patron saint of Leo XIII, pope in 1894. Work on the upper church was undertaken from 1892 to 1894, with the assistance of inmates of Holmesburg Prison. The parish school was opened in 1906, and entrusted to Sisters of Saint Joseph.

Most of the parishes in this region of Northeast Philadelphia were established after World War I, when convenient rail and trolley transportation to and from Center City attracted urban residents to undeveloped areas of the city. In 1911, the parish of SAINT CECILIA was founded in the Fox Chase section of the city adjoining Montgomery County. Large estates that had been built here in the late 1800s were sub-

Saint Cecilia

divided for residential development, which was spurred by the construction of the Fox Chase station on the Pennsylvania Railroad line running toward Newtown. The parish school began in 1912 as a Sunday school conducted by Immaculate Heart Sisters. The first school building was built in 1924, with additions made in 1965, 1971 and 1990. The present church was dedicated in 1955.

As early as 1914, Italian immigrants in Tacony—many of whom hailed from the town of Cosenza in Calabria—met in the chapel at Saint Vincent's Orphanage. Father Cosmas Bruni, resident at Mater Dolorosa church in Frankford, preached and heard confessions in their native tongue. In 1917, the national parish of OUR LADY OF CONSOLATION was founded, and a church built at Wellington and Edmund Streets. A new church/school building was opened at Princeton and Edmund Streets in 1928, and

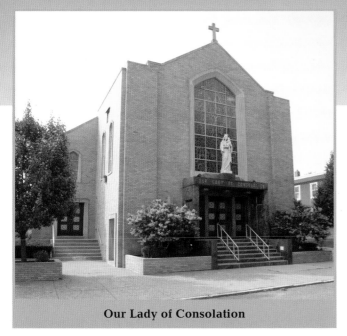

**Our Lady of Consolation**

Franciscan Sisters from Glen Riddle staffed the school. The present church, on Tulip Street, was dedicated in 1956.

The Elite Moving Picture Theatre on Torresdale Avenue was the site of the first Mass celebrated in SAINT BARTHOLOMEW parish, founded in the Wissinoming district in 1919. The parish school, which had a chapel on the ground floor, opened in 1920, and the following year Sisters of Saint Joseph took charge of the school. A new church was dedicated in 1956. The structure, built of Mount Airy granite, is one of the largest churches in the archdiocese.

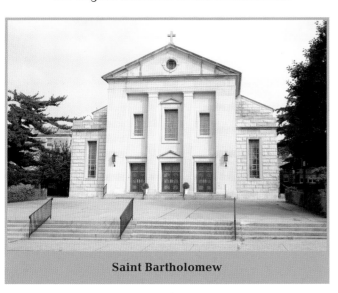

**Saint Bartholomew**

In 1920, the parish of SAINT WILLIAM of Vercelli was founded to serve Lawndale and Crescentville, west of Roosevelt Boulevard. The area was sparsely populated, and some questioned the wisdom of establishing a parish. The small parish community met at the Germania Mannechor on Devereaux Avenue until the parish church and school were opened in 1924. Immaculate Heart Sisters arrived in that year to teach the children of the parish. The construction of new housing along the Newtown Railroad Line (today, SEPTA's R8-Fox Chase Regional Rail Line) steadily increased the parish population after World War II. A lower church was constructed in 1956, and the upper church was completed and dedicated in 1963.

North of Saint William's, the neighborhood adjacent to Oxford Circle developed in a similar manner. In 1923, one of the local home builders, Mr. Matthew Best, offered his home for the celebration of Mass in what was now SAINT MARTIN OF TOURS parish. A church/school building along Roosevelt Boulevard was dedicated in 1928, and the school was staffed by the Immaculate Heart Sisters. The present parish church was constructed from 1947 to 1954. The congregation saw a notable increase after World War II, and by 1963 the parish served more than 15,000 people.

In the early years of the twentieth century, the neighborhood of Mayfair was chiefly inhabited by farmers of German descent. Catholics in the area met at "Mommy" McGraw's farm in 1924

**Saint William**

to found the national parish of SAINT HUBERT. The parish school opened in 1928, administered by Franciscan Sisters from Glen Riddle.

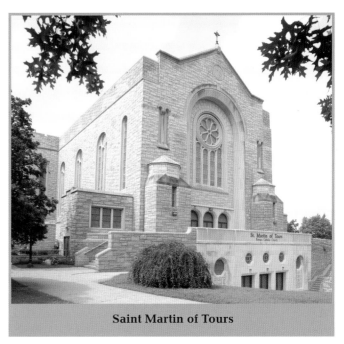

**Saint Martin of Tours**

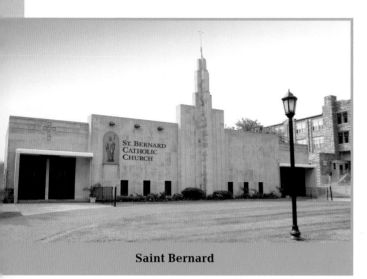

**Saint Bernard**

Mayfair was experiencing rapid development, spurred on by the completion in 1922 of the Market-Frankford elevated line. The parish of SAINT BERNARD was established nearby, in what had been largely farmland between Holmesburg and Tacony. Mass was celebrated in the rectory at Cottage and Saint Vincent Streets until a church/school building was available in 1929. A new church would be dedicated in 1952, although plans for an upper church were never realized.

Saint Bernard School was founded by Sisters of Saint Joseph in 1929. At this time, the pastor, Father Holahan, insisted that non-German-speaking children in the parish attend Saint Bernard's School rather than Saint Hubert's. This fact decimated the enrollment of Saint Hubert's School, and the small number of German-speaking families found it difficult to support the parish, especially during the Great Depression. Saint Hubert's parish was officially suppressed in 1940, and the parish buildings were used for a newly-founded high school for girls, which retained the parish name.

The influx of Catholic families after the completion of the Market-Frankford line prompted the foundation of three more parishes. The parishioners of SAINT MATTHEW parish initially gathered for Mass in a building obtained from the recently-decommissioned naval shipyard on Hog Island. This chapel served until the construction of the lower parish church in 1942, on Cottman Avenue east of the Roosevelt Boulevard. The upper church was dedicated in 1960. Immaculate Heart Sisters founded the parish school in 1937, and the school was enlarged in 1948 and 1962.

In 1928, SAINT TIMOTHY parish was established among the farms and new homes of Lower Mayfair, and the first Masses were celebrated in a store at Barnett and Sackett Streets. A chapel and school were opened in 1930, and Sisters of Saint Joseph took

**Saint Matthew**

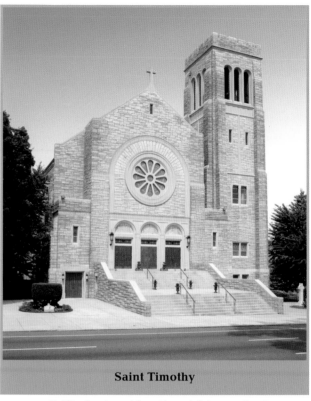

**Saint Timothy**

responsibility for teaching the children. As the parish developed, a lower church was built in 1948 on Levick Street, a main thoroughfare between Frankford Avenue and the Tacony-Palmyra Bridge. The upper church was dedicated in 1952, and the school was enlarged in 1954 and 1960.

When the parish of the RESURRECTION OF OUR LORD was founded in 1928, in the Rhawnhurst neighborhood, across the Roosevelt Boulevard west of Mayfair, a single trolley line ran through the neighborhood of farms along Castor Avenue. The first rectory, which included a chapel, was established in a home in the 2000 block of Bleigh Street, near the side track where outbound trolleys pulled off to allow inbound trolleys to pass. A church/school building was completed in 1929, just

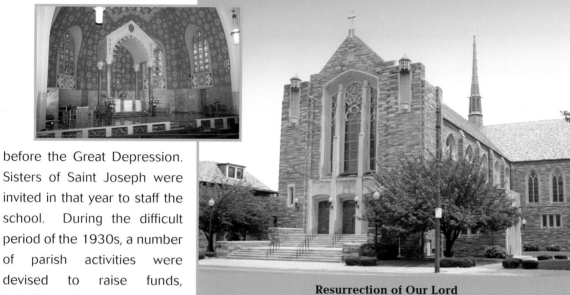

**Resurrection of Our Lord**

before the Great Depression. Sisters of Saint Joseph were invited in that year to staff the school. During the difficult period of the 1930s, a number of parish activities were devised to raise funds, including roller skating parties, fashion shows and frog races. In 1958, the present parish church was dedicated at the corner of Castor Avenue and Vista Street.

The last parish in the archdiocese founded during the Marian Year 1954 was OUR LADY OF RANSOM, established along the Roosevelt Boulevard in the Castor Gardens neighborhood between the parishes of Saint Martin of Tours and Resurrection of Our Lord. Father Paul Larkin celebrated Mass in the Castor Theater until a church/school building was erected in 1955. Immaculate Heart Sisters founded the parish school. Parish boundaries were adjusted in 1961 to include about 200 families from Saint Timothy parish, and the larger congregation celebrated the dedication of the parish church in 1967.

**Our Lady of Ransom**

# Far Northeast Philadelphia

When Philadelphia and Bristol were established in the early 1680s, a well-worn Native American footpath that paralleled the Delaware River became the route of travel between them. Over the next few decades, a road was created and improved with public funds and called the "King's Highway." This road permitted easy travel for government officials and others between Philadelphia and other Middle Atlantic and New England colonies. After the American Revolution, the road was renamed the "Bristol Turnpike," and later, in Philadelphia, "Frankford Avenue."

A stone bridge was built by the colonial government where the King's Highway crossed Pennypack Creek. As stagecoach travel along the road increased in the early 1800s, the bridge was a logical stopping-off point, and a toll house and several taverns were built in the area. John and George Holme bought large tracts of land and subdivided them for farms and residential tracts. The area became known as Holmesburg and developed rapidly in the first half of the nineteenth century.

Bishop Kenrick founded the first parish in Holmesburg in 1849, at the same time that other parishes were being established outside the original borders of the City of Philadelphia. Father John Dominic Berrill, O.P., a Dominican priest serving at Old Saint Mary's, named the new parish SAINT DOMINIC, after the patron and founder of his Congregation. Mass was celebrated in a little stone house until the first

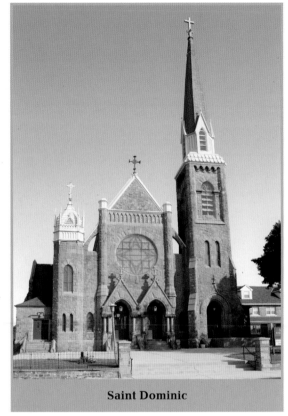

**Saint Dominic**

parish church was dedicated in 1850. This church was destroyed by fire in 1896, and the present church (enlarged in 1957) was dedicated the following year. The parish school, founded in 1874, was entrusted to Immaculate Heart Sisters in 1884, and moved to a new building in 1892.

After Father Berrill was transferred to Saint Stephen's in 1855, the pastors of Saint Dominic's were diocesan priests. The fifth pastor, Father James O'Connor, appointed in 1872, became the spiritual advisor and friend of Katharine Drexel, whose family owned an estate in Torresdale, a short distance away. Father O'Connor was named the Vicar

Apostolic of Nebraska in 1876, and later became the first Bishop of Omaha. There he became familiar with the plight of Native Americans confined to reservations in the Plains states. He shared his concerns with Katharine Drexel, and encouraged her to found the Sisters of the Blessed Sacrament, dedicated to service among African American and Native American communities.

Saint Dominic's was the only parish in the farther northeastern part of the County—and, after 1854, the City—of Philadelphia. In the middle of the century, Mr. John Williams established a calico-printing fabric mill among the farmlands along Pennypack Creek in the Bustleton neighborhood. To work the mill, he brought Irish immigrants with him from Holmesburg. These Catholic families invited priests from Saint Joachim in Frankford to come to Bustleton for Sunday Mass, and Mr. Williams allowed them to use the mill's engraving room as a worship site.

This little mission was the beginning of the parish of the MATERNITY OF THE BLESSED VIRGIN MARY, founded in 1870 on a plot of land donated by Mr. Williams. When the work day was over, the mill workers volunteered their labor to build a small stone chapel, dedicated in December of that year on Bustleton Avenue. A new school building, containing a chapel as well, was dedicated in 1949, and Sisters of Mercy arrived to staff the school. The present church was dedicated in 1964.

**Maternity B.V.M.**

**Saint Christopher**

Mrs. Louise Drexel Morrell. To show his gratitude to Mrs. Morrell—and to honor her sister, Mother Katharine Drexel—Father James Coakley, the founding pastor, chose to spell the name of the new parish with a "K" rather than with a "C".

In June 1922, Cardinal Dougherty established the parish of SAINT KATHERINE OF SIENA at the midpoint between the parishes of Saint Charles Borromeo, Bensalem, and Saint Dominic, Philadelphia. All three parishes are located along the historic Bristol Pike/ Frankford Avenue. For six months, Masses were celebrated in a chapel in the home of

On December 10, 1922, Father Coakley celebrated the first Masses on Saint Katherine's parish property in the combination church/rectory. With founding families numbering fewer than 90, finances were such that Mass was often celebrated by candlelight. However, by the early 1950s, the growth rate of the parish population was notable, and in 1956 the cornerstone of the present church was blessed. Prominent parishioners of Saint Katherine's have included William Green, Mayor of Philadelphia from 1980 to 1984, and Robert Borski, who represented the Third Congressional District in the United States Congress from 1983 to 2004.

An additional six parishes were founded in Far Northeast Philadelphia between 1950 and 1966. Father Christopher Purcell was assigned to found a new parish in the Somerton neighborhood in 1950, and he asked that it be named for his

patron, SAINT CHRISTOPHER. The parish boundaries take in portions of the City of Philadelphia, Huntingdon Valley in Montgomery County, and Feasterville and Trevose in Bucks County. The parish church and school were built on property donated by the Trainer family, whose home in the parish has been converted into the Cranaleith spirituality center, operated by the Sisters of Mercy. These Sisters also founded the parish school in 1953.

The parish of SAINT JEROME was formed from the southwestern area of Saint Katherine parish and near Holme Circle. The first Masses were celebrated in Saint Margaret Vocational School—presently the site of Immaculate Mary Nursing Home—until the parish school building was erected in 1957. For about a year, parishioners gathered for Mass in the school— staffed by Sisters of Saint Joseph—until the parish church was dedicated in 1958.

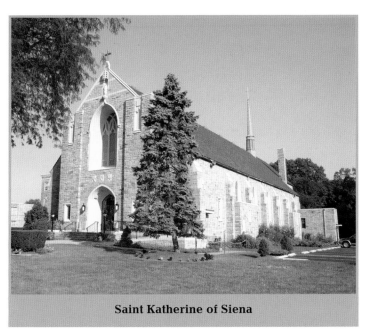
**Saint Katherine of Siena**

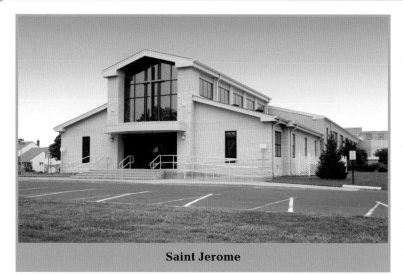

**Saint Jerome**

In 1922, Saint Michael's Mission was established for Polish-speaking Catholics. It was served by priests from Saint John Cantius Church in Bridesburg, who celebrated Mass in the Shrine of the True Cross, on the Drexel family estate on Knights Road. In 1958, this chapel was the site of the first Masses celebrated for the new parish of OUR LADY OF CALVARY. The parish church was constructed in 1960, the same year that the parish school opened under the supervision of the Sisters of the Holy Family of Nazareth. A new school was built in 1964.

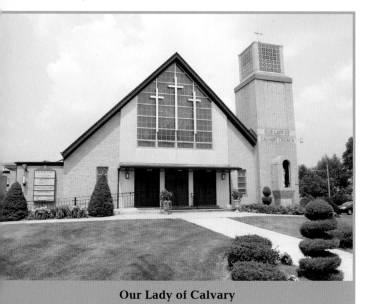

**Our Lady of Calvary**

The original plans for Our Lady of Calvary Church accommodated the 800 families who lived in the community in 1958, but within a few years the Catholic population numbered more than 2,000 families, and in the early 1960s the parish area was divided several times. In 1962, the parish of SAINT ANSELM was founded in the neighborhood of Parkwood Manor. The first Masses were celebrated in a chapel in the rectory, a rowhouse on Chilton Road. A church/school building was dedicated in 1964, and the school was entrusted to the Immaculate Heart Sisters.

In 1963, CHRIST THE KING parish was founded on Chesterfield Road, in the neighborhood of Morrell Park (the former Morrell estate)— roughly the center of existing parishes of the Far Northeast. The first Masses were celebrated in the chapel of the novitiate of the Sisters of the Blessed Sacrament, and in 1964 ground was broken for a church/school building. The school was entrusted to Sisters of Saint Joseph.

While the church and school of Christ the King were under construction, Father Arthur Woods, the founding pastor, lived at Saint Katherine of Siena rectory. Not to impose on his hosts, Father Woods conducted parish business from an outdoor pay phone in a local

shopping center. A parishioner, Mrs. Kathleen Sacks, noticed him doing this, and invited Father Woods to use her home phone as often as he needed to. When the rectory was completed in 1966, Mrs. Sacks became the first parish secretary.

As the population continued to grow, the parish of SAINT MARTHA was established between Christ the King and Saint Anselm parishes, with families and territory also taken from Our Lady of Calvary. At first, the new community gathered for Mass in the lower church of Saint Anselm.

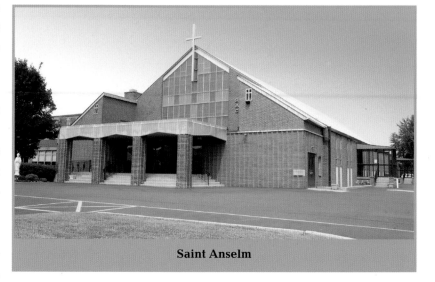

**Saint Anselm**

Later they used the auditorium of Archbishop Ryan High School, located nearby. The parish church was dedicated in 1967, and the parish school opened the same year, staffed by Sisters of Mercy. Franciscan priests from Archbishop Ryan staffed the parish from 1996 to 2002, when an archdiocesan priest was again assigned as pastor.

**Christ the King**

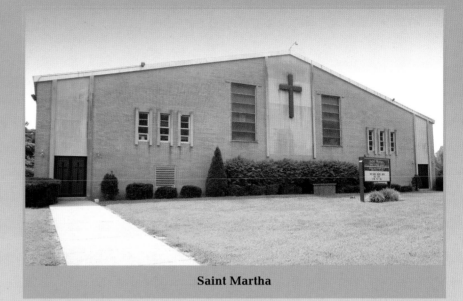

**Saint Martha**

# Fairmount and Spring Garden

One of the earliest maps of the City of Philadelphia—drawn by surveyor Thomas Holme in 1681—shows the grid of streets laid out by William Penn, and a hill along the Schuylkill River to the northwest of the city was labeled "Faire Mount." Also known as Morris's Hill, it became the site of the city's water works and reservoir, and is presently the site of the Philadelphia Museum of Art. This hill also gave its name to the 4,000-acre Fairmount Park, and to the neighborhood adjoining the park to the east, north of Spring Garden Street.

As the Schuylkill Canal brought coal from upstate regions to Philadelphia, large numbers of Irish immigrants settled in Fairmount, attracted by employment opportunities on the wharves. These new Catholic residents traveled in-town to Saint John the Evangelist parish, or to Saint John the Baptist in Manayunk, further up the Schuylkill River. In May 1839, a meeting was held at Saint John the Evangelist Church to discuss plans for a parish in Fairmount. Named for the patron saint of Bishop Francis Patrick Kenrick, the first church of SAINT FRANCIS XAVIER was built at 25th and Biddle Streets in 1839. The first pastor, Father Michael O'Connor, had also been a rector of Saint Charles Borromeo Seminary, and in 1843 would be appointed first Bishop of Pittsburgh. Saint Francis Xavier was the only church in Philadelphia County to celebrate public Mass during the Nativist riots in May, 1844.

In 1894, the Baltimore and Ohio Railroad was

blasting a tunnel near the church, and the explosion cracked the foundation. The damage led to repeated flooding and other problems, and necessitated the demolition of the church. The present church was begun in 1894 by architect Edwin Forrest Durang, who designed many Catholic churches within the city and beyond. The church stands at the corner of 24th and Green Streets, across from the site of the original parish school, built in 1880. Classes had begun in a room under the church in 1845, directed by lay men from the parish;

**Saint Francis Xavier**

the Immaculate Heart Sisters assumed responsibility for the school in 1869. Saint Francis Xavier parish is entrusted to the Congregation of the Oratory of Saint Philip Neri. The Philadelphia Oratory was founded here as an archdiocesan congregation in 1990, and established as an autonomous Congregation of Pontifical Right in 2000.

When Father Charles I.H. Carter, pastor of Saint Mary's, was directed to establish a parish in the area north of Saint John the Evangelist in 1847, the community was still feeling the effects of the Nativist riots which had begun in 1844. The plot of land Father Carter had chosen on Spring Garden Street, east of Twelfth Street, was owned by a Mrs. Russell, known to be unsympathetic to Catholics. Father Carter sought the assistance of Walter Patterson, a recent convert to Catholicism, who purchased the lot from Mrs. Russell on Father Carter's behalf without telling her the purpose for which it would be used. It was here that the church of the ASSUMPTION OF THE BLESSED VIRGIN

MARY was dedicated in 1849. Once the parish debt had been cleared, the church was formally consecrated by Saint John Neumann in 1859.

The parish school was begun in 1852, and a new building erected in 1886. During these years the school and convent would be home to a number of religious communities: School Sisters of Notre Dame, Sisters of Mercy, and Sisters of the Holy Child Jesus. All had their first foundations in the City of Philadelphia at Assumption B.V.M. School. Saint Katharine Drexel was baptized in the parish church in 1858, and Saint John Neumann administered the Sacrament of Confirmation here twice, in 1856 and 1859. Several factors, including a decline in the Catholic population of the area, prompted the closing of Assumption B.V.M. parish in 1995.

After 1855, all of the parishes founded in the Fairmount and Spring Garden area were national parishes for specific ethnic groups. In the second half of the nineteenth century, the area along the Schuylkill north of Fairmount was also the site of more than a dozen breweries. Although all of them were closed by the 1940s, the neighborhood is still known as Brewerytown, and at the turn of the century was home to a large population of German immigrants, who attended Mass and school at Saint Elizabeth's at 23rd and Berks Streets. This journey was difficult in inclement weather, especially for school children. In 1891, the German national parish of SAINT LUDWIG was established, and a church dedicated at 28th and Master Streets. Named for the patron saint of Ludwig Windthorst, M.D., a parishioner and benefactor, a new church was begun in 1901 and dedicated in 1908. The parish school was also founded in 1891, and staffed by Franciscan Sisters from Glen Riddle. By the 1960s and 1970s most descendants of early German-speaking Catholics had moved to other areas, and Saint Ludwig's parish was suppressed in 1975.

A large influx of Polish immigrants to the Callowhill Street area of Spring Garden in the first decade of the twentieth century led to the foundation of the parish of SAINT HEDWIG at 23rd and Wood Streets. The parish church was dedicated in 1908, and the first parish school, staffed by Sisters of the Holy Family of Nazareth, was built at 22nd and Carlton Streets in 1911. Redevelopment of the area in the 1950s forced the relocation of the parish buildings, and in 1956 a new church and school were built at 24th and Brown Streets in Fairmount. As the number of Polish-speaking parishioners and available Polish-speaking priests declined, the parish was suppressed in 2000.

As the African American congregation at Saint Peter Claver's continued to increase, Mother Katharine Drexel sought to establish a new parish for African Americans in Spring Garden. The church of OUR LADY OF THE BLESSED SACRAMENT was founded in 1910 at Broad Street and Fairmount Avenue, and was largely a gift of Mother Katharine and her family.

**Our Lady of the Miraculous Medal Chapel**
*"La Milagrosa"*

Both the parish school and evangelization efforts were conducted by the Sisters of the Blessed Sacrament, the community that Mother Katharine had founded in 1891. Their work continued until the parish school was closed in 1968. The parish of Our Lady of the Blessed Sacrament was suppressed in 1972.

During the 1880s and 1890s—especially at the end of the Spanish-American War in 1898— many Spanish-speaking immigrants arrived in Philadelphia from Latin America, particularly from the Caribbean island of Puerto Rico. Father Antonio Canas, C.M., was among the first Vincentian priests from Spain to take on the work of ministering to these Catholics in their own language. Through the generosity of Sister Agueda Quintana—a Mexican member of the Daughters of Charity who worked as a nurse at Saint Joseph's Hospital—and also the Sisters of the Blessed Sacrament, Father Canas opened a chapel on Spring Garden Street west of Nineteenth Street in 1912. Named for OUR LADY OF THE MIRACULOUS MEDAL (*Nuestra Señora de la Medalla Milagrosa)*, it is often referred to as the "Spanish Chapel" or *"La Milagrosa."*

Spanish Vincentian priests continued to staff the chapel from 1912 to 1977, when it came under the care of the priests of the Cathedral parish. They were assisted for many years by the Trinitarian sisters, who instructed children and conducted outreach programs in the community. Among these programs was the building of houses in the area around 20th and Green Streets, which came to be known as the "Spanish Village." Although many parishioners moved to the neighborhoods of North Philadelphia in the second half of the twentieth century, *La Milagrosa* still serves the pastoral needs of Hispanic families in and around Spring Garden.

The former Machinists' Temple at 13th and Spring Garden Streets was the first meeting place for Lithuanian Catholic immigrants in this neighborhood, and they formed the national parish of SAINT ANDREW in 1924. They built a school and chapel at 12th and Lemon Streets,

**Saint Andrew**

and the volunteer labor of parishioners, who constructed the second and third floors of the building, saved the parish $16,000 ($182,750 in 2005). Sisters of Saint Casimir were entrusted with administration of the parish school. Plans to build a church were delayed because of the Great Depression; however, in 1942, the parish was able to purchase a former Episcopal church at 19th and Wallace Streets. As families of Lithuanian descent moved from this area, the parish school closed in 1960. In 1996, Saint Andrew's was twinned with the Lithuanian parish of Saint Casimir in South Philadelphia.

# Lower North Philadelphia

The district known as Penn Township—north of Spring Garden and west of Kensington and Northern Liberties—was already heavily populated when Assumption B.V.M. parish in Spring Garden was founded in 1849. Only a year later, another parish was established in this neighborhood, which has since come to be known as North Philadelphia. Taken from the territory of Assumption and Saint Michael's, it was named SAINT MALACHY, for the twelfth-century Archbishop of Armagh, Ireland—the homeland of many of the families who made up the new parish. The parish church was built in 1852 on 11th Street above Master Street, and was renovated in 1878 and again in 1900. The parish school opened in 1860, under the direction of Sisters of Mercy, and was enlarged in 1891.

The number of Saint Malachy parishioners of Irish descent began to decline in the 1930s, as the descendants of original

parishioners moved to other sections of the city. African Americans began to predominate in the 1930s, and by the 1960s a sizable Hispanic presence was evident in the neighborhood as well. Father Hubert Cooke, who founded Casa del Carmen—an outreach and evangelization center for Spanish-speaking Catholics—was pastor of Saint Malachy's from 1963 to 1982. With the guidance of his successor, Father John McNamee, the parish is still known for its commitment to the disadvantaged and marginalized members of this North Philadelphia community. Considerable financial support for these efforts is derived from "Irish Nights" that feature prominent Irish musicians and are loyally attended by the families of former parishioners.

In the late 1860s, Father Felix Barbelin, S.J., was responsible for educating the boys and young men of Saint Joseph's College, which had been founded in 1851 at Old Saint Joseph's church on Willings Alley. Father Barbelin wanted a more permanent site for the college, away from the crowded, busy conditions of Center City.

He found a suitable plot at 17th and Stiles Streets—at the time, a sparsely-populated area—and saw to the construction of a new college building that included both a chapel (dedicated to the Holy Family) and a residence for the Jesuit community.

In 1868, this chapel was the site of the first Mass in what would become the parish of THE GESU. Students of the College were joined by families from the area, who were largely of German and Irish descent. The population of the area grew rapidly, and plans were soon developed to build a parish church. Father Burchard Villiger, S.J., who had become the parish priest in 1868, sent the architect to Rome to visit the mother church of the Jesuits, the Church of the Gesù (the Italian form of the name Jesus). The parish church, with walls ten feet thick, was constructed at 18th and Thompson Streets on nearly the same dimensions as its Roman namesake.

By 1873, Saint Joseph's College Preparatory School for boys occupied the basement of the College; however, when the College moved to City Avenue, "The Prep" occupied the entire building. A parish school for girls also began in 1873 under the direction of School Sisters of Notre Dame, and in 1896, Immaculate Heart Sisters arrived to instruct the boys.

The Drexel family contributed generously to the foundation of the parish of SAINT ELIZABETH, named for the patron saint of Elizabeth Drexel,

**Saint Malachy**

one of Francis Drexel's three daughters. The neighborhood of 23rd and Berks Streets, about a mile northwest of the Gesu, was largely ponds and open land when this parish was founded in 1872. A tiny congregation—ten people at most—attended Mass that year on Christmas Day. However, the population increased as roads were paved and houses were built in the vicinity of the new church. A parish school was established on the second floor of the chapel building; in 1874 it was entrusted to Franciscan Sisters from Glen Riddle. The lower church was completed in 1883, and the upper church dedicated in 1890.

The parish boundaries of Saint Elizabeth were soon adjusted to accommodate the rapidly growing Catholic population in North Philadelphia. In 1889, part of the eastern section of the parish became the new parish of OUR LADY OF MERCY. A chapel, at Broad and Susquehanna Streets, was completed quickly, and its second floor housed the parish school until a permanent school was erected in 1894. In that year, Sisters of Saint Joseph were invited to staff the school. The lower church opened in 1891, and the upper church was dedicated in 1899.

In 1895, the western part of Saint Elizabeth's parish, bordering Saint Bridget's parish in East Falls, became the parish of SAINT COLUMBA. The rectory—a converted rowhouse—was the site of Mass until a chapel was dedicated on Easter Sunday of that year. The parish school,

operated by Sisters of Saint Joseph, opened in 1898, and the parish church was dedicated in 1915.

The very visible presence of these new churches drew an even larger number of Catholics to the vicinity. Those who settled along the eastern border of Fairmount Park found it a difficult journey to Saint Columba or Saint Elizabeth, and in 1907 the parish of the MOST PRECIOUS BLOOD OF OUR LORD was established in their neighborhood, at 28th and Diamond Streets. The founding pastor, Father Joseph Kirlin—author of several works on Church history, including *Catholicity in Philadelphia* (1909)—was appointed on the feast day that gave the parish its name. The parishioners used a meeting hall on the second floor of the Titman Building, at 31st Street and Ridge Avenue, until a chapel was dedicated in October 1907. A church/school building was completed in 1908, and Sisters of Saint Joseph assumed administration of the school in 1913. A larger church was dedicated in 1928.

Italian Catholics in these North Philadelphia neighborhoods formed a smaller community than their Irish neighbors. However, with a faith just as strong, these Italian families desired to celebrate devotions and hear sermons in their own language. Accordingly, the national parish of SAINT MARY OF THE ETERNAL was founded in 1911. A chapel was erected at 21st Street and Toronto Streets, and the church and school on West Clearfield Street, just south of Allegheny Avenue, were dedicated in 1930. The school was staffed by Missionary Franciscan Sisters of the Immaculate Conception. By the 1960s and 1970s, many families of Italian descent had moved from the neighborhood, and the parish was closed in 1976.

A few blocks west of Saint Mary's, the parish of CORPUS CHRISTI (Latin for the "Body of Christ") was founded in 1912 at 29th Street and Allegheny Avenue—the "Garden Spot of Philadelphia." Its territory was drawn from the parishes of Saint Columba, Saint Bridget and Our Lady of the Holy Souls. A combination chapel and social hall was constructed in 1914, and served until a lower church was opened in 1928. The large upper church was dedicated in 1955. The parish school opened in 1921 under the direction of Sisters of Saint Joseph,

and for many years, the parish was also the site of the Sisters' Catholic Home for Destitute Children. A decline in the neighborhood's Catholic population, and also in the number of priests in active ministry, led to the closing of Corpus Christi parish in 1987. Some parish buildings are now used by Mercy Vocational High School, founded in 1950 by the Sisters of Mercy.

In 1993, the same problems of diminishing numbers of parishioners and priests necessitated a restructuring of parishes in the North Philadelphia area. Our Lady of Mercy parish had been suppressed in 1984, and Corpus Christi parish in 1987. Now, the Church of the Gesu was closed, and its parishioners became part of Saint Malachy parish. At the same time, the parishes of Saint Elizabeth, Saint Columba and Most Precious Blood were suppressed, and their territories consolidated to form one new parish, SAINT MARTIN DE PORRES, at the site of the former Saint Columba parish. This new parish bears the name of a sixteenth-century Dominican friar who was noted for his humble service to the poor in Lima, Peru. He was canonized by Pope John XXIII in 1962. Born of a Spanish father and a mother who was a slave, Saint Martin de Porres is a beloved patron for the predominantly African American population of the new parish.

Saint Martin de Porres

# Upper North Philadelphia

The neighborhood known as Nicetown, southeast of Germantown, was settled in the early 1700s by Dutch Huguenots. Prominent among them were members of the De Neus family after whom the area was named. The community of farms was also home to a few Catholics; a leading member of this group was the physician John Michael Browne, M.D., who had emigrated from the West Indies in 1725. Priests from Philadelphia frequently came to Doctor Browne's house to celebrate Mass and the sacraments for his family and servants. Among those who were baptized there was Christina, a slave belonging to Doctor Browne. She was one of the first recorded African American converts in Philadelphia.

After Doctor Browne's death in 1750, Catholics in Nicetown were without a priest for long periods. To accommodate an increasing number of Catholic residents—especially recent immigrants—the parish of SAINT STEPHEN was founded in Nicetown in 1843. The following year, a small stone chapel was built at the intersection of Barr and Clinton Streets, at the center of the little village. In 1884, a much larger church opened at Broad and Butler Streets, and a school, operated by Sisters of Saint Joseph, opened at the same location in 1890.

The Episcopal Church of Saint Bartholomew—at Eighth and York Streets, about two miles south of Saint Stephen's—was purchased in 1865 and converted to the parish church of SAINT EDWARD THE CONFESSOR. Drawn from the parish territory of Saint Malachy and Saint Michael, the new congregation established a school in 1886, which was entrusted to Sisters of the Holy Child Jesus. The year after the founding of Saint Edward's, the burgeoning population of German Catholics in Saint Peter's parish (Fifth Street and Girard Avenue) prompted the founding of the parish of SAINT BONIFACE. The church, at Diamond and Hancock Streets, was dedicated in 1867 and enlarged in 1888. The parish school also opened in 1867, staffed by Franciscan Sisters

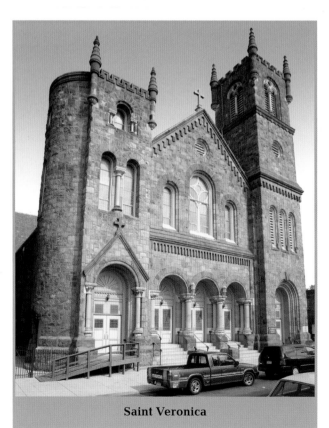

**Saint Veronica**

from Glen Riddle. In 1876, the parish was placed under the care of the Redemptorists, who also staffed Saint Peter's.

A chapel near the site of New Cathedral Cemetery (Second and Butler Streets) was the first worship site for parishioners of SAINT VERONICA parish, founded in 1872. The initial congregation was quite small. In fact, Catholics from other parishes had to be invited to have enough participants to celebrate Benediction of the Blessed Sacrament. The number of parishioners increased, however, from 80 people in 1872 to more than 4,000 by 1889. A resident pastor was appointed in 1878, and a church/school building was completed in 1894 at Sixth and Tioga Streets. Immaculate Heart Sisters were invited in 1904 to staff the school. The present church was dedicated in 1909.

As industry developed along the Delaware River, large numbers of Irish and German laborers were attracted to nearby North Philadelphia neighborhoods. A new church, dedicated to Saint Cecilia, was built at C Street and Cambria Street in 1873. The population of the parish, drawn from Saint Edward's, Saint Michael's, and Saint Ann's in Port Richmond, was small at first. As the number of parishioners increased, the size of this church became inadequate, and a second church was begun in 1876 at Lehigh Avenue and B Street. At this time, the name of the parish was changed to the VISITATION OF THE BLESSED

VIRGIN MARY. The upper church was dedicated in 1880, and the parish school opened in 1883, staffed by Sisters of the Holy Child Jesus. In 1911, these Sisters were succeeded by Sisters of Saint Joseph.

**Visitation B.V.M.**

German immigrants—refugees from the *Kulturkampf* policy which oppressed the Catholic Church in their homeland—continued to settle in North Philadelphia during the 1870s and 1880s, particularly in the area known as Fairhill. They found the 16-block journey to Saint Boniface difficult, and in 1889, Mr. Robert Schaelges wrote to Archbishop Ryan to request a parish for German speakers. The archbishop sent Father Henry Stommel, who had built many parishes for German communities in Bucks and Montgomery Counties, to evaluate the situation. Father Stommel acquired a lot at Ninth and Auburn Streets for a church/school building, which was completed in 1890. Because the foundation had been such a "successful venture"—*bona ventura* in Latin—the parish was named for SAINT BONAVENTURE, a thirteenth-century Franciscan theologian. Work on a lower church began in 1894, and the upper church was dedicated in 1906. The school, founded in 1890, was staffed by Franciscan Sisters from Glen Riddle.

Six more parishes were founded in the Nicetown–Tioga area during the early decades of the twentieth century. The first of these was a Polish national parish, whose members had attended Saint Laurentius in Fishtown. In 1906, with a working capital of only $7.50 ($162.50 in 2005), a committee of 16 parishioners assisted in the founding of SAINT LADISLAUS parish. The Old Oaks Mansion on Deacon Street served as a worship site until a church/school building was opened in 1909 and Bernardine Sisters were invited to staff the parish school. In 1916, a larger church was dedicated at Hunting Park Avenue and Germantown Avenue. The Polish-speaking population of the neighborhood declined in later decades, and between 1997 and 2001 parish membership fell by 76 percent. The parish was closed in 2003, and members were invited to transfer to the national parish of Saint Josaphat in Manayunk.

As Irish families moved from South Philadelphia to North Philadelphia, the farming communities of the Tioga section were developed into residential neighborhoods. The church of the HOLY CHILD, at Broad and Duncannon Streets, was founded in 1909, and a chapel and parish hall dedicated in 1911. The parish school began in the upper levels of the chapel in 1915, staffed by Sisters of Saint Joseph. A large church in the French Romanesque style was dedicated in 1930. In 1936, three years before his election as Pope Pius XII, Cardinal Eugenio Pacelli visited the church during his tour of the United States. Bishop Fulton Sheen, world-renowned for his weekly television broadcasts, was a frequent visitor to Holy Child in the 1950s and 1960s.

Also in 1909, and despite opposition from some non-Catholic neighbors, the parish of OUR LADY OF THE HOLY SOULS was founded at 19th and Tioga Streets. Like its sister parish, it served a large Irish community, drawn from the parishes of Saint Columba, Saint Stephen and Saint Francis of Assisi, Germantown. During the 1940s, the populations of both parishes were becoming predominantly African

American. In 1948, Our Lady of the Holy Souls parish made the decision to integrate the parish school, founded in 1912 by Sisters of Saint Joseph. This integration took place six years before the landmark U.S. Supreme Court decision *Brown v. Board of Education* struck down the notion of "separate but equal" education for whites and blacks.

At the start of World War I, two additional national parishes were founded in North Philadelphia. The church of OUR LADY OF POMPEII, at Sixth Street and Erie Avenue, served a congregation of Italian and Italian-speaking Albanian immigrants. At its founding in 1914, the parish was responsible for all Italian-speaking Catholics north of Girard Avenue and west of Broad Street, and as far north as Fox Chase. The parish school was opened by Immaculate Heart Sisters in 1929.

A third German parish in North Philadelphia, SAINT HENRY, was founded in 1916 on North Fifth Street near the former site of Central Park. The first parishioners, drawn mainly from the growing congregation at Saint Bonaventure's, met in the dance hall in Central Park, and later in a nearby hotel, until the lower church was completed in 1922. In 1917, the parish school was founded on the second floor of the hotel. The school, staffed by the Missionary Sisters of the Most Sacred Heart of Jesus, moved to its own building in 1940.

The Wishart Theatre at Front and Allegheny was the site of the first Mass for the parish of SAINT HUGH OF CLUNY, founded in 1922. A church/ school building for the new parish—formed from the parishes of Saint Veronica, Visitation B.V.M., and the Ascension of Our Lord—was dedicated in 1924. In that year, Sisters of Saint Joseph assumed responsibility

for the parish school. The present church was completed in 1951. The priests, staff and parishioners of Saint Hugh have made great efforts in recent decades to promote community outreach and redevelopment in their neighborhood.

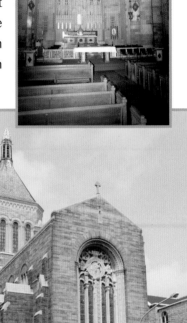

**Saint Hugh of Cluny**

**Our Lady of Hope**

The North Philadelphia Catholic communities of European descent began to move elsewhere in the 1950s and 1960s. In the northwestern neighborhoods of Tioga and Logan, new residents were mainly of African American heritage. In northeastern neighborhoods, newcomers were Spanish-speaking Catholics from the Caribbean and Latin America. The parishes of the area were restructured in 1993. The parishes of Saint Stephen, Holy Child and Our Lady of the Holy Souls were suppressed, and one new parish—OUR LADY OF HOPE— was established at the site of the former Holy Child parish. Today, Our Lady of Hope serves a very diverse community that includes members of African American, Haitian, Vietnamese, Indian and Hispanic descent.

At the same time, Saint Edward, Saint Bonaventure, Our Lady of Pompeii and Saint Henry parishes were all suppressed, and their territory was reassigned to Visitation B.V.M., Saint Veronica, and Incarnation of Our Lord parishes. A Catholic Evangelization Institute was established at the site of the former Saint Henry parish, and a *Casita*, a small outreach center, opened at the site of Saint Bonaventure. Saint Boniface parish was closed in 2006, and consolidated with Visitation B.V.M. The Redemptorists, who had served Saint Boniface for more than a century, were entrusted with the care of Visitation B.V.M. parish.

# Olney

The northernmost section of North Philadelphia was sparsely inhabited at the end of the nineteenth century, when the district—named Olney after the estate of Alexander Wilson on Rising Sun Avenue—attracted Philadelphians who desired to build country homes. Commercial development around Fifth Street and Olney Avenue increased the desirability of the area, as did the improvement of train and trolley transportation between Olney and Center City.

The country estates proximate to the Reading Railroad station in East Oak Lane were subdivided in the late 1800s, and in 1900 the new Catholic residents formed the parish of HOLY ANGELS. Melrose Hall, on the city boundary at Lakeside Avenue, was the site for Sunday Mass until a school and chapel building was completed in 1905. Sisters of Saint Joseph formed the founding faculty of the school. Throughout the following decades, the trolley lines which connected Philadelphia and Willow Grove continued to bring residents into the area. In the later part of the twentieth century, a sizeable population of Korean immigrants established homes and businesses in Olney and East Oak Lane. In 2006, Holy Angels was officially designated a national parish for Korean Catholics.

In 1900, Presentation B.V.M. parish in Cheltenham established the mission chapel of Saint Justin, near the intersection of Tabor Road and Second Street Pike. In 1902, this chapel was renamed INCARNATION OF OUR LORD. Easy access to and from the trolley line on Wyoming Avenue north of Fifth Street prompted the purchase of a plot of land at Fifth and Lindley Streets for a church/school building, which was completed in 1913.

**Incarnation of Our Lord**

The present church was built in 1930, and opened on Christmas Day. The school, staffed by Immaculate Heart Sisters, was enlarged in 1960, and again in 1966. Today, the parish is home to a multi-ethnic community, and Masses are regularly celebrated in five languages—English, Spanish, Portuguese, Creole and Malayalam, which is the language of the Syro-Malankara Rite in India.

The first Mass in the parish of SAINT AMBROSE—founded in 1923—was celebrated in a movie theater on Rising Sun Avenue. Parishioner Francis Lynch offered his home on Wyoming Avenue as a place for worship until a church/school building was erected in 1926. Two years later, Sisters of Saint Joseph were invited to administer the

**Holy Angels**

school. The present parish church, along Roosevelt Boulevard at C Street, was dedicated in 1955. A new parish school opened in 1959. The neighborhood includes many Catholics of Hispanic origin, and Sunday Mass is celebrated in Spanish as well as in English.

In 1924, the growing Catholic population in the Tabor section of Olney called for realignment of the boundaries of Holy Angels, Incarnation and Presentation B.V.M. parishes. The parish of SAINT HELENA had its initial home in a rowhouse on North Fairhill Street, and Sunday Mass was celebrated at the Olney Movie Theatre, at Fifth Street and Olney Avenue. The school building, which included a chapel, was built the following year, and entrusted to Sisters of Saint Joseph. The lower part of the present church was completed in 1936, and the upper

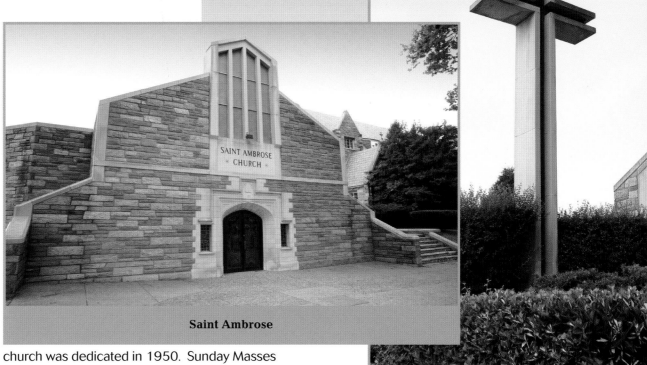

**Saint Ambrose**

church was dedicated in 1950. Sunday Masses are celebrated in English, Spanish and Vietnamese.

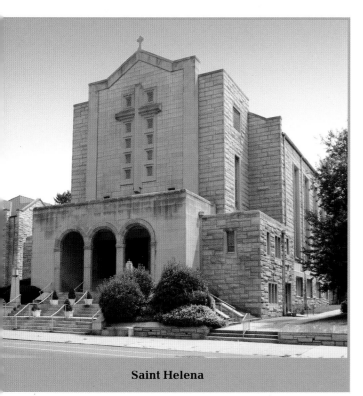

**Saint Helena**

# South Philadelphia

The District of Southwark—located, as its name suggests, just south of the original limits of the City of Philadelphia, and between Passyunk Avenue and the Delaware River—is one of the oldest settlements in Philadelphia County. Originating in the Swedish settlements of Wicaco and Moyamensing, Southwark was settled much earlier than the northern area of the county. Its location along the bank of the river made it the point of entry for a multitude of immigrants during the eighteenth and nineteenth centuries. A sizeable population of Catholics lived here during the decades before and after the American Revolution, and attended Mass at Saint Joseph's or Saint Mary's, about a mile to the north.

A plot of land on Fifth Street was purchased in 1836—with money left to the Bishop of Philadelphia in the estate of Mr. Andrew Steele—for the purpose of building a church in Southwark. In 1840, Bishop Kenrick appointed Father John Dunn, an assistant priest at Saint Mary's, to establish the parish of SAINT PHILIP NERI. The plot on Fifth Street was sold, and the parish church was built in the 200 block of Queen Street, a location centrally placed in the area where most Catholic families lived. The parish school—one of the first free Catholic schools in the nation—was founded in the same year by Sisters of Saint Joseph and Christian Brothers.

The Nativist riots in Southwark in early July 1844 figure prominently in the history of Saint Philip Neri parish. The parish church was besieged for several days; cannon were fired at the church—which was occupied by the militia unit known as the Hibernia Greens— and fighting killed 14 people and injured at least 50 more. The parish was also the site of the first celebration of the Forty Hours Devotion in the Archdiocese of Philadelphia. Saint John Neumann preached at the closing of this three-day period of Eucharistic adoration, on May 26, 1853—the feast day of the parish's patron saint and, that year, the solemnity of Corpus Christi.

Immigration, especially of Irish families, led to rapid development of the southern part of Philadelphia County during the 1830s and 1840s. Three years after the founding of

Saint Philip Neri parish, a parish dedicated to SAINT PAUL was established in the Moyamensing District, west of Passyunk Avenue. In 1843, the parish community was formed of Irish families, attracted by abundant employment in mills and factories along the river, and by commercial ventures along the wide thoroughfare of Christian Street.

**Saint Paul**

The original parish boundaries took in all of the area south of South Street, and between the Schuylkill River and Passyunk Avenue. The construction of the parish church, at Tenth and Christian Streets, was begun in the Spring of

**Saint Philip Neri**

1843, and the first Mass was celebrated in the church on Christmas Day of that year. The tensions provoked by Nativist riots, and the poor economic situation of many parishioners, delayed the completion and dedication of the church until 1847. The parish school was founded in 1904 by Immaculate Heart Sisters, who were later succeeded by Franciscan Missionaries of the Sacred Heart. In the early part of the twentieth century, the original Irish parishioners were outnumbered by Italian families. Today, the parish also includes many families of African American, Polish and Mexican descent.

In the early 1840s, Bishop Kenrick purchased the former Second Presbyterian Church of Southwark, intending to use it as the site of a German national parish. He felt it ill-advised to proceed with this plan during the period of the Nativist riots, but in 1847 he invited the Redemptorists at Saint Peter's Church to open a parish to serve German speakers in Southwark. The Redemptorists initially rejected the idea because they did not have a sufficient number of priests; however, the issue was raised again in the early 1850s when the trustees of Holy Trinity parish found themselves in conflict with the bishop. Bishop Neumann prevailed on his fellow Redemptorists to establish the parish of SAINT ALPHONSUS as a convenient place of worship for the German-speaking members of Holy Trinity, whose parish was under interdict because of issues centering on the trustees.

A small chapel at Fifth and Gaskill Streets was the first worship site, but was quickly succeeded by a church at Fourth and Reed Streets, dedicated in 1854. Because of financial difficulties, the upper church was not completed until 1860. Saint Alphonsus parish was entrusted to the Conventual Franciscan Friars from 1858 to 1861—it was their first foundation in the United States—and later was staffed by diocesan priests, including the famous Father Henry Stommel from 1890 to 1917. Under his leadership the parish school was founded in 1893, and entrusted to Franciscan Sisters from Glen Riddle. Declining numbers of German-speaking families in South Philadelphia prompted the closing of Saint Alphonsus parish in 1972.

A former Methodist chapel on Marriott (now Montrose) Street was the original site of the first Italian national parish in the United States. Named for SAINT MARY MAGDALEN DE PAZZI—a sixteenth-century Carmelite nun and mystic from Florence—the converted chapel was dedicated in 1854. A parish church was built in 1891, and replaced with a larger structure in 1957. The upper part of this church was dedicated in 1964. The parish school was started in 1874, and staffed by Franciscan Missionaries of the Sacred Heart. The parish was suppressed in 2000, and the church was made a worship site of Saint Paul parish.

In the early 1800s, Moyamensing Township around South Broad Street was known as "Cowtown" since the area consisted of grazing fields and only a few scattered houses. Immigration of Irish families, however, increased the local population by more than 20,000 people between 1850 and 1853, when the parish of SAINT TERESA OF AVILA was founded at Broad and Catherine Streets. Anti-Catholics in the area still harbored ill feelings related to the Nativist riots, and the original cornerstone of the parish church was stolen. Parishioners gathered for worship in a private home at Catherine and Watts Streets until the church was dedicated on Christmas Day, 1853.

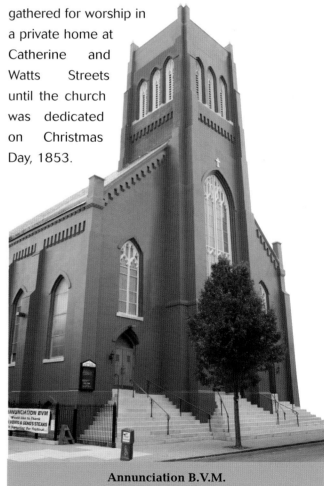

**Annunciation B.V.M.**

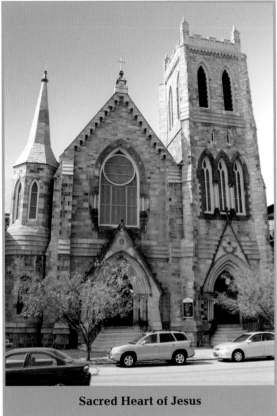

**Sacred Heart of Jesus**

ANNUNCIATION OF THE BLESSED VIRGIN MARY at Tenth and Dickinson Streets. This was the first parish founded by Bishop (later Archbishop) Wood, who named the parish for the feast day on which he had been ordained a priest, March 25, 1844. The lower church was opened on Christmas Day that year, and the upper church was dedicated in 1863. The parish school was founded by Immaculate Heart Sisters in 1869, in rooms in the lower church. The school moved into its own building in 1876. As was the case with many South Philadelphia parishes, the population of Annunciation B.V.M. changed from Irish to predominantly Italian during the early years of the twentieth century.

A small frame chapel was the first home of the parish of the SACRED HEART OF JESUS, founded in 1871 from territory that had belonged to Saint Philip Neri parish. Construction of the parish church began the following year, and the building, at Third and Reed Streets, was dedicated in 1877. The parish school was founded in 1892, and entrusted to Immaculate Heart Sisters.

The parish of the Annunciation B.V.M. was divided in 1889 to create the church of the EPIPHANY OF OUR LORD. The original frame chapel was succeeded by a lower church in 1893; the upper church was dedicated in 1905. The parish school opened in 1897 under the direction of Sisters of Saint Joseph. The lower level of the church, at Eleventh and Jackson Streets, was renovated as a chapel for perpetual adoration in October 2001, when it was rededicated in honor of Blessed Pope John XXIII.

The proximity of the parish to the train station at Broad and Washington Streets prompted the U.S. Army to commandeer the church as a temporary hospital for wounded soldiers returning from the Battle of Bull Run in July 1861. The parish school, founded by Immaculate Heart Sisters in 1869, would later take in students from Saint Peter Claver parish—part of the "Colored Mission" that ministered to African Americans. As the African American population of the area increased in the 1930s and 1940s, Missionhurst Missionaries (also known as Scheut Fathers) were invited in 1949 to staff the parish. Increased financial burdens on a declining Catholic population prompted the closing of the parish in 1972.

The parish of Saint Paul was again divided in 1860 to form the church of the

In the 1870s and 1880s, difficult conditions in their homeland, and abundant employment available in Philadelphia, brought large numbers of Polish immigrants to the city. Many of them settled near the waterfront, especially near the Washington Avenue Immigration Station (which operated from 1870 to 1915), and attended Mass at Saint Alphonsus or at Saint Laurentius, Fishtown. The First Presbyterian Church, at Second and Fitzwater Streets, was purchased in 1891 and converted into the national parish church of SAINT STANISLAUS. New Polish immigrants gravitated toward the church and a large Polish community developed. However,

**Epiphany of Our Lord**

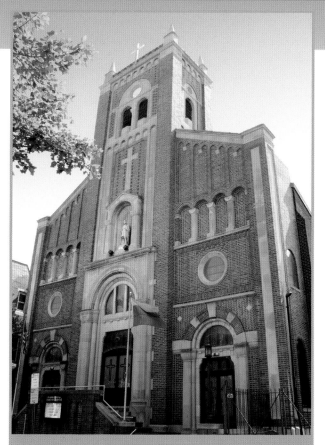

**Saint Casimir**

the Polish-speaking population declined in the second half of the twentieth century. Saint Stanislaus parish was suppressed in 2006, and the church became a worship site of Saint Philip Neri parish.

Lithuanians who were recent arrivals in the city also sought their own parish in South Philadelphia, and in 1893 Father Joseph Kaulakis gathered the parish community of SAINT CASIMIR for Mass in nearby Saint Alphonsus Church. A former Protestant church at Fifth and Carpenter Streets was bought in 1894 and converted to a parish chapel. This was succeeded in 1905 by a new parish church on Wharton Street above Third Street. The church was dedicated in 1906, the same year that the parish school was founded in the church basement by Sisters of Saint Casimir. Fire devastated the church in 1930 and again in 1951. The parish was

twinned with the Lithuanian national parish of Saint Andrew in Fairmount in 1996.

The first chapel of the parish of SAINT MONICA, founded in the Passyunk neighborhood in 1895, had its beginnings about seven miles away from South Philadelphia. It had been the original church of Saint Veronica parish, founded in 1872 in North Philadelphia. That parish had built a new church in 1894, and the chapel was dismantled and reassembled at 17th and Ritner Streets. A permanent church was dedicated in 1903, and the parish school opened in 1908 under the direction of Immaculate Heart Sisters. The parish also operated a business school beginning in the 1920s, and from the 1950s into the 1970s

**Saint Monica**

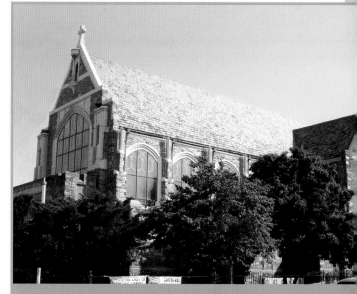

**Our Lady of Mount Carmel**

conducted Camp Saint Monica in Berks County for young parishioners. The parish church was gutted by fire in 1971, and the present church was dedicated in 1975. An original window—dedicated to Saint Eugene, patron of the City of Derry, Ireland—survived the fire and was incorporated into the new church.

A rented house at Third and Wolf Streets housed the original chapel of OUR LADY OF MOUNT CARMEL. Founded on Our Lady's feast day, July 16, 1896, the parish territory was taken from Sacred Heart parish, located about a mile north along Third Street. A church/school building opened in 1901, and Sisters of Mercy arrived in that year to teach in the school. The present church was dedicated in 1922, and a new school building, at Fourth and Shunk Streets, was built in 1965.

When the Italian national parish of OUR LADY OF GOOD COUNSEL was founded on Christian Street in 1898, most of the area was populated by Irish families. Augustinian priests of the Italian province, invited to minister to Italian-speaking Catholics, named the parish church after the miraculous image of Our Lady which is housed in the Augustinian church in Gennezano, Italy. A church/school building was dedicated in 1899, and Franciscan Sisters from Glen Riddle took responsibility for the school.

The parish population of Our Lady of Good Counsel dwindled in the 1920s, at the same time that surrounding parishes had become predominantly Italian. Cardinal Dougherty decided to close the parish in 1932, and this decision sparked controversy. At this time, the mission chapel of SAINT NICHOLAS OF

**Saint Nicholas of Tolentine**

TOLENTINE, which priests from Our Lady of Good Counsel parish had served since 1912, was established as an Italian national parish. The church, dedicated in 1928, was renovated in 1964 and 1987. Sisters of Saint Lucy Filippini arrived in 1951 to staff the parish school, founded in 1925 by the Franciscan Missionaries of the Sacred Heart.

Catholic immigrants from Slovakia who settled in South Philadelphia began meeting at Saint Alphonsus church in 1902, where Father Martin Meres of Reading, Berks County, ministered to them in their native language. In 1906, the congregation purchased the Wharton Street Presbyterian Church, at Ninth and Wharton Streets, and converted it into the parish church of SAINT JOHN NEPOMUCENE. In 1910, members of this parish helped found Saint Agnes parish in Northern Liberties. The parishes of Saint John Nepomucene and Saint Agnes were consolidated in 1980, and the buildings of Saint John's were closed at that time.

In 1907, Augustinian priests from Villanova founded a new parish on South Broad Street, and named it SAINT RITA OF CASCIA for a fourteenth-century Augustinian nun and mystic from northern Italy who had been canonized in 1900. The first Masses were celebrated in a stable on the parish property, and in a rented Protestant church at Broad and Federal Streets, until the parish church was completed in 1908. Much of the money for its construction came from a bequest of parishioner Lucas Burke. Although the neighborhood was predominantly Irish at the time of the parish's founding, its name attracted many Italian families to the area, especially after 1935.

The school was founded in 1910 and staffed by Franciscan Missionaries of the Sacred Heart.

**Saint Rita of Cascia**

Soon after the upper church was dedicated in 1915, the parish began a twice-weekly novena to Saint Rita, a special intercessor for impossible causes. Novena devotions were held 13 times a day each Wednesday and Sunday, and thousands of pilgrims came to what was becoming the National Shrine to Saint Rita of Cascia. Since

2000, the Augustinians have undertaken a major campaign to convert the lower church into a shrine center for devotions, adoration of the Blessed Sacrament, and celebration of the Sacrament of Reconciliation. The shrine is home to a number of original sculptures and paintings depicting Saint Rita and other Augustinian saints. Many of these artworks were created by a parishioner, Anthony Visco.

The area of South Philadelphia west of Broad Street and south of Oregon Avenue was sparsely populated in 1924, when the first chapel of SAINT RICHARD of Chichester was built near 18th and Pollock Streets. Attention was drawn to the area by the Sesquicentennial exhibition (held in 1926 on the site of the future FDR Park and John F. Kennedy Stadium) and especially by the development of the Philadelphia Navy Yard during World War II. The parish school, which had been staffed by Immaculate Heart Sisters since it opened in 1929, had to be enlarged in 1949 and again in 1962. The present church was dedicated in 1951.

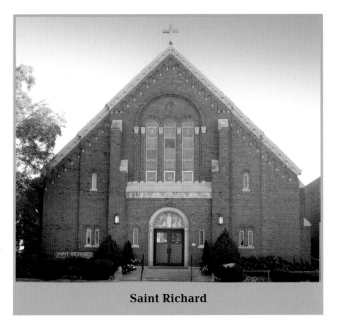

**Saint Richard**

Further development around the Navy Yard brought additional Catholic families to South Philadelphia, and prompted the foundation of two more parishes. The parish of STELLA MARIS was founded in the Marian Year 1954 from the territory of Epiphany of Our Lord and Our Lady of Mount Carmel. Cardinal O'Hara chose the title of the parish, which means "Star of the Sea," because the parish was close to the Delaware River and contained the Philadelphia Navy Yard within its boundaries.

**Stella Maris**

Between 1954 and 1956, Sunday and holy day Masses were celebrated in the Plaza Ballroom at Broad and Porter Streets, which doubled at night as a boxing venue. Parish volunteers set up the altar and chairs before the first Mass in the morning, and broke them down after the last Mass to set up the boxing ring. Children of the parish continued to attend classes at Epiphany School until 1956. A church/school building at Tenth and Bigler Streets was dedicated in that year, and Sisters of Saint Joseph were invited to staff the parish school. The parish has the distinction of being "home" to several professional sports teams, whose stadiums and arenas on South Broad Street are located within the parish boundaries.

In 1964, Catholic families living in military housing and in the Passyunk Homes were a large part of the congregation of HOLY SPIRIT parish, formed from the southern part of Saint Richard's parish. Mass was celebrated in the former Defense Supply Center at 20th Street and Oregon Avenue until the church, on Hartranft Street below 19th Street, was completed in 1965. The parish school was built in that same year, and staffed by the Poor Servants of the Mother of God.

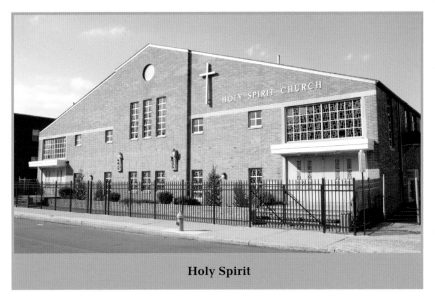

**Holy Spirit**

# Grays Ferry and Point Breeze

The neighborhoods to the southwest of Center City began to take shape after the Civil War, as improved transportation by water and rail along the Schuylkill River brought industry and commerce to the areas of Grays Ferry and Point Breeze. Blocks of new rowhouses were occupied by a largely Irish community throughout the late 1860s and into the 1870s.

The first parish established in the area, SAINT CHARLES BORROMEO, began in 1869 in a frame chapel near 20th and Christian

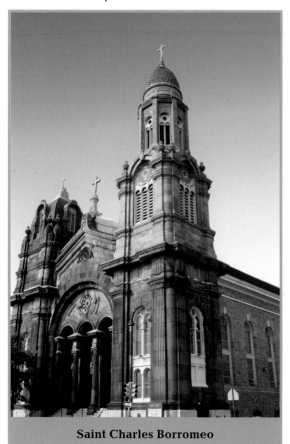

**Saint Charles Borromeo**

Streets. After a number of setbacks, the present church—the third-largest in the city at the time—was dedicated in 1876. The parish school opened in 1886, under the direction of Sisters of Saint Joseph. The school was rebuilt in 1955.

Although the founding families of Saint Charles Borromeo were Irish, by the 1930s and 1940s the community had become predominantly African American. With some success, parish priests and staff worked to evangelize their new neighbors and invite them to become Catholic. Missionhurst Missionaries staffed the parish from the 1950s to the 1990s. These priests worked in many nations in Africa and Asia, and took special care of disadvantaged persons. Today, Saint Charles Borromeo parish is staffed by archdiocesan priests.

When it was founded, Saint Charles Borromeo served most of the western part of South Philadelphia. As more Irish immigrants moved in, the parish boundaries were adjusted to create the parish of SAINT THOMAS AQUINAS at 17th and Morris Streets. A frame chapel was put up in 1885, and the present church—designed by Edwin Forrest Durang in the Italian baroque style—was dedicated in 1904. (Mr. Durang had also planned Saint Charles Borromeo Church, and Saint Monica Church in South Philadelphia.) The parish school was staffed by the Immaculate Heart Sisters when it opened in 1895. New school buildings were erected in 1957 and 1961.

By the 1920s, the original Irish congregation had been replaced by families of Italian descent. Today, Saint Thomas Aquinas parish is home to a mosaic of many cultures. Italian parishioners are joined by new neighbors from

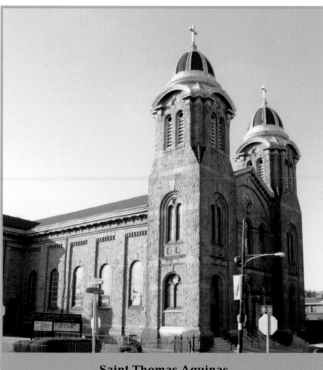

**Saint Thomas Aquinas**

Vietnam, Cambodia, China, Indonesia, the Philippines, Mexico and other Latin American countries. Many of these ethnic groups celebrate Mass and special devotions in their own languages on feast days throughout the year.

The first Mass for parishioners of SAINT ANTHONY OF PADUA parish—the first Catholic church in the Grays Ferry neighborhood—was held in a hall above a livery stable on the south side of Grays Ferry Avenue, between Carpenter and Washington Streets. This hall was home to parishioners from 1886 until the parish church was dedicated in 1893. The parish school was opened by Immaculate Heart Sisters in 1897. During the great Influenza Epidemic in 1918, a parish nursery cared for orphans whose parents had succumbed to the flu.

The German immigrants of Grays Ferry might attend Mass at Saint Anthony's, or choose to travel to Saint Alphonsus or Holy Trinity to be with a German-speaking congregation. In 1894, the German national parish of SAINT ALOYSIUS was established under the leadership of Father William Wachter. With the help of parishioners who volunteered their labor, the first parish church was completed in

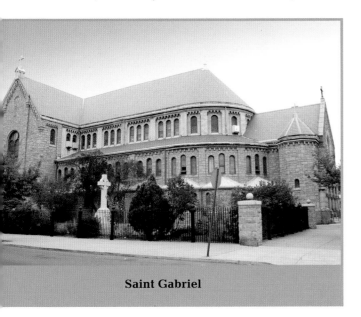

**Saint Gabriel**

December 1894. Women of the parish were often seen carrying lumber on their heads and bricks in their aprons, having salvaged these materials from the wharves along the Schuylkill. Saint Aloysius School—staffed by Sisters of Christian Charity—opened in 1895. In 1913, Father Bernard Phillips built the rectory with his own funds. A new school was erected in 1914, and a new parish church was dedicated in 1924. Saint Aloysius was given territorial boundaries in 1953.

As the immigrant population of Grays Ferry continued to increase, the parish of SAINT GABRIEL was founded in 1895. Parishioners themselves built the first chapel in only 27 days. In 1896, men of the parish volunteered again to dig the foundations for the church. Ground was broken for the school in 1906, and it opened in 1908 under the direction of Immaculate Heart Sisters. Today, the parish is staffed by the Norbertines.

Shortly after becoming the Archbishop of Philadelphia, Archbishop Edmond Prendergast founded a parish south of Saint Gabriel's, which he named for his patron saint, SAINT EDMOND of Abingdon, the twelfth-century Archbishop of Canterbury. The first Mass was celebrated in the Breeze Theater in June 1912, and the first parish church was dedicated in April 1913. The parish school was founded by Immaculate Heart Sisters in 1917. The lower part of the present church was built in 1924, and the upper church was dedicated in 1935.

**Saint Edmond**

KING OF PEACE parish opened at 26th and Wharton Streets in 1926, to serve newly-arrived Italian families. The parish school—founded in 1928 and enlarged in 1956—was served for many years by Franciscan Sisters of the Immaculate Conception.

At the beginning of the twenty-first century, changing demographics and other factors led to a reorganization of the parishes in Grays Ferry. Saint Anthony of Padua closed in 1999, Saint Aloysius in 2003, and King of Peace in 2004. Saint Gabriel parish now cares for the parishioners once members of these other three parishes.

# West Philadelphia

When the Borough of West Philadelphia was incorporated in 1844, relatively few Catholic families were scattered over a wide area of farms, meadows and wooded tracts west of the Schuylkill River. The surrounding neighborhoods of Hamilton Village, the Belmont District and Blockley Township were similarly sparsely populated. However, residential development beginning in the 1840s and 1850s—spurred by improved roads and development of trolley and train service—led to a surge in population, composed largely of Irish families.

The "Mother Parish of West Philadelphia"—SAINT JAMES THE GREATER—was founded in 1850. The first parish Mass was celebrated in

**Saint Agatha—Saint James**

the home of William McBride, in the 3600 block of Locust Street, and construction of the parish church was begun almost immediately. The church was dedicated in 1852, and succeeded by a new, larger structure at 38th and Chestnut Streets, begun in 1881. The lower church was completed in 1884, and the upper church was dedicated in 1887.

At the time, Saint James parish was responsible for all of Philadelphia County west of the Schuylkill River, as well as large sections of Montgomery and Delaware Counties. The original territory of Saint James would eventually be served by 23 parishes. The parish was home to the Immaculate Conception Academy of the Sisters of the Holy Cross, as well as Saint Leonard's Academy, operated by Sisters of the Holy Child Jesus. Holy Child Sisters also staffed the parish school, built in 1868 and enlarged in 1928.

In 1852, Saint Gregory's Chapel in Old Cathedral Cemetery, at 48th Street and Lancaster Avenue, became the center of a second parish in West Philadelphia. Parishioners continued to worship in the chapel until 1867, when a parish church was built nearby. The church was dedicated on September 28, 1873, at which time the name was changed from Saint Gregory's to OUR MOTHER OF SORROWS. In 1878, the parish school was begun in space beneath the church, and Sisters of Saint Joseph made up the founding faculty. The school moved to its own

building in 1885. New school buildings, at 47th Street and Wyalusing Avenue, were built in 1908 and 1922.

**Our Mother of Sorrows**

West Philadelphia experienced continuing residential development at the end of the Civil War, and in 1865 the parish of SAINT AGATHA was founded in the Mantua section. The first church, at 36th Street and Fairmount Avenue, was the former Episcopal Church of Saint Andrew. A new vestibule and bell tower were added to this building in 1867. The cornerstone for a new church, at 38th and Spring Garden Streets, was laid in 1874, and the church was dedicated in 1878.

**Saint Francis de Sales**

In 1976, shifting Catholic populations prompted the consolidation of Saint Agatha and Saint James parishes. The present parish of SAINT AGATHA–SAINT JAMES is at the site of the latter, at 38th and Chestnut Streets. In addition to serving resident parishioners, the parish attends the hospitals of the University of Pennsylvania Health System. The parish also welcomes students, faculty and families from the area, which today is called University City.

Catholics of the Haddington neighborhood of West Philadelphia attended Our Mother of Sorrows parish, and this parish soon established a mission at 65th Street and Haverford Avenues. A new chapel at 63rd and Callowhill Streets became the site of OUR LADY OF THE ROSARY parish, founded in 1886. Construction of the parish church was begun the following year, and the church was dedicated in 1890. Men of the parish dug the foundations of the church and hauled the stone

for its construction. Sisters of Saint Joseph founded the parish school in 1901.

Development of trolley and rail lines increased interest in West Philadelphia residential development in the 1890s, and seven new parishes were founded in this section between 1890 and 1905. The first, SAINT FRANCIS DE SALES, provided pastoral care for many Irish persons who worked as domestic servants in West Philadelphia town houses and on estates, and wanted to attend Mass near their workplaces. A hall at 49th Street and Woodland Avenue served for the celebration of Mass until a church/school building was completed in 1891 at 47th Street and Springfield Avenue. The parish school opened in 1904 under the direction of Immaculate Heart Sisters.

The population of Saint Francis de Sales parish increased rapidly, peaking at over 4,800 families in the early 1950s. In these years the men and boys of the parish choir earned wide renown, under the direction of Monsignor Angelo della Pica. Many families left the neighborhood in the next few decades, however, and by 1990 only 650 Catholic families remained. Saint Francis de Sales is today home to a strong Vietnamese Catholic community.

SAINT IGNATIUS OF LOYOLA parish was founded as a German national parish in 1893. Over the next few decades, most German-speaking families moved out, and were

succeeded by African American families. In 1928, the nearby Holy Savior mission—part of the "Colored Missions" that served African American Catholics, many of whom were converts—was incorporated into the parish of Saint Ignatius. Since 1928, Sisters of the Blessed Sacrament have served both in the parish school and with evangelization efforts.

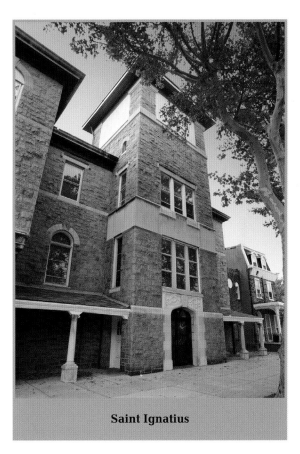

**Saint Ignatius**

The parish was given official territorial boundaries in the early 1970s, and still serves a predominantly African American congregation. Saint Ignatius parish was twinned with Our Mother of Sorrows parish in 2000.

The planned community of Overbrook Farms was developed by the Childs and Drexel Syndicate in 1893, promising large homes in a quiet neighborhood on what were then the outskirts of the city, and with easy access to central Philadelphia by train and trolley. Hoping to attract residents, the developers offered plots of land to any religious denomination that could build a stone church within one year. The archdiocese took advantage of this offer to establish a new parish in 1894. Initial plans were to call the parish Saint Mary Magdalen, but a benefactor—Hugh Sullivan of Merion, who at that time was recuperating in Los Angeles, California—offered to pay $2,000 towards its construction (about $43,300 in 2005 values) if the church were named in honor of OUR LADY OF LOURDES.

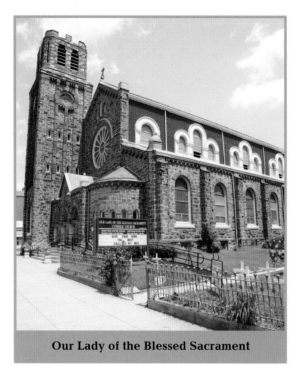

**Our Lady of the Blessed Sacrament**

The first parishioners—many of whom served as domestic staff in the large new homes, and faced a troublesome journey to Our Lady of the Rosary—gathered for Mass at the chapel of Saint Charles Borromeo Seminary until the parish church was opened in 1895. The upper church was dedicated in 1899, and the parish school opened in 1908 under the leadership of Sisters of Mercy. The school was enlarged in 1964. Since 2004, the parish has been entrusted to the Mercedarians.

Continuing development in the area soon led to the division of Our Lady of Lourdes parish and the foundation SAINT GREGORY parish in 1895. The parish church and school (staffed by Sisters of Saint Joseph) were located at 52nd and Warren Streets, not far from the western end of Fairmount Park. In 1899, another parish was founded at 54th and Vine Streets, and Mass was celebrated in a makeshift chapel on the

second floor of an old saw mill. The parish church of OUR LADY OF VICTORY was begun in 1909, and dedicated in 1914. Much of the money for its construction was collected by the founding pastor, Father Patrick McNulty, from his former parishioners at Our Mother of Sorrows. Sisters of Saint Joseph founded Our Lady of Victory School in 1903.

In later years, changes in the Catholic population of these areas led to the closing of these two parishes. Saint Gregory was closed in 1981, and Our Lady of Victory was consolidated with Our Lady of the Rosary in 2005. The present parish of OUR LADY OF THE BLESSED SACRAMENT is located at the site of Our Lady of the Rosary, and entrusted to the Capuchin Franciscan Friars.

**Our Lady of Lourdes**

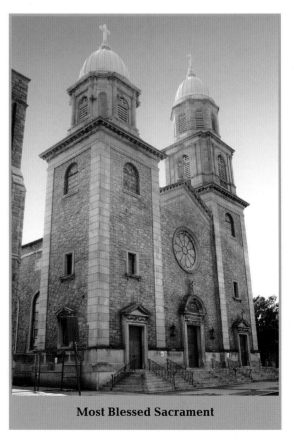

**Most Blessed Sacrament**

The parish of the MOST BLESSED SACRA-MENT was founded in a rented house at the corner of 55th Street and Woodland Avenue in 1901. A chapel at 56th Street and Chester Avenue was built the same year, and served the parish until a church was completed in 1924. The parish school, founded in 1908, was staffed by Immaculate Heart Sisters, and for many years had the largest parish school enrollment in the world. However, many Catholic families had left the parish by the 1970s and 1980s. The parish was twinned with Saint Francis de Sales in 1999. Today, the Theresa Maxis Center provides food and clothing for local families in need.

A wooden chapel at 55th Street and Cedar Avenue was the first home of the parish of the TRANSFIGURATION OF OUR LORD, founded in 1905 from territory of Saint Francis de Sales, Most Blessed Sacrament, Our Lady of the

**Saint Donato**

Rosary and Our Lady of Victory. The original school building—entrusted to Immaculate Heart Sisters and completed in 1907—included a chapel on the first floor. Construction on the parish church began in 1924; the lower church was completed in 1925, and the upper church dedicated in 1928.

In 1907, Our Mother of Sorrows established a mission chapel at 50th and Master Streets for Italian families living in West Philadelphia. The first permanent clergy were assigned to OUR LADY OF ANGELS Church in 1910, and in 1925, Immaculate Heart Sisters arrived to teach in the school. Also in 1910, Father Pietro Michetti built another parish for Italians in West Philadelphia. The parish church was located about a mile and a half to the west of Our Lady of Angels, in the Overbrook section. Many local Italians were from the *paese* of San Donato, and their new church was dedicated in 1910 with the name of their patron, SAINT DONATO.

When Saint Donato School was dedicated in 1911, among the attendees was Saint Frances Xavier Cabrini, whose Missionary Sisters of the Sacred Heart were to take responsibility for teaching parish children. By the 1950s, Saint Donato was much a larger parish than Our Lady of Angels, which was subsequently operated as a mission chapel from 1981 to 2006.

A new parish was founded in 1915, at the intersection of Cedar Avenue and Cobbs Creek Parkway—part of the western border of the City of Philadelphia. The Moving Picture Theatre at 60th and Spruce Streets was the site of the first

Mass, and a church/school building was erected in 1916. It was named for SAINT CARTHAGE, a sixth-century Irish abbot and Bishop of Lismore. Sisters of Saint Joseph taught in the school, which opened the same

**Saint Cyprian**

year. A new church was dedicated in 1925. Its very prominent tower was a response to the Ku Klux Klan's burning of a cross on the parish property.

Transfiguration of Our Lord parish and Saint Carthage parish were both suppressed in 2000. Their territories were consolidated to form the new parish of SAINT CYPRIAN. This parish—named for the Bishop of Carthage, North Africa, martyred in A.D. 258—occupies the site of the former Saint Carthage church. The other parishes of West Philadelphia were all founded in the same year, 1921, during residential development that followed World War I. Father Joseph Wolfe had been a

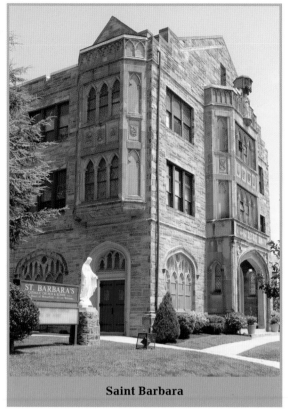

**Saint Barbara**

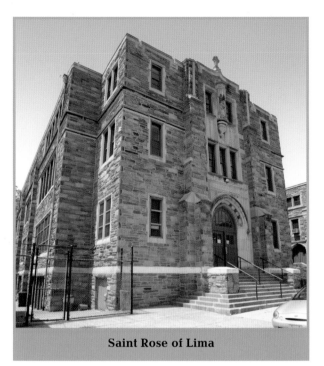

**Saint Rose of Lima**

In the 1950s and early 1960s, Saint Barbara School operated special programs for children with developmental delay and cognitive disabilities. These programs were the origin of Saint Katherine Day School, operated by the Sisters of Mercy.

About a mile to the southwest, SAINT ROSE OF LIMA parish was founded on 59th Street south of Lansdowne Avenue. The parish school building, erected in 1922, included an auditorium in the basement, a first-floor chapel, and classrooms on the second and third floors. Teaching responsibilities were entrusted to Immaculate Heart Sisters. The Great Depression interrupted plans for expanding the parish buildings, and a permanent church was never constructed. The first African American families moved into Saint Rose of Lima in the 1950s, and into Saint Barbara in the middle 1960s. By the 1980s, the areas of both parishes were predominantly African American and non-Catholic. Because of a reduced number of parishioners and priests, Saint Barbara and Saint Rose of Lima were twinned in 2000.

recently-decommissioned Hog Island shipyard was used as a temporary chapel, and a quarry in the parish provided sandstone in abundant quantities for building the parish church, dedicated in 1927. The parish school, opened in 1923, was founded by Sisters of Saint Joseph. The parish is presently entrusted to Capuchin Franciscan Friars.

decorated chaplain in the Great War, and named the parish of SAINT BARBARA after the third-century virgin martyr who is the patron saint of artillery gunners. A temporary chapel at 54th and Diamond Streets was succeeded by a permanent church on George's Lane at Lebanon Avenue in 1929. The school, founded in the 1930s, was directed by Sisters of Mercy.

In 1921, when SAINT CALLISTUS parish was founded in Overbrook, the neighborhood was still a country area, connected to the rest of the city by unpaved streets and one trolley line. The parish founding date was October 14, the feast day of this third-century pope and martyr. A building from the

**Saint Callistus**

# Southwest Philadelphia

When Saint Patrick's parish was founded in Center City in 1839, the priests of the parish were responsible for all of the southern and southwestern parts of Philadelphia County, as well as areas in Delaware County and southern New Jersey. As growing numbers of Catholic families settled in South and West Philadelphia, new parishes were established. In 1865, the last part of this wide expanse—namely, the southwestern part of Philadelphia between the Schuylkill River and Darby Creek, and the adjoining section of Delaware County—was organized into a new parish as well.

In late 1864, a wooden frame chapel, named for Saint Catherine, was constructed on the western side of Darby Creek. Early the following year, land was secured for a more permanent structure at 71st Street and Woodland Avenue, in the neighborhood of Paschallville. The site was donated by a parishioner, Clement Erwig, and the new parish church was named for his patron, Pope SAINT CLEMENT, the third successor of Saint Peter.

The first church of Saint Clement was dedicated in 1896. When a new church was built in 1959, it included the stained-glass windows from this original church. The parish school was built in 1890, and Immaculate Heart Sisters arrived in 1898 to administer it. A new school welcomed staff and students in 1927.

The original boundaries of Saint Clement included all of Southwest Philadelphia, from the Schuylkill River to Kellyville, Delaware County. It was the "mother parish" of ten other churches. The first two were Holy Spirit, Sharon Hill, and SAINT RAPHAEL, in the "Meadows" at 86th Street and Tinicum Avenue. Saint Clement's had established a mission chapel here in 1893. In 1904, it was raised to the canonical status of a parish. Immaculate Heart Sisters founded the parish school in 1915. Changing demographics led to the closing of Saint Raphael in 1989.

Several more parishes were founded in this part of Philadelphia after World War I. Father James E. Dougherty had served as chaplain at the U.S. Navy shipyard on Hog Island, South Philadelphia, during the war. In 1919, he built a brick and stone rectory and chapel for the new parish of SAINT BARNABAS, at 63rd Street and Buist Avenue. As the congregation increased, parishioners gathered for Sunday Mass at the Benn Theater, 64th Street and Woodland Avenue, until the lower church was completed in 1921. The school opened in 1927, under the direction of Immaculate Heart Sisters. The present church was dedicated in 1952.

**Saint Barnabas**

A small wooden chapel was the first location for Sunday Mass for the parish of the GOOD SHEPHERD, established at 67th Street and Chester Avenue in 1925. This neighborhood developed after World War I, and 300 new homes were built in 1925 alone. Prior to this time, Catholics faced a long journey to either Saint Clement or Saint Barnabas. The parish school was opened in 1930 under the direction of Immaculate Heart Sisters, and a second school building was erected in 1960. The present church was dedicated in 1951.

Since 1910, immigrant Polish families in Southwest Philadelphia and Grays Ferry had sought a parish of their own. Their efforts were finally successful in 1927, when Father Boleslas Zywicki celebrated Mass for the first time for the parishioners of SAINT MARY OF CZESTOCHOWA parish. That first Mass took place in the Polish Hall on Elmwood Avenue at Millick Street. By July of that year, the congregation had moved to the McIlvaine Estate at 59th Street and Elmwood Avenues. The McIlvaine mansion provided space for a church, rectory, convent and school, which was administered by Sisters of the Holy Family of Nazareth. After a fire in 1935, a new parish church was dedicated in 1937.

The national parish of OUR LADY OF LORETO was founded in 1932 for Italian-speaking families in Southwest Philadelphia. The first church was built at 63rd Street and Grays Ferry Avenue in 1932, and a larger church dedicated in 1938. Bernardine Sisters taught in the school when it opened in 1960.

At the end of the twentieth century, the population of the ethnic communities that originally attended these national parishes diminished in number. Smaller congregations could not maintain parish buildings and activities, and reduced enrollment made it unfeasible to keep individual schools open. Saint Mary of Czestochowa and Our Lady of Loreto were closed in 2000, and consolidated with Saint Barnabas parish.

In the 1950s and early 1960s, residential development after World War II transformed the neighborhoods of Eastwick and the Meadows, with nearly 1,000 new residents arriving every year. The boundaries of Saint Clement and Saint Raphael were adjusted in 1966 to establish SAINT IRENAEUS parish. Parishioners worshipped in the auditorium of Saint Clement School until 1968, when a church was dedicated on South 73rd Street. In that same year, Immaculate Heart Sisters established Saint Irenaeus/Saint Raphael School.

Parishes in West and Southwest Philadelphia experienced many difficulties in the late twentieth century, not least of which was a continuing decline in the number of Catholic parishioners. In 2004, Cardinal Rigali approved a plan to consolidate the parishes of Southwest Philadelphia. Saint Clement, Good Shepherd and Saint Irenaeus were suppressed, and one new parish, named DIVINE MERCY, was established at the site of the former Good Shepherd. The parish church of Saint Irenaeus serves as a worship site for Divine Mercy parish. Children attend Mary, Mother of Peace Area Catholic School, at the site of the former Saint Barnabas School.

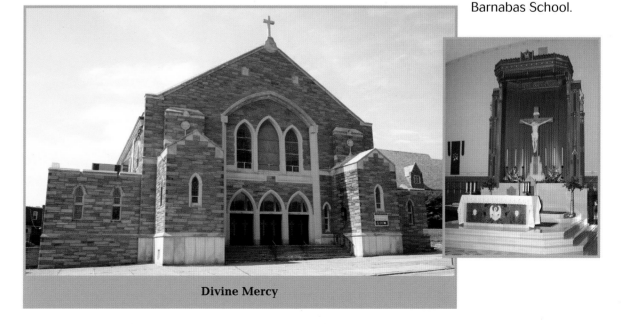

**Divine Mercy**

# BUCKS COUNTY

# Upper Bucks County

In the 1730s and 1740s, Jesuit missionaries like Father Theodore Schneider, S.J., and Father Ferdinand Steinmeyer—known in America as Father Farmer—rode circuits of 150 to 250 miles to tend scattered flocks in Pennsylvania, New Jersey and New York. As early as 1741, Father Schneider recorded a baptism in the German farming community of Revere, located along the Delaware River in northern Bucks County. Albertina Kohl was the first child baptized in the mission of SAINT JOHN THE BAPTIST, founded in 1743.

**Saint John the Baptist, Ottsville**

Albertina later married Nicholas McCarty, son of Edward McCarty, a farmer whose 500 acres of land at the foot of Haycock Mountain were the first home of Saint John's mission. In 1776, Mr. and Mrs. McCarty built the wooden structure known as the Mass House, which included a large first-floor chapel and a room on the second floor for circuit-riding priests. In 1796, their son John donated an acre of land for the church, dedicated in 1798. The McCarty homestead also included a schoolhouse, which had operated since at least 1784. The Immaculate Heart Sisters taught in the school during the 1860s, and were succeeded by Franciscans from Glen Riddle.

Over the years, the parish of Saint John was administered by Jesuits (1742-1829), Redemptorists (1848-1856) and archdiocesan priests. Missionaries of the Sacred Heart have served the parish since 1912. A fire destroyed the original church in 1853, and this church was replaced in 1855. The present church was dedicated in 2003.

The parish of Saint John the Baptist was responsible for a number of missions in the surrounding countryside. Father Henry Stommel, a German-speaking archdiocesan priest who was pastor of Saint John's from 1871 to 1875, took special interest in these missions, which were home to largely German-speaking farming families. Even after he was appointed in 1875 as pastor of Our Lady of Mount Carmel, Doylestown, Father Stommel continued to visit these missions in Upper Bucks County.

In 1881, Father Stommel gathered the Catholic community in Quakertown at the home of James Cox. This little band of nine people would help to plan a parish named for SAINT ISIDORE of Madrid, also known as Saint Isidore the Farmer. A church with room for 200 people was built in 1886, and in 1921 the rectory housed the first school, founded by Sisters of Saint Joseph. Despite anti-Catholic attitudes among some local residents, the Catholic community continued to grow, necessitating a larger church, which was built in 1953. Residential development continued and the present church, built on a recently-acquired site outside the town, was dedicated in 2005.

Work on the Bethlehem branch of the Reading Railroad attracted large numbers of immigrant Irish families to Perkasie, East Rockhill Township. Priests from Saint John's had been celebrating Mass there as early as 1863. At first, the German and Irish families met for Mass in parishioners' homes, until arrangements were made to meet above Hendrick's General Store in Perkasie. In 1868, a small church in Sellersville was dedicated in honor of SAINT AGNES. It was served by priests from Saint John's (1868–1877), Saint Stanislaus, Lansdale (1877–1908), and Saint Isidore,

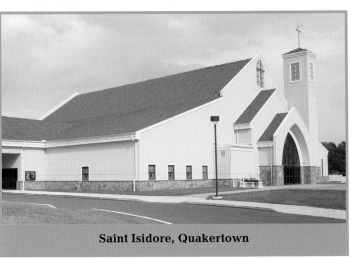

**Saint Isidore, Quakertown**

**Saint Agnes, Sellersville**

donated by the du Mees. A church was built that year, and in 1929 the Missionary Sisters of the Most Sacred Heart of Jesus opened a small school on the second floor of the church. Faced with anti-Catholic attitudes, Father Charles Knittle encouraged parishioners to move closer to the parish site, and when possible he helped them to find land. A church/school building was opened in 1979, and restored following a fire in 1988. In 2000, this building was renovated again and dedicated as a permanent church.

Quakertown (1908–1919), until it was canonically established as a parish. A second church was built in 1952, and the present church was dedicated in 1985. The parish school, which opened in 1922 under the direction of Immaculate Heart Sisters, was consolidated with Our Lady of the Sacred Heart School in 1978.

In October 1918, Edward and Anna du Mee offered their house for the first Mass in Hilltown. The following April, the parish of OUR LADY OF THE SACRED HEART was founded on land

Father William Wappeler, S.J., had established a mission at Saint Paul, Goshenhoppen (later renamed Blessed Sacrament Church, Bally) in Berks County in 1737, and priests from Bally ministered to Catholics living near the iron and steel forges known as Durham Furnace. Here, in 1872, Father Stommel established the mission church of SAINT LAWRENCE, patron saint of ironworkers. The Borough of Riegelsville was incorporated in 1916, and the

mission at Saint Lawrence continued until the parish was canonically established in 1974. The present church was dedicated on August 10, 1958, the feast of Saint Lawrence.

**Saint Lawrence, Riegelsville**

**Our Lady of the Sacred Heart, Hilltown**

# Doylestown and Vicinity

From the early days of the Commonwealth of Pennsylvania, present-day Easton Road (Route 611) was a stage coach route between Philadelphia and points north. William Doyle built a tavern at the meeting of this road and the turnpike that connected Norristown and New Hope (Route 202), and the community of Doylestown grew up around this intersection. In 1813, Doylestown became the county seat of Bucks County, and in 1838 was incorporated as a borough.

The German and Irish immigrants of Doylestown attended Mass either at Saint John the Baptist, Haycock, or in Lambertville, New Jersey—a journey of about 12 miles over unpaved roads. In 1834, Father Herzog of Saint John's celebrated Masses at the Union Academy, preaching in German and English. In 1850, the parish of Saint Mary's was founded, and Father Francis George celebrated Mass there twice a month. A church was dedicated in 1855 and renamed in honor of OUR LADY OF MOUNT CARMEL.

In 1876, parishioners saw to the founding of Saint Bernard's School, the name of which was subsequently changed to Our Lady of Mount Carmel. Classes were taught by Franciscan Sisters from Glen Riddle, and the school was expanded in 1950 and 1958. In 1968 the present church was dedicated, with furnishings and stained-glass windows designed by parishioner Edward Byrne. His studio has created windows for several other churches in the archdiocese.

Father Henry Stommel became pastor of Our Lady of Mount Carmel in 1875. Within a few years, he took pastoral responsibility for the growing Catholic community in the Borough of New Hope, situated along the Delaware River and 12 miles northeast of Doylestown. Baptisms had been celebrated in New Hope as early as 1741, and Catholics often attended the mission church of Saint John the Evangelist in Lambertville, New Jersey, across the river.

After the Diocese of Newark was founded in 1853, Catholics in New Hope continued to travel to Saint John's; however, in 1880 a committee of New Hope residents

**Saint Martin of Tours, New Hope**

petitioned Archbishop Wood for a parish of their own. Priests from Saint Andrew's, Newtown, celebrated Mass in New Hope twice a month until 1883, when Father Stommel saw to the construction of a parish church. The church was dedicated, and the parish of SAINT MARTIN OF TOURS formally established, in 1885. The original church underwent a thorough renovation in the 1960s, and parishioner George Nakashima, a world-renowned woodworker, donated time and materials to fashion sanctuary furnishings. A

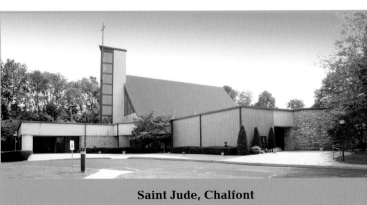

**Saint Jude, Chalfont**

...

**Our Lady of Mount Carmel, Doylestown**

new school, parish office and church were constructed along Route 179, and dedicated in December 2000.

The parish of SAINT JUDE in Chalfont was founded in 1962 with only 325 families; however, the population multiplied five times over in the first thirty years. A farmhouse along Route 202 served as the first rectory and chapel, and parishioners met for Sunday Mass at Forest Park, a local amusement park. The original church, dedicated in 1963, contained a Shrine of Saint Jude—the patron saint for "impossible cases"—which drew as many as

**Saint Cyril of Jerusalem, Jamison**

5,000 pilgrims for weekly devotions. In 1982, this church burned down. A new church—including a new shrine—was dedicated in 1984. In 1963, Sisters of Mercy formed the first faculty of the parish school.

An anticipated increase in population within Warminster and Warwick Townships, east of Doylestown, prompted the founding of SAINT CYRIL OF JERUSALEM parish in

Jamison in 1965. However, home construction was much slower than expected, and with few families the parish faced difficulties in its early years. Until the first church was dedicated in 1969, the Saint Cyril parish community met for Sunday Mass in the Warwick Township Fire House and also the Bucks County Country Club. Residential development accelerated in the 1980s and 1990s, and a new church was dedicated in 2004.

In 1968, a new parish, drawn from the territory of Saint Cyril and of Saint Bede, Holland, was founded in Richboro. One of the priests on the archdiocesan College of Consultors—which met with Cardinal John Krol to discuss plans for the new parish—commented that a parish in a place called Richboro ought to be named for a saint who ministered to the poor. The cardinal immediately selected the name of SAINT VINCENT DE PAUL, the French priest known for his care for needy persons. The

**Saint Vincent de Paul, Richboro**

450 families who founded the parish celebrated Sunday Mass in the Churchville Elementary School until the dedication of their church in 1970.

By the late 1990s, the parish of Our Lady of Mount Carmel served more than 5,000 families, and continuing residential expansion in Buckingham and Plumstead Townships was a sign that the Catholic population would continue to increase. On July 1, 2000, a new parish was created from the territory of Our Lady of Mount Carmel, and named for OUR LADY OF GUADALUPE, the Patroness of the Americas. The parish established offices in Buckingham Township, and parishioners met for Mass in the auditorium of Central Bucks East High School and Holicong Middle School. At the time of this writing, plans are underway for the construction of a parish church and office at Durham Road and Cold Spring Creamery Road.

**Our Lady of Guadalupe, Buckingham (proposed)**

# Warrington, Warminster and Vicinity

Warrington Township, on the border of Bucks and Montgomery Counties, was developed after World War I, in part because of the availability of "kit homes"—pre-fabricated houses that could be ordered by mail from manufacturers around the country. To attend Sunday Mass, Catholics in these new developments faced the choice of journeying either to Our Lady of Mount Carmel, Doylestown, or to Saint David, Willow Grove—a five-mile trip in either direction. In 1922, the parish of SAINT JOSEPH was founded at Easton Road and County Line Road in Warrington, the midpoint between these two parishes. Immaculate Heart Sisters founded the parish school in 1925, and in 1950, the present church/school building was dedicated. A second school building was constructed in 1961.

**Saint John Bosco, Hatboro**

During the 1950s and 1960s, the Warrington and Warminster area underwent development, as the G.I. Bill made home construction and ownership affordable. Seven new parishes were founded in the area within fifteen years. Industries associated with World War II, particularly aviation, attracted workers to the area, and Saint Joseph's established several chapels in the Hatboro area to care for new residents. The parish of SAINT JOHN BOSCO was founded in Hatboro, Montgomery County, in 1953, from the territory of Saint Joseph's and Saint David's, Willow Grove. A church/school building was dedicated the following year, and Immaculate Heart Sisters were invited to teach in the school. The present church was constructed over three years, and dedicated in 1991.

In May 1956, a chapel dedicated to Our Lady of Perpetual Help was built on Fir Street in Warminster. A carriage house at Street Road and York Road was converted in September of that year to serve as a chapel for the new parish of the NATIVITY OF OUR LORD. The parish church and school were dedicated in 1958, and a new church and hall in 1963. Increased enrollment in the school, staffed by Sisters of Saint Joseph, made it the second-largest parish school in the archdiocese outside the City of Philadelphia during the 1980s and 1990s.

In 1963, the boundaries of Saint Joseph's and Saint David's were adjusted to establish the parish of SAINT CATHERINE OF SIENA in Horsham, Montgomery County. Saint Joseph's had provided priests for this mission chapel in Horsham since 1931. At the time, anti-Catholic hostility made it difficult to find a site for Mass. Finally, a barn was made available on the estate of C. Howard Thomas, founder of the National Publishing Company, which printed the "Gideon

**Saint Joseph, Warrington**

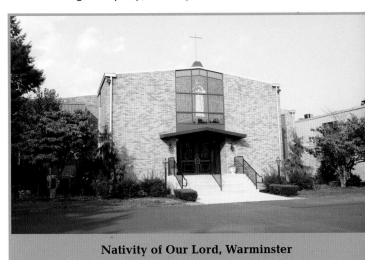

**Nativity of Our Lord, Warminster**

**Saint Catherine of Siena, Horsham**

Bibles" commonly found in hotel rooms. The mission was established as a parish in 1963, and a church/school building was dedicated in 1966. Sisters of Mercy arrived to teach in the school in the same year.

In 1968, Saint Joseph's was divided again, and parishioners of the new SAINT ROBERT BELLARMINE parish in Warrington worshipped in the Barn Cinema movie theater on Easton Road. The parish church and school were dedicated in 1970. A larger church followed in 1982. In 1974, the parish school was consolidated with Saint Joseph's School.

**Saint Robert Bellarmine, Warrington**

# Bristol, Bensalem and Vicinity

Founded by Samuel Clift in 1681 as Buckingham, the town of Bristol is one of the oldest communities in Pennsylvania. As the principal town in the area, Buckingham it gave its name to the surrounding county, which became known as Buckinghamshire. (The abbreviation for this name—Bucks.—eventually was used as the name of the county.) Clift established a ferry and tavern, and in 1720 the town that grew up around this Delaware River port was incorporated as Bristol. Industry in the 1700s centered on mills and wharves along the river. Fertile land made farming in the area very successful, and Bristol was one of only three Market Towns in Pennsylvania. Still, in 1790 the community had fewer than 300 people and 50 households. Bristol experienced an economic expansion in 1837 when ground was broken for the Delaware Division of the Pennsylvania Canal. Along these canals, which ran parallel to the Delaware River from Easton to Bristol, mules pulled barges bearing coal from the Lehigh Valley in upstate Pennsylvania. The work of digging canals, manning barges and unloading coal attracted immigrant laborers, many of whom were from County Donegal, Ireland. By 1830, the population of the borough numbered 1,200 persons.

In 1844 or 1845, Father John Mackin, from County Armagh, Ireland, established a mission in Bristol. He named the mission chapel for SAINT MARK, and this chapel was dedicated in 1846. In December 1855, Saint John Neumann celebrated the Sacrament of Confirmation here for 93 men, women and children.

When the church was damaged by fire in 1867, the pastor, Father Edmond Prendergast, saw to its rebuilding. Father Prendergast, pastor of Saint Mark's until 1870, became in 1897 the first Auxiliary Bishop of Philadelphia. He was appointed the third Archbishop of Philadelphia in 1911. Immaculate Heart Sisters founded the parish school, which opened in 1887.

Saint Mark's is the "mother church" of many parishes in Bristol and its vicinity. The first was the parish of SAINT CHARLES BORROMEO, founded in Cornwells Heights, Bensalem Township, in 1903. Money, land and construction costs for the original brownstone church were donated by parishioner Charles

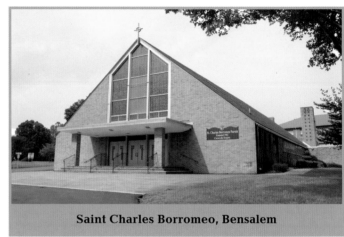

**Saint Charles Borromeo, Bensalem**

McFadden and his family, and the parish was named for Mr. McFadden's patron saint. This first church was destroyed by arson in 1924, and for a brief time parishioners worshipped at Saint Elizabeth's Convent—the nearby motherhouse of Mother Katharine Drexel's Sisters of the Blessed Sacrament.

The connection of the parish to the Drexel family antedates 1903. Prior to his appointment

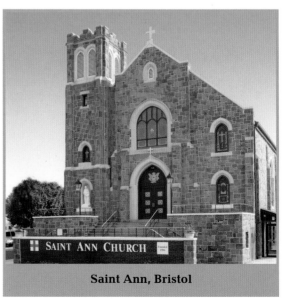

**Saint Ann, Bristol**

**Saint Mark, Bristol**

as founding pastor, Father Andrew McCue had been chaplain at the motherhouse across the road. In addition, Mother Katharine's sister, Mrs. Louise Drexel Morrell, opened her estate—the present site of Morrell Park, Philadelphia—to area children whom she tutored in religion. The parish school was founded by Immaculate Heart Sisters in 1920, and a new building was erected in 1926. The present church of Saint Charles was dedicated in 1963.

Numerous Italian immigrants began to arrive in Bristol in 1868, attracted by opportunity for employment connected to the canal. Initially they attended Saint Mark's, where Father Paul Gentile was assigned to preach and instruct them in their native language. In 1906 he established a little chapel for the Italian community, which became the national parish of SAINT ANN. The lower church was completed in 1907, and the upper church was dedicated in 1916. The parish school was founded in 1920 by the Holy Trinity Sisters, and care of the parish is entrusted to Trinitarian priests.

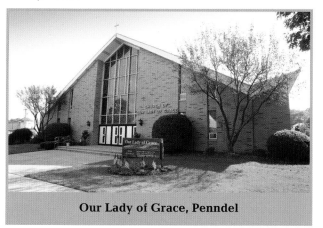
Our Lady of Grace, Penndel

The Reading Railroad began service to Langhorne in 1876, and the small farming community around the Langhorne train station witnessed commercial and residential development. The district of the Eden Post Office was incorporated as the Borough of Attleboro in 1899, and renamed Penndel in 1947. Holy Ghost Fathers from Bensalem established a mission here in 1906, and in 1908, an archdiocesan priest, Father Miles Keegan, was appointed the first pastor of OUR LADY OF GRACE parish. In 1923, Immaculate Heart Sisters arrived to staff the parish school, at Bellevue Avenue and Crescent Street. New school buildings were erected in 1949 and 1958. The present church—built in 1961—replaced the old mission chapel.

After World War I, the area of Croydon in Bristol Township developed as a commuter suburb easily accessible from Philadelphia. The parish boundaries of Saint Mark were adjusted in 1922 to found the parish of SAINT THOMAS AQUINAS. In 1922 the first school opened, under the direction of Immaculate Heart Sisters, and a small wooden church on Emily Avenue was dedicated in 1925. A new church/school building was built in 1926 at the corner of Bristol Pike and Belmont Avenue. After the Second World War, new school buildings were constructed, and the present church was dedicated in 1956.

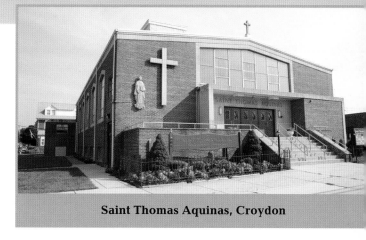
Saint Thomas Aquinas, Croydon

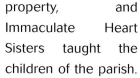

The post-World War II period was a time of population development in Bensalem Township, and three new parishes were founded. The first, OUR LADY OF FATIMA, was established in 1954, during the Marian Year designated by Pope Pius XII to commemorate the centennial of the definition of the dogma of the Immaculate Conception. The first Mass was celebrated in a farm house on the parish property, and Immaculate Heart Sisters taught the children of the parish.

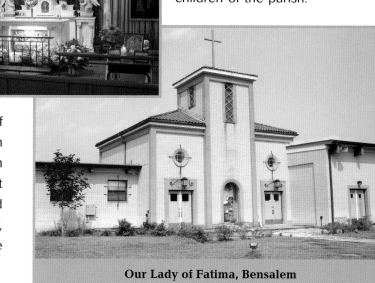
Our Lady of Fatima, Bensalem

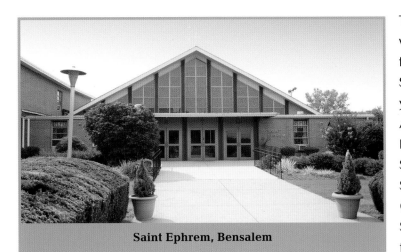

**Saint Ephrem, Bensalem**

The youngest parish in Bensalem was founded in 1976, and named for SAINT ELIZABETH ANN SETON, canonized the previous year—the first native-born American woman to be so honored. Parishioners met for Sunday Mass in the chapel of Saint Francis Vocational School (now part of the Saint Francis—Saint Joseph Homes for Children) from 1976 to 1978. In that year Masses were celebrated in the newly-completed parish church, which was formally dedicated in 1981.

Sunday Masses were held at Butch's Auction House until 1956, when a church/school building was dedicated.

Ten years later, the parish of SAINT EPHREM was established from territory served by Saint Charles Borromeo, Bensalem, and Our Lady of Grace, Penndel. The Newportville Fire House was the site for Sunday Mass until the dedication of a church/school building on Hulmeville Road, opposite the tract that would become Resurrection Cemetery. The school, which opened in 1969, was staffed by Immaculate Heart Sisters, and was enlarged in 1986.

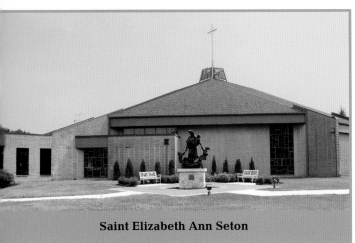

**Saint Elizabeth Ann Seton**

# Newtown and Vicinity

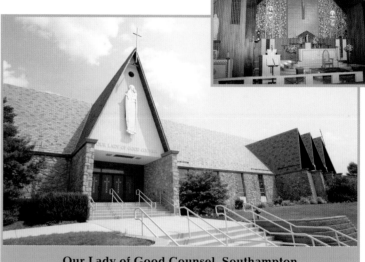

**Our Lady of Good Counsel, Southampton**

The town of Newtown Creek was established in 1684 by William Penn to provide a place for country homes for residents of the City of Philadelphia. Newtown was the county seat of Bucks County from 1725 to 1813, and was incorporated as a borough in 1838. The few Catholics in the borough faced challenging journeys—a round trip of as much as 25 miles, on foot or horseback—to attend Mass in Trenton or Lambertville, New Jersey, and later in Doylestown or Bristol.

Industrial development after the Civil War—related to the development of railroads and canals along the Delaware River—increased the population of Newtown, where a mission was established in 1864. Priests from Saint Mark's in Bristol celebrated Mass once a month in the Township House Hotel or the Free Church (now Newtown Hall) until SAINT ANDREW church was built in 1874. The church was dedicated in 1880, and the parish was established in that same year. The parish school opened in 1927 under the supervision of Immaculate Heart Sisters, and new buildings were constructed in 1953 and 1957. As farms were sold off for housing development in the 1970s, the Catholic population of Newtown rapidly increased. The number of registered families more than doubled between 1978 and 1982. In 1984, the parish moved to its present location on Swamp Road, where the church was dedicated in 1985.

Saint Andrew's parish was responsible for a large part of Bucks County, as far south as Southampton on the boundary with Montgomery County. For years, priests from Saint Andrew's celebrated Mass for about a dozen Catholic families in the neighborhood at Fitzpatrick's Hall, Street Road and Second Street Pike. By 1923, the number of families had increased to fifty, and the parish of OUR LADY OF GOOD COUNSEL was established in Southampton. Local residents were initially reluctant to sell property for a Catholic church; however, once the site was purchased, parish volunteers acted quickly to dig the foundations for the church, dedicated in 1924. The community grew rapidly after World War II, and a parish school, staffed by Felician Sisters, opened in 1954. A second church and school were built in 1957, and the present church was dedicated in 1962.

In 1923, a frame clubhouse in Trevose was converted into the chapel of Saint Thérèse the Little Flower, as a place for summer residents to attend Mass. In 1927, Our Lady of Good Counsel parish took responsibility for this mission and also for Saint Mary's chapel on Elmwood Avenue in Trevose Heights. The area was transformed after World War II from summer resort to residential suburb, and a parish was founded in Feasterville on November 3, 1950. This parish was named for the ASSUMPTION OF THE BLESSED VIRGIN MARY, the dogma that had been solemnly defined by Pope Pius XII only two days before. The new parish used Saint Mary's Chapel until a church/school building was dedicated in 1956. The founding faculty was made up of

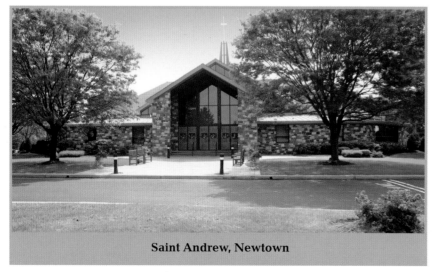

**Saint Andrew, Newtown**

Immaculate Heart Sisters. The altar and sanctuary furnishings were designed by George Nakashima, a woodworker and parishioner of Saint Martin of Tours, New Hope.

The parish of SAINT BEDE THE VENERABLE was founded in Holland on May 16, 1965—the date then celebrated as his feast day (now observed on May 25). Members of the new parish, who had previously belonged to Saint Andrew's, Newtown, met on Sundays in the auditorium of Villa Joseph Marie High School, a private school operated by the Sisters of Saint Casimir. These Sisters also founded the parish school of Saint Bede's in 1966, and at first utilized classrooms in Our Lady of Good Counsel School, Southampton. The present church and school were dedicated in 1967.

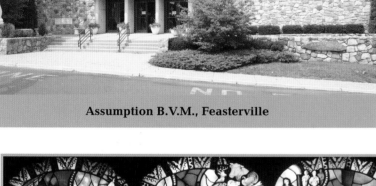

Assumption B.V.M., Feasterville

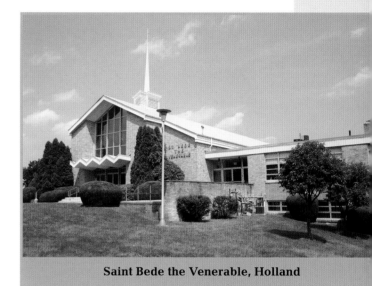

Saint Bede the Venerable, Holland

199

# Morrisville, Levittown and Vicinity

The extension of the Pennsylvania Railroad towards New York in the 1870s included construction of a railroad bridge across the Delaware River, connecting Morrisville, Pennsylvania, with Trenton, New Jersey. Plentiful jobs in the construction of this bridge, and of a railroad spur into the Borough of Morrisville, attracted immigrant laborers to the area. Priests from Saint Mark's in Bristol had established a mission here in 1863, and in 1901 the church of the HOLY TRINITY was built on Washington Street. This first church was razed in 1951 to make way for the construction of the U.S. Route 1 bridge across the Delaware. A new church/school building was constructed in 1952, and Immaculate Heart Sisters arrived that year to administer the school. The present church was dedicated in 1957.

**Holy Trinity, Morrisville**

The 1920s saw industrial development in the Morrisville area, as manufacturers like the Vulcanized Rubber and Plastics Company and Robertson Manufacturing set up plants. As families built homes in the area, the boundaries of Holy Trinity were adjusted, and in 1920 the parish of SAINT IGNATIUS OF ANTIOCH was founded in Yardley, about four and a half miles from Morrisville along the Delaware River. The parish had been a mission of Saint Mark's, and this mission church served until a church and school were built in 1958. The Glen Riddle Franciscans were invited that year to teach in the school.

The 1950s were a time of growth for the steel industry in this part of Bucks County. The Fairless Works Steel Plant, part of the United States Steel Corporation (U.S. Steel), was built in 1951. At the same time, U.S. Steel contracted the Danherst Corporation to build tracts of prefabricated homes for sale to employees. The residential development—Fairless Hills—was named for the president of U.S. Steel, Benjamin Fairless. Catholic residents of the new community were organized into a parish named for SAINT FRANCES CABRINI, the Italian-American missionary nun who had been canonized in 1946. Initially, Mass was celebrated at the Fairless Hills Fire Company, until the completion of a chapel and school in 1954. Immaculate Heart Sisters arrived in 1955 to staff the school, and a new school was built in 1966. The present church was dedicated in 1976.

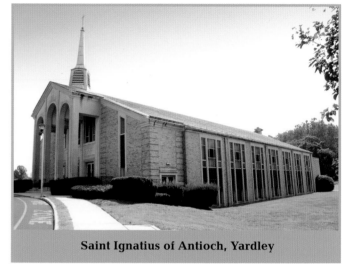

**Saint Ignatius of Antioch, Yardley**

Steelworkers and their families also found homes in the much larger community developed by William J. Levitt and Sons. Levittown, as it is named, is often cited as one of the first modern suburbs: large tracts of single-family homes, with few exterior variations, and each surrounded by a lawn and having built-in appliances and conveniences. The houses were quick and inexpensive to produce. The ready availability of jobs, and easy financing through the G.I. Bill, meant that Levittown developed very rapidly. In two years,

**Saint Frances Cabrini, Fairless Hills**

**Saint Michael the Archangel, Levittown**

more than 16,000 homes were built for a population of 68,000 people.

Part of Levitt's plan to encourage sales of new houses was to offer land at minimal cost for public schools and religious institutions. The archdiocese benefited from this offer and so established three parishes for the increasing local Catholic community. The first parishioners of SAINT MICHAEL THE ARCHANGEL parish initially attended Mass at the Italian chapel of the Sacred Heart in Tullytown, and soon after at the Edgely Fire House. The first school was built in 1954 and staffed by Sisters of Mercy. Sunday Masses were celebrated in the school auditorium until the completion of a church in 1966. From 1,200 parishioners in 1954, the parish had grown to more than 2,600 parishioners by 1955.

The Edgely Fire House was also home to the second parish in Levittown, IMMACULATE CONCEPTION OF THE BLESSED VIRGIN MARY. A church/school building was com-

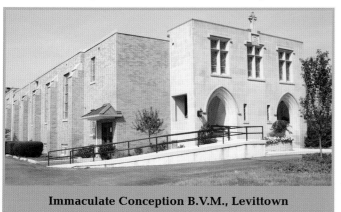

**Immaculate Conception B.V.M., Levittown**

pleted in 1955, and Immaculate Heart Sisters served on the faculty of the school. At first, the parish comprised only a few hundred families, but the expansion of Levittown saw an accelerated increase in the parish population. A similar situation affected the parish of QUEEN OF THE UNIVERSE, founded in 1955 in what

**Saint Joseph the Worker, Fallsington**

had been a rural area between Fairless Hills and Penndel, north of Levittown. As the development moved north, a church and school, conducted by Sisters of Saint Joseph, were built on land bought from Levitt and Sons. The church—named for the feast of the Queenship of Our Lady, added to the General Roman Calendar by Pope Pius XII in 1954—was dedicated in 1958. The present church was dedicated in 1985.

Employees of the steel plants perhaps provided the inspiration to name the fourth parish founded in the area in as many years: SAINT JOSEPH THE WORKER, located in the community of Fallsington. In 1955, Pope Pius XII

**Queen of the Universe, Levittown**

had established a feast day with this title on May 1, to contrast with May Day celebrations observed in Communist nations. In 1956, a barn on the newly-acquired parish property on Newportville–Fallsington (now New Falls) Road became the first daily Mass chapel, and the auditorium of the Manor Public School on Penn Valley Road was made available for Sunday Mass. The church and school were completed in 1957, and Bernardine Franciscans were invited to teach the children.

As the interstate highway system expanded in the 1960s, Archbishop (later Cardinal) Krol surmised that further development would take place along the route of Interstate 95. He established the parish of SAINT JOHN THE EVANGELIST in Lower Makefield Township, located between the boroughs of Yardley and Morrisville. Parish territory was taken from Saint Ignatius, Holy Trinity, and Saint Joseph the Worker. A church/school building was dedicated in 1966, and Bernardines arrived that year to staff the school. The present church was dedicated in 1982.

**Saint John the Evangelist, Lower Makefield**

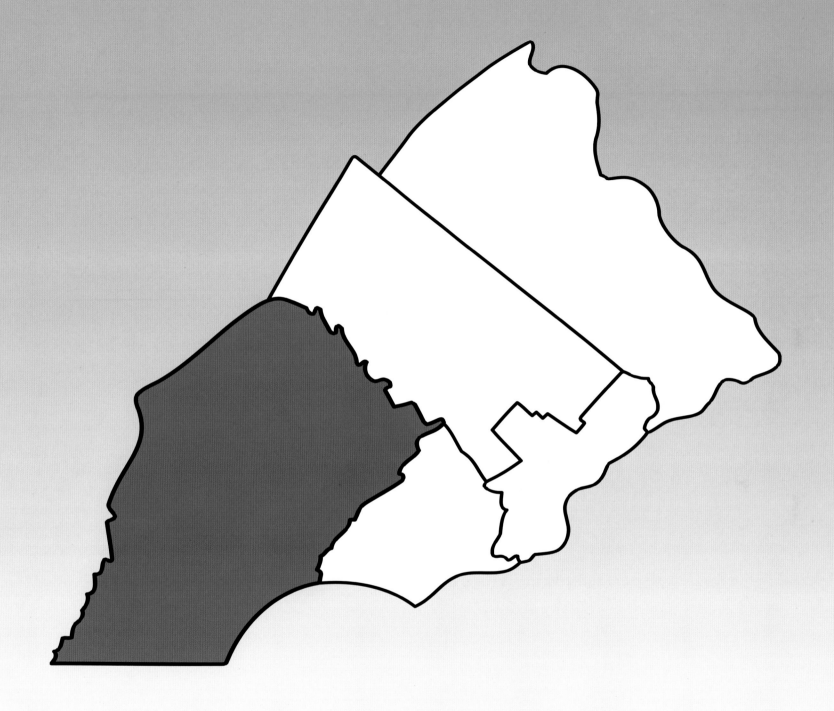

# Chester County

# West Chester, Downingtown and Vicinity

Chester County was one of the original three counties founded by William Penn in 1682. Colonial settlements clustered around the village of Turk's Head, called after the inn of the same name. Turk's Head was renamed and incorporated as the Borough of West Chester in 1782, and became the county seat in 1789.

In 1793, John and Mary Hannum sold a plot of land to Philadelphia Catholic and Revolutionary War hero Stephen Moylan for a Catholic church in the borough. Originally known as Christ's Church, it was a mission church attended until 1808 by priests from Old Saint Joseph's and Old Saint Mary's in Philadelphia. For the next two decades, it was served by Father Patrick Kenny, who also tended to several other mission churches in Delaware, until his death in 1840. Eleven visiting pastors were appointed during the 1840s.

In 1852, Father John Prendergast was appointed the first resident pastor in West Chester. He organized the construction of a church, dedicated in 1852 and named SAINT AGNES. Even in its earliest days, the small parish served a racially diverse community—an African American parishioner was buried in the parish cemetery as early as 1830. Father Prendergast also took an active role in promoting the cause of the Union during the Civil War. Saint John Neumann celebrated the Sacrament of Confirmation at Saint Agnes five times during the 1850s.

Saint Agnes School welcomed its first students in 1872. They were taught by Immaculate Heart Sisters, whose motherhouse had been transferred from Reading to West Chester in 1871. School buildings were erected in 1892 and 1910. The present church was dedicated in 1927. The parish still celebrates the Solemnity of the Assumption (August 15) with a solemn procession—a tradition begun by Italian parishioners in 1919. Today, the community is home to a large Spanish-speaking population, and Masses are celebrated every Sunday in Spanish as well as in English.

In 1851, Saint Agnes parish established a mission church in the Borough of Downingtown, a mill town on the main road

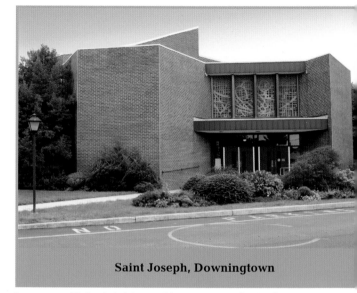

**Saint Joseph, Downingtown**

between Philadelphia and Lancaster. Catholics assembled for Mass at the home of Michael McFadden, on Bradford Avenue, as well as in McFadden's Railroad Hotel. In 1852 the church of SAINT JOSEPH was dedicated in the west end of the town, an area inhabited pre-dominantly by Irish families. Saint Joseph's remained a mission church—one of six for which Saint Agnes parish was responsible—until 1870, when a resident pastor was appointed.

Immaculate Heart Sisters were teaching the children of Saint Joseph's before 1940, and in 1954 the first parish school was built. A new school was erected in 1987. Pastor and parishioners broke ground for the present parish church in 1968. The parish site was an 82-acre plot donated by Gunard and Margaret Carlson. Mr. Carlson, an engineer, was not a Catholic; however, his daughter was a member of the parish. This church opened in 1972.

**Saint Agnes, West Chester**

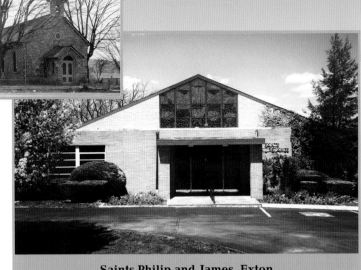

In 1873, Saint Joseph's parish established a mission of its own, Saint Mary of the Immaculate Conception. This little chapel was located in the community of Exton, at the intersection of the Lancaster Road (present-day Route 30) and the road from Pottstown (Route 100). The building had been a stable belonging to two sisters, proprietors of the nearby Ship Inn, who donated the stable for the nominal fee of $1 a year for five years. This chapel served a community of farmers, quarry workers and domestic servants. A parishioner would meet the visiting priest, who arrived by train, and bring him to the chapel in a horse-drawn wagon. Unfortunately, there was not a railroad station in Exton; accordingly, the priest had to ask the conductor to slow the train as it approached Ship Road to permit the priest to jump off.

Saint Mary's remained a mission of Saint Joseph's until 1959, when the parish of

**Saints Philip and James, Exton**

SAINTS PHILIP AND JAMES was established in Exton on May 12. Although two parishes (in West Philadelphia and Elkins Park) had been named for Saint James the Greater, this was the first named for Saint James the Less, who shares a feast day with Saint Philip, then observed on May 11. A church/ school building was erected in 1960, and the school was staffed by Immaculate Heart Sisters. The parish church was dedicated in 1966.

Only two apostles remained who were not honored with a

church named for them in the archdiocese, and in 1961 a new parish in West Chester was named SAINTS SIMON AND JUDE. (A second parish named for Saint Jude would be founded the following year in Chalfont.) A small community—only about 350 families—met for Mass at the Goshen Fire Company meeting hall until a church was dedicated in 1962. That same year a school was established under the direction of Immaculate Heart Sisters. The parish population grew quickly—multiplying more than five times in the first 25 years—and by the year 2000 it had outgrown the original church. Cardinal Rigali dedicated the present church in 2005.

**Saints Simon and Jude, West Chester**

**Saints Peter and Paul, East Goshen**

Saint Maximilian Kolbe, West Chester

The population growth of the West Chester area during the 1960s and 1970s made it necessary to adjust boundaries of existing parishes to form the parish of SAINTS PETER AND PAUL in East Goshen Township, between West Chester and Malvern. The chapels of Immaculata College (now Immaculata University) and Villa Maria Academy—both on the campus of the motherhouse of the Immaculate Heart Sisters in Immaculata—were gathering places for the first parishioners. Construction began in 1968 on the parish church, dedicated in 1970. A parish religious education program began in 1974, and the parish school opened its doors in 2001.

Soon, two additional parishes were needed in this part of Chester County. SAINT MAXI-MILIAN KOLBE parish in West Chester was established in 1986. The population of this new parish—named for the Polish Franciscan priest and martyr at the Auschwitz concentration camp who had been canonized in 1982—doubled within the first five years. Parishioners met for Sunday Mass at the Newman Center of West Chester University and at Stetson Middle School until the parish church was dedicated in 1988.

A parish named for SAINT ELIZABETH, the mother of Saint John the Baptist, was founded in 2000 within Uwchlan Township, north of Downingtown. The parish church was dedi-cated in 2005, and the parish school opened in 2006.

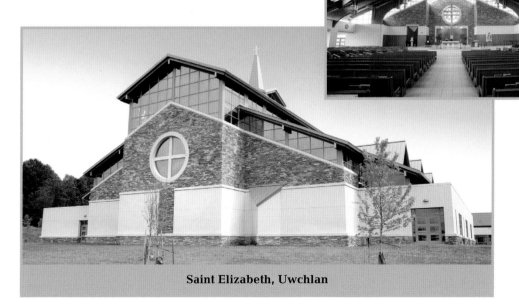
Saint Elizabeth, Uwchlan

# Phoenixville and Vicinity

The village of Phoenixville—a mill town situated at the confluence of French Creek and the Schuylkill River—was settled in the 1730s. The arrival in 1851 of the Phoenix Iron Works transformed this small community of farmers and millers. This manufacturer of cannon and other armaments for the Civil War drew Irish, and later Italian and Eastern European immigrants in search of employment. These new arrivals built homes in the newly-incorporated borough.

The mother church of SAINT MARY OF THE ASSUMPTION had been built in 1840, and was visited monthly by priests from Saint Patrick parish in Norristown. On other Sundays, parishioners either walked to Norristown, or gathered for the Rosary and Litany of the Blessed Virgin Mary at Saint Mary's Church. The first resident pastor, Father Philip O'Farrell, was appointed in 1846.

**Sacred Heart, Phoenixville**

In time, Saint Mary's Church could no longer accommodate the parish population. The expanded church was dedicated in 1854, and was the site, in 1857, of the first celebration of the Forty Hours devotion outside the City of Philadelphia. The Immaculate Heart Sisters opened the parish school in 1890, in a former public school.

Slovak immigrants working at the Phoenix Iron Works lived in company-built housing and attended Mass at Saint Mary's. Father Joseph Kasparek, a Slovak priest from Reading, Berks County, traveled to Phoenixville to celebrate Mass and the sacraments for these immigrants,

and encouraged them to petition for a parish of their own. In 1900 the national parish of the SACRED HEART was established for Slovak-speaking Catholics, in what had been the Phoenixville Public Library. This church, renovated in 1920, was damaged by fire in 1923, and the present church was built later that year. The parish school was founded by Immaculate Heart Sisters in 1906, and a new school building opened in 1959.

A community of Polish immigrants also worshipped at Saint Mary's, and later at Sacred Heart. Visiting priests served this community from 1901 to 1903, when a delegation of Polish Catholics met with Archbishop Ryan to ask him to establish a Polish national parish in Phoenixville. HOLY TRINITY parish had its first home in a former public school on Dayton Street until the parish church was dedicated in 1910. Men of the parish volunteered in the evenings after work to dig the foundation and assist in the construction of the church. Early years were turbulent at times—seven pastors served the parish in its first decade—but the situation improved in the 1920s and 1930s. Bernardine Sisters taught in the parish school, which opened in 1930. In 1999, Holy Trinity was twinned with Sacred Heart.

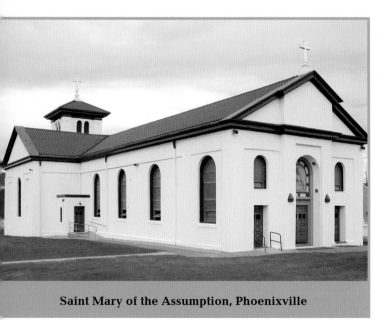

**Saint Mary of the Assumption, Phoenixville**

**Holy Trinity, Phoenixville**

Irish-born Thomas Byrne became a licensed machinist with the Phoenix Iron Works in 1875. He was a creative and skilled inventor, and money he made from various patents enabled him to build the Byrne Knitting Mill—one of the largest in the country—which, in turn, brought him a large fortune. In 1905, he obtained permission from Archbishop Ryan to build SAINT ANN Church in Phoenixville as a memorial to his mother, Ann Byrne, who had died nine days after giving birth to Thomas in 1854.

Mr. Byrne, his wife and six other family members are entombed in the crypt of Saint Ann's Memorial Church, together with the founding pastor, Father John Wagner. A new, larger church, known as Saint Ann's Chapel, was built a block away in 1967. The parish school opened in 1922 under the

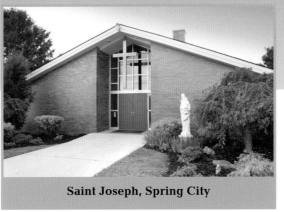

Saint Joseph, Spring City

direction of the Immaculate Heart Sisters. It was renamed Holy Family School, and today serves as a consolidated school for the parishes in Phoenixville and Spring City.

This last town, originally known as Pump Town or Springville, was settled around 1815, as the Schuylkill Navigation Company dug canals along the Schuylkill River to transport coal from Reading to Philadelphia. The canals, grist mills and saw mills in the area stimulated local commerce as well as opportunities for employment, and these factors attracted immigrants. In 1891, Mrs. Frances Sherry opened her home to fellow Catholics who gathered for Mass with Father Thomas Quinn of Saint Mary's, Phoenixville. In 1916, Saint Mary's acquired property in Spring City for a mission church, named for SAINT JOSEPH. The church remained a mission until 1919, when a canonical parish was founded. The parish school was opened in 1955, and staffed by Sisters of Saint Joseph.

In the 1960s, northern Chester County underwent development, and two additional parishes were founded. Parishioners of SAINT BASIL THE GREAT—founded in 1965 in Kimberton, west of Phoenixville—first gathered at the Kimberton Grange Hall and Roberts' Spring House until a church/school building

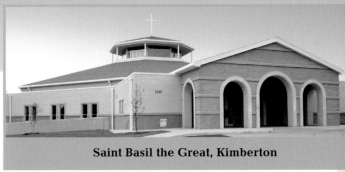

Saint Basil the Great, Kimberton

was opened in 1966. The school was initially staffed by Holy Child Sisters, who were succeed in 1983 by the Glen Riddle Franciscans. In 2005, Cardinal Rigali dedicated the present church.

The parish of SAINT THOMAS MORE in South Coventry Township was established in 1968 from the territory of Saint Aloysius, Pottstown, Montgomery County. Prior to the founding of Saint Aloysius in 1856, settlers in the area had to travel for Mass either to Phoenixville or to Bally, Berks County. The years following World War II witnessed suburban development that transformed the area. Catholic residents petitioned Cardinal Krol to found a parish, and they volunteered time and labor to renovate the Old Coventryville School House on Route 23 as a temporary parish church. A permanent church was dedicated in 1969.

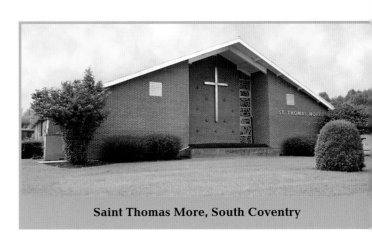

Saint Thomas More, South Coventry

Saint Ann, Phoenixville

# Parkesburg, Coatesville and Vicinity

In 1731, the Fountain Inn opened along the Gap-Newport Pike (present Route 41), which ran north from New Castle, Delaware. A small community grew up around the Inn, and included a number of Irish families. A chapel named for Saint Malachy was founded here in 1771. A log chapel was built in the area of Doe Run in 1800, and a church in 1838.

In 1831, the Philadelphia and Columbia Railroad extended tracks to the area, and in 1836 the Fountain Inn became the first post office for the Borough of Parkesburg. In the 1840s and 1850s, employment with the railroad—which had established a repair shop at the Parkesburg station—triggered rapid settlement. The parish church of Seven Dolors was founded in the borough in 1853. When a second church was dedicated in 1905, the

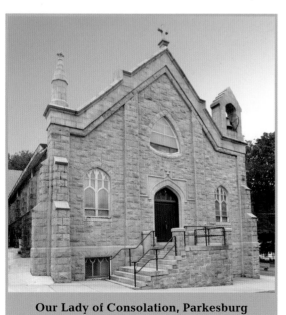

**Our Lady of Consolation, Parkesburg**

name of Seven Dolors was changed to OUR LADY OF CONSOLATION.

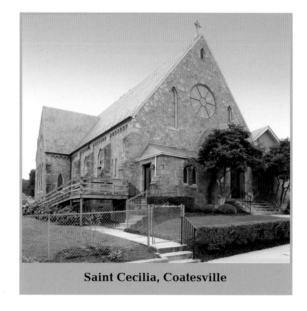

**Saint Cecilia, Coatesville**

The farm of Moses Coates, which straddled the Brandywine River near Lancaster Pike (Route 30), became the center of the town which bears his name. Coatesville—since 1915 the only incorporated city in Chester County—was developed circa 1810 along the recently-opened turnpike. Coates' nephew, Jesse Kersey, formed a partnership with Isaac Pennock, a local ironmaster, and they transformed a saw mill into the Brandywine Iron Works and Nail Factory. Pennock's daughter, Mrs. Rebecca Lukens, purchased the mill in 1825, and well into the 1960s, Lukens Steel was the largest employer in Coatesville.

As was the case in other Philadelphia-area localities, the steel mill attracted many immigrant families to Coatesville, especially after

the Philadelphia-Columbia Railroad reached the area in 1834. By 1854 priests from Saint Malachy in Doe Run were celebrating Mass in Mechanics' Hall in the west end of Coatesville. In 1869 the parish of SAINT CECILIA was founded to serve the predominantly Irish population. The parish church was dedicated in 1874, and Immaculate Heart Sisters arrived to administer the parish school in 1906.

In 1907, Polish-speaking Catholics established the church of SAINT STANISLAUS KOSTKA, named for a Polish Jesuit novice who died in 1568. The parish school, where Bernardine Sisters taught both Polish and Slovak children, began in 1912, and the first school building was erected in 1917. A new parish church was built in 1927.

**Saint Stanislaus Kostka, Coatesville**

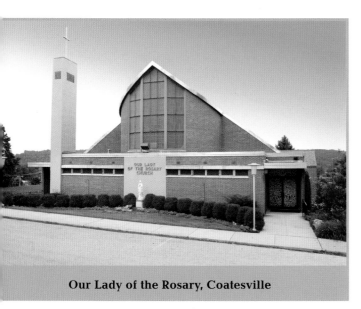

**Our Lady of the Rosary, Coatesville**

Italian immigrants petitioned for a national parish of their own, and in 1917, the church of OUR LADY OF THE ROSARY was constructed at the intersection of Coates Street and Black Horse Hill Road. The present church was dedicated fifty years later, in 1967.

Slovak Catholics worshipped at Saint Cecilia's until the opening of Saint Stanislaus in 1907. Often this growing community prayed the Rosary together in Slovak after Mass. However, on Sundays many still traveled to Sacred Heart, Phoenixville, where homilies were preached in Slovak. In 1924, parishioners of the newly-founded SAINT JOSEPH parish raised $5,000 (about $57,100 in 2005) to build a temporary church on Strode Avenue. This church was replaced with a permanent church in 1926. Father Michael Metro served as pastor of Saint Joseph for over forty years—from 1929 to 1970—and oversaw the construction of the

parish school, which was staffed by Immaculate Heart Sisters. The present church was dedicated in 1965. Saint Joseph's was twinned with Saint Stanislaus in 1998.

The likelihood of residential development in West Brandywine Township was the motivation for the foundation of SAINT PETER parish in 1963 in the area known as Honey Brook. The parish originally encompassed ten townships and boroughs—an area of 120 square miles—and the population grew from fewer than 100 families in 1963 to more than 1,000 families forty years later. The parish church and hall were dedicated in 1967. At the time of writing, the parish is planning the construction of a new church.

The parish schools in Coatesville were consolidated in 1971 to form Coatesville Area Catholic Elementary School (CACES), under the direction of the Immaculate Heart Sisters. In

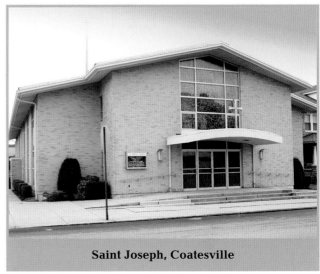

**Saint Joseph, Coatesville**

January 2007, students from CACES joined children from Saint Peter's parish—who had attended school at Saint Joseph School, Downingtown—in the new Pope John Paul II Regional Catholic Elementary School. This school, on the parish campus of Saint Peter's, is also staffed by the Immaculate Heart Sisters and lay teachers.

**Saint Peter, West Brandywine**

# Kennett Square and Vicinity

In 1810, the farming community of Kennett Square was a tiny village of only eight dwellings. By the 1850s, however, it had grown large enough to incorporate as a borough. The area was the birthplace of a number of technological innovations in agriculture, and manufacturers like S. & M. Pennock and Sons—the future American Road Machinery Company—helped to build the local economy and attract settlers. Kennett Square was also an important stop on the Underground Railroad, which provided shelter and aid to African American slaves who had escaped from Southern plantations.

For many years, Catholics in the new borough were visited by priests from Saint Thomas the Apostle parish in Chester Heights, Delaware County. In 1868, Father John Wall collected funds from Kennett Square Catholics to build a church, which was dedicated in 1872. Because many of the residents were from Ireland, Father Wall chose SAINT PATRICK as the name of the church, which remained a mission until 1893. A second church was dedicated in 1908, and the parish school was founded in the convent of the Sisters of Saint Joseph in 1922. A new school building was opened in 1927.

Known as "The Mushroom Capital of the World," Kennett Square is still home to many farms, and immigrant workers still find seasonal employment here. Typically, today's immigrants come from Mexico and other countries of Central and South America. Mass is celebrated in Spanish at Saint Patrick's every Sunday for Hispanic parishioners.

The development of the Philadelphia and Baltimore Railroad in 1860 brought change to the small village of West Grove, southwest of Kennett Square. By the 1880s, West Grove had become a flourishing community, home to three flour mills, a large rose nursery, and the Paxson Comfort casket factory, along with other industrial and commercial endeavors. Convenient transportation and ready employment led to residential development as well, and in 1873 the parish of the ASSUMPTION OF THE BLESSED VIRGIN MARY was founded. The first parish church, on Evergreen Street, was dedicated in 1876, and utilized original pews from Old Saint Mary's, Philadelphia. The parish school opened in 1922 under the direction of Immaculate Heart Sisters. A larger school building was erected in 1959, and the present church was dedicated in 2001.

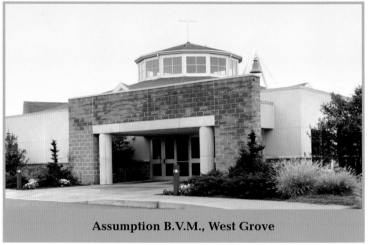

**Assumption B.V.M., West Grove**

**Saint Patrick, Kennett Square**

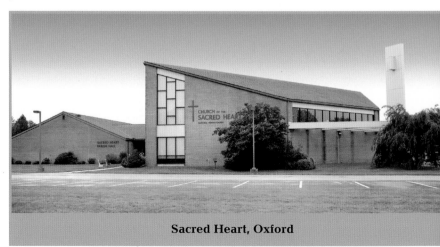

**Sacred Heart, Oxford**

Assumption B.V.M. parish established a mission in the Borough of Oxford in 1877. Over the next 30 years, as industry and the railroad spread to the area, the borough also benefited from a population increase. The parish of the SACRED HEART was founded in 1915 at the site of the mission church on Broad Street (now the Broad Street Community Center). During the 1960s and 1970s, the parish population outgrew the original facilities. A larger parish church was built on Church Street near Route 10, and was dedicated in 1985.

A little stone chapel with a green tile roof, located along U.S. Route 202 in Chadds Ford, was built in 1919 as a mission chapel of Saint Thomas the Apostle, Chester Heights. The mission became a canonical parish in 1963, named for SAINT CORNELIUS, a martyr and pope from 251 to 253. A church/hall building was dedicated in 1966. In 1986, ground was broken for a permanent church, which was dedicated in 1991.

In 1893, the mission chapel of Saint Francis Xavier was established in New Garden Township, about eight miles southwest of Kennett Square. When the mission was moved to Avondale in 1965, many Italian parishioners suggested that it be renamed for SAINT GABRIEL OF THE SORROWFUL MOTHER, a novice in the Passionist community at Gran Sasso in central Italy who died in 1862 and was canonized in 1920. A church/school building was erected in 1966, and the mission was established as a parish in 1988. The present church, dedicated in 2002, received an Award of Merit for architectural design from the Southeastern Pennsylvania Chapter of the Associated Builders and Contractors.

**Saint Cornelius, Chadds Ford**

LA MISIÓN SANTA MARIA, MADRE DE DIOS (the Mission of Holy Mary, Mother of God) was established in 1992 to provide pastoral care for thousands of Spanish-speaking Catholics who live and work in southern Chester County. Monsignor Francis Depman and the Servants of the Lord and the Virgin of Matara staff this mission, which provides opportunities for worship as well as social services in Spanish. To serve this widely-spread community, Mass is celebrated at the churches of Saint Patrick, Assumption B.V.M., Saint Gabriel, Sacred Heart, and Our Lady of Consolation, Parkesburg.

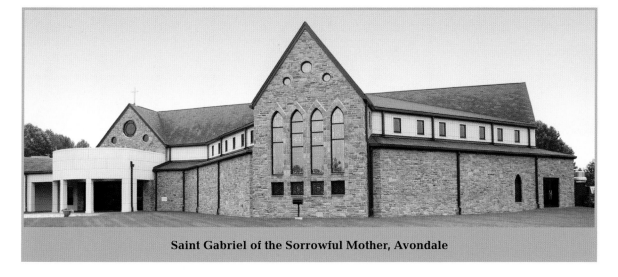

**Saint Gabriel of the Sorrowful Mother, Avondale**

# DELAWARE COUNTY

# Chester Heights, Media and Springfield

In 1704, Jesuit missionaries from England established the mission of Saint Francis Xavier at the Maryland estate known as Bohemia Manor. This was located in Cecil County, about 13 miles south of the border with Pennsylvania, and about a 50 mile journey to Philadelphia. From Bohemia Manor, Jesuits visited missions throughout the Middle Colonies, including several in Pennsylvania. One of these missionaries was Father Joseph Greaton, S.J., who arrived at Bohemia Manor in 1720 and was responsible for the missions in Conewago, Lancaster and Philadelphia.

On his way to Philadelphia, Father Greaton often stopped at the estate of Thomas Willcox, who operated a paper mill on the West Branch of Chester Creek, in what is now Concord Township, Delaware County. "Ivy Mills" became well known as a source of paper for newspaper printing—Benjamin Franklin was a regular customer—as well as for colonial and United States currency. The Willcox family were also respected leaders among Catholics in the area,

and the Willcox house behind the mill became a meeting place for local Catholics. It also served as a place of worship when Father Greaton arrived to celebrate Mass and the sacraments.

In 1729, the Willcox home was formally recognized as a mission chapel. Father Greaton and other Jesuits made regular visits here throughout the eighteenth century, and, beginning in 1790, Augustinians from Saint Mary's in White Clay Creek, New Castle County, Delaware, also journeyed to Ivy Mills. The original Willcox house was demolished in 1837, and a larger house served as the parish chapel until the first church was dedicated by Saint John Neumann in 1853 and named SAINT THOMAS THE APOSTLE. Thomas Willcox's patron saint, this apostle is well-known for his own missionary journeys.

The parish church underwent renovations in 1897 and 1937. A new, much larger church—initiated by Father Francis Corkery—was dedicated in 1991, to serve a parish population that had now reached 1,200 families. The parish school, founded by Sisters of Saint Joseph, welcomed its first students in 1956.

The Borough of Media was incorporated in 1850, as a new county seat for Delaware County. Named for its location in the middle (Latin *media*) of the county, the town expanded as government, legal and commercial buildings

Nativity B.V.M., Media

were built around the new court house. Priests from Saint Thomas the Apostle parish established a mission in Media, and in 1868 the first parish church, on Franklin Street, was dedicated to the NATIVITY OF THE BLESSED VIRGIN MARY.

The present parish church was dedicated in 1882. The parish school dates to 1912, and was originally directed by Sisters of Saint Francis of Philadelphia. School buildings were erected in 1949, 1953 and 1960. Sisters, Servants of the Most Sacred Heart of Jesus taught in the school from 1994 to 2006.

Saint Thomas the Apostle, Chester Heights

In the 1880s, priests from Saint Thomas the Apostle established another mission, in the village of Lenni, between Chester Heights and Media. In 1889, plans were drawn up for a new church, but an economic depression delayed church construction for several years. In 1894, the mission was canonically established as a parish, and the church was dedicated the following year with the title of SAINT FRANCIS DE SALES.

Saint Francis School began in 1895 in the lower part of the parish church, and each day three Franciscan Sisters traveled by horse and buggy from their motherhouse in nearby Glen Riddle. A school building went into service in 1925, and was renovated following a fire in 1977.

**Saint Francis de Sales, Lenni**

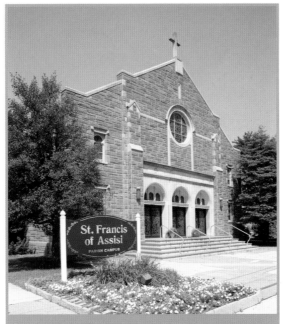

**Saint Francis of Assisi, Springfield**

At the beginning of the twentieth century, improvements to Baltimore Pike facilitated commercial development along the "Golden Mile" in Springfield Township, east of Media. Easy transportation by rail and trolley, and abundant opportunities for work made this part of Delaware County attractive to Philadelphia residents wishing to move out of the city. As the population of Springfield Township grew, the parish of SAINT FRANCIS OF ASSISI was founded in 1923.

Named for the patron saint of the first pastor, Father Francis Conway, the church was built on land purchased from the Johnston family. The first parish Mass was celebrated in their home on June 10, 1923. The first parish building, the present Conway Hall, was built during that year,

and the parish school was opened in 1929 by Sisters of Saint Joseph. The present church was dedicated in 1952 by Bishop Joseph McShea—an auxiliary bishop of Philadelphia and the first Bishop of Allentown—who was a former parishioner of Saint Francis.

Residential development in Springfield continued after World War II, particularly in the area known as Westbrook Park. Consequently, the parish of the HOLY CROSS was founded in 1948, and parishioners celebrated the first Mass at the Knights of Columbus Hall on Baltimore Pike. The Clifton Heights Fire House was also made available for Sunday Mass. The founding pastor, Father Louis Meyer, had been a chaplain in World War II with the 20th General Hospital Unit, sponsored by doctors from the University of Pennsylvania. He was injured in Assam, India, and flown home to Philadelphia in a body cast.

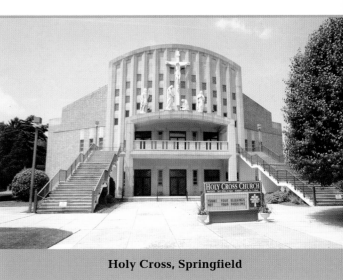

**Holy Cross, Springfield**

Housing sales in Westbrook Park had slumped in 1949, until the developers posted signs on the corners of their property announcing the construction of Holy Cross School. New home buyers were attracted by the prospect of a Catholic school in their neighborhood, and the Westbrook Park development boasted a population that was about 75 percent Catholic. Sisters of Mercy staffed the school when it opened in 1950, and the school hall was used for Sunday Mass until September 14, 1963, the feast of the Triumph of the Cross. The lower church was dedicated the following year, and the upper church in 1967.

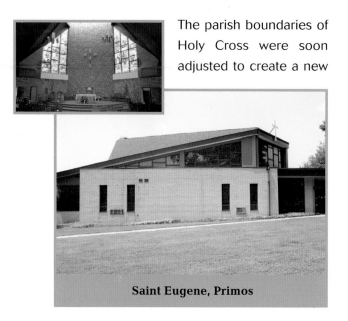

The parish boundaries of Holy Cross were soon adjusted to create a new

**Saint Eugene, Primos**

parish in the neighborhood of Primos, south of Baltimore Pike. The parish of SAINT EUGENE was named for Saint Eugene I, pope from 654 to 657, and the patron saint of Pope Pius XII, born Eugenio Pacelli. Pope Pius XII blessed and sent two bricks—which had walled up the Holy Door at Saint Peter's Basilica between the Holy Years in 1933 and 1950—to be placed in

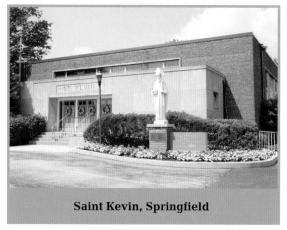

**Saint Kevin, Springfield**

the cornerstone of the original church/school building, dedicated in 1957. Immaculate Heart Sisters taught in the parish school. The original church was converted to a parish hall when the present church was dedicated in 1980.

In 1955, another parish was created in Springfield. SAINT KEVIN church is located on Sproul Road not far from the Springfield Mall. Parishioners initially met for Sunday Mass at the Springfield Country Club (next to the parish property) until the church was dedicated in 1957. That same year the parish school

opened under the direction of Sisters of Saint Joseph.

Nativity B.V.M. parish was the only Catholic church in Media until 1963, when the parish of SAINT MARY MAGDALEN was established on Providence Road. Father Gilbert McDevitt celebrated the first parish Mass in a stable on Feathering Road in June of that year. A church/school building was opened in 1965; this school was the first one established by the Dominican Sisters from Elkins Park. A second church was dedicated in 1970, and at the time of this writing, the parish is planning the construction of a larger church to serve the more than 1,600 Catholic families who now live within the parish boundaries.

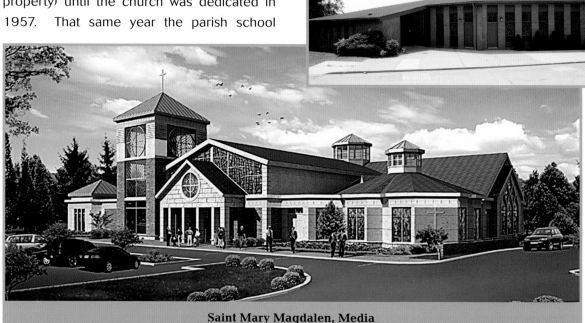

**Saint Mary Magdalen, Media**

# Havertown and Vicinity

In 1806, Dennis Kelly—a very successful merchant—his wife, Mary, and their daughter, Margaret, emigrated from County Donegal, Ireland, to Philadelphia. After spending a few weeks in the city, Mr. Kelly arranged for a business venture in Pittsburgh. The first leg of the journey was a stagecoach ride along the Haverford–Darby Road to connect to the Lancaster Pike beyond Philadelphia. As the stage neared the little village of Coopertown, the teamster was using loud, vulgar and obscene language. Mrs. Kelly asked the man to stop his offensive talk. When he refused, she insisted that the coach stop immediately so that she and her family could get off.

The Kellys walked to the nearest inn to consider their situation. They had no place to live, and they could not get back the money they had paid in advance for the trip to Pittsburgh. Mr. Kelly found work in powder and textile mills along Cobbs Creek, and over the next few years accumulated sufficient funds and connections to go into business for himself. He established a family home on what was known as the Hermitage Farm, which was also the site of several of his mills. As immigration from his native Ireland increased, many of his countrymen arrived in Philadelphia with one piece of advice in mind: "If you want to go to America," the saying went in Donegal, "see Dennis Kelly." Soon a large community of fellow Irish was established in the area of Mr. Kelly's mills and homestead, forming the district now known as Havertown.

While in Philadelphia, the Kelly family had attended Old Saint Augustine's Church, and Mr. Kelly had befriended the Augustinian priests who served there. Around 1815, he invited the Augustinians to celebrate Mass in his house for his family and employees. In 1822, he donated land to Bishop Conwell for a parish church and cemetery. The church was built in 1825 and named for SAINT DENIS, a martyr and the first bishop of Paris, who was also Mr. Kelly's patron saint. Mr. and Mrs. Kelly signed the deed over to Bishop Conwell, who dedicated the church in 1828.

Augustinians continued to serve the parish as a mission from Villanova until 1873, when a resident pastor was appointed. In 1858, ground was broken for a new church, dedicated in 1869. The present church was dedicated in 1948. The first parish school building opened in 1864, and another building was constructed in 1924, when Sisters of Mercy arrived to serve on the faculty. Augustinians served the parish until the 1990s, when archdiocesan priests were appointed to the parish.

Between the two World Wars, development of efficient transportation along West Chester Pike (Route 3) drew Philadelphia residents to central Delaware County. When a parish was founded in Newtown Square in 1912, the Pike was often washed out and muddy, and trolley tracks were uneven. However, as conditions improved the

**Saint Denis, Havertown**

**Saint Anastasia, Newtown Square**

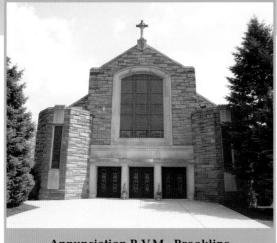
**Annunciation B.V.M., Brookline**

population increased. Father William Maguire, the founding pastor, sought permission to name the new parish for his mother's patron saint, SAINT ANASTASIA. Parishioners met for Mass in the home of Patrick and Margaret Hurley until a former Protestant chapel in Morton was dismantled and moved to the parish property in 1914.

A building comprising the parish school, staffed by Immaculate Heart Sisters, and a chapel for Sunday Mass was opened in 1930. A new school building was erected in 1955, and the present church followed in 1957. From a small population of only 30 families in 1927, the parish population has increased ten-fold to more than 3,300 at the beginning of the third millennium.

For more than a century, Catholics in the Brookline section of Haverford Township attended Mass at Saint Denis. In 1927, an additional parish was founded about a mile away, on Brookline Boulevard. Father John Cahier, the founding pastor of the parish of the ANNUNCIATION OF THE BLESSED VIRGIN

MARY, had to cope with anti-Catholic hostility as he saw to the construction of the first church/school building in 1928. Ground was broken in 1953 for the present church, dedicated in 1955. Sisters of Mercy staffed Annunciation B.V.M. School, which was enlarged in 1958.

A second parish was founded in Haverford Township in 1927, in the community of Manoa, just south of Brookline along West Chester Pike. SACRED HEART parish also faced anti-Catholic activity from neighbors—the Ku Klux Klan burned crosses on the parish property. Despite opposition, parish members volunteered their labor and built a church/school building in less than six months. Immaculate Heart Sisters arrived in 1928 to instruct the children of the parish. The original community of 43 families had grown by the 1960s to more than 1,800 families, many of Irish descent. The present parish church was dedicated in 1952, and a new school was built in 1961.

Suburban growth after World War II occasioned the foundation of another parish in the area between Sacred Heart and Saint Anastasia. In 1955, 700 families in the community of Broomall, Marple Township, formed the new parish of SAINT PIUS X, pope from 1903 to 1914, who was canonized in 1954.

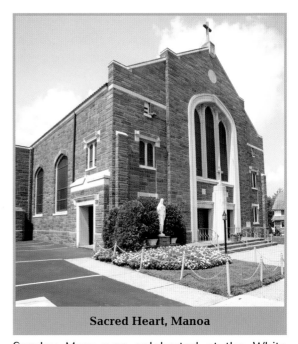
**Sacred Heart, Manoa**

Sunday Mass was celebrated at the White Manor Country Club until a church/school building was opened in 1956. Immaculate Heart Sisters established a convent in 1957 and took responsibility for the parish school. The present church was dedicated in 1971.

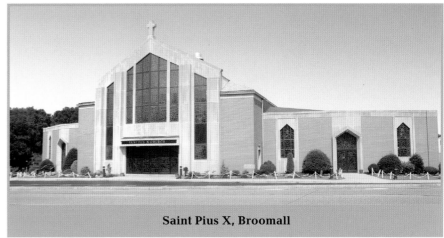
**Saint Pius X, Broomall**

# Chester and Vicinity

The area that became the City of Chester was settled by Swedish explorers in the seventeenth century, and known as Finlandia and, later, Upland. It was here in 1682 that William Penn first set foot on Pennsylvania soil; he renamed the village after the English city of Chester. It became the first capital of Pennsylvania, and first county seat of Chester County. When Delaware County was established in 1789, Chester became its county seat. Chester was a center for shipbuilding during the Civil War and both World Wars, and the wharves and shipyards along the Delaware River made it an important manufacturing center well into the twentieth century.

Early Catholics in Chester faced a 15-mile journey along the river to parish churches in Philadelphia, until the city's first parish, SAINT MICHAEL, was founded in 1842. The first parish church was dedicated the following year, and the parish school—the first in Delaware County—opened in 1867, staffed by a lay faculty. In 1881, Sisters of the Holy Child Jesus took responsibility for the school; they were succeeded by Sisters of Saint Joseph in 1913. A granite church was built in 1874.

A little frame chapel on Second Street served Catholics in the western end of Chester. In 1873, this became IMMACULATE HEART OF MARY parish, and a larger church was built that year. The parish school, built in 1882, was operated by Immaculate Heart Sisters. As the west end developed in the years before World War I, the parish of the RESURRECTION OF OUR LORD was established at 9th Street and Highland Avenue to serve German-speaking parishioners. The founding pastor, Father Augustine Ganster, had been ordained in Innsbruck, Austria. A church/school building was constructed in 1918, and Franciscan Sisters from Glen Riddle were invited to staff the school. A school annex was built in 1956, and a new church was dedicated in 1949. Today, the convent is home for Mother Teresa's Missionaries of Charity.

At the beginning of the twentieth century, plentiful employment in Chester's factories drew large numbers of immigrants to the city,

and several national parishes were established to care for them. Forty Polish families—many of whose members worked in Chester's pipe mills—faced a two-hour trip by trolley or boat to Saint Stanislaus, Philadelphia, the closest Polish parish. They consequently sent a delegation to Archbishop Ryan in 1902, to ask him to send a Polish-speaking priest to Chester. Father Mieceslaus Kopytkiewicz gathered the community at Thurlow House until the parish church of SAINT HEDWIG was dedicated in 1917. The parish school, founded in 1911, was operated by Sisters of the Holy Family of Nazareth.

Beginning in 1908, Italian-speaking families in Chester met in rooms beneath Saint Michael Church, where visiting priests preached and instructed the people in Italian. When the church of SAINT ANTHONY OF PADUA was dedicated in 1914, it was the first Italian parish in Delaware County. The parish school was placed in the care of Missionary Franciscan Sisters of the Immaculate Conception. In 1924, about a half-mile to the east, Lithuanian families formed the parish of OUR LADY OF VILNA, at Fourth and Madison Streets.

In the 1920s, Chester benefited from the industrial demand associated with the First World War, and the city continued to grow. The parish of SAINT ROBERT was founded in 1922

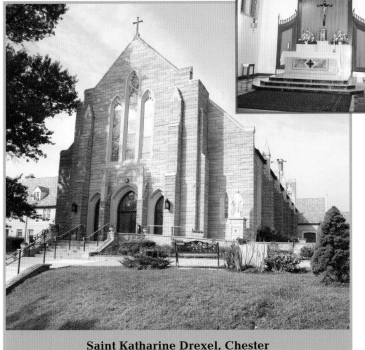

**Saint Katharine Drexel, Chester**

at 20th Street and Providence Road, on a tract donated by parishioners John and Peter Nolan. Mass was celebrated at the Good Will Fire Company until 1924, when a church/school building was completed. Sisters of Saint Joseph arrived that year to instruct the children. A new church was dedicated in 1940.

The City of Chester also experienced growth during and after World War II, and the population of the city peaked in 1950 at about 66,000 inhabitants. However, the post-war years saw a serious decline in the manufacturing and steel industries that formed the backbone of Chester's economy. As industries relocated, so did many residents who had depended on the factories and mills for employment. The Catholic population diminished as many new residents—predominantly African American families—did not share the Catholic faith of the descendants of Chester's immigrant communities.

Faced with the economic realities of caring for aging parish buildings, and declining numbers of parishioners and available priests, the archdiocese needed to reorganize the Catholic parish presence in Chester. Our Lady

**Holy Saviour, Linwood**

of Vilna had already been closed in 1972, and in 1993 the other parishes of Chester were suppressed as well. Saint Hedwig's church became a chapel of Sacred Heart, Clifton Heights, and one new parish was established at the site of Saint Robert's to serve all of Chester's Catholics. This new parish includes descendants of European immigrants, a vibrant African American community, and a growing population of Spanish-speaking families. This parish was named Blessed Katharine Drexel after Philadelphia's own saint, who spent her life in service to the African American community and was beatified in 1988. When Mother Katharine was canonized on October 1, 2000, the name of the parish became SAINT KATHARINE DREXEL.

A number of parishes in southern Delaware County started as missions of parishes in Chester. In 1914, Father Ganster of Resurrection parish established a chapel on Chichester Avenue in Linwood, and in 1915 this mission became the parish of HOLY SAVIOUR. The present church was dedicated in 1942. A parish school began in 1918 under the direction of Sisters of Saint Joseph, and a school building was erected in 1951.

**Saint Joseph, Aston**

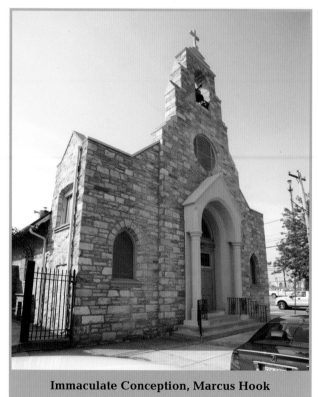

**Immaculate Conception, Marcus Hook**

Italian residents of the Borough of Marcus Hook initially attended Holy Saviour parish, where they started the tradition of a solemn procession on the feast of the Assumption of the Blessed Virgin Mary. Mrs. Morris, a midwife from Marcus Hook, impressed by the devotion of the Italian community, approached the pastor of Saint Anthony of Padua about forming an Italian parish in her own community. A meeting of Italian Catholics in the Cadorna Society Hall formed a committee to collect funds for the church of the IMMACULATE CONCEPTION OF LOURDES, dedicated in 1917. The church was a mission of Saint Anthony's until 1924, when a resident pastor was appointed. Franciscan Sisters from Glen Riddle arrived in 1960 to staff the parish school.

Post-war residential expansion led to the foundation of several parishes north of the City of Chester. In 1947, 68 families in the Green Ridge section of Aston Township petitioned Cardinal Dougherty for a new parish. A lot on Concord Road was donated by the Jurich family as the site of SAINT JOSEPH parish, and a church was built in 1949. The parish school was founded by Immaculate Heart Sisters in 1951, and moved to a permanent building in

**Our Lady of Charity, Brookhaven**

1954. The present church was dedicated in the year 2000, and incorporates beautiful opalescent windows from the church of the Assumption B.V.M., Philadelphia.

Five years after the foundation of Saint Joseph's, two parishes were established on the same day. OUR LADY OF CHARITY, in the Borough of Brookhaven, bordered Saint Joseph's to the east, and was created largely from the territory of Saint Robert's. Parishioners initially gathered at the Upland Civic Club and the Parkside Fire Hall for Sunday Mass, and in a chapel in the rectory basement on weekdays. Immaculate Heart Sisters arrived to staff the parish school in 1954, and a church/school building was dedicated in 1955.

Development along the Media/West Chester line of the Pennsylvania Railroad contributed to development in the area of Wallingford. Like their neighbors in Our Lady of Charity parish, the parishioners of SAINT JOHN CHRYSOSTOM gathered for Mass in a small

**Saint John Fisher, Boothwyn**

chapel in the basement of the rectory. Sisters of Saint Joseph founded the school in 1952, and a school building, which included a chapel for Sunday Mass, was opened in 1955. The parish church was dedicated in 1970.

Home building spread towards the southwest in the 1960s, and in 1971 the territory of Holy Saviour, Linwood, was divided to create the parish of SAINT JOHN FISHER in Boothwyn. The parish was named for the sixteenth-century Bishop of Rochester, England, who died a martyr at the Tower of London in 1535. The parish church was dedicated in 1973, and the parish population more than doubled in its first twenty years. Children from the parish attend Holy Savior–Saint John Fisher School, in Linwood.

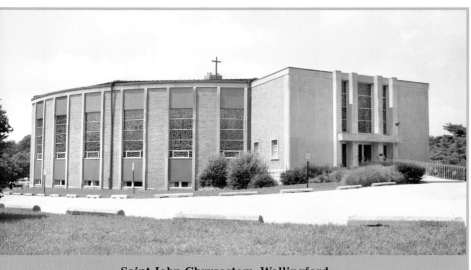

**Saint John Chrysostom, Wallingford**

# Drexel Hill, Upper Darby and Vicinity

The community of Irish immigrants that had established itself around Dennis Kelly's mills in Havertown included several members of his extended family. As the Cobbs Creek mills became more successful, Dennis Kelly's nephew Charles Kelly decided to try his hand at operating cotton mills on the nearby Darby Creek. His homestead, about six miles west of the City of Philadelphia, became known as Kellyville, and was soon populated by a number of Irish families from the Donegal village of The Crossroads.

Charles Kelly donated an acre of land in Kellyville for a parish church, named for his patron, SAINT CHARLES BORROMEO. The parish, founded in 1849, was served by priests from his uncle's parish, Saint Denis, Havertown; and the first Masses were celebrated in the mill office. The first parish church was dedicated in 1850, and a school opened in 1869. Immaculate Heart Sisters arrived in 1892 to assume responsibility for the school. As the community increased, larger parish buildings became necessary. The present church was dedicated in 1892, and a school was built in 1910.

The building of the Darby Road Station of the Pennsylvania Railroad, about three-quarters of a mile to the east of Kellyville, made the area attractive to developers who were planning "commuter suburbs." City residents who wanted a large home in a quiet neighborhood would still be able to commute to work in Philadelphia. The name of the station was changed to "Lansdowne Station"—after the Marquess of Lansdowne, a prominent British diplomat—and the surrounding community was incorporated as the Borough of Lansdowne in 1893.

Catholics in the new borough often found it difficult to get to Saint Charles Borromeo church, because the journey included fording Darby Creek and climbing a steep bank on the opposite side. In 1898, a delegation met with Father Matthew O'Brien from Saint Charles to discuss plans for a parish church in Lansdowne. The founding pastor, Father Francis Markee, chose the name of SAINT PHILOMENA, a virgin martyr whose relics had been discovered in a Roman catacomb in 1802. He gathered residents for Mass in Lansdowne Hall (site of the present Borough Hall) until the church was completed in December 1898.

Immaculate Heart Sisters opened the parish school in 1907. Soon after, the rectory was built

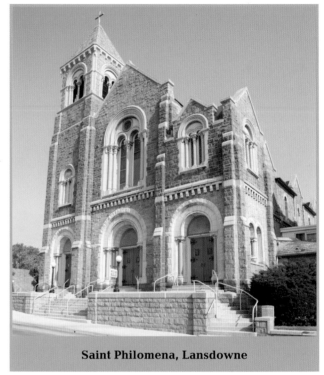

**Saint Philomena, Lansdowne**

with money donated by parishioner Thomas Fitzgerald. This wealthy businessman—the benefactor of Mercy Fitzgerald Hospital in Darby—also donated the main altar in memory of his wife, May. While Father Markee was waiting for the rectory to be completed, he lived in a house on Nyack Avenue owned by the Hughes family. The Hughes' grandson, Edward, would become a priest, and later an auxiliary bishop of Philadelphia. In 1987, he was installed as second Bishop of Metuchen, New Jersey.

In the late nineteenth century, Polish immigrants to the Philadelphia area found work in the mills and factories along Darby Creek, and many settled in the Borough of Clifton Heights, just west of Kellyville (later called Oakview or Drexel Hill). A

**Saint Charles Borromeo, Drexel Hill**

one-room public school was the first meeting place for parishioners of the Polish national parish of the SACRED HEART, founded in 1910. A small wooden church was built that year on Edgemont Avenue. Following a fire, a new church was constructed in 1937 with the help of a $50 donation from each parish family (worth about $680 in 2005). Bernardine Franciscan Sisters originally staffed the parish school—founded in 1952—and were succeeded by the Little Sisters of the Immaculate Conception in 1986. Sacred Heart parish was assigned territorial boundaries in 1968, but it still serves Polish-speaking Catholics in Delaware County. Priests of Sacred Heart parish also tend the chapel of Saint Hedwig, the former Polish parish in Chester which closed in 1993.

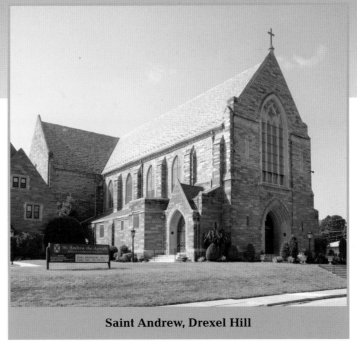
**Saint Andrew, Drexel Hill**

The area between Darby Creek and the City Line continued to be attractive to home builders in the first decades of the twentieth century. Consequently the parish of SAINT ANDREW was founded in 1916 to serve Catholics in the Drexel Hill region of Upper Darby Township. A temporary chapel served until 1920, when a church/school building was opened. Sisters of Saint Joseph arrived in 1922 to staff the school, which was expanded in 1928 and 1964. The

present church was dedicated in 1928.

The area of Highland Park, along West Chester Pike (Route 3), was sparsely populated farmland until developers planned another commuter suburb. The parish of SAINT LAURENCE was founded on West Chester Pike in 1917 by Father Maurice Cowl. He was one of several Episcopal clergymen received into the Catholic Church in 1908, after the difficulties surrounding the "Open Pulpit Controversy." He studied for the priesthood at Saint Charles Seminary, and was ordained for the Archdiocese of Philadelphia in 1910. Immaculate Heart Sisters founded the parish school in 1919. The lower church was dedicated in 1926, but the Great Depression and World War II delayed completion of the upper church for several decades.

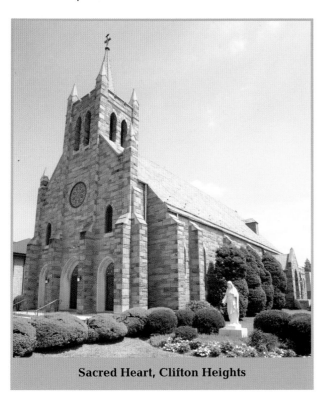
**Sacred Heart, Clifton Heights**

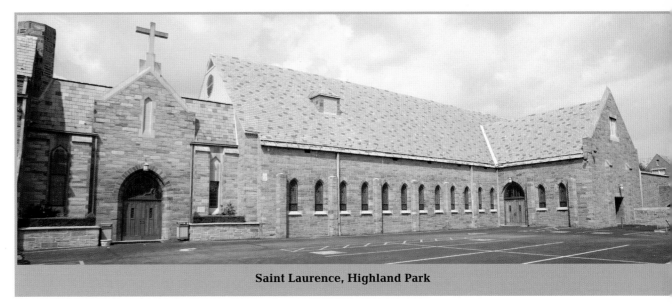
**Saint Laurence, Highland Park**

As Upper Darby Township continued its expansion, the parish of SAINT ALICE was established in the Stonehurst neighborhood, near the commercial areas surrounding 69th Street Station. A chapel was built on the Old Sellers Homestead in 1922, and later that year Immaculate Heart Sisters from Saint Laurence arrived to teach in the school. The first church was dedicated in 1925; the present church was completed in 1950. In the 1950s and 1960s, Saint Alice's large social center was well-known throughout the area for weekly dances with nationally famous bands. In recent decades, the parish community has changed to include many residents of Asian descent, and Sunday Mass is celebrated at Saint Alice in Vietnamese, as well as in Spanish and in English.

Saint Alice, Upper Darby

The Borough of Yeadon was incorporated in 1893, the same year as its neighbor, Lansdowne. The walk to Saint Philomena's was difficult in bad weather, especially for children, and in 1928, Catholic families petitioned Cardinal Dougherty for a church and school in their own community. Louise Drexel Morrell was an early benefactor, and the church/school building—dedicated to SAINT LOUIS—was completed in 1929, just weeks before the stock market crash that precipitated the Great Depression. As a result, the parish carried a heavy debt for years, and it was not until 1955 that a permanent church was dedicated. The 1970s and 1980s brought new economic hardships, as a decline in local industry and steep tax raises led to a loss of more than 1,000 parish families. The parish school, which had been staffed by the Immaculate Heart Sisters since 1929, was forced to close in 1995.

At the same time that Saint Louis was founded, the boundaries of Saint Philomena and Saint Alice were changed to establish the parish of SAINT CYRIL OF ALEXANDRIA in the Borough of East Lansdowne. A church/school building was dedicated in December 1928, and the economic realities of the Great Depression forced the pastor to take creative steps to keep the parish financially solvent. To generate income,

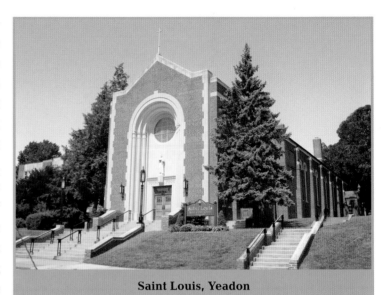

Saint Louis, Yeadon

Father Edmond O'Shea rented the vacant part of parish property for a gas station, and constructed several garages. The neighborhood and parish recovered after World War II, and a large church was dedicated on Penn Boulevard in 1955.

The post-war recovery led to further home construction in Drexel Hill, and two parishes were founded here in 1947. SAINT BERNADETTE parish erected a church/

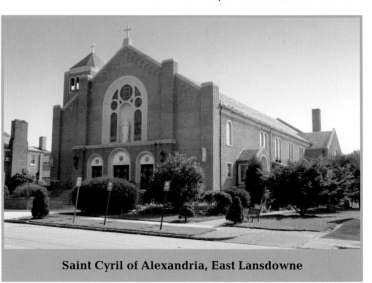

Saint Cyril of Alexandria, East Lansdowne

**Saint Bernadette, Drexel Hill**

**Saint Dorothy, Drexel Hill**

school building in 1947, and a permanent church was built at Bond and Turner Avenues in 1953. In 1948, Sisters of Notre Dame de Namur arrived to staff the school. They were later succeeded by Sisters of Saint Joseph (1972-83) and Oblate Sisters of Saint Francis de Sales. The first church of SAINT DOROTHY, on Belfield Avenue, was built in only 85 days. A permanent, Colonial-style church was erected on Township Line and dedicated in 1961. Immaculate Heart Sisters founded the parish school in 1949.

229

# Eddystone, Ridley Park and Vicinity

In the 1830s, Philadelphia jeweler Matthias Baldwin turned his attention to steam engineering, and perfected a steam locomotive that revolutionized rail service. Over the next several decades, his business developed rapidly, and in the late nineteenth century he began the process of moving his Baldwin Locomotive Works from cramped quarters on Broad Street to a large facility in the newly-incorporated Borough of Eddystone, about six miles south along the Delaware River.

The Baldwin plant soon became the largest manufacturer of steam locomotives in the United States, and ample employment opportunities attracted many residents. Accordingly, the parish of SAINT ROSE OF LIMA was

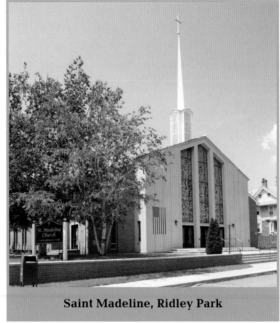

**Saint Madeline, Ridley Park**

founded in 1890. The first Masses were celebrated in a corner store in Crum Lynne, and the first parish church was built in 1892. A new church on Chester Pike was dedicated in 1907, and renovated following a fire in 1952. The parish school, staffed by the Immaculate Heart Sisters, opened in 1916.

In 1906, priests from Saint Rose parish established a mission in the neighboring Borough of Ridley Park. In 1908, Frederick and Madeline Mitchell donated land at Penn and Tome Streets for a parish church, named SAINT MADELINE. The parish school was founded in 1924 under the guidance of Immaculate Heart Sisters; it was enlarged in 1957. Saint Madeline School merged with Saint Rose of Lima School in 1981. The present church, at Penn Street and Morton Avenue, was dedicated in 1965.

In 1907, a year before the founding of Saint Madeline, the parish of OUR LADY OF PERPETUAL HELP was founded in the Borough of Morton, on the site of Farady Park. The church was dedicated in 1908. Parishioner Bernard O'Connell donated his homestead on Amosland Avenue for the parish school, which opened in 1935 and was staffed by Franciscan Sisters from Glen Riddle. A second, large church was dedicated in 1981, and construction on a new rectory and parish office complex began in 1989. The original church and rectory were destroyed by fire in January 1990, just prior to the dedication of the new buildings.

As early as 1891, Saint Rose of Lima parish was responsible for a mission in the Borough of Norwood. Mass was celebrated for parishioners in this northern end of the parish—about three miles distant from Saint Rose of Lima Church—

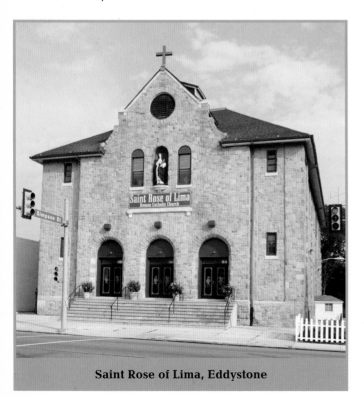

**Saint Rose of Lima, Eddystone**

**Our Lady of Perpetual Help, Morton**

**Saint Margaret Mary Alacoque, Essington**

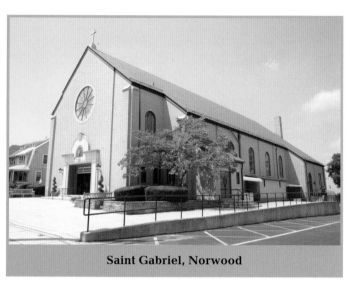

**Saint Gabriel, Norwood**

children of the parish. A second church was dedicated in 1954, and a school in 1960. By 1990, parish membership included nearly 3,000 families.

Beginning in 1917, Saint Madeline's was also responsible for the founding of a mission in the neighborhood of Ridley Heights, now called Milmont Park. In 1922 this mission was established as the parish of OUR LADY OF PEACE. In 1917, during the turmoil of World War I, Pope Benedict XV had added the invocation, "Queen of Peace, pray for us," to the Litany of the Blessed Virgin Mary. A church/school building was constructed in 1929, and placed in the care of Sisters of Saint Joseph. The present church was dedicated in 1956, and a new school building opened in 1960.

When the parish of SAINT MARGARET MARY ALACOQUE was established in Essington in 1921, the parish community found a novel way to provide a building in which to worship. In 1917, a major shipyard had been built on Hog Island—a short distance up the Delaware River—where more than 120 warships were built for the U.S. Navy. The shipyard closed and was dismantled in 1921, and Saint Margaret Mary parish secured a dormitory building from the site to use as a temporary church. A permanent church was dedicated in 1950, and a school building in 1951. The school was staffed by Immaculate Heart Sisters until it closed in 1990.

The area of Ridley Township adjacent to the Borough of Swarthmore experienced intensive home building during the 1950s. The parish of NOTRE DAME DE LOURDES was founded in 1959. For the next year, the College Movie Theater served for Sunday Mass. A small house on the parish property served as a rectory, and a barn was put to use for daily Mass.

The parish church was dedicated on the solemnity of the Immaculate Conception, December 8, 1960. The date recalls the words of Our Lady of Lourdes, who told Saint Bernadette, "I am the Immaculate Conception." In 2004, the former convent was converted to the parish business center, and named in honor of the pastor emeritus, Father William Benonis.

in private homes until a small wooden chapel was constructed in 1893. The chapel became a mission of Saint Madeline when that parish was founded in 1907, and remained a mission until 1914, when Father Joseph Smith became the first pastor of SAINT GABRIEL parish. The 71 founding families in the new parish erected a church/school building in 1914, and in 1922, Sisters of Saint Joseph were invited to teach the

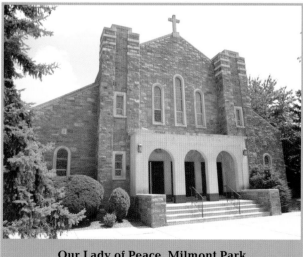

**Our Lady of Peace, Milmont Park**

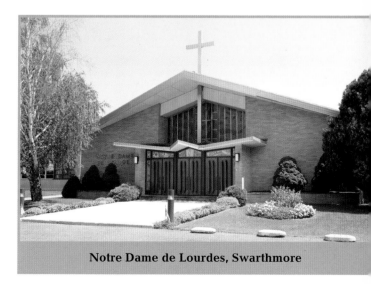

**Notre Dame de Lourdes, Swarthmore**

# Sharon Hill, Darby and Vicinity

At the turn of the twentieth century, convenient trolley service from the center of the city made the area of Delaware County across the border of Southwest Philadelphia an attractive place for new homes. When the Borough of Sharon Hill was incorporated in 1890, Catholic residents of this new "commuter suburb" had to journey to Saint Charles in Drexel Hill or Saint Clement in Philadelphia—

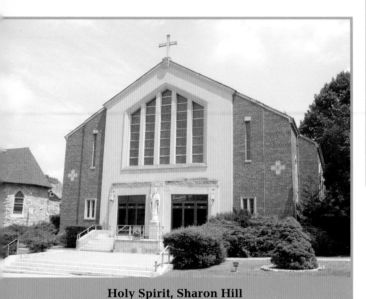

Holy Spirit, Sharon Hill

either church about two miles away. In 1891, the Sisters of the Holy Child Jesus gave land belonging to their Sharon Female Academy (established in 1864) for a mission chapel of Saint Clement's. In 1894, the original "dear little church," as it came to be called, was dedicated with the title of the HOLY SPIRIT.

The Catholic population of Sharon Hill grew rapidly, from 145 Catholics in 1897 to more

Blessed Virgin Mary, Darby

than 700 in 1906. A parish school was founded in 1901, and entrusted to the Holy Child Sisters who lived nearby. A second school building was erected in 1917, and enlarged in 1949. The present parish church was dedicated in 1961, and may be the only Catholic church to have a stained-glass window that depicts John F. Kennedy, who was inaugurated that year as the first Catholic President of the United States.

Development in southeastern Delaware County occurred rapidly during the next few decades—115 new homes were built in 1927 alone—and three new

Saint Joseph, Collingdale

parishes were established from the territory of Holy Spirit. The Borough of Darby had become an important business center because of its location between Philadelphia and industrial areas along the Delaware River. The population expanded, and the parish of the BLESSED VIRGIN MARY was founded in 1913. A chapel and parish hall were built in 1914, and in 1917, the Bunting Mansion was converted to the first parish school, staffed by the Immaculate Heart Sisters. The present church was dedicated in 1930, and a new school building opened in 1955. In 1920, newly-ordained Father Vincent Gallagher arrived as curate at Blessed Virgin Mary, and spent his entire priestly ministry at the parish. He was appointed pastor in 1934, and served the parish until his retirement in 1972.

Just west of Darby, the Borough of Collingdale developed rapidly, and the parish of SAINT JOSEPH was founded in 1916. It was originally conceived as a mission chapel of Holy Spirit, but the population of the area was growing so

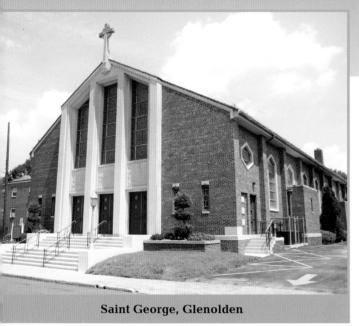
**Saint George, Glenolden**

quickly that the decision was made to establish it as a parish immediately. Masses were celebrated in the Collingdale Fire Hall until a church/school building was completed. The Immaculate Heart Sisters staffed the parish school, which opened in 1917 and was expanded in 1959. The present church of Saint Joseph was dedicated in 1955.

In 1923, when plans were developed to found a parish in Glenolden, there were some non-Catholics who did not welcome a Catholic church in their neighborhood. The archdiocese hired real-estate agent John Metz to secure a lot on which to build the new church of SAINT GEORGE. Mr. Metz noticed that he was being followed on his scouting trips by local residents seeking to find out what properties he was trying to buy. Their plan was to purchase small lots at various places on large tracts of land so that Mr. Metz could not find a contiguous plot large enough for the parish buildings.

Mr. Metz was eventually successful, and a church/school building was opened in 1927. Parishioners had attended Sunday Mass for nearly four years in the Williamson Hall, at Chester Pike and Logan Avenue, while a plot was found and the church constructed. Educational responsibilities were entrusted to Sisters of Saint Joseph. A new church, on Lamont Avenue, was dedicated in 1955, and a new school opened in 1965.

A former locker house of the Tully-Secane Golf Course served as the temporary chapel for OUR LADY OF FATIMA parish when it was founded on October 13, 1952—the 35th anniversary of the final apparition of the Blessed Mother to three shepherd children in Fatima, Portugal. The communities of Secane, Briarcliff

**Our Lady of Fatima, Secane**

and Holmes had been built up in the post-war years, and new parishioners quickly formed a "Cyrenian Society" to share the burden of building the new church. (This society was named for Simon of Cyrene, who helped Jesus to carry His Cross.) The parish school opened in 1953 under the direction of Immaculate Heart Sisters. The present church was dedicated in 1961. In 1979 the lower level of the church was converted to a daily Mass chapel, dedicated to Saint John Neumann.

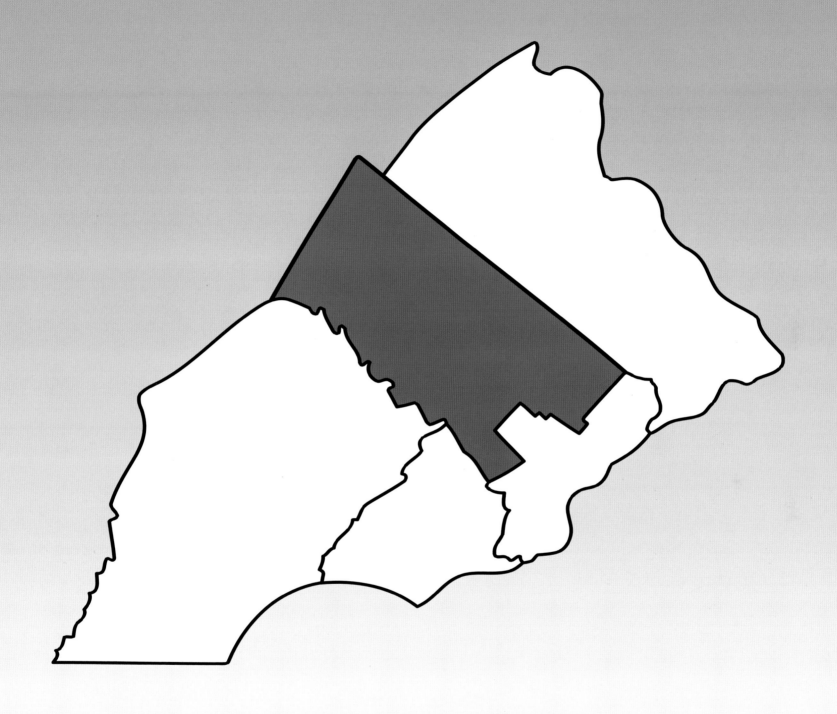

# MONTGOMERY COUNTY

# Norristown and Vicinity

Located along the Schuylkill River about 16 miles northwest of Philadelphia, Norristown became the county seat of Montgomery County in 1784, and was incorporated as a borough in 1812, with a population of about 500 people. Many residents worked in mills along the river, or were employed in digging canals that would soon make the Schuylkill River the means of transporting coal from the Reading area to the port of Philadelphia. The 1830s saw the construction of the Philadelphia and Reading Railroad, which followed the course of the river. The need for workers to lay tracks and build stations attracted laborers from Philadelphia, many of whom were recently arrived Irishmen.

The first stage in the construction of the railroad was between Reading and Norristown, and many railroad families established homes in the

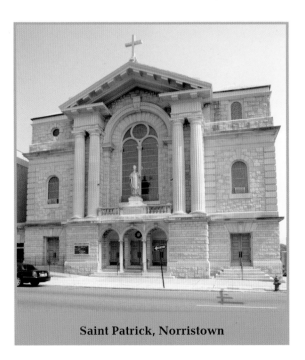

**Saint Patrick, Norristown**

small borough. The closest Catholic church was Saint John the Baptist, Manayunk—about 8 miles away. Such a distance was a difficult journey to make on foot, and Catholics in Norristown desired to attend Mass in their own locality. In 1832, Father Charles I.H. Carter, a priest at Saint John's, began celebrating Mass at Saint John's Episcopal Church in Norristown. By 1833 the congregation moved to the home of local resident, Patrick Flynn. In 1835, SAINT PATRICK was established as the first Catholic parish in Norristown.

Bernard McCready, a cotton mill owner, offered to donate land for the church provided parishioners could raise $1,000 for its construction. Collections among the railroad workers brought in all but $100 of the required sum. The remaining amount (about $2,000 in 2005 values) was donated by Patrick Flynn. It is said that Saint Patrick Church was named after his patron saint in gratitude for this act of generosity. The name of the patron saint of Ireland, of course, also well suited the large Irish population of the area. The first church building was completed in 1839. The present church was dedicated in 1907.

Saint Patrick's school welcomed its first students in 1875, and was conducted by Immaculate Heart Sisters. A parish high school opened in 1941; in 1955, it was renamed Bishop Kenrick High School and made part of the archdiocesan high school system. Since 1985, the parish convent has been home to the

**Holy Saviour, Norristown**

Missionaries of Charity—a religious congregation of women founded by Blessed Teresa of Calcutta—who tend to the needs of the poor and homeless. A large Hispanic community—including many immigrants from the Puebla region of Mexico—now lives in Norristown, and Sunday Mass is celebrated here both in Spanish and in English.

Large numbers of people from Italy moved into the area in the early twentieth century. Italian missionary priests initially met with Italian families in Saint Patrick Church. In September 1903, this growing community established the first Italian national parish in the suburban counties. Many parishioners came from the town of Montella, about 40 miles east of Naples, where there was a shrine dedicated to

San Salvatore—which in English is HOLY SAVIOUR. They gave this name to the new parish, and enshrined there an image of the "Christ of Montella," depicted as a youth wearing a crown. The founding pastor, Father Michael Maggio, himself an immigrant, encouraged his parishioners—who came from Campagna, the Marches, Naples, and Sciacca in Sicily—to celebrate their traditional feasts with public processions.

The lower church of Holy Saviour—located on Main Street on the eastern end of the borough—was completed in 1903, and the upper church in 1908. The 1920s saw the establishment of Holy Saviour School, under the direction of Immaculate Heart Sisters, as well as the SS. Salvatore Settlement House, which helped recent immigrants to make the transition to life in America. In 1940, the parish opened a mission chapel, Our Lady of Mount

**Saint Helena, Blue Bell**

Carmel, on Fairfield Road in the Black Horse neighborhood of Plymouth Township.

By the end of World War I, more than 30,000 people lived in Norristown and surrounding communities. Three additional parishes were founded at this time to care for the burgeoning Catholic population. At the turn of the century, the small community of Port Kennedy, located along the Reading Railroad line west of Norristown, became popular as a summer resort for Philadelphia residents. As more Catholics made the area their permanent home, the parish of SAINT TERESA OF AVILA was founded in 1918. A second church was built in 1952, and Immaculate Heart Sisters founded the parish school in 1958. The present church was dedicated in 1983. The parish borders include a large area of the Valley Forge National Historical Park—the site of the Continental Army's encampment in the winter of 1777—and today the entire area is commonly known as Valley Forge.

North of Norristown, the town of Blue Bell—also called Center Square—was experiencing similar development. When the parish of SAINT HELENA was founded in 1919, there were residents of the area who were suspicious of or hostile to the idea of a Catholic church in the neighborhood. Since many land owners would not sell to a Catholic priest, the first pastor, Father Francis Higgins, had to wear lay clothes while he searched for a parish site.

Eileen Duddy, a local farmer, donated two acres of her land for construction of a church. The old farm buildings served as the first chapel, and it was not uncommon for farm animals to wander into the church during the celebration of Mass. When Miss Duddy died in 1922, she left the rest of the farm—about 90 acres and livestock— to the parish. During the difficult years of the Depression, the parish often made more money from the sale of eggs than it was able to collect from parishioners.

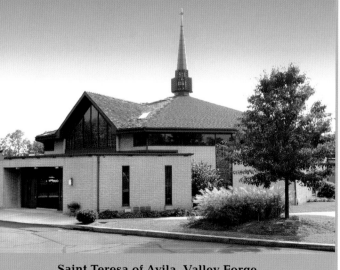

**Saint Teresa of Avila, Valley Forge**

**Saint Francis of Assisi, Norristown**

**Visitation B.V.M., Trooper**

The first school at Saint Helena's was begun in the convent of the Sisters of Mercy in 1949, and a new school building opened in 1950. A church was built in 1952, and the present church was dedicated in 2004.

In 1923, further development within the borough occasioned the establishment of SAINT FRANCIS OF ASSISI parish. The first Masses were celebrated outdoors on the lawn of the McAvoy family, at George and Main Streets, and parishioners soon moved to a barn on the Kemmer farm, on West Main Street above Centre Avenue. In December 1923, a wooden chapel at the present site—Marshall and Buttonwood Streets—was completed. The first school, operated by Sisters of Saint Joseph,

opened in 1927. The present church was dedicated in 1955, and houses a replica of Michelangelo's statue of Moses.

The suburban expansion in the years following World War II led to further home building in the Norristown area; accordingly, several new parishes were founded. VISITATION OF THE BLESSED VIRGIN MARY parish, in the Trooper neighborhood of East Norriton Township, was founded during the Marian Year, 1954. The school, originally staffed by Sisters of the Holy Family of Nazareth, opened in 1957. The lower portion of the present church was completed in 1962, and the upper church was dedicated in 1971.

In the 1950s, development of the Plymouth Meeting Mall, as well as high-tech companies such as Univac and Honeywell, encouraged residential development in Plymouth Township, to the east of Norristown. The parish of the EPIPHANY OF OUR LORD was founded in Plymouth Meeting on January 7, 1957, and named for the feast that had been celebrated on the preceding day. Mass was celebrated in the Plymouth Township municipal building until

**Epiphany of Our Lord, Plymouth Meeting**

the first church/school building was ready in 1958. Sisters of Saint Joseph arrived that year to teach in the parish school. The present church was dedicated in 1970.

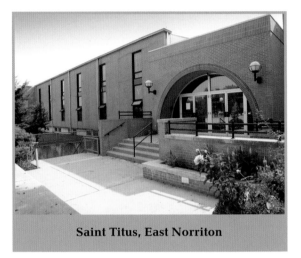

**Saint Titus, East Norriton**

The parish of SAINT TITUS was founded in East Norriton Township in 1962, in territory that had formerly been part of Saint Helena parish. Parishioners met for Sunday Mass in the East Norriton Fire House for several years prior to

the dedication of a church/school building in 1964. Bernardine Sisters were invited to serve on the faculty. Saint Titus saw a population increase of over 200 percent in the first fifteen years of its existence.

In 1963, another parish was founded in the area. SAINT PAUL parish was formed from the territory of Saint Titus, as well as from Saint Patrick and Epiphany parishes. The 800 families in the new parish met for Sunday Mass in the auditorium of Bishop Kenrick High School. A church/school building was completed in 1964, and the present church was dedicated ten years later. The school was founded with the assistance of Sisters of Mercy.

**Saint Paul, Norristown**

239

# Conshohocken and Vicinity

Located one mile east of Norristown, the Borough of Conshohocken (a Lenape word meaning "pleasant valley") was incorporated in 1850. Its position on the Schuylkill River made it an attractive location for textile and grist mills. The development of canals and railroads brought the Alan Wood iron-rolling mill to the borough. Numerous Irish and German immigrants moved to the area to take advantage of employment opportunities.

To attend Mass, Catholics in the area had to walk several miles to Saint Patrick's in Norristown, or to Saint John's in Manayunk, until SAINT MATTHEW parish was founded in

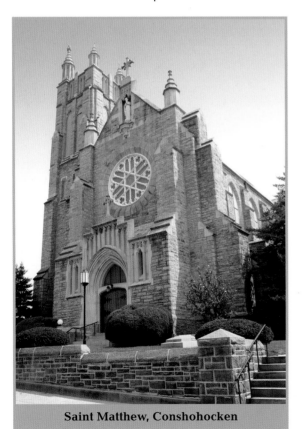
Saint Matthew, Conshohocken

Conshohocken in 1851. The original church was built largely by parishioners, who assisted the hired craftsmen with laborious tasks like digging the foundation. Parish members likewise took part in building a parish elementary school, which opened in 1864. Sisters of Saint Joseph arrived in 1915 to serve on the faculty. Saint Matthew's High School—the first parish high school in the archdiocese—operated from 1866 to 1955, when it became part of the archdiocesan secondary school system. It was renamed Archbishop Kennedy High School in 1966, and merged with Bishop Kenrick High School in 1993. The present church of Saint Matthew was dedicated in 1919.

Priests from Saint Matthew's soon established a mission in the village of West Conshohocken. This mission became SAINT GERTRUDE parish in November 1888, on the saint's feast day. Immaculate Heart Sisters founded the parish school in 1889 in a room below the church; a school building opened in 1954. Decline in parish population led to the closing of Saint Gertrude's School in 1977.

Across the Schuylkill River from Saint Patrick's, the Borough of Bridgeport was home to about 3,000 persons by the end of the nineteenth century. Catholics who worked in the mills and factories of the borough took part in the foundation of SAINT AUGUSTINE parish in 1892, and met for Sunday Mass in the "Bonnet Factory" at Fifth and Ford Streets. Parishioners

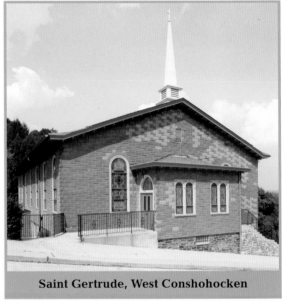
Saint Gertrude, West Conshohocken

dug the foundation for the church/school building, which was completed within the year. A new school was opened in 1896, and Immaculate Heart Sisters took responsibility for the school in 1911. The present church was dedicated in 1935.

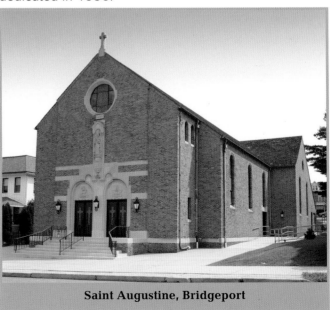
Saint Augustine, Bridgeport

Several national parishes were opened in the first decades of the twentieth century to serve ethnic communities in Conshohocken and Bridgeport. SAINT MARY parish in Conshohocken was originally a mission of Saint Josaphat parish in Manayunk. In 1905 the mission chapel was established as the parish church for Polish-speaking people in the area, and Bernardine Sisters staffed the parish school. Saint Mary's was twinned with Saint Gertrude parish in 2001.

Polish immigrants were also drawn to the area of Swedesburg, east of Bridgeport, by the many jobs available in local quarries, textile

**Sacred Heart, Swedesburg**

mills and steel mills. In 1907, SACRED HEART parish was founded for Polish residents of Swedesburg, Bridgeport and King of Prussia. The parish school, founded the same year, came under the direction of the Bernardine Sisters in 1922. The present church, completed in 1927, stands near the site where George Washington camped with Polish General Casimir Pulaski on the way to Valley Forge in 1777.

The mills also attracted Italian immigrants to the Conshohocken area. Many of these immigrants were from the Italian province of Isernia, and they named their parish after the patrons of their local shrine, SAINTS COSMAS AND DAMIAN. The new parishioners met at the

Opera House at First and Fayette Streets until the church was completed in 1913. A second church was built in 1926, and the present church was dedicated in 1952. Sisters of Saint Joseph, Immaculate Heart Sisters and Bernardine Sisters provided religious education at various times until a parish school opened in 1954 under the direction of Missionary Sisters of the Sacred Heart, a congregation founded by the Italian-born Saint Frances Xavier Cabrini. The school building now serves the primary grades of Conshohocken Catholic School.

**Saints Cosmas and Damien,
Conshohocken**

**Saint Mary, Conshohocken**

OUR LADY OF MOUNT CARMEL parish was founded in Bridgeport in 1924. At first, Masses were celebrated in Salvatore Paschall's garage, as well as in the Bonnet Factory that had been home to the first parishioners of Saint Augustine's some 30 years before. The lower church was completed in 1927, and the upper church was dedicated in 1949. Immaculate Heart Sisters operated an elementary school from 1952 to 1977.

**Saint Philip Neri, Lafayette Hill**

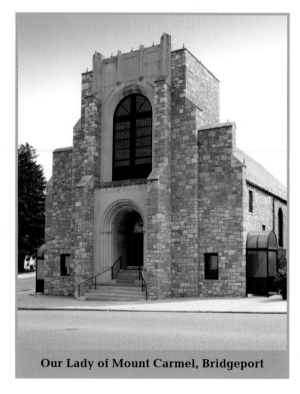
**Our Lady of Mount Carmel, Bridgeport**

The Bonnet Factory would be home to one more Catholic community in Bridgeport, as immigrants from Slovakia found work in the Alan Wood Steel mills and in the area's mines and quarries. At first the Slovak community attended Sacred Heart Church in Phoenixville, but the ten-mile journey was difficult. Consequently, the national parish of OUR MOTHER OF SORROWS was founded in 1926 to care for Slovaks in Bridgeport, Conshohocken, Norristown and King of Prussia. A church/school building located at the intersection of Holstein, Hurst and Coates Streets was dedicated in 1928, and was debt-free in less than a year. Sisters of Saint Cyril and Methodius were the founding faculty of this parish school. Declining numbers of Slovak-speaking priests and parishioners led to the suppression of Our Mother of Sorrows parish in 2001.

Further development in the Conshohocken area occurred in the years after World War II. In 1945, SAINT PHILIP NERI parish was founded in the area of Barren Hill, on Ridge Pike southeast of Conshohocken. The locality was later renamed Lafayette Hill, after the French general the Marquis de Lafayette who served with George Washington. The first church building was dedicated in 1946, and the first school opened in 1950, entrusted to Sisters of Saint Joseph. The present church was completed in 1982.

The growth of the Interstate Highway System in the 1950s brought commercial and industrial development to the town of King of Prussia, located near the intersection of the Schuylkill Expressway and the Pennsylvania Turnpike. In 1954, Cardinal John O'Hara founded the parish of MOTHER OF DIVINE PROVIDENCE in this developing region. The cardinal had known the Sisters of Our Lady of Providence during his years at the University of Notre Dame, and named this last parish of the Marian Year to honor this title of Our Lady. Mass was celebrated in a second-floor chapel in the parish school from 1958 until 1963, at which time the church was dedicated.

**Mother of Divine Providence, King of Prussia**

# Pottstown and Vicinity

Priests from Saint Mary's Church in Phoenixville, Chester County, established a mission church in Pottstown in 1856. The church was named for SAINT ALOYSIUS, on whose feast day it was founded. The following year, the Catholic population in this mill town on the Schuylkill River had grown large enough to support a resident pastor, Father J. D. Davis. The parishioners quickly outgrew the small mission church, and a second church was dedicated in 1891. A parish school followed in 1913, staffed by Franciscan Sisters from Glen Riddle. The present church was dedicated in 1952.

The steel mills of Pottstown also attracted immigrants from Slovakia, who came to the United States to escape religious and cultural oppression in their homeland. Slovak priests from Reading, Berks County, established a mission chapel in Pottstown in 1899, and saw to the construction of HOLY TRINITY Church in 1901. The first resident pastor was appointed in 1905. A new church was built in 1916, and the parish school was founded in the lower area of the church in 1950. Holy Trinity was twinned with Saint Aloysius in 1998, and suppressed in 2004. Holy Trinity Church now serves as a worship site of Saint Aloysius parish.

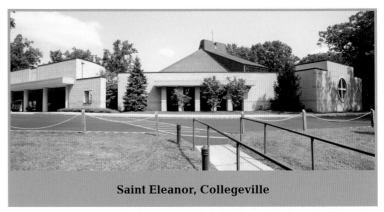

**Saint Eleanor, Collegeville**

The Borough of Collegeville, between Pottstown and Norristown, grew up near the campus of Ursinus College, founded in 1870. The church of SAINT ELEANOR was founded on Main Street in 1911. For many years, parish students were bussed to Saint Francis of Assisi School in Norristown, until a parish elementary school was ready in 1948. The present church was dedicated in 1971, at Sixth and Locust Streets. In that year, Immaculate Heart Sisters were invited to staff the parish school.

In the 1740s, German Catholic pioneers had settled the area of Pennsburg and East Greenville, and for many years they traveled to Blessed Sacrament Church in Bally, Berks County. In 1889 priests of the Bally parish established a mission chapel in Pennsburg. Responsibility for the mission was assumed by Saint Aloysius parish in 1910, and by Saint Eleanor parish from 1911 to 1917. This mission was canonically established as SAINT PHILIP NERI parish in 1919, and a second church was completed in 1922. A parish school was founded in 1951 by Sisters of Mercy, and the present church was dedicated in 1968. The area continues to grow as farms give way to residential development.

Pottstown's steel mills had attracted many Polish immigrants to the borough in the late nineteenth century, and from 1901 they attended Mass with the Slovak community at Holy Trinity. A Polish-speaking priest from Philadelphia or Reading might come to Pottstown during Lent to hear the people's confessions; however, Polish Catholics in Pottstown were without a priest of their own. In 1924 members of the local branch of the Polish National Alliance petitioned Cardinal Dougherty to establish a Polish national parish, and later that year ground was broken for SAINT PETER Church. Bernardine Sisters were soon invited to teach in the parish school.

**Saint Aloysius, Pottstown**

**Saint Philip Neri, Pennsburg**

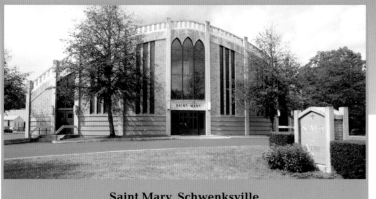
**Saint Mary, Schwenksville**

At the start of the twentieth century, visiting priests from Saint Aloysius celebrated Mass at the Perkiomenville farm of Max von Lang. By 1905 the worshipping community had outgrown the farmhouse, and the congregation moved to the stable of the Green Lane Hotel. A mission chapel was built in 1917, and in 1923 a creamery at the foot of Spring Mountain was converted to a church, staffed by priests from Saint Eleanor's. In 1926, this mission was established as the parish of SAINT MARY in Delphi. Development after World War II warranted the establishment of a parish school in 1959, staffed by Glen Riddle Franciscans. The present church of Saint Mary in Schwenksville was dedicated in 1984.

Another mission of Saint Aloysius parish was established to serve 30 families who lived several miles away in Stowe. From 1926 to 1929, Mass was celebrated in the home of the Bucciaglia family, and also in the West End Fire Company Hall. The parish of SAINT GABRIEL OF THE SORROWFUL MOTHER was formally established in 1929, and a church was completed in 1930. The parish school opened in 1950 under the direction of Glen Riddle Franciscans and closed in 1989. The present church of Saint Gabriel was built in 1961.

The first Masses in the farming community of Linfield were celebrated in 1925 by priests from Saint Joseph parish in Spring City, Chester County. The development of this mission was due in large part to the request of local resident Monica Balciunas, who asked the pastor of Saint Joseph's to celebrate Mass for Linfield's increasing Lithuanian community. A mission church was built in 1927, and post-war development of the area led to the foundation of SAINT CLARE parish in 1963. In its early days, the parish was very poor, and the first pastor, Father Henry McNulty, made many requests for financial assistance to parishes where he had previously been assigned.

In the 1990s and early years of the 21st century, continuing development of the area meant that both Saint Peter's and Saint Clare's churches were too small to accommodate worshippers.

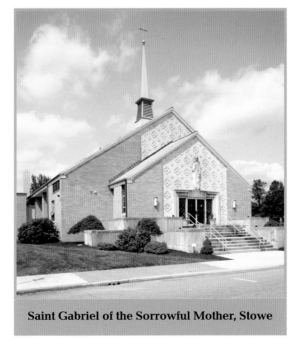
**Saint Gabriel of the Sorrowful Mother, Stowe**

**Sacred Heart, Royersford**

These two parishes were consolidated in July 2006 to form BLESSED TERESA OF CALCUTTA parish, the first in the archdiocese named for Mother Teresa, who was beatified in October 2003.

The youngest parish (after Blessed Teresa) in the Pottstown area actually traces its history back to 1891, when the mission church of the SACRED HEART was established in Royersford. Initially staffed by priests from Saint Ann's in Phoenixville, this mission became the responsibility of Saint Joseph's in Spring City in 1919. A church was built at the corner of Fifth and Walnut Streets in 1923, and a second church in 1954. The parish school welcomed its first students in 1954. Sacred Heart mission was established as a parish in 1973, and Sisters of Saint Joseph arrived that year to staff Sacred Heart School.

# Lansdale and Vicinity

By 1839, the Reading Railroad connected Reading, Berks County, with the City of Philadelphia, and passed through Norristown on its way along the Schuylkill River. In 1853, the North Pennsylvania Railroad Company began construction on a new line connecting Norristown with Doylestown, the county seat of Bucks County, some 17 miles to the northeast. About halfway along the route, railroad workers and their families established a village in 1856 that they named for the chief surveyor of the North Penn Railroad, Philip Lansdale Fox. The Borough of Lansdale was incorporated in 1872.

For the farmers and railroad workers of the new borough, attending Mass meant an all-day journey to Our Lady of Mount Carmel parish, Doylestown, or to Saint Patrick, Norristown. In 1875, Father Henry Stommel, pastor of Our Lady of Mount Carmel, established a mission that he called Marienfeld, at that time just outside the Lansdale borough limits. In 1876 this mission was established as the parish of SAINT STANISLAUS. A parish school was founded in 1891; in 1901, Immaculate Heart Sisters arrived to serve on the faculty, and were succeeded some years later by Franciscan Sisters from Glen Riddle. In 1911, the mission chapel was replaced with a larger church. The parish opened a high school, named Little Flower, in 1949. Its name was changed to Lansdale Catholic High School in 1951, and it became part of the archdiocesan secondary school system in 1983. The present church of Saint Stanislaus was dedicated in 1964.

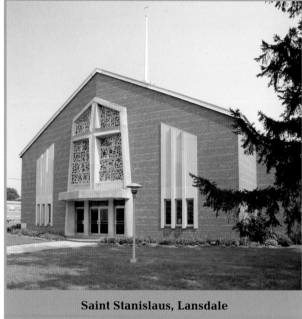

Saint Stanislaus, Lansdale

A decade after the founding of Saint Stanislaus, Father Stommel established a parish in the Borough of Ambler, about seven miles southeast of Lansdale. The site he chose for SAINT ANTHONY OF PADUA church, at the corner of Forest Avenue and Hendricks Street, is the highest point in the borough. Father Stommel's church was dedicated in 1886, and in 1956 it was transformed into the sanctuary of a larger church. Saint Anthony's was gutted by fire on Christmas Eve 2000; a new church was dedicated in 2004. Saint Anthony's School, founded in 1886 by Franciscan Sisters from Glen Riddle, was operated by Sisters of Saint Joseph after 1923.

A second parish in Ambler, dedicated to SAINT JOSEPH, was founded in 1920 to

Saint Anthony of Padua, Ambler

respond to an influx of Italian immigrants to the borough. The Keasbey and Mattison Company, producers of chemicals and asbestos products, had relocated to Ambler in 1881, and the availability of employment at the company's plant attracted many workers. Although it was not officially a national parish, the boundaries of Saint Joseph's included areas where many Italians had settled. Most of the Ambler Italians were from the town of Maida, in the region of Calabria. Both the first church, built in 1923, and the present church, dedicated in 1976, include shrines to Saint Francis of Paola, the patron saint of Calabria.

In 1912, Saint Stanislaus parish established a mission in North Wales, a borough which grew up around the train and trolley lines that connected Norristown and Doylestown. A lower church was built in 1915, and in 1919 the parish of SAINT ROSE OF LIMA was officially established, with about 100 member families. The post-World War II period saw a

**Saint Joseph, Ambler**

population increase in North Wales, and a parish school was founded in 1955 by Sisters of Mercy. The present church was dedicated in 1966.

The post-war decades were likewise a time of intensive home construction in the farming community of Hatfield, just to the west of Lansdale. A parish was founded in 1953 and named for SAINT MARIA GORETTI, the Italian virgin and martyr who had been canonized in

1950. The 200 families of the new parish met for Sunday Mass in the Hatfield Fire Hall and also in Hen's Restaurant on Souderton Pike, until a church/ school building was erected in 1954.

Immaculate Heart Sisters were invited that year to teach the children of the parish. Angelo Goretti, the brother of Saint Maria, attended the dedication of the first church in 1960. Rapid growth in population—an eight-fold increase by 1990—made it necessary to build a much larger church, which was dedicated in 1995. The Vietnamese Catholic community in Montgomery County gathers for Sunday Mass at Saint Maria Goretti Church.

**Saint Maria Goretti, Hatfield**

In 1964, a new parish was needed in Upper Gwynedd, just west of the boroughs of Lansdale and North Wales. CORPUS CHRISTI parish began with only 230 families, but the population grew to more than 2,000 families by 1990, and to almost 4,000 families in 2005. Parishioners met at the farm of John Curtin until a church/school building was completed in 1965. The parish school was entrusted to Sisters of Saint Joseph. Construction of the present church was begun in 1998, and the church was dedicated in 2000.

**Saint Rose of Lima, North Wales**

Residential development in Upper Dublin Township led to the founding, in 1963, of SAINT ALPHONSUS parish in Maple Glen, from the parish area of Saint Anthony, Ambler, as well as from Saint David, Willow Grove, and Saint John of the Cross, Roslyn. The church, built in 1965, was expanded and rededicated in 2004. Sisters of Mercy inaugurated the parish school in 1964.

The population of the North Wales area continued to grow throughout the 1980s, and in 1987 Cardinal Krol established the parish of MARY, MOTHER OF THE REDEEMER from territory that had been part of Saint Stanislaus. This new parish was named after the encyclical *Redemptoris Mater* ("Mother of the Redeemer") that Pope John Paul II had issued during the

**Saint Alphonsus, Maple Glen**

than 200 parish volunteers served without salary. The parish church, dedicated in 1991, received widespread recognition and design awards from architectural associations. The parish school opened in 2003 with a lay faculty.

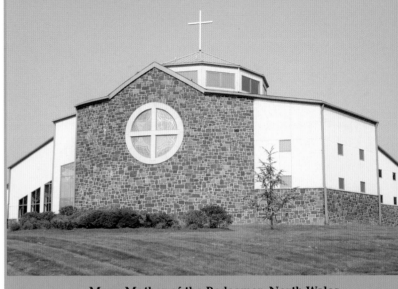

**Mary, Mother of the Redeemer, North Wales**

Marian Year in 1987. Sunday Mass was initially celebrated at the clubhouse of the Neshaminy Village development, and later at Gwynedd Mercy High School. Daily Mass was held in a farmhouse donated by Mrs. Nora O'Connor, and this building still serves as the rectory. For the first ten years of the parish, a staff of more

**Corpus Christi, Upper Gwynedd**

# Glenside and Vicinity

At the beginning of the twentieth century, the village of Glenside was little more than a country outpost. Its business district, concentrated in the space of two blocks, was largely surrounded by farms. The location of Glenside was along the railroad line that brought Philadelphians for summer holidays in Willow Grove Park. This location made it attractive and convenient to people looking for a suburban home. Both the rail line and the Germantown–Willow Grove Turnpike (now Easton Road) encouraged the development of Glenside as a "commuter suburb" for people who worked in Philadelphia.

Mass for the first parishioners of SAINT LUKE THE EVANGELIST parish was celebrated in the Tierney Hotel on Christmas Eve, 1905. This hotel and the Glenside Inn were used until the first parish church was dedicated in 1910. Further building was delayed by World War I and the influenza epidemic, but the parish school was finally opened in 1920, under the direction of the Sisters of Saint Joseph. The parish encountered anti-Catholic prejudice in its early years, including a march by the Ku Klux Klan in September 1927. An influx of families during the 1950s and 1960s necessitated several expansions to the school. The present church was dedicated in 1971.

Saint Luke's parish established several mission churches during the first decade of the twentieth century. A small mission church was built on Willow Grove Avenue in Wyndmoor in 1907, and in 1916 it became the parish church of SEVEN DOLORS. Immaculate Heart

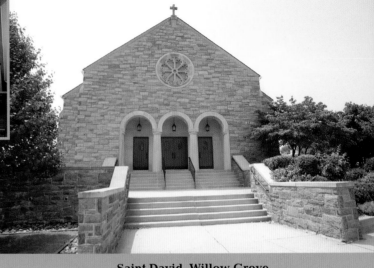

Saint David, Willow Grove

Sisters opened the parish school in 1918, in the former Saint Mark Lutheran Church. A permanent school building was built in 1921. A former Protestant church was refurbished and opened as the parish church in 1950, and a new church was built in 1963. Twinned with the parish of Saint Genevieve, Flourtown, in 2000, Seven Dolors was officially suppressed in 2003.

The little chapel of Saint Louis, on Penn Street in Hatboro, was established in 1890 by Father Augustine Rufe, then pastor of Saint Anthony in Ambler. This chapel ceased to function in 1892; however, when Father Rufe became pastor of Saint Luke in 1909, he resumed the celebration of the liturgy in this chapel. The Ku Klux Klan remained openly hostile to this activity, and in 1916 the mission chapel was relocated to Willow Grove on the

Saint Luke the Evangelist, Glenside

**Holy Martyrs, Oreland**

Doylestown Pike (now Easton Road). Every afternoon, after working in his general store, parishioner David Nolan came to help with the construction of the church. In gratitude for his dedication, Father Rufe named the new church in honor of Mr. Nolan's patron, SAINT DAVID.

Saint David's mission was established as a parish in 1919. Immaculate Heart Sisters began religious instruction in the chapel in 1920, and a school building opened in 1926. The area became a center of the aviation industry during World War II, and the presence of both aircraft manufacturers and the Willow Grove Naval Air Station encouraged housing development in the 1940s and 1950s. The present church was dedicated in 1952.

In 1946, a third mission from Saint Luke's parish was established on Oreland Mill Road in the village of Oreland, just west of Glenside on the North Penn Railroad line. This was the beginning of HOLY MARTYRS parish, formally established in 1949. A church/school building was completed in 1953, and Sisters of Mercy formed the founding faculty.

In the 1950s, the benefits provided to veterans by the G.I. Bill encouraged home building in this part of Montgomery County. Four new parishes were founded within ten years to serve the expanding Catholic population. SAINT GENEVIEVE in Flourtown was founded in 1949 by the Augustinians, as a mission of Our Mother of Consolation in Chestnut Hill. The mission was made a parish in 1953, and a church/school building was erected in 1955. The school was under the direction of Sisters of Saint Joseph, while Augustinian priests continued to serve the parish until 1998. In that year, an archdiocesan priest was appointed pastor of Saint Genevieve, which was twinned with Seven Dolors, Wyndmoor, in 2000. The former church of Seven Dolors is now a worship site of Saint Genevieve parish.

An empty store on Easton Road belonging to

William Koenig was the first home of SAINT JOHN OF THE CROSS parish, Roslyn, formed from the territory of Saint David's and Saint Luke's in 1953. Although he was not Catholic himself, Mr. Koenig donated the building for the use of the new parish. The auditorium of the parish school, founded in 1954, was the location for Sunday Mass until the church was dedicated in 1965. Education of the parish children was entrusted to Immaculate Heart Sisters.

**Saint Genevieve, Flourtown**

**Saint John of the Cross, Roslyn**

the pastor, the name of the street was soon changed to Marian Road.

Another parish in the area dedicated to the Blessed Mother was established in 1954. The Cannon family farm became the site of the chapel of QUEEN OF PEACE, in the area known as Fitzwatertown but commonly referred to as Ardsley. The school, founded by Sisters of the Holy Family of Nazareth, began in an old carriage house on the property, and a new building was completed in 1955. The present church was dedicated in 1963.

**Our Lady Help of Christians, Abington**

During the Marian Year—observed from December 8, 1953, to December 8, 1954, to celebrate the centennial of the declaration of the dogma of the Immaculate Conception of the Blessed Virgin Mary—Cardinal O'Hara founded ten parishes dedicated to Our Lady. The first, OUR LADY HELP OF CHRISTIANS parish in Abington, began with Mass in a nineteenth-century house that served as a rectory. A school building was erected in 1954, and Sunday Mass was celebrated in the school hall until the parish church was completed in 1962. Sisters of the Congregation of the Holy Cross—the religious congregation to which Cardinal O'Hara also belonged—founded the parish school in 1953, and were succeeded by Sisters of Saint Joseph in 1968. The parish property was located on Folly Road in Abington, but at the suggestion of

**Queen of Peace, Ardsley**

# Jenkintown and Vicinity

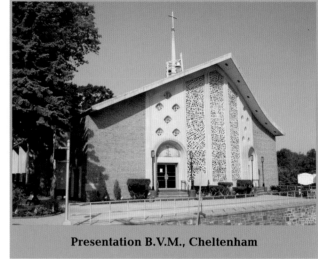

**Presentation B.V.M., Cheltenham**

By 1857, the North Pennsylvania Railroad extended from Philadelphia as far north as Bethlehem, Lehigh County, and many towns grew up along the rail line. In the eighteenth century, Sarah Jenkins' Tavern had been a stage coach stop on the route to New York, and the arrival of the railroad spurred development in the area near the tavern. The town became known as Jenkintown.

A mission church had been planned for the Jenkintown area in 1857, when priests from Our Mother of Consolation in Chestnut Hill, four miles away, came to celebrate Mass in the Jenkintown Lyceum. A stock market crash in 1857, and the Civil War from 1861 to 1865, made it impossible to follow through with these plans. Priests continued to visit, however, first from Our Mother of Consolation and, from 1864 to 1866, from Saint Joachim parish in Frankford, Philadelphia. In 1866 the mission, with its congregation of about 70 families, was established as the parish of Saint Mary.

In the following year this parish was renamed for the IMMACULATE CONCEPTION OF THE BLESSED VIRGIN MARY. The first church was dedicated in 1868, but was destroyed by fire sixty years later. The present church was completed in 1929. Sunday School classes were conducted in the home of the Elcock family of Glenside until the first school building was finished in 1895. Sisters of Saint Joseph formed the original faculty. Another school was built in 1982.

In the 1890s, access to the City of Philadelphia via the railroad made the surrounding countryside an attractive place for the development of commuter suburbs. Large residential tracts transformed the area of Cheltenham, just across the city boundary, and Cheltenham Township was incorporated in 1900. At the time, the only churches available to Catholic residents of Cheltenham were Immaculate Conception and Saint Joachim, both several miles away.

In 1890, the parish of the PRESENTATION OF THE BLESSED VIRGIN MARY was founded in Cheltenham. The church was dedicated in 1891, and a parish school followed in 1923, staffed by Sisters of Saint Joseph. A second parish in Cheltenham, named for SAINT JOSEPH, was founded in 1953, in response to the home construction made possible by the G.I. Bill. Saint Joseph was

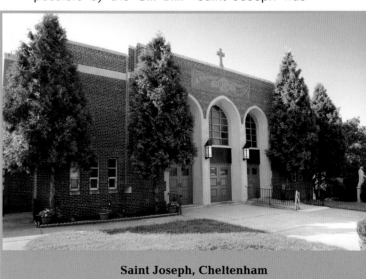

**Saint Joseph, Cheltenham**

**Immaculate Conception B.V.M., Jenkintown**

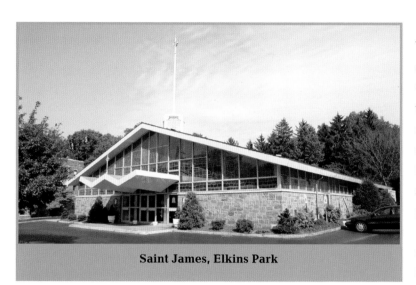

**Saint James, Elkins Park**

**Saint Albert the Great, Huntingdon Valley**

Two more parishes in this section of Montgomery County were established in the 1960s, from territory that originally was part of Immaculate Conception, Jenkintown. Lower Moreland Township saw a five-fold increase in population in the 1950s and 1960s. Many young families moved to the area from Northeast Philadelphia. The U.S. Marine Corps auditorium at Red Lion Road and Philmont Avenue was the first home for the parishioners of SAINT ALBERT THE GREAT parish, founded in the Huntingdon Valley section of the township in 1962. A school opened in 1964 under the direction of School Sisters of Notre Dame, and the parish church was dedicated in 1965. The parish boundaries encompass some territory in the City of

Philadelphia, making Saint Albert the Great one of the few parishes that cross county borders

Similar growth in Abington Township led to the foundation of SAINT HILARY OF POITIERS parish in the Rydal area, also in 1962. The community gathered for Mass in the auditorium of Saint Basil Academy, on Fox Chase Road in Jenkintown, until the church was completed in 1963. The parish school also opened that year, staffed by the Sisters of Saint Joseph.

established in the Oak Lane Manor Neighborhood from territory of Presentation B.V.M. as well as Saint Helena and Holy Angels parishes in Philadelphia. A church/school building was dedicated in 1955, and Sisters of Saint Joseph formed the founding faculty. Saint Joseph was twinned with Presentation B.V.M. in 2000.

Presentation B.V.M. parish was divided in 1923 to create the church of SAINT JAMES the Greater in Elkins Park. The new parish lay about halfway between Immaculate Conception and Presentation, and also developed around a train station on the Reading Railroad line. The initial congregation met for Sunday Mass at Johnson's Hall on Stahr Road, and during the week in a chapel in the rectory on Cadwalader Avenue. A chapel/school building was erected in 1924, built of stone from a quarry located within the parish boundaries. The present church, dedicated in 1968, is built on a filled-in quarry. Sisters of Saint Joseph arrived in 1936 to staff the parish school.

**Saint Hilary of Poitiers, Rydal**

# The Main Line

The vicinity of Radnor Township, about 13 miles west of Philadelphia in present-day Delaware County, was a farming community when William Penn founded the township in 1682. The completion in 1795 of the Philadelphia and Lancaster Turnpike—the first long-distance paved road in the United States—made the area attractive to wealthy Philadelphia families for building country estates to escape the heat and diseases that often plagued the city. One such family was that of John Randolph, a lieutenant in the Continental Army, who made a fortune as a merchant in Burlington, New Jersey. He and his wife, Elizabeth, built "Belle Aire" on 100 acres of land along Lancaster Pike in 1806.

**Saint Thomas of Villanova, Villanova**

The Randolphs were Catholics, and to attend Sunday Mass from Belle Aire they had to travel back to Philadelphia, to Saint Augustine's church at Fourth and Vine Streets. When the Augustinians founded the parish of Saint Denis, Havertown, in 1825, the Randolphs were able to cut their journey in half, but it was still a lengthy trip. Having become friendly with the Augustinian priests, Mr. Randolph invited them to come to Belle Aire whenever possible to celebrate Mass for his family, their servants, and Catholic neighbors. He fitted out a parlor in his mansion with an altar and an organ, which he often played himself during the Mass.

In 1841, three years after John Randolph's death, his Belle Aire estate came up for public sale. By now the "Main Line" of the Philadelphia and Columbia Railroad, which connected Philadelphia to the state capital in Harrisburg—and which, as the Pennsylvania Railroad, would eventually reach all the way to Pittsburgh—was in full operation. The Augustinian community in Philadelphia knew the estate, and realized that its position along both the railroad and Lancaster Pike would make it an ideal location for the college and motherhouse that they had been planning. They arranged to buy the property the day before the public sale was to be held, and benefited greatly from the generosity of Mrs. Randolph. The estate had been estimated to bring $40,000 at auction (about $755,000 in 2005 values), but Mrs. Randolph sold it to the Augustinians for less than half of that amount. The Augustinians renamed the estate "Villanova", after the childhood home of a well-loved Augustinian saint, the scholar and bishop Saint Thomas of Villanova.

In 1843, the Randolph mansion was officially recognized as the motherhouse of the Augustinian's American province. On August 28 of that year—the feast of Saint Augustine—the first Mass was celebrated in the newly-renovated chapel of SAINT THOMAS OF VILLANOVA. Present at that Mass were Mrs. Randolph and many members of the estate staff, including Mr. and Mrs. William Moulden, the first known African American Catholics in the area.

The mansion also housed the first students of the new Villanova College, which struggled in

**Our Mother of Good Counsel, Bryn Mawr**

**Saint Katharine of Siena, Wayne**

its first years as a consequence of the devastation of Saint Augustine's in Philadelphia by the Nativist riots in 1844. A chapel was constructed that year, and eventually became one of the buildings of the college, today known as Villanova University. The first baptism was celebrated in this chapel in 1848, and marked the beginning of Saint Thomas of Villanova as a canonical parish.

The Gothic-style church of Saint Thomas of Villanova was begun in 1883, and was dedicated by Archbishop Ryan in 1887. Twenty years later, as the community around Villanova continued to increase, the parish established a mission chapel and school in Rosemont, about a mile east on Lancaster Pike, and invited Sisters of Mercy to staff the school. The Rosemont chapel has had a resident priest since 1921. A new chapel and school were built here in 1956, and the chapel continues to serve as a second worship site of Saint Thomas parish.

In 1885, the Augustinian community also established a mission in the area of Bryn Mawr, along Lancaster Pike east of Rosemont. Area Catholics first met for Mass in an old wooden schoolhouse that was used as a Sunday school for the local Episcopal church. A Catholic chapel was dedicated in 1886 and named OUR MOTHER OF GOOD COUNSEL. Since the fifteenth century, a miraculous painting with this title has been housed in the Augustinian church in Gennezano, Italy, and Augustinians are especially devoted to the Virgin Mary under that title. The first parish school was established by Sisters of Mercy in 1889 in the lower part of the church; a proper school building was erected in 1908. The present church was dedicated in 1897.

Priests from Saint Thomas also established several missions to the west of Villanova, as residential communities continued to spring up along the Main Line. Augustinians celebrated Mass at the Wayne Opera House—also known as the Lyceum Hall, at Wayne and Lancaster Avenues—until the mission chapel of SAINT KATHARINE OF SIENA was founded in 1893. The church was built on land donated by George Childs and Anthony Drexel. The spelling of the name of Saint Katharine may allude to Mr. Drexel's niece, the future Saint Katharine Drexel.

Many parishioners worked as domestic servants on Main Line estates, and the church included a shrine to Saint Zita, patron saint of housekeepers and cooks. A parish elementary school and a high school were established in 1916, under the direction of Immaculate Heart Sisters. By the late 1950s, the parish community was too large for the original buildings. A new school was erected in 1958, and the present parish church was dedicated in 1966.

In Reeseville, about eight miles west of Villanova, the house of James Kelley served as the first site for Catholics in that area to gather for Mass with priests from Villanova. The Augustinians named this mission—which soon moved to the Town Hall on Church Avenue—after SAINT MONICA, the mother of Saint Augustine. When Saint Katharine's was founded in 1893, it became responsible for Saint Monica's, until the latter was established as a parish in 1897. Immaculate Heart Sisters staffed the school, which opened in 1917; the present school was constructed in 1958. The original church, built in 1889 on the estate of George Tobler in what came to be known as the town of Berwyn, was heavily damaged by fire in 1991. The present church was dedicated in 1993.

**Saint Monica, Berwyn**

Main Line communities closer to Philadelphia likewise experienced growth at the beginning of the twentieth century, as efficient rail service led to the development of planned suburbs. Like their neighbors farther out along the Main Line, these parishes served not only the wealthy families who owned the estates, but also those who worked as household staff or in the various trades and commercial enterprises that this development brought with it. These new communities provided ample employment opportunities for recent immigrants, many of them Catholic.

The Borough of Narberth was incorporated in 1887, along the "Paoli Local" route of the Pennsylvania Railroad. The nearest parishes at the time were Our Mother of Good Counsel, Our Lady of Lourdes in Overbrook, Holy Family in Manayunk, and Saint Denis in Havertown.

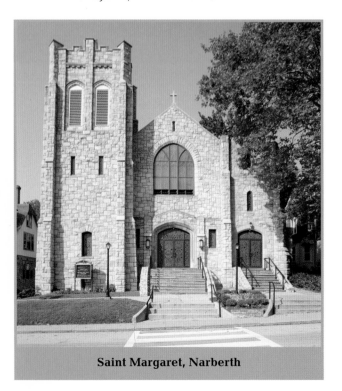

**Saint Margaret, Narberth**

The parish of SAINT MARGARET of Antioch was founded in Narberth on Christmas Day, 1900, to provide pastoral care for this growing community.

The first Christmas Mass was celebrated in the home of Nicholas Thouron, and in the following months parishioners gathered for Mass both in the Elm Hall fire station and in the rectory chapel on Forrest Avenue. Anti-Catholic attitudes among some residents made it difficult to find property on which to build a church. Consequently, the parish was forced to settle for a plot in the middle of the block, rather than a more prominent corner lot that other Narberth churches occupied. The lower church was completed in 1902, and the upper church was dedicated in 1922. Saint Margaret School opened in 1922 under the direction of Sisters of Mercy. A parishioner of Saint Margaret parish, Mr. Robert McGovern, is a renowned sculptor and wood worker. His panel carvings and statues can be found in more than 50 churches, hospitals, schools and other institutions in the archdiocese. He has created religious artwork for churches in 24 other dioceses, in 13 states, and often serves as consultant to pastors and architects.

A few years later, John Lonergan—a manufacturer of "steam specialties"—opened his home at Union Avenue and Conshohocken State Road in Bala Cynwyd for the first Mass celebrated in the new parish of SAINT MATTHIAS. Founded in 1906, the parish was drawn from the territory of Saint Margaret's and Our Lady of Lourdes, and situated on the site of an old sausage factory at

Bryn Mawr and Union Avenues. Ground was broken almost immediately for the church, which was dedicated in 1908. Sisters of Mercy—whose motherhouse in Merion was only a few miles away—began Sunday school instructions in 1914, and the first parish school was built in 1916. A new school was dedicated in 1971.

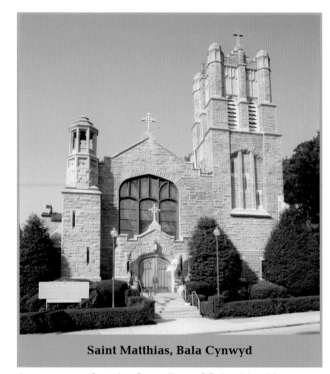

**Saint Matthias, Bala Cynwyd**

Just a year after the founding of Saint Matthias, the boundaries of Saint Margaret's were adjusted again to form the new parish of SAINT COLMAN in Ardmore. The Merion Title and Trust Building on Lancaster Avenue served as the site for the first parish Masses, and three weeks later the congregation moved to the Masonic Hall on Ardmore Avenue. A church/school building was dedicated in 1909, and a separate school was built in 1915. Sisters of Saint Joseph arrived at this time to staff the school.

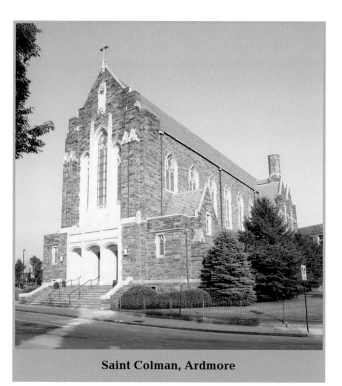

**Saint Colman, Ardmore**

The parish church was dedicated in 1926, and bears the name of the fifth-century Irish monk and bishop who baptized Saint Declan, the first Archbishop of Ardmore, County Waterford. The name was suggested by Father James Carton, a native of County Tyrone, who was mindful of the large number of Irish families in the area.

Italian immigrants were also attracted to the Main Line by the work to be found in the construction or maintenance of estates. Many men were employed by the Pennsylvania Railroad in the work of laying tracks and building stations. Others plied their trades as masons, stone cutters and plasterers on the large homes that were being built. Still others found work as landscapers and gardeners, chauffeurs, barbers, tailors or musicians in the service of the wealthy residents of the Main Line.

Father Aemilius Landolfi recognized the need for a national parish to minister to these Italian Catholics in their native language, and in May 1908 he organized the Italian-speaking community in the town of Strafford, part of Tredyffrin Township, Chester County. A chapel was built there in June of that year, and dedicated to OUR LADY OF THE ASSUMPTION. The present church was dedicated in 1922, and still serves Catholics of Italian descent living along the Main Line. The parish school was founded in 1955, and served by Grey Nuns of the Sacred Heart.

At this time, there were only about 50 resident Catholic families in the Borough of Malvern, the last railroad stop at the western end of the Main Line. However, their number was greatly increased during the summer by Philadelphia families who had vacation homes in the

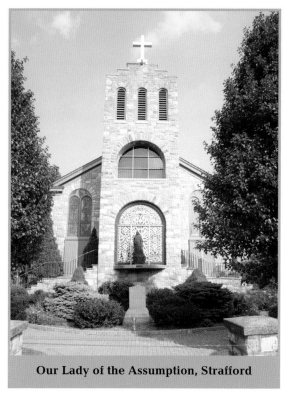

**Our Lady of the Assumption, Strafford**

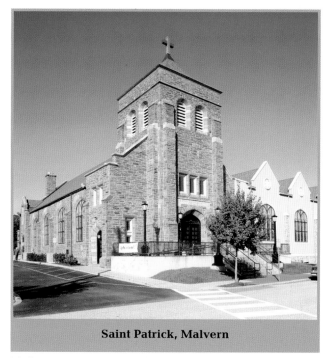

**Saint Patrick, Malvern**

Malvern area. The first church of SAINT PATRICK parish, dedicated in 1917, was renowned for its architectural style, and when the growing parish population necessitated a larger church in 1990, the original structure was incorporated into the new building. Parish children were taught by Sisters of Saint Joseph as early as the 1920s, and the parish school—built in 1954 and enlarged in 1965—was staffed by these Sisters.

The little village of Gladwyne—part of Lower Merion Township, between Narberth and Conshohocken—consisted almost entirely of farms and large estates until 1927, when the township set up plans for residential development. A handful of Catholic farmers and domestic servants faced a three-mile walk to Saint Margaret's, and the hardship involved inspired local resident John Doran to write to Cardinal Dennis Dougherty. Catholics were falling away from the practice of the faith, Mr. Doran said, and he asked a very pointed question: "If we were dying, where would we turn for a priest?" In response, the cardinal sent Father Augustine Schulte to visit Mr. Doran and investigate the possibility of founding a parish in Gladwyne.

The house of Thomas Barker, at the intersection of Conshohocken State Road (Route 23) and Youngsford Road, served as the first rectory and chapel for the parish of SAINT JOHN BAPTIST VIANNEY, founded in 1927. The parish church, built in 1940, was designed to resemble an English country church, to complement the architecture of nearby estates. Further development occurred in the 1950s, as large estates were sold off, and the building of the Schuylkill Expressway (Interstate 76) brought easy transportation and commercial opportunities to the area. A parish school was built in 1963, and placed in the care of Bernardine Sisters.

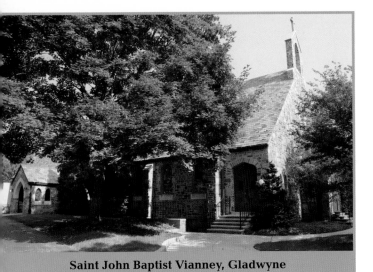
Saint John Baptist Vianney, Gladwyne

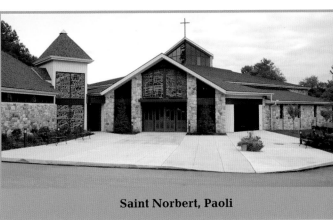
Presentation B.V.M., Wynnewood

In the 1950s, development spurred by the G.I. Bill and the reality of the "Baby Boom" affected the Main Line as much as it did any other suburban community. The parish of the PRESENTATION OF THE BLESSED VIRGIN MARY was founded during the Marian Year 1954 in the Penn Wynne–Wynnewood section of Lower Merion Township. The first school, staffed by Sisters of Mercy, included a chapel for Sunday Mass. The present church was dedicated in 1967. For many years, Presentation parish was a center of the Charismatic Renewal in the archdiocese.

The Norbertines had served in South Philadelphia since 1934. In 1950 they purchased the Cassatt estate on Berwyn-Paoli Road for a new foundation, which came to be known as Daylesford Abbey. Several years later, in 1956, Cardinal O'Hara established a new parish from the territory of Saint Patrick's and Saint Monica's, and entrusted it to the care of the Norbertines from Daylesford. The logical choice for the name of the new parish was the community's founder and patron, SAINT NORBERT.

The first parish Mass was celebrated in the Paoli Firehouse in July 1956, and a church/school building was dedicated in 1957. The Grey

Nuns of the Sacred Heart provided the founding faculty of the school, which was enlarged in 2005. The present church, completed in 1985, is still in the care of the Norbertines. The Abbot of Daylesford Abbey nominates a priest to be pastor of Saint Norbert's parish, who is confirmed and officially appointed by the Archbishop of Philadelphia.

Two more Main Line parishes were founded in 1964. SAINT JUSTIN MARTYR, in Penn Valley, between Narberth and Gladwyne, was formed from the territory of the parishes of Saint John Vianney and Saint Lucy, Manayunk. Ground was broken the following year for the parish church, which was dedicated in 1971. Father Louis Giorgi, the pastor who oversaw the construction of this church, intended it to be a shrine honoring Saint Justin and other Fathers of the Church—bishops and priests of the first centuries of Christianity who defended the faith against heresy and persecution. The stained glass windows of the church depict a number of the Church Fathers, and Father Giorgi traveled to Rome to obtain relics of some of these saints for veneration by the faithful. The parish of Saint Justin was twinned with Saint John Vianney parish in 2000.

Saint Norbert, Paoli

A second parish in Bryn Mawr—which also includes territory in Haverford Township, Delaware County—was founded in 1964 and named for Blessed John Neumann, beatified by Pope Paul VI in 1963. Renamed SAINT JOHN NEUMANN after his canonization in 1977, the parish has several links to the saint. The property on which the parish buildings stand had once belonged to the Sisters of Saint Francis of Philadelphia, the community which Saint John founded in 1855. William Zintl, M.D., a parishioner, had been present as one of the medical witnesses when Saint John's body was exhumed from its resting place in Saint Peter's Church in preparation for his beatification. Another parishioner and physician, William McNamee, M.D., was the surgeon who attended Michael Flanigan, the young boy whose miraculous cure from bone cancer in 1963 was attributed to the intercession of Saint John and was important in the process of his canonization.

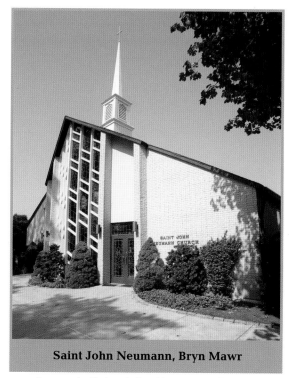

**Saint John Neumann, Bryn Mawr**

enrollment in Saint John Neumann School and Saint Colman School led to the decision to consolidate the two schools in 1976.

The youngest parish on the Main Line was named for another saintly priest who ministered in North America. SAINT ISAAC JOGUES was among the first French Jesuits to serve the missions of New France, in the region of the modern-day Canadian provinces of Ontario and Québec. He worked among the Huron and Algonquin nations there, and in northern New York State, until he was martyred by hostile Indians in 1646. The parish which bears his name was founded in 1970 in the New Centerville district of Wayne, about a mile from Valley Forge National Historic Park. Parishioners

were drawn from the parishes of Saint Monica, Saint Norbert, Our Lady of the Assumption, Saint Teresa of Avila, Valley Forge; and Saint Ann, Phoenixville.

At first, Masses were celebrated in parishioners' homes, and also in the auditorium of the Valley Forge Junior High School. Reverend Menno Good, pastor of Saint Matthew Methodist Church, invited the parishioners of Saint Isaac's to celebrate Mass in his church throughout the summer of 1970. The church of Saint Isaac Jogues was opened for Mass on Christmas, 1971, and dedicated early the following year. Continued residential development in the late 1970s—particularly in the Chesterbrook community—tripled the parish membership in its first two decades. A church annex, which houses the parish religious education programs, was constructed 1979, and a new chapel was dedicated in 1980.

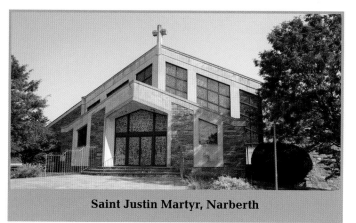

**Saint Justin Martyr, Narberth**

The parish church was built in 1967, and the parish school opened in the same year. The founding faculty was made up of Sisters of Saint Joseph, who were succeeded by Franciscan Sisters from Glen Riddle. Dwindling

**Saint Isaac Jogues, Wayne**

## FOR FURTHER READING

*Any attempt to tell the story of the Catholic Church in Philadelphia must rely on two histories published in the twentieth century and edited by Philadelphia priests. The first*—Catholicity in Philadelphia from the Earliest Missionaries down to the Present Time—*was written by Monsignor Joseph L.J. Kirlin and published in 1909.* The History of the Archdiocese of Philadelphia *was prepared in conjunction with the Bicentennial of American Independence in 1976. Edited by Monsignor James F. Connelly, a professor of Church history at Saint Charles Seminary, it includes essays from a number of priests, religious and laymen, all professors of history at Philadelphia Catholic colleges and universities.*

*In addition to these two works, the authors have consulted a number of other books and articles. While no attempt has been made to reference these works in the text, they are included here and recommended for further reading.*

**Monsignor Joseph Kirlin**

**Monsignor James Connelly**

Baldwin, Lou. *St. Katharine Drexel: Apostle to the Oppressed.* Philadelphia: The Catholic Standard and Times, 2000.

Black, Gregory D. *The Catholic Crusade Against the Movies*, Cambridge University Press, 1997.

Casino, Joseph J. "Anti-Popery in Colonial Pennsylvania." *The Pennsylvania Magazine of History and Biography*, CV (July 1981), 279-309.

_____. "Religious Freedom and the Early Catholic Experience." *All Imaginable Liberty: The Religious Liberty Clauses of the First Amendment.* Edited by Francis Graham Lee. Philadelphia: Saint Joseph's University Press, 1990.

Casterline, Gail Farr. "St. Joseph's and St. Mary's: The Origins of Catholic Hospitals in Philadelphia." *The Pennsylvania Magazine of History and Biography*. CVIII (1984): 289-314.

Chinnici, Joseph P. *Living Stones: The History and Structure of Catholic Spiritual Life in the United States.* New York: Macmillan, 1989.

Clark, Dennis. "A Pattern of Urban Growth; Residential Development and Church Location in Philadelphia." *Records of the American Catholic Historical Society of Philadelphia*, 82 (1971): 158-170.

_____. *The Irish in Philadelphia: Ten Generations of Urban Experience.* Philadelphia: Temple University Press, 1973.

Connelly, James F. *Saint Charles Seminary, Philadelphia. A History of the Theological Seminary of Saint Charles Borromeo, Overbrook, Philadelphia, Pennsylvania, 1832–1979.* Philadelphia: Saint Charles Seminary, 1979.

Contosta, David R., *Villanova University 1842-1992.* Pennsylvania State University Press, 1992.

Curley, Michael J. C.SS.R, *Bishop John Neumann, C.SS.R.* Bishop Neumann Center, 1952.

_____. *Venerable John Neumann, C.SS.R.: Fourth Bishop of Philadelphia.* Washington, D.C.: The Catholic University of America Press, 1952.

DeCock, Mary D. "Terence J. Donaghoe: His Missionary Career." In Kathryn Lawlor, ed., *Terence J. Donaghoe: Co-founder of the Sisters of Charity, B.V.M.* Dubuque, Iowa: Mount Carmel Press, 1995.

DeMayo, John B. and Casino, Joseph J. *The Forty-first International Eucharistic Congress, August 1–8, 1976: A History.* 1978.

Dolan, Jay. *The American Catholic Experience: A History from Colonial Times to the Present.* New York: Doubleday, 1985.

Donaghy, Thomas J., F.S.C. *Conceived in Crisis: A History of LaSalle College 1863–1965.* Philadelphia: LaSalle College, 1966.

_____. *Philadelphia's Finest: A History of Education in the Catholic Archdiocese, 1692-1970.* Philadelphia: The American Catholic Historical Society, 1972.

Feldberg, Michael. *The Philadelphia Riots of 1844: A Study of Ethnic Conflict.* Westport, Connecticut: Greenwood Press, 1975.

Fink, Leo Gregory. *Buckingham Palisades of the Delaware River: Historical Symposium of the Catholic Church in Bucks County, Pennsylvania.* New York: The Paulist Press, 1960.

Gabriel, Angelus. *The Christian Brothers in the United States, 1848-1948.* New York: Declan X. McMullen Company, Inc., 1948.

Gavigan, Kathleen. "The Rise and Fall of Parish Cohesiveness in Philadelphia." *Records of the American Catholic Historical Society of Philadelphia,* 86 (1975): 107-131.

Geffen, Elizabeth M. "Industrial Development and Social Crisis, 1841-1854." In Russell F. Weigley, ed., *Philadelphia: A 300 Year History.* New York: W.W. Norton & Company, 1982.

Griffin, Martin I.J. "History of Rt. Rev. Michael Egan, D.D., First Bishop of Philadelphia." *American Catholic Historical Researches* IX (1892): 65-80; 113-128, 161-176; X (1893): 17-32, 81-96, 113-128, 161-192.

_____. "Life of Bishop Conwell of Philadelphia." Revised and edited by L.B. Norton. *Records of the American Catholic Historical Society* XXIV (1913): 16-42, 162-178, 217-250, 348-361; XXV (1914): 52-67, 146-178, 217-248, 296-341; XXVI (1915): 64-77, 131-165, 227-249; XXVII (1916): 74-87, 145-160, 275-283, 318-259; XXVIII (1917): 64-84,150-183, 244-265, 310-347; XXIX (1918): 170-182, 250-261, 360-384.

_____. "Reverend Joseph Greaton, S.J." *American Catholic Historical Researches,* XVI (1899), 59-106.

Hawks, Edward. *William McGarry and the Open Pulpit: An Intimate History of a Celibate Movement in the Episcopal Church and of its Collapse 1870–1908.* Philadelphia: Dolphin Press, 1935.

Hennesey, James. *American Catholics: A History of the Roman Catholic Community in the United States.* New York: Oxford University Press, 1981.

Herbermann, Charles G. "Der Neue Welt-Bott." *Historical Records and Studies,* Vol. VIII (New York: United States Catholic Historical Society, 1915), 157-167.

Jeffrey, Edith. "Reform, Renewal, and Vindication: Irish Immigrants and the Catholic Total Abstinence Movement in Antebellum Philadelphia." *The Pennsylvania Magazine of History and Biography.* CXII (1988): 407-432.

Kauffman, Christopher. *Faith and Fraternity.* Harper & Row, 1982.

Kite, St. Albans. "William Penn and the Catholic Church in America." *Catholic Historical Review.* New Series, VII (1927), 480-496.

Laurie, Bruce. *Working People of Philadelphia, 1800-1850.* Temple University Press. Philadelphia, Pennsylvania, 1980.

*Letters* of Archbishop Edmond Prendergast, Dennis Cardinal Dougherty and John Cardinal O'Hara, Philadelphia Archdiocesan Historical Research Center.

Light, Dale. "The Reformation of American Catholicism, 1830-1860." *The Pennsylvania Magazine of History and Biography.* CXII (1988): 375-405.

_____. *Rome and the New Republic: Conflict and Community in Philadelphia Catholicism between the Revolution and the Civil War.* Notre Dame: University of Notre Dame Press, 1996.

Mahoney, Daniel H., ed. *Historical Sketches of the Catholic Churches and Institutions of Philadelphia: A Parish Register and Book of Reference.* Philadelphia: Daniel J. Mahoney, 1895.

Martino, Joseph F. *Positio, Catharinae Mariae Drexel,* Rome, 1986.

_____. *A Study of Certain Aspects of the Episcopate of Patrick J. Ryan, Archbishop of Philadelphia 1884–1911.* Rome: Pontifical Gregorian University, 1982.

McAvoy, Thomas T., C.S.C. *Father O'Hara of Notre Dame.* Notre Dame University Press, 1966.

McCauley, Janet, S.C.C. "Labors of Pioneer German Jesuits in Colonial Pennsylvania." M.A. Thesis, Seton Hall University, 1960.

McGreevy, John T. *Parish Boundaries.* University of Chicago Press, 1996

Miller, Kerby A. *Emigrants and Exiles: Ireland and the Irish Exodus to North America.* New York: Oxford University Press, 1985.

Morris, Charles R. *American Catholic.* Random House, 1997.

Nash, Gary B. "Reverberations of Haiti in the American North: Black Saint Dominguans in Philadelphia," *Explorations in Early American Culture Pennsylvania History* 65 (1998): 44-73.

Nolan, Hugh J. *The Most Reverend Francis Patrick Kenrick, Third Bishop of Philadelphia, 1830-1851.* Philadelphia: American Catholic Historical Society of Philadelphia, 1948.

O'Donnell, George E., *St. Charles Seminary 1832-1964,* American Catholic Historical Society, 1964.

Ray, Sister Mary Augustina, B. V. M. *American Opinion of Roman Catholicism in the Eighteenth Century.* New York: Columbia University Press, 1936.

Richardson, Edgar P. "The Athens of America." In Russell F. Weigley, ed., *Philadelphia: A 300 Year History.* New York: W.W. Norton & Company, 1982.

Schrott, Lambert. *Pioneer German Catholics in the American Colonies, 1734-1784.* New York: United States Catholic Historical Society, Monograph Series XIII, 1933.

Smith, Sara Trainer. "Sketch of Mary Brackett Willcox, of Ivy Mills, Pa. 1796-1866." *Records of the American Catholic Historical Society of Philadelphia* VII (1896): 395-401.

Taves, Anne. *The Household of Faith: Roman Catholic Devotions in Mid-Nineteenth Century America.* Notre Dame: University of Notre Dame Press, 1986.

Tourscher, Francis E. *The Hogan Schism and Trustee Troubles in St. Mary's Church Philadelphia, 1820-1829.* Philadelphia: Peter Reilly Co., 1930.

Wainwright, Nicholas B. "The Age of Nicholas Biddle, 1825-1841." In Russell F. Weigley, ed., *Philadelphia: A 300 Year History.* New York: W.W. Norton & Company, 1982.

Weigley, Russell F. "The Border City in the Civil War, 1854-1865." In Russell F. Weigley, ed., *Philadelphia: A 300 Year History.* New York: W.W. Norton & Company, 1982.

# ILLUSTRATIONS

Permission to use the following illustrations is gratefully acknowledged:

Cover photograph (right) by Gerard Burns, used with permission of Saint Michael Church, Philadelphia, Pennsylvania.

Photographs of Pope Benedict XVI on pages 11 and 123, and photos on pages 113 (top right) and 121 (top left), courtesy of *L'Osservatore Romano*.

Architectural drawing of the Cathedral of Saints Peter and Paul on page 54, courtesy of The Athenaeum of Philadelphia.

Photograph of Agnes Repplier on page 59, courtesy of The Agnes Repplier Papers, Rare Book & Manuscript Library, University of Pennsylvania.

Photograph of Sister Anselm Jennings, S.S.J., on page 62, courtesy of the Archives of the Sisters of Saint Joseph of Philadelphia.

Photograph of Bishop William O'Hara on page 64, courtesy of *The Catholic Light*, the diocesan newspaper of the Diocese of Scranton.

Photographs of Katharine Drexel on pages 71 and 72, courtesy of The Archives of the Sisters of the Blessed Sacrament.

Cover of *The Ring* magazine on page 91, courtesy of Kappa Publishing Group, Inc.

Cover of *Time* magazine on page 94, Copyright © 1937 Time, Inc. Reprinted with permission.

Photograph of Mr. and Mrs. John Connelly on page 105, courtesy of The Connelly Foundation.

Photograph of the Wall and Gutherman families on page 117, courtesy of *The Bucks County Courier-Times*.

Photograph of the Mission Center on page 117, by Robert J. Borton, courtesy of The Archives of the Sisters of the Blessed Sacrament.

Photographs on the cover (bottom left) and on pages 39 (left), 79 (all), 87 (top right, bottom left, bottom right), 88 (bottom right), 90, 93, 96 (all), 97 (both), 98 (all), 103 (both), 104, 105, 106 (all), 107 (all), 112 (all), 115 (right), and 123 (left) are from the collection of Robert S. Halvey, and provided courtesy of the Philadelphia Archdiocesan Historical Research Center, Archdiocese of Philadelphia.

Photographs on pages 114 (both), 115 (top left, bottom left), 116 (both), 117 (top right), 118 (bottom), 120, 121 (bottom left, bottom right), and 122 are provided courtesy of *The Catholic Standard and Times*, the archdiocesan newspaper of the Archdiocese of Philadelphia.

Church photographs on the cover and on pages 1--10, 41, and 124--261 by John Glover .

All maps by Father Philip G. Bochanski, C.O.